"This book is a tour de force—it's the best phenomenological treatment of the selected topics I've ever read."

Søren Overgaard, *University of Copenhagen, Denmark*

"The reception of Husserl's thinking has suffered from the complexity of his ideas and the awkwardness of his jargon. At long last our suffering is at an end. Walter Hopp has created an introduction to phenomenology that is at the same time a pleasure to read and accurate to its subject-matter. Here begins a new era of Husserl scholarship."

Barry Smith, *University at Buffalo, NY, USA*

Phenomenology

The central task of phenomenology is to investigate the nature of consciousness and its relations to objects of various types. The present book introduces students and other readers to several foundational topics of phenomenological inquiry, and illustrates phenomenology's contemporary relevance. The main topics include consciousness, intentionality, perception, meaning, and knowledge. The book also contains critical assessments of Edmund Husserl's phenomenological method. It argues that knowledge is the most fundamental mode of consciousness, and that the central theses constitutive of Husserl's "transcendental idealism" are compatible with metaphysical realism regarding the objects of thought, perception, and knowledge.

Helpful tools include introductions that help the reader segue from the previous chapter to the new one, chapter conclusions, and suggested reading lists of primary and some key secondary sources.

Key Features:

- Elucidates and engages with contemporary work in analytic epistemology and philosophy of mind
- Provides clear prose explanations of the necessary distinctions and arguments required for understanding the subject
- Places knowledge at the center of phenomenological inquiry

Walter Hopp is Associate Professor of Philosophy at Boston University. He is the author of *Perception and Knowledge: A Phenomenological Account* (2011).

ROUTLEDGE CONTEMPORARY INTRODUCTIONS TO PHILOSOPHY

Series editor:
Paul K. Moser
Loyola University of Chicago

This innovative, well-structured series is for students who have already done an introductory course in philosophy. Each book introduces a core general subject in contemporary philosophy and offers students an accessible but substantial transition from introductory to higher-level college work in that subject. The series is accessible to non-specialists and each book clearly motivates and expounds the problems and positions introduced. An orientating chapter briefly introduces its topic and reminds readers of any crucial material they need to have retained from a typical introductory course. Considerable attention is given to explaining the central philosophical problems of a subject and the main competing solutions and arguments for those solutions. The primary aim is to educate students in the main problems, positions and arguments of contemporary philosophy rather than to convince students of a single position.

Recently Published Volumes:

Virtue Ethics
Liezl van Zyl

Philosophy of Language
3rd Edition
William G. Lycan

Philosophy of Mind
4th Edition
John Heil

Philosophy of Science
4th Edition
Alex Rosenberg and Lee McIntyre

Philosophy of Western Music
Andrew Kania

Phenomenology
Walter Hopp

For a full list of published Routledge Contemporary Introductions to Philosophy, please visit https://www.routledge.com/Routledge-Contemporary-Introductions-to-Philosophy/book-series/SE0111

Phenomenology

A Contemporary Introduction

Walter Hopp

 Routledge
Taylor & Francis Group

NEW YORK AND LONDON

First published 2020
by Routledge
52 Vanderbilt Avenue, New York, NY 10017

and by Routledge
2 Park Square, Milton Park, Abingdon, Oxon OX14 4RN

Routledge is an imprint of the Taylor & Francis Group, an informa business

Library of Congress Cataloging-in-Publication Data
Names: Hopp, Walter, author. Title: Phenomenology : a contemporary introduction / Walter Hopp. Description: New York, NY : Routledge, 2020. | Series: Routledge contemporary introductions to philosophy | Includes bibliographical references and index. | Identifiers: LCCN 2020002908 (print) | LCCN 2020002909 (ebook) | ISBN 9780367497385 (hardback) | ISBN 9780367497392 (paperback) | ISBN 9781003047216 (ebook) | ISBN 9781000069464 (adobe pdf) | ISBN 9781000069686 (epub) | ISBN 9781000069570 (mobi) Subjects: LCSH: Phenomenology. Classification: LCC B829.5 .H66 2020 (print) | LCC B829.5 (ebook) | DDC 142/.7–dc23 LC record available at https://lccn. loc.gov/2020002908 LC ebook record available at https://lccn.loc.gov/2020002909

ISBN: 978-0-367-49738-5 (hbk)
ISBN: 978-0-367-49739-2 (pbk)
ISBN: 978-1-003-04721-6 (ebk)

Typeset in Times New Roman
by Taylor & Francis Books

In loving memory of William John Hopp (1976–2013) and Dallas Willard (1935–2013).

Contents

Illustrations

Figures

Table

Acknowledgments

I have had the privilege of presenting much of the material presented herein at various venues over the past several years, including Tongji University (2019), the International Conference on Phenomenology and Philosophy of Mind at Huaqiao University (2019), the Workshop in Phenomenological Philosophy at Assumption College (2019), the Boston Phenomenology Circle Symposium on Phenomenology & Aesthetics (2019), the Center for Subjectivity Research at the University of Copenhagen (2018 and 2014), the Reinach Centennial Conference at Ludwig-Maximilians-University (2017), the conference on Husserl in a New Generation at Kent State University (2017), the Workshop in Phenomenological Philosophy at Fordham University (2017), the Boston Phenomenology Circle Symposium on the Varieties of Phenomenology (2017), Rice University (2016), the Conference in Honor of Dallas Willard at Boston University (2015), the Workshop in Phenomenological Philosophy at Creighton University (2015), the Conference on Perception in Phenomenology at the University of Fribourg (2014), the 37th Annual Wittgenstein Symposium at Kirchberg am Wechsel (2014), the conference on The Phenomenology of Thinking at the Internationales Wissenschaftsforum Heidelberg (2013), the workshop on Perceptual Intentionality at the Norges Teknisk-Naturvitenskapelige Universitet in Trondheim (2013), the workshop on Thought Experiments in Science: Four Blind Spots at the University of Toronto (2012), and the conference on Defending Realism at the Università di Urbino (2011). I am extremely grateful to the organizers and attendees of these events for allowing me to present portions of the following material and for their constructive feedback on it.

I am incredibly fortunate to have been assisted in thinking about these topics over the last few years by numerous people. I am especially indebted to the following individuals: Derek Anderson, Philipp Berghofer, Jason Bell, Andrew Butler, Marco Bettoni, John Brough, Tian Cao, Kuei-Chen Chen, Colin Cmiel, Benjamin Crowe, Steven Crowell, David Decosimo, Steven DeLay, John Drummond, Troy Dujardin, Andreas Elpidorou, Christopher Erhard, Juliet Floyd, Joseph Gamache, Aaron Garrett, Brian Glenney, Paul Goldberg, Charles Griswold, Artem Gureev, Tanner Hammond, Mirja Hartimo, George Heffernan, Ryan Hickerson, Burt Hopkins, Hanne Jacobs, Anthony Jannotta, Emma Jerndal, Greg Jesson, Zachary Joachim, Paul

Katsafanas, Michael Kelly, Victor Kestenbaum, Chad Kidd, James Kinkaid, Jordan Kokot, Manfred Kuehn, Tarjei Larsen, Rebecca Leiby, Zhongwei Li, Ka-wing Leung, Jesse Lopes, Takaaki Matsui, Molly McGrath, Michaela McSweeney, Brian Moen, Dermot Moran, Kevin Mulligan, Søren Overgaard, Anne Ozar, Aaron Preston, Jake Quilty-Dunn, Sonja Rinofner-Kreidl, Elliott Risch, David Roochnik, Ethan Rubin, Jacob Rump, Alessandro Salice, Guy Schuh, Sally Sedgwick, Erin Seeba, Adam Shmidt, Charles Siewert, Barry Smith, David Woodruff Smith, Ryan Sosna, Allen Speight, Susanne Sreedhar, Daniel Star, Thomas Szanto, Tadashi Tamura, James Van Cleve, Corijn van Mazijk, Judson Webb, Donn Welton, Dallas Willard, Harald Wiltsche, Steve Wu, Ying Yao, Jeff Yoshimi, Dan Zahavi, and Gina Zavota. This is of course just a partial list.

I warmly thank Jeff Yoshimi for encouraging me to write this rather partisan introduction to phenomenology from a realist, Willardian perspective. I am also grateful to Søren Overgaard and Barry Smith for their extensive and insightful comments and suggestions. I thank David Kasmier for providing me with such extensive feedback and enriching conversations, and for his invaluable moral support. I owe an incalculable debt to Daniel Dahlstrom for his many insights, his help translating, and for discussing these matters with me almost every day for the past several years.

This work would have been impossible without the extensive and sustained help of Dallas Willard, whose knowledge far surpassed even what was documented in his significant body of published work, and who generously shared it with those of us fortunate enough to have been his students. In addition to his encouragement, he provided me, over many years, a way of understanding phenomenology that would surely never have occurred to me without his insights. I am grateful for the continued support of Jane Willard and Becky Willard Heatley.

Finally, a heartfelt thanks to my wife Maita and my children Amelia and David for their patient, loving, and unlimited support.

Preface

Before my own acquaintance with phenomenological philosophy as a graduate student, "phenomenology" had an imposing and unappealing ring to it. "Philosophers are supposed to clarify," says Iris Murdoch, "and should attempt to write in ordinary language and not in jargon" (Murdoch 1993, 172). Not only did "phenomenology" sound like a piece of jargon, but whenever I encountered the term, it seemed to travel in the company of even less appealing jargon: "epoché," "noema," "transcendental ego," "Dasein," and so on. I also had no real interest in finding out about "phenomena." I wanted to learn about reality. The first major work in the phenomenological tradition that I tried to read, Heidegger's *Being and Time*, corrected many of these misconceptions, but did little to endear me to phenomenology. Whatever else can be said about that remarkable work, which certainly does manage to say a great deal about the world, it is not the creation of someone trying his very best to be understood. Heidegger himself would later say—after, to be fair, abandoning the conception of philosophy as a science—that "Making itself intelligible is suicide for philosophy."[1] It's hard to get on board with that. Figuring out what is true in philosophy is hard enough without the added burden of deciphering what is even being said.

My initial impression of phenomenology was a tangle of unsupported prejudices. It turns out that making things intelligible is exactly what phenomenologists, especially those working prior to the publication of Heidegger's master work, took themselves to be in the business of doing. Many continued and continue to do so. Husserl himself had a refreshingly dim view of "profundity." In a 1931 letter to Alexander Pfänder, Husserl writes of Heidegger, "philosophically I have nothing to do with this Heideggerian profundity, with this brilliant but unscientific genius," adding that "he may be involved in the formation of a philosophical system of the kind which I have always considered it my life's work to render impossible forever."[2] "Genuine science," he wrote two decades earlier, "so far as its real doctrine extends, knows no profundity" (PRS, 144). The famous phenomenological injunction to return to "the things themselves" is motivated by the felt need to replace obscurity with clarity, to measure our claims not against this or that theory, but against the objects that they are about.[3] Husserl does not always succeed in reaching the heights of lucidity, but when he does, the results are extraordinarily rewarding. In light of Husserl's own suspicion of "profundity," I have adopted in what follows a general interpretive principle, kindly suggested to me by David Kasmier: if a claim of Husserl's permits of both a profound and an obvious reading, always choose the obvious one.

When done in accordance with the plain intentions of its founding figures, phenomenology is dedicated to achieving clear insights regarding cognitively accessible phenomena and expressing those insights in perspicuous language. In this respect it bears many similarities with the conception of philosophy endorsed by some early analytic philosophers. Like Bertrand Russell, Husserl—especially in his earlier phenomenological writings—was optimistic about philosophical progress, if not on all issues, then at least on a significant range of them. Both opposed system building in favor of detailed work on well-defined problems, preferably through collaborative efforts. Husserl characterizes the central topics addressed in his (in my estimation) greatest single work, the *Logical Investigations*, as a "field of *attainable* discoveries, fundamentally involved in the possibility of a *scientific* philosophy," whose central questions could be resolved by "resolute cooperation among a generation of research-workers." He adds: "Such discoveries have indeed nothing dazzling about them."[4] Russell writes that "to build up systems of the world ... is not ... any more feasible than the discovery of the philosopher's stone," and proposes instead a "piecemeal and tentative" approach to philosophical problems. If philosophers could achieve "successive approximations to the truth" in the manner of the sciences, the importance for philosophy "would be almost impossible to exaggerate" (Russell 1917, 113). Both prized clarity and rigor, and had a corresponding distrust of obscurity. Since then, "analytical philosophy" and "the phenomenological school" have gone their separate ways; Michael Dummett famously compares them to the Rhine and the Danube (Dummett 1994, 26). But there have been and remain numerous members of both traditions more or less committed to this vision of philosophy, and quite a few contemporary philosophers bringing the two back together.

So what exactly are the "things themselves" to which phenomenology is supposed to turn? Among the early practitioners in the Munich and Göttingen groups, the answer is not that phenomenology is concerned exclusively or even primarily with consciousness—though of course much of their work was so concerned.[5] For them, rather, "phenomenology" designates a certain way of tackling philosophical problems. In the editors' Forward to the first *Jahrbuch für Philosophie und phänomenologische Forschung* in 1913, Husserl, together with Moritz Geiger, Alexander Pfänder, Adolf Reinach, and Max Scheler, writes:

> It is not a school-system which unites the editors or which should to be presumed by all future co-workers. Rather, what unifies us is the mutual conviction that the great traditions of philosophy come to be evaluated by reference

to concepts and problems through a regress to originary sources of intuition
and to eidetic insights generated therefrom.[6]

That is to say: we should tackle philosophical problems by grounding our
discussions in an appropriate type of *encounter* with "things themselves," as
they are given, and not just theories about them. Obviously this method—like
any method suitable for the conscious—can only deal with objects of which
we can be consciously aware, and the insistence that the objects be *given*
requires that at least some attention be paid to consciousness itself. But the
primary objects dealt with need not themselves be conscious experiences.
Reinach (2012a) treats in detail the foundations of civil law and the essence of
social acts such as promising, and those kinds of things are essentially not
private or within any single sphere of consciousness. As he puts it in his 1913
lecture "Concerning Phenomenology," "The first thrust of phenomenology
has been to trace out essence relationships in the most various domains in
psychology and aesthetics, ethics and law, etc. New domains open up to us on
all sides" (Reinach 2012b, 163). Phenomenology, then, is not defined by any
particular "domain." To practice phenomenology, rather, is to proceed *phenomenologically* in one's philosophical thinking. We'll hopefully gain a sense
of what that amounts to in the chapters that follow.

It is in Husserl's work, above all, that conscious experience stands as the
preeminent, but not the sole, "thing itself" or subject matter of phenomenological inquiry. That will be the primary focus of this introduction as well.
Husserl summarily defines phenomenology to be "a descriptive doctrine of
the essences of pure experiences" (Ideas I, §75, 134). That is true, but without
further elaboration it is highly misleading. The reason is, as we will see, is that
phenomenological inquiry does not only concern itself with consciousness,
but with its *objects* as well—real objects, I might add, out there in the world
(Zahavi 2003a, 63; Alweiss 2013, 464). And even that only expresses two
thirds of the truth. Phenomenology's principal business, in Husserl's hands at
least, consists in investigating the essential interrelationships among:

a   mental acts or experiences,
b   their objects—what they are about—
and
c   their "contents" or (in many cases) "meanings,"

and he says so repeatedly. "To elucidate these connections between veritable
being and knowing and so in general to investigate the correlations between
act, meaning, object is the *task of transcendental phenomenology*."[7]

Despite the jargon—yes, I'm afraid it is unavoidable, though I will try to
clarify it as we go along—the idea here is fairly straightforward. If I am
conscious of an object, there is something about my mind that makes me
conscious of it. A lot of those mental (and neural) features of my mind are

the proper objects of empirical psychology, cognitive science, and neuroscience. But some of those features of my mind are the proper objects of a different kind of science. Right now, for instance, I think my table is wobbly and unstable. My present thought about my table has a certain character, a nature, and given that it has this character or nature, it is of a table and not, say, of Socrates's beard or a piano sonata. The connection between this experience's character and the table does not seem to be just contingent or accidental.[8] It is not only a matter of my having some sort of subjective response, never mind which, thanks to standing in causal relations with the table. Something more seems to be involved. That's what we want to find out about—whether and how experiences, their characteristics or natures, and objects of different types are non-accidentally, essentially, related to one another.

At this point I cannot expect such sweeping claims to mean much, which is why I will repeat them often in what follows. The best way to learn about phenomenology is phenomenologically, that is, by extensive acquaintance with phenomenological analyses and arguments. Before diving in, then, here is an example of the kind of phenomenological insight that I enjoy discovering. We have bodies, but just how we are related to our bodies is and always has been a philosophically perplexing issue. In addressing it, Shaun Gallagher points out that for any object we perceive, we can ask how far it is away from us. That means that we can ask of any two objects whether one is closer or further to us than the other one. We cannot, however, sensibly pose those questions with respect to the parts of our bodies. "Whereas one can say that this book is closer to me than that book over there, one cannot say that my foot is closer to me than my hand" (Gallagher 2005, 138).

There are a few things to notice about Gallagher's insight. The first is that, despite couching this in terms of what we "cannot say," this is neither a (false) descriptive claim about what cannot be said nor a (true) prescriptive claim about what we should not say. It's a claim about spatiality and embodiment themselves: no part of my body is spatially further from *me* than any other part of my body. It is not made true by our linguistic conventions. It is not just a claim about our "concepts." It's true because of what the relevant words and concepts are about. And it doesn't look like something that just happens to be true, but something true because of the nature of embodiment itself.

The second is that Gallagher's insight is deeply obvious. This claim will probably be resisted; many philosophers have a tendency to be open-minded, sometimes even a bit too credulous, when it comes to incredible propositions, and suspicious of those which are evident. That's okay. We could and should try to find counterexamples, raise various skeptical possibilities, worry about being envatted brains, and so forth. We should ask whether and in what sense this is true in cases such as "out of body" experiences. (Gallagher's answer, I think, would be that in such cases the body we perceive is our body as an object, and he is talking about the body when it functions as a subject of perception.) But, as a description of how we experience our own bodies in the vast majority of non-pathological cases, it's still obvious. It's obviousness, however, is of a distinctive kind. It's not obvious in the way that someone saying "The phone's ringing" while the phone is ringing is obvious. Rather, its obviousness is more like the way the punch line of a joke or the answer to a riddle is obvious. It's obvious and insightful. The difference between getting a point like Gallagher's and coming up with a point like Gallagher's is like the difference between getting a great joke and coming up with one.

Third, it's philosophically significant. It's not, of course, a concise theory of everything, and it's not surprising or shocking either. That speaks in its favor, I think. Surprising claims are worthwhile to consider but the most likely to be mistaken, and the surprising theories that survive do so because the evidence in their favor is powerful enough to override the features that make them surprising. But Gallagher's claim matters. Not only does it appear to be inconsistent with what many very capable philosophers have said about the body and its relation to the self but, more importantly, it has rich implications for how we inhabit space, the way we conceive of ourselves, and what we are. It isn't a conversation stopper. It presents opportunities for positive and detailed, perhaps even systematic, philosophical work. It invites us to make further distinctions, to ask whether this is always true of our bodies or only of certain parts or in certain contexts or attitudes, whether there are ever contexts in which the same is true of things which are not parts of our bodies, and so on. Even if it should turn out false—and some things that strike us as obvious do turn out false—it will almost certainly point us in the direction of truth. Far from being philosophical suicide, this sort of intelligibility is what keeps philosophy going. And this is real intelligibility, not lost-in-the-flow intelligibility. It's the kind of thing that will still make sense to you and motivate further philosophical reflection long after you've shut the book's cover.

Fourth, Gallagher's phenomenological observation is not a subjective report of the happenings within Shaun Gallagher's private sphere of consciousness. It is not an attempt to provide an introspective report on subjective processes, to describe "qualia," or anything of that nature. Rather, it simultaneously draws our attention to both the world and our relationship to it, to the fact that we are subjects, but live in and among objects. Furthermore, many of the objects that Gallagher has in mind are physical ones, out there in space. There is no hint that the things that are further and closer to us are "in" our minds. As we will see, phenomenologists have produced a number of comparable insights. The chapters that follow will certainly advance claims much less obvious than Gallagher's insight. But hopefully some such truisms will orient the discussions.

Finally, a few words about this introduction. First, this is not an overview of the phenomenological movement or tradition. Happily, excellent accounts of that movement already exist (Spiegelberg 1960; Moran 2000). The concerns here are more theoretical. As is often pointed out, the term "phenomenology" refers to both a historical movement or tradition and a discipline unified by its subject matter and methods (D.W. Smith 2018, §1). The movement's brightest figures include, among others, Edmund Husserl, Max Scheler, Edith Stein, Martin Heidegger, Jean-Paul Sartre, Emmanuel Levinas, Aron Gurwitsch, and Maurice Merleau-Ponty. It is often said to have come into its own with the publication of Husserl's *Logical Investigations* in 1900–01—though it is worth noting that Alexander Pfänder's *Phänomenologie des Wollens* was published in 1900. In any case, the unity of the phenomenological movement or tradition is largely historical and sociological, a unity provided primarily by personalities and their influences and interactions and only secondarily, if at all, by the "things themselves" and an agreed upon way of accessing them. The differences among, say, Reinach or Daubert, on the one hand, and Heidegger or Fink, on the other are vast—much more significant, philosophically, than the differences between Husserl and Frege. So, while the work of key figures within that tradition will be discussed as needed, it will be because of the phenomenological value of their contributions to the topics covered rather than their status within the phenomenological tradition.

Second, there is the question of coverage. One option is to survey a large portion of the topics dealt with in phenomenology. Another is to provide a bit more in-depth coverage of a smaller range of topics, chosen for a combination of their fundamentality to the field as a whole and their susceptibility to intelligible treatment. I have elected to pursue the second strategy. One reason is, again, that there exist numerous outstanding introductions to phenomenology that pursue the first option, and I cannot add to or improve upon them. A second is that this book is aimed at philosophers with a fairly advanced familiarity with philosophy already in hand—advanced undergraduates and beyond—and I think that a fair amount of moderately detailed treatment is in order. A third reason is that many of the topics in phenomenology are just so immensely difficult and founded on so many presuppositions that I think it would be beneficial to provide a firm footing in the fundamental concepts and commitments of the field rather than try to address the more difficult topics in an introductory text. This is similar to the way many introductions proceed, especially in the sciences. An introductory course in physics or logic does not typically survey the whole field, but covers topics fundamental to the discipline.

Third, and finally, there is the question of whether an introduction should be neutral or opinionated. I have decided to write an opinionated introduction, for several reasons. The first is just empirical: in my teaching experience, students (and I myself) seem to learn more from works in which theses are asserted and defended than from surveys of the space of a debate or reports on someone else's views. D.M. Armstrong's own *Universals: An Opinionated Introduction* (2018) is an excellent introduction to the problem of universals, whether or not one agrees with Armstrong's conclusions. One of the most successful books in my own courses is Michael Huemer's *Skepticism and the Veil of Perception* (2001). It advances strong theses in strong terms—which makes some students very eager to refute him, and others just as eager to defend him—but also functions as an outstanding introduction to epistemology. The second reason to write an opinionated introduction is that many of the discussions in later chapters presuppose conclusions drawn in earlier ones. That is much more difficult to make happen if no conclusions are drawn. The third reason, finally, is that while I am not optimistic about phenomenology or any other branch of philosophy rising to the heights of a "rigorous science," I do think that at least some areas of philosophy can be branches of humanly attainable and fairly systematic knowledge, and also think that much of what Husserl and other phenomenologists say and have said does constitute such knowledge.

The central topics of this introduction will be consciousness, intentionality, meaning, perception, and, at the heart of it all, knowledge. I situate myself within a realist phenomenological tradition, similar in many ways to the realism endorsed by most members of the Munich and Göttingen circles, along with contemporary realist phenomenologists such as John Drummond, Ronald McIntyre, Kevin Mulligan, Barry Smith, David Woodruff Smith, Robert Sokolowski, and Dallas Willard. Nevertheless, I think that a great many of the theses advanced in what follows regarding the nature of intentionality and the primacy of intuition and knowledge are fully compatible with idealism.

Notes

1 Heidegger 1999, 307. Heidegger is, nevertheless, capable of tremendous clarity. His discussion of "The Sense and Task of Phenomenological Research" in the Preliminary Part of his *History of the Concept of Time* (1985, 13–89) is one of the most lucid overviews of Husserlian phenomenology anywhere.

2 Heidegger 2007, 403. Translated by Burt C. Hopkins.

3 LI, Introduction to Vol. Two, §2, 252.

4 LI, Introduction to Vol. Two, §3, 256.

5 See Salice 2016b for an outstanding overview of the Munich and Göttingen phenomenologists.

6 Husserl et al. 1913, V–VI. Translation courtesy of Bob Sandmeyer: http://husserlpage.com/docs/hus_jahr_forward.pdf.

7 ILTK, 434.

8 See Smithies 2019, 96. This marvelous book only came to my attention as I was finishing the present work. Smithies' view that knowledge is grounded in phenomenal consciousness, along with many of his reasons for thinking so, overlap with Husserl's views, and those defended in what follows, to a considerable degree. It is one of several examples in which classical phenomenology and contemporary philosophy of mind and epistemology converge.

1 Consciousness

The central subject matter of transcendental phenomenological philosophy is, in Daniel Dahlstrom's words "the structures and make-up of conscious experiences" (2016, 141). Describing them should be easy. Whatever else one thinks of Descartes—and the twentieth century did not treat him kindly—he seems to have been on to something in insisting that our access to our own states of consciousness is unlike our access to anything else.

Descartes famously challenges us to establish a basis on which to believe that physical objects, including our own bodies, exist. Let's consider his question with respect to one part of our bodies that, we know, has a lot to do with consciousness: our brains. How do you know that you have a brain? This is not a skeptical question, a "puzzle." Of course you know you have a brain. I'm only asking you to reflect on the nature and quality of your evidence that you do. Speaking for myself, my best evidence that I have a brain is based on the informed and unbiased testimony of scientific authorities that human beings, of which I am one, have brains. I haven't actually observed my brain or anyone else's. My evidence is on a par with my evidence that I have kidneys and a gall bladder. This becomes especially clear when I consider my evidence that I have various brain parts, such as an amygdala or a fusiform gyrus.

My knowledge that I have a brain has a number of characteristics. First, it is based on testimony from qualified and trustworthy sources. Second, the evidence that these researchers have about brains is, ultimately, perceptual evidence: they see, handle, and experiment upon them. Third, it is *conceivable* that I am mistaken. This, again, is not a skeptical point. I do not have any *actual* evidence that I am mistaken, and the mere possibility that I am does not entail that I do not actually know. But there are *conceivable* scenarios in which I *would be* mistaken, and conceivable scenarios in which I would change my mind. Descartes's own scenario in his First Meditation involving a maximally deceptive evil genius is one (Descartes 1984, 14–15). Fourth and finally, there is nothing special about *my* knowledge of *my* own brain. Third parties can have the same or better evidence than I do about its existence and nature, as they in fact do.

My evidence that I am conscious, however, is rather different (see D.W. Smith 2004a, 51). First, very smart people did not have to tell me so. And if very smart people told me I wasn't, I wouldn't believe them, because I would know that they are mistaken. My knowledge is immediate, something based directly on experience (Chalmers 1996, 199). Second, my knowledge is not based on *perceptual* experience. I can know that I see something, but I do not see my experience of seeing itself, nor do I access it through any of the familiar senses. Third, it's hard to see how I could be mistaken about being conscious. I may be mistaken that I really do *see*, rather than hallucinate, the appearing cup in front of me, but I can't really conceive of a case in which it seems to me that I am conscious, but I'm not (Ideas I, §46). Finally, it seems I do have a distinctive kind of access to my own consciousness that no third party can have. I can be absolutely sure that *I* am conscious in a way that no one else can, and in a way that I cannot be sure that anyone else is.

Such, at least, is the Cartesian orthodoxy. Descartes concluded from such considerations that the mind is a distinct substance from matter. That isn't our concern. What is our concern is that despite the special access we seem to enjoy to our own conscious experiences, it is *not* easy to describe them, nor is it clear that there is even much there to describe. Do conscious experiences even have a "structure" or "make-up"? And if so, are they accessible through phenomenological reflection? In this chapter, we will cover two widely recognized features of conscious experiences: their intentionality and their phenomenal character. We will then turn to the widely endorsed claim that conscious experiences are transparent, and show why this poses a problem for phenomenology. We will then examine an argument that consciousness is not, in fact, transparent.

1.1 Intentionality and Phenomenality

In most contemporary treatments of consciousness, two features are singled out as especially salient.[1] First, when you are conscious, there is *something that it is like* to be you, and something that it is like to undergo the experiences you undergo (Nagel 1974). There is something that it is like to consciously see a color, feel a tickle, or hear a note; each of these types of experience has a distinctive *phenomenal character*.

A second and equally conspicuous feature of many, and perhaps all, conscious experiences is *intentionality*. This term is misleading, but unfortunately it has stuck. To say that conscious experiences exhibit intentionality is to say that they are *of* or *about* something. It does not imply they must be voluntary or deliberate (Graham, Horgan, and Tienson 2009, 521). When I see a book, for instance, my seeing is *of* the book, and when I desire a pay raise, my experience of desiring is *directed at* my getting a raise. In accordance with established usage, I will frequently refer to such experiences as "acts," and refer to those things they are directed upon as their "objects," with the understanding that such acts need not be voluntary *actions* (LI 5, §13, 563), and that their objects need not be *things*, but can belong to any ontological category whatsoever. The "object" of an "act" is just whatever that act is directed upon. In the case of my act of desiring a pay raise, the object of my conscious desiring is the state of affairs of *my getting a pay raise*.

Just what sorts of "objects" are we capable of being conscious of? We can get an idea by listing a few: colors and sounds; gorges and mountains; tigers and grasshoppers; tables and computers; money and contracts; fads and fashions; sensations and emotions; ourselves and others; values and moral laws; numbers and deductive arguments; symphonies and constitutions; photons and quantum fields; Santa Claus and Frodo Baggins; a square circle and the greatest prime number; individuals, properties, processes, relations, events, wholes, parts, and states of affairs. Even unknowable "things in themselves" can in some fashion or other be the objects of intentionality, otherwise it would be impossible to assert their existence or nonexistence. And so, of course, can consciousness itself. That gives us some idea of the diversity of the kinds of objects upon which we can direct our consciousness. You can add to the list by thinking of something. Interestingly, nothing whatsoever—not even *being* or even *being possible*—seems to unite them. This gives us a sense of the "complete unrestrictedness of intentionality with regard to the kind of object it may have as a term" (Willard 1984, 56).

The distinction between acts of experiencing and their objects is typically quite obvious. It is not, however, a philosophically barren one. Once we distinguish the act of awareness from its object, we usually also remove whatever temptation there might be to treat them as identical. The air conditioning unit of which I am currently conscious might, let us temporarily suppose, be "mental" or "subjective" in some sense. Maybe it's a bundle of sensations. Maybe it owes its existence to my imposing a concept on it. But there is one mental entity with which it is definitely not identical, and that is my present conscious experience *of* it. It is hard to discover many features that the two share. My consciousness of the air conditioner is an event. The air conditioner is not. My experience is *of* the air conditioner. The air conditioner is not *of* anything. The air conditioner has a certain shape and color. It can be turned on or off, picked up, or put in a box. My consciousness of it does not and cannot. The air conditioner cools the room. My experience does not. In the case of some objects of consciousness, it is even more obvious that they and the acts directed upon them are not identical. Acts of thinking about square circles exist. Square circles do not. It is upon such platitudes that phenomenology is built.

But how will this help us discover the structure and composition of consciousness? One way to begin examining consciousness would be to select some paradigmatic instance of conscious experience and simply describe its properties. But this is not an easy thing to do. What can I say about the intentionality of my visual experience of my lamp beyond citing its object, the lamp, along with those features of the lamp of which I am conscious? And what can I say about the experience's phenomenal character except that what it's like is what it's like to see a lamp with these and those features? If you've had such an experience, you know what I'm talking about. If you haven't, you don't. I can provide increasingly careful and precise descriptions of the lamp's features. But in doing so, I will be describing the lamp of which I am conscious rather than my consciousness of it.

This is a pattern among those attempting to describe the nature of experience: we frequently end up describing features of what we are aware of, not the experience itself. Just ask someone to describe their experience of an air conditioner, lamp, or whatever, and watch as they describe the object (Harman 1990, 39). For instance, David Chalmers, no stranger to the make-up and structure of consciousness, writes that "Some color experiences can seem particularly striking, and so can be particularly good at focusing our attention on the mystery of consciousness" (Chalmers 1996, 6). He continues: "In my environment now, there is a particularly rich shade of deep purple from a book on my shelf, an almost surreal shade of green in a photograph of ferns on my wall," and so on (ibid.). I do not want to pretend that I don't have any idea of what Chalmers finds striking, puzzling, and wondrous about conscious experience in general and the consciousness of colors in particular. He's right about that. Nevertheless, what Chalmers has characterized as "striking" here are the colors that he sees, the objects of which he is visually aware. The experiences themselves may be striking as well, but from what's been said, they may have simply inherited their striking character from that of their objects. Chalmers turns our attention to the experience itself when he asks, "How could I possibly convey the nature of this color experience to someone who has not had such an experience?" (Chalmers 1996, 7). That is an excellent question. But so is the question of how one could convey the nature of the colors themselves to someone who has not seen them. Nothing has really emerged about the nature of the experience of color beyond the fact that it is of something which is striking and incommunicable to those who have not seen it, namely color.

One might think that some progress has been made in describing consciousness if it should turn out that sensuous colors somehow exist "in" consciousness, as many believe. If colors are "subjective," then won't describing them be a description of experience? Perhaps they are "ideas" in Locke's sense, where an idea both resides in the mind and serves as an "*immediate* object of Perception, Thought, or Understanding" (Locke 1975, 134). But this does not get us any further. Colors are *objects* of sight, what we see, not experiences of seeing. The latter are not red, do not cover any region of space, and are not seen. And so situating the color red, or anything else, in the mind as an "idea" or "immediate object" still does not bring us any closer to characterizing the experiences in which we are conscious of them. Such things as Lockean ideas are what Laird Addis calls "secondary mental entities" sitting over against conscious experiences, the primary mental entities (Addis 1989, 5–6). And it is the primary mental entities, experiences themselves, that we want to understand. As we will see several times in what follows, putting things in the mind explains next to nothing about perception, intentionality, or knowledge.

1.2 Transparency

In light of these considerations, it is not difficult to see why many regard consciousness to be *transparent*. The problem, one might reasonably think, is not that Chalmers has not tried hard enough to describe the consciousness of color rather than the colors of which he is conscious. The problem, rather, is that no one can describe the consciousness of color any further. The consciousness-of relation has, as it were, a left-hand and a right-hand side.[2]

Experience → Object

On the left side sits the consciousness-of something, the experience or act, and on the right the object, that of which one is conscious. Whenever we try to describe what is on the left side, however, we find to our frustration that we are describing what's on the right. G.E. Moore famously makes the point as follows: "When we try to introspect the sensation of blue, all we can see is the blue: the other element is as if it were diaphanous" (Moore 1903, 450). Gilbert Harman agrees:

> Look at a tree and try to turn your attention to intrinsic features of your visual experience. I predict you will find that the only features there to turn your attention to will be features of the presented tree, including relational features of the tree "from here" (Harman 1990, 39).

What we do *not* find are any intrinsic features of our experience.

It seems abundantly clear that in Harman's scenario there is nothing more to be *seen*, visually, than the seen object and its features. Whether one selects physical or immaterial entities as the objects of sight, I don't seem to *see* my experience itself or of any of *its* features.[3]

However, it does not follow that I cannot be aware of or attend to my experience and its features. It seems, rather, that I can and must in order to discover what Moore and Harman want us to discover. One thing I must realize if I follow Harman's instructions is that *I am trying to turn my attention to my visual experience*. In order to do that, I must first realize that *I am having a visual experience*. And one thing I will allegedly find is that *I can only find tree-features to attend to*. But if I realize all of *that*, then I will have succeeded in finding—though not visually *seeing*—a great deal besides features of the tree and its environment. And if I do *not* find those things, then I will not be able to follow the procedure needed to verify that introspection will not make me aware of anything but features of the tree.[4] If it were a fact that the tree and its features are all I can be aware of whenever I try to introspectively examine my experience of the tree, I could never be aware of *that* fact through introspection or reflection.

For now, I will not treat this as a serious worry, nor do I think that making this point really disarms the threat that the transparency of consciousness poses to the types of inquiries we wish to pursue. Most advocates of transparency admit that we are sometimes aware of at least *some* properties of our experiences or, at the very least, of the fact that we have experiences. Moore himself, after declaring that "When we try to introspect the sensation of blue, all we can see is the blue," then says that "introspection *does* enable me to decide that something else is also true: namely that I am aware *of* blue."[5] Even Sartre, who more than any other phenomenologist insists on the emptiness or intrinsic nothingness of consciousness, maintains that every intentional consciousness-of something is at the same time a non-objectifying consciousness of itself (Sartre 2018, 11). On any credible view of consciousness, if I am conscious of a tree, I can know that my conscious awareness of the tree exists, and that it is of a tree. And if advocates of transparency admit that, they would probably not deny that I can also be aware that my act of *introspection* exists, and that *it* is of my experience of a tree.

We need a somewhat more precise characterization of the thesis that consciousness is transparent, one that accommodates the fact that we are not blind to the existence and intentional direction of our experiences. I will understand it as follows:

> Transparency: We cannot be aware, through either pre-reflective or reflective introspection or inner awareness, of anything concerning an intentional conscious experience beyond (a) its existence, (b) its intentional directedness upon its object(s), and (c) various non-intentional relations—temporal and causal, perhaps—that it bears to objects and other experiences.[6]

I can know, for instance, that my present experience of my lamp exists, that it is of a lamp, that it is simultaneous with an auditory experience of music and later than an experience of the scene outside my window, and so on. What I cannot know are the intrinsic properties of my experience—those intrinsic features and properties, if any, in virtue of which it is about what it is about, and in virtue of which it has the phenomenal feel that it does.

1.3 A Dilemma for Phenomenology

As phenomenologists intent on describing consciousness, Transparency, together with some other plausible propositions, confronts us with a dilemma. On the one hand, one may believe in the *authority of inner awareness*. According to this view, inner awareness, understood to include both reflective and pre-reflective awareness of our own conscious experiences, is a good way to discover the properties of conscious experiences. It is capable of disclosing many of those central or essential features in virtue of which a conscious state is the conscious state that it is. Together with Transparency, this supports the view that the nature of intentional experiences *just is* to be directed to their objects.

On the other hand, one might believe in the *intrinsic complexity of the mental*, according to which all or at least most mental states, whether conscious or unconscious, are intrinsically complex, and possibly extremely complex, entities. Together with Transparency, this supports the view that the real nature of experience, and our mental lives generally, is almost entirely beyond the reach of our reflective grasp.

On either alternative, there does not seem to be a lot of work for the phenomenologist to do. This appearance is, I think, partly mistaken. A great deal of valuable phenomenological work, not only in Husserl but especially in the phenomenological writings of Heidegger, Sartre, and Merleau-Ponty, consists of rich descriptions of the world that our experiences are of rather than the experiences *per se*. Still, if we want to investigate the structure and composition of consciousness itself, Transparency seems to leave us without much to look at.

Turning to the first horn of the dilemma, if Transparency is true, and if inner awareness has the power of disclosing the essential features of experiences fully or nearly fully, then the reason we cannot discern the intrinsic features and structures of experience is not because of the limitations of us or our powers of reflection. Rather, it is because they do not *have* such features or structures. Christopher Hill attributes such a view to G.E. Moore, who not only denies that consciousness has a "representational structure," but that "it has an internal organization of any kind" (Hill 2009, 77). On this view, "there is nothing about consciousness of any one object that distinguishes it from consciousness of any other object, save only the differences between the objects themselves" (ibid.). A similar view was held, at one point at least, by Russell. "At first sight," Russell writes, "it seems obvious that my mind is in different 'states' when I am thinking of one thing and when I am thinking of another. But in fact the difference of object supplies all the difference required" (Russell 1984, 43).

These are both exceptionally clear statements of what Smith and McIntyre call an "object-theory" of intentionality.[7] The object-theory construes intentional acts to be like spotlights, and locates all differences in the shinings of those spotlights in the objects upon which the beam happens to fall. Sartre's view is similar, but nicely brings out the dynamic nature of consciousness. Consciousness, he says,

> is clear as a strong wind. There is nothing in it but a movement of fleeing itself, a sliding beyond itself. If, impossible though it be, you could enter "into" a consciousness you would be seized by a whirlwind and thrown back outside, in the thick of the dust, near the tree, for consciousness has no "inside."
>
> (Sartre 1970, 4–5)

Even Husserl, himself no advocate of Transparency, admits that when we try to look in at our perceptual experience, it initially strikes us as "devoid of an essence, a case of an object being emptily looked upon by an empty 'ego' that is remarkably [merkwürdig] in touch with that object" (Ideas I, §39, 69).

This view of consciousness as internally featureless may appear to have one advantage. It may seem to support the claim, which enjoys overwhelming phenomenological support, that we are *open* to the world, that the public objects that we seem to perceive, know, and act upon really are perceived, known, and acted upon, immediately and directly (see Kennedy 2009). That is certainly Sartre's view. The tree I see is not a "content" of consciousness. The tree is in the world, "at the side of the road, in the midst of the dust, alone and writhing in the heat" (Sartre 1970, 4). Not only are the objects of perception and thought not "in" consciousness, but neither is anything else, nothing that could eclipse, veil, distort or be projected upon them. As Sartre puts it, "The first procedure of a philosophy ought to be to expel things from consciousness and to reestablish its true connection with the world, to know that consciousness is a positional consciousness of the world." Consciousness is not enclosed within a sphere of immaterial shadows and imposters, but "transcends itself to reach an object, and it is exhausted by just this act of positing" (Sartre 2018, 10). One lesson that G.E. Moore draws is that "There is ... no question of how we are to 'get outside the circle of our own ideas and sensations'. Merely to have a sensation is already to *be* outside that circle" (Moore 1903, 451).

To the extent that Transparency dispenses with mental imposters of the worldly objects of thought and perception, it supports the commonsense view. The view that consciousness is *featureless*, however, does not in any obvious way support the view that we are open to the world, or to anything else. Things which are "open" to other things are able to enter into relations with them. And wherever we look, it seems to be a general truth of ontology that things enter into relations with other things, at least in part, by virtue of having a nature of their own. Keys open locks, atoms form bonds with other atoms to form molecular compounds, organisms take in and utilize energy from their environments, and planes fly. These things do not happen because the entities in question lack a nature, but because they have one. It would be exceedingly puzzling if the same were not true in the case of consciousness. As Dallas Willard puts it, "Consciousness is not some sort of ontological odd-man-out over against everything else," as it would have to be if it were able to relate to things without having properties of its own (Willard 2003a, 170).

This is not, admittedly, much of a *phenomenological* argument for the claim that consciousness is structured and contentful. But if we take it seriously— and upcoming phenomenological data will vindicate our doing so—this leaves us with the second horn of the dilemma, according to which conscious states do have intrinsic features, and possibly very complicated intrinsic features. If that is right, and if Transparency is correct, then virtually none of these features is discoverable through inner perception, introspection, or reflection upon our conscious life. This position, unlike the object-theory, cannot be faulted for treating consciousness as something magical, something that can relate to things despite having no nature of its own. It is, nevertheless, mistaken. The problem is not that the mind is internally complex—it almost surely is—or that some of its features are not accessible to phenomenological reflection. The problem, rather, is that there are many features of conscious experience that can be uncovered in reflection. That is, the problem is Transparency itself.

1.4 Transparency and Intentionalism

A number of philosophers have argued that Transparency entails representationalism or intentionalism about experience.[8] According to intentionalism, the phenomenal character of an experience supervenes on, or is completely determined by, its "content."[9] That is: if two experiences differ experientially, if what it is like to undergo them differs, then they have different "contents."

Unfortunately, the term "content" is ambiguous. It is sometimes used to pick out the object of an experience, what that experience is about or represents. Alex Byrne, for example, writes, "the phenomenal character of a perceptual experience is entirely determined by the experience's propositional content—that is, by what it represents" (Byrne 2001, 199). And sometimes it is used to designate something else—not the object an experience is about, but something on the left-hand side of the intentional nexus, the object's mode of presentation, or perhaps some property of the experience in virtue of which it is about the object.[10] Sometimes the term is used to designate both things.[11] From this point on, however, I will adhere to Husserl's advice by never referring to the *object* of consciousness as its "content" (LI 5, §17, 580).

More will be said about the existence and nature of mental content in what follows. For now, we can distinguish two versions of intentionalism. *Object intentionalism* is the view that the phenomenal character of an experience is determined by *what* that experience represents, its object. If an experience represents a spatial object, its phenomenal character is determined by that object and its represented properties. If an experience represents the state of affairs of a tree being tall and green, then that state of affairs determines the experience's phenomenal character.

Content intentionalism, by contrast, is the view that an experience's phenomenal character is determined by its *content*, and not (just) by its object. On some views of content, content intentionalism entails object intentionalism. But on many it does not. For, as we will see, many correctly maintain that experiences can have exactly the same objects but different contents.[12]

So which view does Transparency support? The answer, I think, is *object* intentionalism (see Shim 2011, 200). One of the clearest versions of the argument from Transparency to intentionalism is due to Jeff Speaks. On Jeff

Speaks' formulation, to say that experiences are transparent is to say that "Nothing is available to introspection other than the objects represented as in one's environment, and the properties they are represented as having" (Speaks 2009, 542). Speaks' argument then runs as follows:

1 If two experiences differ in phenomenal character, there is an introspectable difference between them.
2 If there is an introspectable difference between two experiences, then there is a difference in the objects and properties those two experiences represent as in one's environment. (Transparency/Difference Principle)
3 If there is a difference in the objects and properties two experiences represent as in one's environment, there is a difference in the content of the two experiences.
C If two experiences differ in phenomenal character, they differ in content.

(Speaks 2009, 543)

Premise 2, the Transparency/Difference Principle, follows straightforwardly from Transparency as Speaks understands it. It also follows, with some trivial modifications, from Transparency as we have understood it. Any introspectable difference between experiences above and beyond differences in their intentional directedness, along with various non-intentional relations that each bears to objects and other experiences, is a difference in their objects. If all that is available to introspection or inner awareness beyond the existence, intentional direction, and non-intentional relations that the experience bears to other things and experiences are entities on the right-hand side of the intentional nexus, then any phenomenal difference between two experiences must be a difference in their objects.

Although Speaks' conclusion states that experiences that differ in phenomenal character differ in "content," it should be clear that they must (also) differ in their *objects*. That is, Transparency entails *object* intentionalism: if two experiences differ in phenomenal character, they represent things as being different.

1.5 Against Transparency

Now we turn to the case against Transparency, which will hopefully allow us to escape the dilemma discussed above. The present strategy will be to show that object intentionalism is false, and so, therefore, is Transparency.

Let's again "look at a tree" (Harman 1990, 39) or, if no trees are on hand, at any other material object in space. Now turn to the experience of the tree. As we have already seen, this experience is something of which we are conscious. We must at least know that this experience exists, that it is *of a tree* (or whatever), that it arose after reading the instructions to look at a tree, and so on. No problems (we will suppose) for Transparency there. But is this all we can say about the experience? It is not.

The first and most evident feature of the experience is that it is a case of *looking at* a tree. It is a *perceptual* experience. And perceptual experiences possess a number of noteworthy features. The first and most salient is that perceptual experience is a type of *intuitive* experience rather than an *empty* one. "Intuitive" here does not mean that it is an unsupported hunch or a gut feeling or something one "feels" to be true. It means that it is an experience in which something is *presented* rather than merely represented.

The distinction between empty and intuitive experiences is, if not the very most important distinction among intentional experiences, a close runner-up. It is both phenomenally and epistemically relevant, as later chapters will show. In the example, I see a tree, and see it as being green, tall, in the yard, and so on. Are there any other ways that I could be conscious of it? Yes. I am conscious of the tree right now while writing these words, but it's several miles away from me. What I am now thinking and writing about is that very tree that I have so many times looked at. Furthermore, I can merely think that it is just the way it presents itself to me while I am looking at it. I can think that it is green, tall, in the yard, and so on while perceiving something else, something completely unrelated to the tree. My thoughts about the tree might vary among themselves. Some may be beliefs, others doubts, others guesses, and others mere entertainings of propositions. In none of them, however, is the tree intuitively *present* to me as it is in the case of perception.

Perception is not the only kind of intuitive experience. We can also intuitively present objects in imagination, by visualizing them, for instance. And we can imaginatively present the same tree that we are looking at. So now we have three different types of experiences of the tree: perceptual, empty, and imaginative. They are all experiences of the same object. And yet they differ markedly from one another in their phenomenal character. Evan Thompson makes precisely this objection to intentionalism (Thompson 2007, 285): imaginative visualization and perception can have the same objects, but differ in their phenomenal character. Jan Almäng presents a similar objection to intentionalism, this time appealing to the intuitive/empty distinction:

> [T]he distinction between full and empty content is not a distinction that can be made by the transparency theorist. For according to the transparency theorist, a perceiver is only aware of the object of perception and its properties. And this is what explains the phenomenal character of the perception. But if this is correct, it would not matter to the phenomenal character whether a part of content was given in full mode or in empty content.[13]

By the "full mode" here, Almäng means the intuitive mode. If Almäng is right, then one of the most fundamental phenomenological distinctions cannot be accommodated within a very prominent contemporary theory in the philosophy of mind.

Let's take a closer look at the argument, focusing only on the empty/intuitive distinction. Here is my reconstruction of the Thompson/Almäng argument against Transparency:

1   If Transparency is true, then objection intentionalism is true.
2   If object intentionalism is true, then if two experiences have the same intentional object, they have the same phenomenal character.
3   For some perceptual experiences, there is a possible empty experience with precisely the same object as that experience.
4   In at least some cases, a perceptual experience of an object O does not have the same phenomenal character as an empty experience of O.
5   So, object intentionalism is false.
6   So, Transparency is false.

Premise (2) is true by definition, and Speaks' argument discussed above establishes premise (1). Premise (4) should also be obvious upon a moment's reflection. What it's like to perceive an object is not, in all cases, what it's like to emptily think about it. And really, premise (4) is an understatement. The truth is far more likely to be that *no* conscious perceptual experience of an object has even remotely the same phenomenal character as an empty thought of that object. But (4) will suffice.

The most questionable premise is (3). Are there any perceptual experiences whose objects can also be emptily thought about? The answer, I believe, is that there are. In fact, I think a much stronger claim is true, namely that *anything whatsoever* that can be presented intuitively can in principle be emptily thought of, and that this constitutes a fundamental phenomenological law: "corresponding to every mode of intuition is a possible mode of empty presentation."[14]

If we consider the sorts of objects that we typically take ourselves to perceive, each can be emptily thought about. Trees, mountains, people, basketball games, sonatas, colors, sounds, and so forth are the objects of empty thoughts on a regular basis. Against this, one strategy might be to try to find some sorts of objects that are proprietary to perception, objects that can only be perceived but not thought of emptily. Traditional sense data might seem to be promising candidates. But, apart from the fact that most contemporary defenders of Transparency rightly refuse to identify the objects of perception with sense data, it seems clear that we can emptily think about those too. One family of sense data that seem clearly to exist are bodily sensations, and these, both as a class and individually, can easily be thought about in their absence. I do not need to relive the pain I felt during a slip and fall a few years back to have it, that very pain, as an intentional object. It can be thought of emptily, and thought of as the quite awful thing that (I assure you) it was. Such things as qualia can be thought of emptily as well. And so, merely being *of* a sense datum or a quale cannot fix an experience's phenomenal character. All of those things can be thought of emptily. This is why, for instance, one does not need to be in pain to comprehend philosophical articles about the phenomenal character of feeling pain.

Some have argued that what distinguishes perception from thought is its "richness" (Heck 2000) or "fineness of grain."[15] I may for instance, think of the tree in my yard as being brown and green and tall. In perception, however, I will see it as being a very precise size and each of its seen parts as being a very determinate shade of color. "My desk," writes Heck, "exhibits a whole host of shades of brown, for which I have no names."[16] Appeals to the richness of perceptual experience are typically employed to show that perceptual experiences have a different kind of "content" than thought, a type of nonconceptual content. I will argue later (§8.2.2) that some such arguments succeed in showing this. If one can be aware of a determinate shade of color C without possessing or exercising a concept of C, then not all intentionality employs conceptual contents.

What this argument does not establish, however, is that thought and perception are, as such, distinguished from one another on the basis of their richness or fineness of grain. As Husserl points out, "Empty intentions can also be determinate."[17] And they can be far more determinate than perception. We can think of and even determine sizes down to nanometers, weights down to atomic mass units, and so on. But we cannot perceive things to be a determinate number of nanometers long or a determinate number of atomic mass units in mass. We cannot perceive a unit of Planck time.

Perhaps, then, it is not the determinacy of perceived properties but the richness of a perceived environment that cannot be captured in thought. In seeing the tree, I not only see it as having quite determinate characteristics, but I also see it as embedded in an environment of co-existing objects, situations, events, and states of affairs.[18] It's hard to see, however, why these entities and states of affairs could not also be thought about emptily. One can think that the tree is next to a bush, 30 feet from the street, and so on. There are empirical limitations on just how many propositions about our environment any of us can emptily entertain. But these limitations seem entirely contingent, not grounded in the very nature of thought or perception.

Furthermore, in the case of some perceptual experiences, the arguments from fineness of grain and richness have no grip. Consider a visual experience of looking at a navy blue circle on a completely white, evenly illuminated wall. Thinking about this scenario emptily poses no great challenges. Nevertheless, this perceptual experience has a radically different phenomenal character than the experience of emptily thinking about that same circle and wall. But both are about the very same objects.

A final objection can be made. Claude Romano, concerned about "what it means to describe our experience *as such*," and struck by experience's tendency to "withdraw[] before [one] like the sea" whenever one tries to describe it, suggests that characterizing experiences phenomenologically does not involve doing anything more than describing "*the way* things look to us" (Romano 2015, 263). (As anyone who has read his work can attest, Romano himself is highly skilled at describing experiences as such, so this worry seems a bit unclear to me.) Romano writes that we enter phenomenological territory when, instead of confining our descriptions of the way things look to their "objective" features, we include various subject-relative features as well. So, instead of just describing the color, shape, and so on of what I see,

> I can also say that it looks close or far away, on a slant, to my right, shinier or duller than it was just now, and, when I move, taking on a reflected sheen that moves slowly along its edge, then dulls out.
>
> (Romano 2015, 263)

All of these features, despite being subject-relative, are on the right-hand side of the consciousness-of relation. They are among the objects of which we are aware. Perhaps, then, Transparency can be defended, provided we enrich the object of our awareness with this stock of subject-relative features.

It may be that Transparency really is true of perceptual consciousness. The problem with this approach as a general defense of Transparency, though, is that every one of the subject-relative features that Romano attributes to what he sees—its looking close, slanted, and so on—is one that can be emptily thought of as well. In fact, in understanding Romano's own descriptions, a reader is doing exactly that. But the phenomenal character of seeing a pen, or a tree, or anything else, as having these subject-relative features is completely different from emptily thinking that it does.

We could even add some further subject-relative features to the object and still not fix an experience's phenomenal character. When I see something, for instance, it not only appears to have a set of intrinsic properties and a set of subject-relative properties. It also appears *to be seen*, and *seen by me*. But I can merely think that something is seen by me. Right now, I can emptily entertain the thought that my tree is green, in the garden, ten feet in front of me, and is presently perceived by me. I can think that it is given, that it exists right here and right now. That the thought is self-evidently false doesn't make it unthinkable. On the contrary, I can only recognize its falsity because I can think it. And one might try to explain the difference by adding that only when something really is seen by me will I believe that it is. That may be so. But it seems clear that the belief in such a case is not constitutive of its appearing perceptually, but a rationally motivated consequence of its appearing perceptually.

Romano is right that part of the task of phenomenology is to describe how things appear. That claim, however, is ambiguous. When we characterize the way things look, or how they appear, or how they are represented, we could mean several different things. In describing how things look, or how they are represented, I might describe how things look or are represented *to be*. That's what Romano focuses on. He quite rightly expands the properties that objects are perceived to have to include not only their intrinsic properties but also their subject-relative properties. But I might also describe the way—or rather the ways—in which they are represented to be the way that they are. My visual experience of the tree represents it as being in the yard. So does my empty thought. They represent it *to be* the same way—in the yard. But they do not represent it *as being in the yard* in the same way.

This is a familiar phenomenon. Ronald McIntyre (1999, 437–438) provides the following example. Suppose we want to know how Degas depicted his subjects, and were given the following answers: he depicted them as dancers, and he depicted them impressionistically. The first answers the question of how he depicted his subjects to be. The second does not. Degas did not depict his subjects as being impressionistic. He depicted them impressionistically. Similarly, a graph and a sentence can both represent a rise in interest rates over a five-year period, but they represent the same thing in different ways; they represent the world to be the same, but differ*ently*. Despite the intuitions underlying Transparency, the same is true of at least some experiences. For any perceptual experience, there is a possible empty thought that represents the world *to be* exactly as it does. But it does not represent the world to be that way *in the same manner* as the perceptual experience presents it. Emptiness and intuitiveness are features of the experiences themselves, not their objects (Pietersma 1973, 96). And they are not posited or inferred or introduced for theoretical purposes. This is a difference that is right there, manifest to us even before any reflection on our consciousness.

1.6 Conclusion

Transparency does not, if the argument above is right, confront phenomenology with an insurmountable dilemma. There are features of experience which are manifest upon and even prior to reflection, and which help determine the phenomenal character of our experiences. This does not mean, however, that intentionality and phenomenal character can come apart. For all that's been said, the difference between perceiving and thinking of the very same thing is an intentional difference, since intentionality involves a lot more than just representing things to *be* a certain way. It also essentially involves representing them *in* a certain way. For every *what* of consciousness, there is a *how* (Zahavi 1999, 121).

I conclude this chapter with a proposal that we have uncovered two phenomenological laws. The first is that in the case of any intentional experience directed upon an object that can possibly be intuited, the phenomenal character of that experience is not determined by the mere fact that it is of that object. That is, merely specifying the object that an intentional experience is of, no matter how finely, is not sufficient to specify that experience's phenomenal character. The reason is that no matter what we keep fixed on the right-hand side of the consciousness-of relation, it is always possible to vary what's on the left, and in doing so to change the phenomenal character of the experience. Merely knowing that someone is consciously aware of a green tree, a vivid color, an intense pain, a phenomenal quale, or anything else tells us very little about the phenomenal character of her experience. It doesn't even tell us whether the object in question is present or absent, to say nothing of the various species of acts falling under those broad headings.

Nevertheless, Transparency does contain an important truth, which is a second phenomenological law, and that is that it is also impossible to specify the phenomenal character of an intentional experience without specifying its object.[19] "This truth is what the transparency metaphor aims to convey" (Thompson 2007, 287). Husserl agrees. It is, he writes, "impossible to describe referential acts without using expressions which recur to the things to which such acts refer."[20] Or again: "the description of the essence of consciousness leads back to what, in consciousness, one is conscious of" (Ideas I, §128, 254). It would be more accurate to say that the description of the essence of any conscious experience *begins* with a description of what that experience is of, and never loses sight of it. I cannot describe the nature of my visual experience of the color blue or a tree, my fear of fire, or my memory of a concert I attended without mentioning the color blue, the tree, fire, or the concert. I cannot even describe my imaginary experience of a dragon without mentioning the dragon. No other characteristic of an experience seems nearly as important.

For what it is worth, many properties that have been proposed as capturing the essential character of mental states do not seem nearly as important. One can know a great deal about the essential character of an experience without knowing where it sits in the causal or associational nexus, what sorts of stimuli prompt it or what sorts of behaviors result from it, or what its functional role is. One can know a great deal about an experience without knowing which physical state it is identical with or supervenes upon, or even whether it is identical with or supervenient upon any physical state at all. But if you do not even know what an experience is of, what it is aiming at, or at least what *type* of thing it aims at, you are basically in the dark concerning the nature of that experience. If it should turn out that one could know, say, the functional role or neural/physical correlate of an experience without thereby knowing what its intentional object is, that would be a significant objection to any theory according to which the functional role or physical correlate of an experience constitutes its essence or nature. But since no one has yet succeeded in identifying either, we are left to speculate.

Notes

1 See, for instance, Georgalis 2006, 1 and Chalmers 2010, 339.
2 See Fasching 2012, 124–125; also PICM, 218.
3 See Tye 2002, 138 and Siewert 2004, 24.
4 I owe this objection to Dallas Willard, who makes essentially the same point against Colin McGinn's (1996, 14) position. See Willard 1994b. Related objections can be found in Kriegel (2009a, 372, n. 28), Janzen (2006), and Montague 2016, 79.
5 Moore 1903, 450. Also see Dretske 2003 and Harman 1990, 42.
6 For related formulations, see Janzen 2006, 325 and Kind 2003, 230.
7 Smith and McIntyre 1982, 47. Also see Crane's discussion (2013, 10ff.) of *"purely relational conceptions of intentionality."*
8 For example, Tye 2000, Chapter 3, Byrne 2001, Tye 2002, Speaks 2009.
9 See Tye 2000, 45: "necessarily, experiences that are alike in their representational contents are alike in their phenomenal character."
10 David Woodruff Smith (1989, 8) characterizes the content of an experience as "the 'mode' of presentation, the conceptual or presentational structure of the experience itself." This will be our conception of content in later chapters.
11 Peacocke 2001, 241; Pautz 2010, 257–258.
12 For a rich discussion of some of the possible varieties of representationalist or intentionalist views, see Chalmers 2004. The distinction between object and content intentionalism discussed above corresponds closely with his distinction between Russellian representationalism (§6) and Fregean representationalism (§8). Another sophisticated discussion of some of the varieties can be found in Almäng 2014, 3–5.
13 Almäng 2014, 14. One of the best treatments of representationalism and transparency in relation to Husserl's thought can be found in Shim (2011).
14 PAS, 113; also see LI 6, §21, 728 and LI 6, §63, 824. Also see Willard 1984, 56.
15 Peacocke 1992, 83; Kelly 2001.
16 Heck 2000, 489–490; also see Evans 1982, 229.
17 TS, §18, 49. See also A. D. Smith 2001, 285–286.
18 Kelly (2001) rightly emphasizes the "context-dependence" of perceptual experience, and argues that it provides a better reason than the fineness of grain to maintain that experiences have nonconceptual content.
19 See Thompson 2007, 287, along with Siewert 2004, 35–37, whom Thompson cites in this connection.
20 LI Introduction to Vol. II, §3, 256. Also see Willard 1984, 195.

Recommended Readings

Chalmers, David. 1996. *The Conscious Mind.* Oxford: Oxford University Press.

Harman, Gilbert. 1990. "The Intrinsic Quality of Experience." *Philosophical Perspectives* 4: 31–52.

Moore, G.E. 1903. "The Refutation of Idealism." *Mind* 12: 433–453.

Sartre, Jean-Paul. 1960. *The Transcendence of the Ego: An Existentialist Theory of Consciousness.* Forrest Williams and Robert Kirkpatrick, trans. New York: Hill and Wang.

Sartre, Jean-Paul. 2018. *Being and Nothingness.* Sarah Richmond, trans. New York: Routledge.

Siewert, Charles P. 1998. *The Significance of Consciousness.* Princeton: Princeton University Press.

2 Consciousness—A Look Inside

In the previous chapter, I examined the widespread claim that consciousness is transparent, discussed how this might pose troubles for phenomenology if true, and argued that while Transparency does contain an insight, it is incorrect. The goal of this chapter is to provide a further look "inside" of consciousness. What we will not find is a mental replica of the world, or a place in which we are trapped and must struggle to escape. Moore, Sartre, Harman, and other advocates of Transparency are right that the nature of consciousness is to be outside of itself. What we will examine instead are some of the features of consciousness that help determine the manner in which it is outside of itself, how its objects are present to it.

2.1 Some Discoverable Features of Intentional Experiences

It is incredibly difficult to simply gaze inwardly at one's conscious experiences. One of the helpful lessons of the last chapter is that we might have more luck if we instead compare and contrast experiences with other ones, especially if we hold some of their features constant, such as being directed at a particular object, while varying the others.

Let's consider again the experience of looking at a tree. In it we can find a number of features. First, as we have seen, perceptual experiences are *intuitive*. Second, they are *positing*; they present their objects as actual. Third, they are *intentionally direct*. And fourth, and most importantly, they are *originary*.[1] These features, while perhaps discoverable through a simple act of introspection, stand out in relief when we compare and contrast perceptual experiences with other types of experiences, such as mere thought, imagination or "phantasy," memory and "presentification," and image consciousness (see Levinas 1995, 65). I recognize that this jargon might be unfamiliar and cumbersome. But the phenomena themselves are very familiar, and the jargon is justified because (but only because) we do not have ordinary terms that unambiguously capture them.

2.1.1 Intuitive Character

We have already discussed the intuitive character of perception. Perception is a *presentational* experience. Intuitiveness alone does not distinguish perception from other experiences, however. There are many other types of intuitive experiences. I can, for instance, close my eyes and form a "mental image" of the tree. I can, that is, reproduce my perceptual experience of it and behold the tree in "my mind's eye." I do not suggest that we take these phrases literally. Imagination is not at all the same thing as image consciousness. As Andreea Smaranda Aldea (2013, 372) notes, many of the objects of phantasy are not the sorts of things that could be given in sense perception or acts modeled on it, such as image consciousness. Nevertheless, this is an intuitive rather than an empty consciousness of the tree. Familiarly, if I imagine the tree, then I will imagine it as presenting a certain side to me rather than others. I will imagine it from a certain point of view and in a certain orientation. In the case of emptily thinking about it, however, I do not need to do this (Davis 2005, 42). Of course I might. I may, for instance, imaginatively picture the tree as green while I think of the proposition that it is green. But this act of thinking is distinct from the imaginative picturing that it accompanies. We can vary the imaginative act without varying the thought. I can imaginatively circle the tree, all the while thinking the same proposition. I can imaginatively picture a ham sandwich and still entertain the proposition that the tree is green. Or I can cease imaginatively picturing altogether and still think that proposition. "A comparison of a few casually observed imaginative accompaniments will soon show how vastly they vary while the meanings of words stay constant" (LI 1, §17, 299–300).

Imaginative acts cut across two classes of acts that, I think, are more helpful to focus upon for phenomenological purposes (see LI 5, §40, 646). The experience in which I visualize or imagine the tree in my yard is what Husserl calls a "presentification" (PAS, 110), and presentifications can, as this example shows, be positing—that is, they can represent their objects as actual. This is not to be confused with a different type of act also called "imagination," namely "phantasy." I can form a phantasy-consciousness of a tree, and situate the tree within a phantasied world. Unlike the presentification discussed above, in this case there is no question of me regarding the phantasied tree or the world in which it resides as actual. It would be disastrous if I did, since any attempt to put it into the world would require me to put it along with its phantasied surrounding environment in the world, and that would result in a conflict with my perceived surroundings (see Marbach 2013, 440).

One important point to note, though, is that phantasy experiences can be either intuitive or empty with respect to their objects, a fact that renders the term "imagination" unsuitable for them. I can, in phantasy, project myself into a phantasy-world in which the tree in question is the unseen destination of an arduous quest, or one that is plagued by an elusive dragon that I do not ever see. Phantasy experiences can be *either* intuitive or empty with respect to their objects; in them "there is constituted a single *quasi-world* as a unique world, partly intuited, partly intended in empty horizons" (EJ §40, 171).

The same holds of acts of remembering and acts of anticipation. Many are intuitive. I can remember a hike I took by re-living or reproducing the experience or parts thereof, though usually sketchily. But I can also simply think about that event emptily. Similarly, I may anticipate the motion of the tree blowing in the wind by imagining it, or by simply thinking about it. Memory and anticipation may be either intuitive or nonintuitive. In no case, however, are they the same as perceiving.

One type of act that is *essentially* intuitive is image consciousness.[2] In fact, it involves the intuitive consciousness of three distinct objects.[3] They are:

   i The "physical image."
   ii The *"image object"* or "representing image."
   iii The *"image subject"* or "depicted object."[4]

If someone photographs or paints the tree, then in looking over the image I will, if things go well, be intuitively conscious of the tree depicted therein, the image subject. I will not merely think about the tree, or be reminded of the tree. Nor will I imagine the tree. I will, rather, *see* the tree.

Second, I see the two-dimensional image itself, the "image object," and I see the depicted tree in virtue of seeing this; *"in the image* one sees the *subject."*[5] Unlike the tree, it is only ten inches tall, does not have roots extending into the soil, and is not in my yard. It can rest on my lap or hang on my wall. Unlike the depicted tree, the image object is in many cases perceived. But it need not be. I can, in phantasy or memory, intuitively represent an image of a tree (Ideas I §99, 201). Still, such an act is essentially intuitive with respect to both the imagined image object and its image subject. Merely thinking about an image of a tree is not a way of being image-conscious of the tree.

In viewing the photograph, I will also be intuitively and perceptually conscious of the mere "physical image" or "Dingbild," the "physical thing made from canvas, marble, and so on" (PICM §9, 21). This is distinct from the image object, for several reasons.[6] First, the complete set of ways in which the physical image can present itself in perception—its perceptual manifold—is not identical with the set of ways in which the image object can present itself (PICM, 586). I can inspect the physical image further by turning it over or looking closely at its top right corner, by feeling the material out of which it is made, or by throwing it off a ledge to see how it descends. But in doing those things I do not disclose further features of the image object.

A second reason for distinguishing the physical thing and the image object is that changes in the orientation of one do not necessarily constitute changes in the orientation of the other. This is made clear by John Dilworth. According to his *"oriented subject matter invariance* or *OSMI* principle," "the field orientation of the subject matter does not change even if the field orientation of the picture does change" (Dilworth 2005, 172). If I turn the photograph of the tree upside down, I will then have an inverted picture of an upright tree, not an upright picture of an inverted tree.[7]

A third reason for distinguishing them is that the image object is not type-identical with the same class of objects with which the physical image is type-identical. Suppose I scan the photograph and save the resulting image as a Jpeg file. Then I will have two type-identical copies of the image object. But the physical Jpeg file is not type identical with the physical photograph. It is not, for instance, made of celluloid, does not have sharp corners, and cannot be hung on a wall. But if the image object and the physical thing were token-identical—if they were the very same individual—then anything with which one of them was type identical would have to be type identical with the other. Since that's not the case, they are not identical.[8]

So far we have looked at perception, phantasy, memory and anticipation, and image consciousness. Now we turn to thinking. Thinking is intuitively empty. Of course, many but not all of the possible objects of thoughts—the objects of judgments, beliefs, doubts, surmises, and so on—can be intuited. There is, moreover, such a thing as "thinking in presence" (Sellars 1997, 65). In attentive perception, for instance, we also typically entertain at least some thoughts about the objects and states of affairs presented to us. Nevertheless, the objects of thought are intuited through *other* acts, such as perceptual experiences, that present what they merely represent. Thoughts can borrow, as it were, the intuitive character of other acts, especially in acts of "fulfillment," which will be discussed in more detail in Chapters 5 and 9. Nevertheless, just about any act of thinking in presence can retain its character as a thought of its object, represented precisely as that object is represented to be, in the intuitive absence of its object.

This is compatible with the fact that some propositions can only be entertained by someone if he or she has intuited the object or objects that the thought is about. If someone says, "That tree in the garden looks quite lovely," I cannot fully apprehend the proposition expressed without knowing which tree is being referred to, and that requires that I at perceive it at some point and realize that it is the object referred to. And, more generally, our ability to represent things and properties authentically does require a grounding in intuition. But I do not need to continue looking at the tree to understand the proposition; its sense will not evaporate for me if I turn my gaze to some other object, or if I remember it being uttered the next day. Similarly, having an authentic conception of the color red, or the phenomenal character of an experience of red, very likely depends on intuitively beholding it at some point. But once we are able to do that, we can think of those things without intuiting them at all. "Once the intention to an object has been formed on a suitable intuitive basis, it can be revived and exactly reproduced *without* the help of a suitable act of perception or imagination" (LI 6 §5, 684). There are, with only a couple of possible exceptions, no cases in which a proposition requires a sustained and uninterrupted intuition of its object in order to be thought and understood.

2.1.2 Positing Character

My perceptual experience of the tree is not only intuitive. It is also *positing* with respect to the tree, its parts, and its features. That is, the tree is presented to me as existing, as something real (see Marbach 1993, 52–53). In normal circumstances, the tree will be presented to me with the positing character of "straightforward, naïve certainty" (PAS, 75). In ordinary perception, we take things to exist, and to be as they appear to be. This positing character can, however, be modified. In the case of discovered perceptual illusions, for instance, the positing character of a perceptual experience changes. The two lines of the Muller-Lyer illusion, for instance, still perceptually appear to be unequal in length after I have discovered them to be equal. Nevertheless, the positing character of this experience has been "overwhelmed by stronger counterforces" (TS, 251). My visual experience is still, however, a positing consciousness of the lines and their inequality. Not only does it retain its "affective pull," but it generates an inclination on my part to judge that the lines are unequal (EJ, 303). It has been overridden, but were I to discover that it was my experience of measuring the lines to be equal that was illusory, the experience of them as unequal would reassume its original force.

Other types of mental acts can also be positing. Thinking, quite obviously, can have a positing character. In fact, it may be that the shifts in positing or thetic character described above were really shifts in my thoughts about the lines—what I lost and gained confidence in, perhaps, were propositions about the lines, propositions which figured as the contents of acts of thinking. In any case, such transformations and fluctuations in the thetic character of our beliefs occur all the time. Secure beliefs are cast into doubt, what started as hunches transform into convictions, and our body of beliefs is constantly being updated as we take in information.

In the *Logical Investigations*, Husserl identifies positing acts as those which are "existentially committed" (LI 5, §36, 634). This would situate beliefs as positing acts, but would exclude doubt. As Husserl makes clear in his account in *Ideas I*, however, belief and doubt sit on a continuum, and *all* acts along this continuum are, in their own way, positing. This is because all such acts are attitudes towards how things actually are, and are subject to the rational motivating force of other acts that represent how things actually are. Like beliefs, doubts, when rational, are motivated by evidence, evidence concerning how the world is. Doubt is also normally incompatible with firm belief in the same state of affairs. If I doubt that a dog ate a student's homework, that is because I find it more likely that the student failed to do the work than that he owns a dog, that the homework sat for sufficiently long within the dog's reach, that this dog has a taste for ink and paper, etc. My doubt is nevertheless a positing attitude; in it I represent a state of affairs, alleged to have actually taken place, as unlikely. And this doubt can be converted into belief by suitable evidence, such as eyewitness testimony, video footage, or seeing the dog eagerly devour some other documents. Even many acts of merely entertaining a proposition lie along this continuum. If I merely think the proposition that the stock market will decline next week, regarding that state of affairs as equally likely or unlikely, my act has a positing character. It lies within "reason's jurisdiction" (Ideas I §110, 214), and can be converted into belief or doubt of various degrees by the consciousness of evidence that bears upon it.

Like perception, memory, anticipation, and all other presentifications that purport to represent how things are, have been, or will be are essentially positing. In memory, objects, events, and states of affairs are represented as having actually existed or occurred, and, as a consequence, are represented as bearing definite temporal relations to the present. Intuitively contentful memory, as a "reproductive modification" of perception, "points back to perception in its own phenomenological essence."[9] Acts of remembering may also undergo modifications, but they never lose their positing character, and to doubt the deliverances of memory does not thereby relieve them of their positing character, but is instead to oppose them with the positing character and force of one's present beliefs. To misremember something is not to really have "imagined" it in the sense of an act of *phantasy*. It is, rather, to have made an error about the actual world, and acts of phantasy are not errors about the actual world.

Standing opposed to all positing acts are acts of phantasy, whether imaginative or intuitively empty. Phantasy, as Husserl puts it, "is set in opposition to perceiving and to the intuitive positing of past and future as true; in short, to all acts that posit something individual and concrete as existing" (PICM, 4). If I imagine a tree in phantasy I do not, in that act, posit its existence in any way. This does not mean that my consciousness of it falls short of belief, or that the existence of the tree is in some way doubtful for me. Rather, I simply do not situate it within the actual world at all, as something either present or missing. This is why changes in my positing attitudes, whether in perception, belief, or memory, do not have any rational bearing on how I imagine the tree to be (see EJ §39). If I imagine the tree to be bathed in sunlight, my actual belief that it is presently raining imposes no rational requirements on me to alter my attitude towards the imagined tree. My consciousness of the imagined tree neither coheres nor conflicts with my positing experiences—though it *would* conflict if I attempted to situate it in the real world (Marbach 2013, 440). I can, of course, imagine that the tree is in the actual world—I can imagine it as sitting in an existing meadow that is in fact empty. But the actual emptiness of the meadow in question does not cancel or defeat my imaginative act. I don't find myself rationally required to abandon this imaginative presentation in light of the actual nonexistence of any tree in the meadow. More generally, just as phantasy presentations are not confirmed by what one genuinely believes, neither are they *at odds* with what one believes, since what is presented therein is not a competitor in the real world.

Phantasied objects, events, and states of affairs are not represented as actual, nor are they all represented as occupying one common world. Of any two events posited as actual, we can sensibly ask which occurred first, and how far away they took place. This, however, is not true of every pair of phantasied events. While the question of what happened first makes perfect sense with respect to events that are imagined to take place in one imagined world, it makes no sense otherwise. "The centaur which I now imagine, and a hippopotamus which I have previously imagined, and, in addition, the table I am perceiving even now have no connection among themselves, i.e., they have *no temporal position in relation to one another*" (EJ §39, 168). This is why it is senseless to ask whether Frodo destroyed the ring before or after Zeus imprisoned Cronus (see EJ §40, 173).

It should be clear that phantasy does not sit on a continuum with the positing characters discussed earlier. If I firmly believe that the stock market will dip next week, and ensuing events prove me wrong, my attitude toward the refuted proposition will not transition into phantasy. Phantasy is not an attitude of denial or doubt aimed at the actual world. It is, rather, an over-arching attitude towards an ensemble of states of affairs—a world—that is regarded as quasi-real (EJ §40,171). As we will see, all of the doxic attitudes discussed above—belief, doubt, and everything in between—can be reproduced in modified form within phantasy itself.

Image consciousness, finally, can be either positing or non-positing with respect to *any* of its three objects.[10] If I am aware of a painting of a tree, for instance, I may adopt a nonpositing attitude toward the tree. In the case of manifest fictions—an image of a dragon, say—my attitude towards the image subject will be non-positing. If I genuinely perceive a photograph of a tree, however, my attitude will in all likelihood be positing with respect to the tree. Again, we generally take a nonpositing attitude towards the states of affairs depicted in movies, and a positing attitude towards televised sporting events. Because image consciousness can be reproduced in phantasy, we can also take a nonpositing attitude toward the image object and the physical image that serves as its vehicle. One can even take a positing attitude toward the image subject while taking a nonpositing attitude toward the image object. I may, for instance, carry out an act of phantasy in which I see an image of the actual tree in my yard.

2.1.3 Directness

When I look at the tree in the yard, the object that I perceive is perceived directly. The "commonsense" view is that what I perceive directly is the tree itself. Philosophers, however, have proposed a number of arguments that things such as trees cannot be perceived directly, and that the only objects which can be perceived directly are those which depend in some critical way on our subjectivity—ideas or mental images or sense data, for instance. Those arguments will be examined in Chapters 6 and 7. For now, the important point is just that whatever it is that I perceive, I perceive that thing directly. This is bound to sound implausible or unacceptable to those who do think that we perceive such things as trees, but only perceive them indirectly. If what I've said is right, this is a mistake—there is no such thing as indirectly perceiving. And I think it is right on a suitable understanding of what directness amounts to (see §6.6).[11]

What, then, is indirect intentionality? The clearest case of it is undoubtedly image consciousness (Aldea 2013, 374). In seeing a tree in an image, I see the tree in virtue of seeing something else, namely the image object hanging on my wall. And it may seem that perception can be indirect, since we often perceive one thing in virtue of perceiving something else. On Frank Jackson's characterization, for instance, one sees some object x indirectly just in case there is some other object y such that one sees x in virtue of seeing y (Jackson 1977, 19–20). This definition can be generalized to all intentional acts. It is not, however, a plausible one. We hear melodies in virtue of hearing their constituent notes, and we see and hear written sentences in virtue of seeing and hearing their constituent words. But we hear melodies and perceive sentences directly, not indirectly. More generally, spatial and temporal wholes are the kinds of things that are perceived *directly* in virtue of perceiving their parts arranged in a certain manner.

There is a further problem with Jackson's characterization of indirect intentionality. In image consciousness, I see the tree in my yard by virtue of seeing an image of it. My consciousness of the tree is *founded on* my consciousness of the image object, since if the image object did not show up for me as it does, the tree could not show up for me as it does. Although Husserl himself appears to disagree (PICM §19, 42–43), my consciousness of the image-object is also founded on the consciousness of the image-subject. The image of the tree would not appear as *it* does if the tree were not visible in it. It is, of course, possible to perceive something that just happens to be an image, such as an ultrasound or an MRI, without thereby seeing anything in it. But that would only be the case if its representational or depicting features did not appear either, in which case it would not appear as it does within the context of image consciousness.

The mutually founding character of our experience of image-object and image-subject means that the image-object and image-subject are not presented by means of two separable experiences. Our consciousness of the image-object and image-subject is an "integrated whole" (Hopkins 1998, 16) whose elements are "inseparably linked" (Dilworth 2005, 115). Richard Wollheim, correctly in my view, says that rather than two experiences, we are dealing with "two aspects of a single experience" (Wollheim 2003, 3; also 13).

Since we see the image subject in virtue of seeing the image object *and* see the image object in virtue of seeing the image subject in it, it follows from Jackson's definition that our awareness of each is indirect, and indirect in virtue of our awareness of the other. That, however, seems like the wrong answer. If one is indirectly conscious of something, one must be directly conscious of something else.

What the awareness of temporally and spatially extended wholes and image consciousness share in common is that they are *phenomenologically founded* acts. An act A is phenomenologically founded when the following conditions are met:

  i A contains other acts a_1, a_2, ... a_n as parts;
  ii A could not exist if those part-acts a_1, a_2, ... a_n did not; and
  iii A is intentionally directed upon an object O which is not the object of any of the constituent acts a_1, a_2, ... a_n.[12]

In the case of hearing a melody, the act of hearing a melody over time is made up of acts of hearing each note, but is itself directed upon something that none of those founding acts is directed upon. I *directly* hear the melody in virtue of directly hearing its component parts.

One clue that indirect and founded acts are distinct is that there are some objects which, as a matter of necessity, can only be given in founded acts, but there are no objects which can only be given indirectly. What can be given in an image, for example, can in principle be perceived directly. As Husserl puts it,

> A picture or sign points to something lying outside it, something that could be apprehended "itself" via a transition into another manner of presentation, that of the affording intuition. A sign (or a picture) is not, in itself, the way what is designated (or, respectively, depicted) "manifests" itself."
>
> (Ideas I §52, 96)

Contrast that with founded intentionality. There are certain objects that can *only* be directly given in founded acts. Melodies and sentences, for instance, just are the kinds of things whose direct givenness depends on the givenness of their parts in suitable acts of intuition. The same is true of such things as states of affairs, sets, disjunctions, and other "categorial" objects (LI 6 §46, 788).

All indirect acts are founded acts. But not all founded acts are indirect. What makes image consciousness an *indirect* form of intentionality vis-à-vis the image subject, but not the image object, is that not only is one aware of the image subject by virtue of perceiving the image object, but that one takes the image object to be *about*, to *represent*, the image subject. This typically happens quite passively; "the image is immediately felt to be an image" (PICM §12, 28). More generally, an act A is *indirectly* of O just in case:

a   A is of O in virtue of being of some other object O*, and
b   the subject of A takes O* as a representation of O.[13]

Perceiving a whole by virtue of its perceiving its parts and properties does not work this way, since the perceived parts and properties by virtue of which we perceive the whole are not taken to represent or be about the whole. The shape of a tree is not about the tree, and the words in the sentence "The tree is green" are not about the sentence itself. Similarly, perceiving a state of affairs is a founded act, but not an indirect one. We can only perceive that the hood is scratched if we see the hood and the scratch, but neither the hood nor the scratch *represents* the state of affairs of the hood's being scratched.

In the case of image consciousness and all other forms of indirect consciousness, the latter condition (b) is essential. One is not indirectly conscious of an object just because one is directly conscious of something that just happens to depict or represent it. Trained experts can be image conscious of tumors in MRI images, for instance, but most of us cannot. The word "bone" represents bones, but a dog who sees that word is not thereby indirectly aware of any bones. What is missing in these cases is the subject's taking one thing to be a representation of another.

It is worth pointing out, however, that while O* must be taken as a representation of O, O* does not actually have to *be* a representation of O. John Kulvicki points out that image consciousness or seeing-in "can also occur when looking at oil in a puddle, dirt on a wall, or clouds in the sky."[14] Moreover, even when something is an image, what you see in it may not be what its producer intended you to see in it. Robert Hopkins notes that a friend of his saw the Batman logo as "two hunched figures moving away from one another" rather than a bat (Hopkins 1998, 71). And we might recognize the person who served as a sitter for a genre painting, in defiance of the depictive norms of the genre. As Gadamer notes, "it destroys the meaning of the picture of a figure if we recognize the painter's usual model in it" (Gadamer 1975, 145). But it does not destroy image consciousness.

With these distinctions in mind, it seems clear that while thinking, memory and anticipation, and phantasy can be indirect, none of them is *essentially* indirect. If I remember a past event, for instance, I can be directly conscious of that event, since there need not be any more immediate object such that I am conscious of it, and take it as a representation of the past event. Of course, as we have seen, intuitive memory is in its nature a *reproduction* of a past experience. That does not mean, however, that its intentional object, what the memory is about, is in the first instance a past experience. If I remember a tree, whether intuitively or emptily, it is the tree, not my past experience, that is the object of my memory experience (PCIT §27, 60). I don't need to first represent my past experience of the tree, and then take *it* as a representation of the tree. Similar remarks go for phantasy.[15]

Before moving on, however, it is important to forestall a potentially serious misconception. Philosophers often refer to experiences themselves as "representations." This might suggest (though it need not) that we are only ever directly aware of our experiences, and only indirectly aware of their objects. That, however, is a mistake—and one of the virtues of Transparency consists in warding it off. We can, of course, make objects of our own experiences. But when one is living through an experience, it does not function at all like a representation. Our consciousness of representations exhibits two features that our consciousness of our ongoing conscious experiences lacks.

First, in the case of indications and representations—tree rings, words, maps, images, icons, symbols, and so on—we are aware of *their* objects by virtue of being aware of the indications and representations themselves. But in the case of experiences, the dependence relation is reversed (Dretske 1995, 40). In having an experience, I am not aware of the object of that experience by virtue of being aware of the experience itself. In order for me to be aware, in the required way, of an experience, it must exist. But if my experience exists, I am *thereby* and without further ado aware of the object that it is about. I don't become aware of trees in virtue of representing my experiences of trees. Rather, I represent my experiences of trees only in virtue of undergoing experiences of, and thereby being conscious of, trees. Experiences, or at least one's own living experiences, are not like tree rings or inscriptions on stone tablets; we don't first need to make them objects of awareness in order to be conscious of what they are about. In having an experience, one is aware, and often directly aware, of its object. This makes experiences completely unlike every other sort of "representation."

Second, when we are aware of an indication or representation, there is always the possibility that our awareness might not go through the representation or indication to that representation's object. We might simply fail to be conscious of it as a representation or indication at all. Tree rings indicate the age of a tree, but that doesn't mean whoever is aware of tree rings is thereby aware, consciously or unconsciously, of the age of a tree.

Furthermore, if we take something as an indication or representation, it is possible to take it as a representation of something that it does not in fact represent. Words, icons, traffic signs, and so on require interpretation, and are sometimes misinterpreted. But this is not true of one's own present experiences. To have an experience is just to be aware of *its* object. We might misidentify or misclassify the object of an experience. We might ascribe properties to it that it does not have. But in order for that to occur, we must already be aware of the experience's object. I can only misclassify a crocodile that I see as an alligator, or see it as gray rather than green, if I am aware of the crocodile. I can only misidentify Stan as his twin Dan if I am aware of Stan. Here I am not misinterpreting the experience. Rather, I am just mistaken about the object of the experience—the crocodile or Stan. When, however, I misinterpret a sign or indication or representation, I do not misinterpret *its* object, but the representation itself. If I think the word "crocodile" refers to alligators, it is not crocodiles who have been misunderstood, but a word of the English language.

One final point is in order, and that is that the epistemic status of a mental act, such as a belief, can within wide limits vary independently of its intentional directness. Merely thinking that President Obama has more gray hair than he used to is an intentionally direct act. But by itself, it has no epistemic credentials whatsoever. Comparing a recent photograph of Obama with one from a decade ago, by contrast, involves two intentionally *indirect* acts of image consciousness, yet provides considerable evidence that his hair has grayed. We cannot conclude, then, that because a certain mental act's content is not known or even justified, or that a certain experience is fallible, that it is intentionally indirect. Nor can we conclude that because an act is intentionally direct, it has any positive epistemic status.

2.1.4 Originary Character

Now, finally, we turn to what is the defining feature of perception: its originary character. Perception presents its objects "in the flesh" (PAS, 140), "*in an originary way*" (Ideas I §1, 9). Perceptual experience "is characterized by the fact that in it, as we are wont to express the matter, the object 'itself ' appears, and does not merely appear 'in a likeness'" (LI 6 §14a, 712). The originary character of perception entails the three aforementioned features—every originary consciousness is intuitive rather than empty, positing rather than nonpositing, and direct rather than indirect. Nevertheless, those features do not entail that an act is originary. I can close my eyes and enjoy an intuitive, positing, and intentionally direct consciousness of the tree in my yard. But that is not perception. The originary character of perception is very likely primitive.[16]

Image-consciousness is also essentially non-originary with respect to the image-subject depicted therein. The reason is that in originary perception, objects are presented as bearing perceptible relations to one's own body. "The 'far' is far from me, from my Body; the 'to the right' refers back to the right side of my Body, e.g., to my right hand" (Ideas II §41a, 166). In image-consciousness, by contrast, the image-subject does not bear any perceptible spatial relations to oneself or one's body.[17] If I see a picture of Pike's Peak off to my right, I also see Pike's Peak. But although Pike's Peak is seen, and seen on my right, it is not seen as being on my right. I only perceive where the image-object is. Where on Earth Pike's Peak itself might be is completely unspecified in my experience of an image of it. In perception, the relative locations of things might be misperceived. But in image-consciousness, they are not perceived at all.

It might seem that only perception is an originary act. This is the feature that seems most clearly to set perception apart from all other intentional experiences. Perception just is that mode of consciousness that presents its objects in the flesh. Things are more complicated, however. Image-consciousness, for instance, is not an originary consciousness of the image subject. But it is, in most cases, originary vis-à-vis both the physical image and the image object.

Phantasy is non-originary. Husserl goes so far as to say, "Not to give the object itself is the very essence of phantasy" (PCIT §19, 47). But, while phantasy is not an originary consciousness of the individual objects and states of affairs toward which it is directed, it can be an originary consciousness of properties and their possible and necessary relations with one another. I can discover in phantasy, for instance, that it is possible for something to be both round and red. In such an act, the respective essences are intuited, presented directly, posited, and given originarily. Phantasy or "fiction," writes Husserl, *"makes up the vital element of phenomenology, as it does of all eidetic sciences"* (Ideas I §70, 127). In such acts individuals are not given originarily, but universals are. That is why, as Husserl writes, "In a consideration of essence, perception and imaginative representation are entirely equivalent— the same essence can be seen in both" (IdPh, 50). What distinguishes perceptual acts, then, is not that they alone are originary, but that *they alone are originary with respect to everything intuitively presented in them*: individuals, states of affairs, properties, property-instances, relations, and so on.

Thinking, finally, is as such not an originary mode of consciousness. The reason is that, with perhaps a few exceptions, every content suitable to serve as the content of a thought can be entertained in the intuitive absence of what that thought is about. Thought can, of course, certainly accompany intuition, and can even enter into distinctive forms of unity with it—a fact of the utmost importance when it comes to understanding how intuitive acts function in meaning and knowledge. And in the case of those thought contents that can only be entertained when their objects are intuitively present— thoughts involving certain indexicals and demonstratives, such as "I am here now"—the intuitive character of those acts is due to other, accompanying intuitive acts.

There are two further features of perceptual experience that must be noted, and that follow from its originary character. One is that perceptual experience is a "de re" or "definite" mode of intentionality.[18] This is a somewhat dangerous characterization since it is widely held that de re intentions entail the existence of their objects. For now, we will bracket that commitment, and focus on the definite, nondescriptive character of perceptual intentionality. Perceptual intentionality is not a mode of consciousness in which its objects are picked out by description, as *just whatever* has such-and-such properties or satisfies a description. When I see a tree T, it is T, this very individual tree, that is presented in perception. I do not see *some tree or other*. T is not presented to me as *just whatever* thing, or even just whatever *tree*, out there is responsible for the experiences I am undergoing when I see it. That is because I have "direct and immediate acquaintance" with it (Smith & McIntyre 1982,

20). If a different tree T* were there, I would see T*, not T, even if T* looked like T, and even if I believed or judged that what I see is T.

This reveals a second feature of perceptual experience: it is largely autonomous and independent from other kinds of intentionality, such as thought and judgment. Often times what I perceive is identical with what I *think* I perceive. But not always, and certainly not as a matter of necessity.

Consider a case: suppose Dan, unbeknownst to me, has an identical twin Stan.[19] Stan is walking down the hall, and I form the judgment that Dan is walking down the hall. Whom do I see? That is, which person is the intentional object of my perceptual experience? If we take our cue from my *beliefs about* whom it is that I see, then my experience is *of Dan*. In that case, my experience would have to be nonveridical, since Dan is nowhere around. But that is not the correct answer. I have a veridical experience of Stan, not a hallucination of Dan. My error is one of *misrecognition* or *misidentification*, not *misperception*.[20]

The quick and easy answer as to why I see Stan, despite thinking I see Dan, is that Stan's presence is partly causally responsible for my experience. That is undoubtedly true. Of course, some might object that such a claim, even if true, is not permissible when doing phenomenology because we are supposed to "bracket" all claims about existence, causal relations, and so forth. That might be true too. But at this point that objection may be premature. Methods are ways of accessing subject matters. Our subject matter is the nature of conscious intentionality, and *if* the best way of understanding intentionality does require us to posit existing particulars and causal relations, then the method of bracketing is not the right method. So far we have no good reason to think that the method that Husserl proposes is the right one. This is not a skeptical or critical point, either. It's simply that that's not the kind of thing we could possibly know until we *already* know quite a bit about the subject matter to be investigated, and we're only getting started. You can only craft a method for disclosing a domain of objects if you know something about that domain to begin with. If someone has no idea what a Klein bottle is, they would rightly feel unqualified to propose any method for studying its properties.

In any case, the justification for the claim that I see Stan rather than Dan is not solely or even principally because of any causal relation. It's a claim with phenomenological teeth. We can bracket the claim that Stan is causally responsible for my experience and leave only the unproblematically phenomenological observation that Stan is presented *as* bearing causal relations to me and my experience, and still get the result that I see Stan.[21] And even that is more than we need; the reason why Stan is presented as bearing causal relations to my experience *depends* on the fact that I am perceptually conscious of Stan. I cannot see an object O as standing in causal relations with me if I do not see O.

To see that my experience is of Stan, even when I think it is of Dan, suppose that as I watch Stan approach me, Dan emerges from his office and walks down the hall on Stan's right. Dan then says, "This is Stan, my twin brother." Now I both see and recognize Dan as Dan and Stan as Stan. But I do not first come to see Stan merely upon gaining this knowledge. Rather, the person to Dan's left is the same person I tracked walking down the hall, and is given *as* the same person I tracked down the hall. And what I learn is that *he*, the person I've been perceiving the whole time, is Stan. But I must have perceived Stan the whole time to *learn* that, since it would be false if it were not Stan I saw the whole time. If Dan were the object of the perceptual experience, I could not, even on my own terms, learn that the person I see is Stan. This is not a transformation from hallucination to perception. Furthermore, I do not see Stan in virtue of the fact that this sort of further verification and identification occurs. Nor is it because such acts could *possibly* occur. Actual and merely possible acts of future recognition and identification are not what make it the case that my actual experience, right now, is of Stan. Rather, those merely possible acts are possible in virtue of the fact that I actually see Stan now (see Mulligan and Smith 1986, 126).

Note that it is on my own terms, that is, the terms of my very experience itself, that I saw Stan the whole time. This is not a conclusion foisted on me from an external perspective, as though God, or a philosopher occupying a transcendental standpoint, were the only ones keeping score. The whole time I was looking at Stan, even though I thought it was Dan. The conflict here is not between my perspective and that of an outside onlooker. The conflict is between *my* perspectives, between two intentional acts both carried out by me: perception and belief. And it is on the terms of those experiences themselves, given their natures, that the intentionality of perception is not parasitic on that of belief.

An important result of this discussion is that two acts that seem the same, introspectively, can have *different* intentional contents and objects. And that should really not come as a surprise. Lots of things look like other things. Experiences of those things are accordingly a lot like experiences of those other things.[22] We do not need to appeal to elaborate thought experiments involving "Twin Earth," where there's a Doppelgänger for every earthly item, to see this.[23] The real world is full of things that look a lot like other things— socks, actual twins, and so on. We know this and, in many cases, ensure it by design. On our own terms, in terms "internal" to our own experiences and our own knowledge and beliefs, it is not the case that our perceptual acts are directed at just whatever we *believe* them to be directed at—though we can be led to believe that in cases of reflection (see Dretske 2000a, 102). We know that we can misidentify things. We can be very unsure that the first sock we put into the washer is the last sock that we take out of the dryer. Obviously in cases in which we have doubts—like this—the identity of the object we see is not determined by our beliefs, or by how things cognitively "seem," since there is no suitable belief or seeming at all (Dretske 1969, 22). If I am sure that I see one of eight particular socks, but unsure which one it is, it doesn't follow that it's at all indeterminate, or that there's no fact of the matter, which of the eight socks I see. I don't see all eight, and I don't see none of them. I see one of them, and I don't know which (ibid., 8–9).

This can be taken to be an anti-Cartesian point. To some extent it is. If I undergo an experience E1 at t1, and E2 and t2, I might be unable to tell whether E1 and E2 have the same or different contents and objects, especially if they are of very similar looking socks or golf balls. However, there is a sense in which I know perfectly well which object I am aware of in each of those experiences: I am aware of precisely the individual that is *given* in those experiences (see McDowell 1998a, 266–267). That I cannot "identify" the object, in *one* sense of "identify," does not mean I do not *see* that very object, or that I don't know *which* object I see. As P.F. Strawson notes, there are acts of "distinguishing" identification, in which one thing is distinguished from all others. There are also "reidentifying" acts of identification—or, better, acts of "relational identification."[24] An example of relational identification would be thinking that Stan is walking down the hall, when that depends on knowing that (a) *he* is walking down the hall and (b) he = Stan (see Evans 1982, 180). In this example, the knowledge that *he* is walking down the hall, where "he" is a content founded on my visual experience of the individual I see, is an act of distinguishing identification. Perception itself, as a mode of acquaintance or originary intuition, is also an act of distinguishing identification.

As Strawson (1959, 60) and Evans (1982, 181) point out, relational identification and relational *mis*identification depend on successful acts of distinguishing identification. In order to identify, or misidentify, *a* with *b*, you must first of all have established an intentional fix on *both* *a* and *b* (or rather two independent intentional fixes on *a*, in the veridical cases). Relational identification is a double-rayed act that is founded on, and so presupposes, the single-rayed acts of distinguishing identification. An act of distinguishing identification cannot fail in the same way an act of relational identification can. You either distinguish an object from others, and thereby "identify" it, or you do not (see Evans 1982, 218). If you do, that's a success—you are now conscious of it rather than of some other thing. But in relational identification, in which you identify *a* with *b*, your act fails if *a* ≠ *b*.

So, in the case involving Stan, I undergo a successful and veridical act of distinguishing identification aimed at Stan. I perceive him, and perceive him as he is. My problem is that my act of relational identification fails: I misidentify him with Dan. If, by contrast, my perceptual experience were of Dan, then my act of relational identification would be fitting (though not veridical), but I would be undergoing a hallucination. But that is not at all plausible for the reasons given above.

There is much more to say about the nature of each of the types of acts discussed above. For now, though, we can express the preliminary results of our initial foray into consciousness as follows:[25]

Table 2.1 Some Conscious Intentional Experiences

	Intuitive	*Positing*	*Direct*	*Originary*
Perception	+	+	+	+
Image Consciousness[26]	+	+/-	-	-
Phantasy[27]	+/-	-	+/-	-
Memory/Anticipation	+/-	+	+/-	-
Thought	-	+/-	+/-	-
Imagination	+	+/-	+/-	-

These are discoverable and phenomenally conspicuous similarities and differences among conscious intentional experiences. These similarities and differences are, moreover, grounded in features of experience that can, to a large extent, be varied independently of an experience's object. And while some of the experiences above essentially differ in their *total* objects—image consciousness, for instance, can never have precisely the same total object as a perceptual experience—all of them can overlap at least partially in their objects. What can be perceived can be thought of, remembered, anticipated, or imagined, for instance. And because anything whatsoever can be emptily thought of, so can any of the objects of any other type of act.

2.2 Some Further Features of Consciousness

The features discussed in the previous section all pertain to the *intentionality* of consciousness, and we will pay closer attention to many of them in following chapters. There are further features of consciousness which deserve our attention as well, many of which Husserl very helpfully discusses in the Second Chapter of the Third Section (Ideas I §§76–86) of *Ideas I*. In what follows, I will discuss them in varying degrees of detail, but will not attempt to provide full accounts of their nature.

2.2.1 The For-Structure of Consciousness

Consciousness has, as Donn Welton (2000, 22) puts it, a "for-structure." When we are consciously aware of something, in any of the intentional modes described above, that object is present or absent *to* or *for* us. Or, as Zahavi and Kriegel (2016, 36) put it, conscious experiences exhibit "for-me-ness." When I perceive a scratched car hood, the car hood is not just originarily given. It is originarily given *to* or *for me*. "It is part of the sense of appearing that appearing is always an appearing-*to*" (Drummond 2006, 199). The scratched hood may be originarily given to others as well, but in each case there will be a different for-structure implicated in each instance of givenness, one for each customer. The same is true of every other conscious intentional experience. What is consciously present or absent, believed or doubted, imagined or perceived *by* me is present, absent, and so on *to* me. This is why it is immediately evident, when I perceive or remember something, that *I* am the one who perceives or remembers, and that I am perceiving or remembering rather than, say, imagining or predicting (Ideas I §80, 154). Husserl refers to this as the "two-sidedness" of conscious experience.[28] As he puts it,

> In the course of observing something, *I* perceive it; likewise in remembering, *I* am often "pre-occupied" with something; in fictionalizing phantasy, *I* closely follow goings-on in the imagined world, in a quasi-observation of them.
>
> (ibid.)

The upshot of this is that whenever we are consciously aware of an intentional object, we are also consciously aware of ourselves, and consciously aware of our awareness itself.

Self-consciousness plays a critical role in our apprehension of the world. Not only does it enable us to distinguish, say, merely thinking about something and having it given, it is also essential for the consciousness of certain kinds of objects and states of affairs. Without self-consciousness, for instance, we could not consciously count things. To give Dallas Willard's example, as I count the trees in a park, the trees become progressively separated into two groups: the counted and the to-be-counted.[29] But *being counted* is not a property of the trees in themselves. It's a property they have in relation to my act of counting. If I were totally unaware that I was counting, it is difficult to see how the trees could present themselves as counted. And if they did not present themselves as counted, I could not count them. It is a matter of considerable debate, however, just what form that self-awareness takes.

If we think of all awareness-of as having an act-object structure characteristic of every type of experience so far discussed, then we will regard our awareness of ourselves and our experiences as an *objectifying* form of awareness—we and our experiences will be among the *objects* or which we are aware whenever we are consciously aware of anything.

According to one broad family of objectifying views, conscious experiences are the objects of distinct *higher-order acts* directed upon them. As David Rosenthal puts it,

> Conscious states are simply mental states we are conscious of being in. And, in general, our being conscious of something is just a matter of our having a thought of some sort about it. Accordingly, it is natural to identify a mental state's being conscious with one's having a roughly contemporaneous thought that one is in that mental state.
>
> (Rosenthal 1986, 335)

In the case of a conscious mental act A, then, its structure looks like this:

$$HOA \rightarrow A \rightarrow O$$

If all mental states were conscious, this would give rise to an infinite regress of higher-order experiences (Brentano 1995, 121–122). Rosenthal addresses that worry by denying the Cartesian view that all mental states are conscious (Rosenthal 1986, 339–340). In the case above, HOA is unconscious, since it is not the object of any higher order act.

On this view, consciousness is not an intrinsic feature of a conscious experience (see Zahavi 2006, 20). Nor is it an essential feature. If the light cast upon it by the higher-order state were withdrawn, the lower-order experience could persist, but unconsciously. The consequences of such a view are, however, unfortunate. Not only does consciousness seem to be intrinsic (Gennaro 2012, 57), so do a number of other consciousness-entailing features of experiences. Consider, again, the distinction between intuitive and empty acts. This is not a distinction between the objects of acts, but between the acts themselves. We can be conscious of an object as *intuited*, but that is different from being conscious of that object *intuitively*—one can, after all, emptily represent an object as intuited. Moreover, the distinction between empty and intuitive experiences is a distinction between types of *conscious* experiences, and one that can be and is made on the basis of our first-personal acquaintance with them.

This is most obvious in the case of intuitive experiences, in which something is given or present *to* a perceiving subject. As Wolfgang Fasching has argued, no matter how tight the causal connection between one's experience and an object or state of affairs, no matter how much the two covary with one another, no matter how reliably the former tracks the latter, without phenomenal consciousness nothing can be intuited. "Without consciousness, nothing is present to anyone" (Fasching 2012, 127). Empty acts, however, must be conscious as well (Pietersma 1973, 96). Emptiness, the lack of "fullness," is a "privation" (LI 6 §21, 729), and like many privations, it is in some measure a felt one. This is not to say that it's a kind of feeling or sensation.[30] It is, rather, that emptiness and intuitive fullness are discoverable, and discoverable as features that were *already* present in the experience before reflection upon them.[31] As Sartre nicely expresses it, "To be empty, an intention must be conscious of itself as empty, and precisely as empty *of* the precise matter it aims at."[32] If this is right, we cannot even draw the distinction between intuitive and empty acts among phenomenally unconscious mental states, for the simple reason that unconscious states could not possibly be either intuitive *or* empty. They are not the kinds of things that could be either. And in that case, phenomenally unconscious acts cannot be perceptions, or phantasies, or image-consciousnesses—or even, perhaps, thoughts.

If acts which are intuitive or empty are *necessarily* intuitive or empty, and therefore necessarily conscious, and if it is not essential to a conscious state that it be targeted by a higher-order act, then the extrinsic higher-order view must be false. But even if fullness and emptiness are simply intrinsic but non-essential features of acts, there are serious problems with the higher-order view. The reason is that the higher-order act must be responsible for *bestowing* phenomenal consciousness, and with it such properties as intuitiveness and emptiness, on the first-order act (Gallagher & Zahavi 2012, 59). But that, it seems, is not how intentionality works. There is a view on which consciousness endows its objects with intrinsic properties. Dallas Willard calls it the "Midas touch" account. According to Midas touch theories of intentionality, "to take something as our 'object' automatically transforms it in some essential way" (Willard 2000b, 38). But the Midas touch account is, to say the least, implausible.

First, as many have pointed out, things like rocks and numbers do not become conscious when we aim our thoughts at them; intentionality does not make its objects conscious, but makes us conscious of them (Gennaro 2006, 225). More importantly, representing an object does not endow it with any properties. Trees don't become green because we see them to be green (or because we call them "green"), and fossils don't become old because we know (or say) that they are old. The function of intentionality, or at least representational intentionality, is to apprehend how things are, not to make them be that way. That's the job of *action*. It's hard to see, then, why and how a first-order act could acquire properties in virtue of being the object of another intentional act—apart, that is, from the relational property, sometimes also possessed by rocks and numbers, of being the object of consciousness.

We turn now to "one-level" accounts of self-consciousness, many of which can account for the fact that conscious states are intrinsically conscious and even essentially conscious.[33] Here there are several contenders. Following Michelle Montague (2016, 56), I will focus on Brentanian self-representational views and Husserlian non-representational views. According to "self-representational" views, every conscious act *represents* itself.[34] In the case of an act of hearing, says Brentano, "We can say that the sound is the *primary object* of the *act* of hearing, and that the act of hearing itself is the *secondary object*" (Brentano 1995, 128). And so on in each case: the "secondary object" of each act is just the act itself. Like higher-order theories, self-representational views treat pre-reflective self-consciousness as having an act-object structure, like this:

$$\curvearrowleft$$
$$A \rightarrow O$$

Now, however, we need to determine the *manner* in which conscious states represent themselves, since not just any consciousness of a mental act will render that act conscious. According to Uriah Kriegel (2009b, 157), "mental states are conscious when they represent themselves *in the right way*." According to his account, the "right way" involves representing itself (a) non-derivatively, (b) specifically, and (c) essentially (2009b, 163).

Representations such as words and sentences are derivative. They owe their representational properties to being interpreted in a certain way. Their intentionality is, as Searle (1983, 27) says, "derived." Mental states, by contrast, have non-derived or intrinsic intentionality (ibid.; Kriegel 2009b, 158). A representation is *specific* when it "purports to represent a particular" (Kriegel 2009b, 160). Finally, a mental state is *essentially* self-representing when it represents itself in a way that is not accidental or contingent. To illustrate, Kriegel (2009b, 161) appeals to John Perry's famous example of making a mess in a grocery store by leaking sugar all over the floor, without realizing that he is the one doing so. It is one thing for Perry to think "I am making a mess" and another thing to think "the shopper with the torn sack is making a mess" (see Perry 1979, 3). The latter representation only contingently picks Perry out, whereas Perry's I-thoughts necessarily pick him out, and do so in an "epistemically necessary" way (Kriegel 2009b, 161). It is not epistemically necessary for Perry that he is the shopper with a torn sack of sugar. After all, for some time he does not realize *his* sack of sugar is torn. But Perry's I-thoughts epistemically necessarily pick him out; he cannot, via such a thought, confuse himself with anyone else. Our I-thoughts are, as Sydney Shoemaker (1968, 556) points out, "immune to error through misidentification." I can, in thinking that I like reading phenomenology, find out that I really don't. But I cannot discover that it was really someone else who likes reading phenomenology rather than me (ibid.).

In addition to these three features, pre-reflective self-consciousness has another, one that arguably partially explains the other three: it is an *originary* form of consciousness. This has been contested. Kenneth Williford claims that "an episode of consciousness represents itself in a[] ... nonpropositional, nonsensory, 'empty' way" (2006, 121)—much like the way in which unseen parts of a perceived object are represented. However, the fact that self-consciousness is nonsensory does not entail that it is empty or non-intuitive, much less non-originary. Sensory consciousness is not the only kind of intuitive consciousness. Furthermore, if consciousness represented itself emptily, we should expect there to be a way of representing itself which fulfills that empty intention, on pain of consciousness being something that, perhaps like various theoretical entities, can *only* be intended emptily. But it does not seem that there is any conceivable way to have a better or more authentic or intimate relation with an experience than to undergo it.

In hearing a tone, I don't emptily think that I hear a tone. Nor do I pick out the hearing of the tone by description. Nor, finally, is my self-consciousness empty in the unique way that my consciousness of the unseen portions of a perceived object are empty. As David Woodruff Smith puts it, "The mode of presentation 'I' is a form of presentation by *acquaintance*" (D.W. Smith 1989, 74, my emphasis), and so is the awareness of my hearing of the tone (ibid., 86). In that respect, at least, it is very much like perception. One reason for thinking so is that it is a source of significant and robust knowledge about the existence and nature of ourselves and our experiences. While there is a great deal that we do not know about ourselves and our own occurrent conscious states, our knowledge that they exist, that they are directed upon this object rather than that one, and that they do so in a certain way, such as intuitively rather than emptily, is about as good as knowledge gets. It would be a disturbing sign to somehow confuse the hearing or a tone with thinking about one, or the thinking of a tone with thinking about the effectiveness of hoplites in battle.

Furthermore, pre-reflective self-consciousness enables us to acquire knowledge of the phenomenal character of our experiences.[35] The phenomenal character of an experience is not identical with and does not supervene upon the bare fact that it is directed upon its object, as we have seen, since co-directed acts can differ massively in their phenomenal character. This is also true when the object in question is the *phenomenal character of an experience itself*. I can emptily think about the phenomenal character of the intuitive, originary experience of bungee jumping. In doing so, I am not intuitively acquainted with the phenomenal character of the intuitive experience of bungee jumping. I don't thereby know what that experience is like. How could I find out? By *having* the intuitive experience of bungee jumping. Merely undergoing an experience E, and thereby being pre-reflectively conscious of E, is a sufficient condition for knowing what it's like to experience E. As Galen Strawson puts it,

> There is, to repeat, a fundamental respect in which *the having is the knowing*. This is because the knowing is just—just is—the having (it involves no "introspection"). The having is all there is to the knowing, in this fundamental sense of "know"; it's (non-discursive) knowledge "by acquaintance".[36]

If I go bungee jumping, and somehow remain conscious while doing so, I will thereby know what it's like to bungee jump, which is something I cannot know by either emptily thinking about bungee jumping or emptily thinking about the *experience of* bungee jumping.

This gives us an additional reason to reject all higher-order theories. That is, in addition to failing to explain how conscious experiences are intrinsically conscious, they fail to account for the originary character of self-consciousness. All originary acts are intuitive, and all intuitive acts are conscious. Therefore, whatever act is responsible for the self-appearance of conscious states must *itself* be conscious. But on higher-order views, this series must terminate in a higher-order act that is unconscious. This criticism extends, not only to higher order thought (HOT) views, but also to higher order perception (HOP) views. William Lycan, for example, points out that self-awareness is a "presentational" form of consciousness, and appeals to this fact, among others, to argue for the superiority of HOP views.[37] However, these acts of higher order "perception" cannot all be conscious. If they all were, then we would encounter the regress with which we started. But, as we have seen, originary, presentational acts must be conscious. Just as we cannot explain how a color is intuitively and originarily present in visual perception by appealing to an unconscious experience of it, so we cannot explain how a conscious experience is intuitively and originarily present by appealing to an unconscious experience of *it*. Calling such experiences "perceptual" or "presentational" is a promising start, but the label doesn't fit if they aren't even conscious.

This criticism also extends to Rocco Gennaro's wide intrinsicality view. Unlike Rosenthal's higher-order view, the wide intrinsicality view maintains that "what makes mental states conscious is *intrinsic* to conscious states." The reason is that:

> a kind of *inner* self-referential relational element is also present *within* the structure of such states. In contrast to standard HOT theory, the WIV says that *first-order* conscious mental states are *complex* states containing both a world-directed mental state-part M and an unconscious metapsychological thought (MET).
>
> (Gennaro 2012, 55)

Since this metapsychological thought is unconscious, however, it cannot provide us with the originary consciousness of subjectivity that pre-reflective self-consciousness possesses.

If right, this puts to rest all higher-order views. It also limits the range of possible first-order or self-representational views: any viable self-representational view must construe the self-directed component of the act as an originary intention. One self-representational view that satisfies this constraint is Brentano's. On his view, every conscious state—indeed every mental state—is essentially conscious. And he characterizes the consciousness of a "presentation of sound" as a "presentation of the presentation" (Brentano 1995, 127). On his view, we "perceive [Nehmen ... wahr] the mental phenomena which exist within us" (ibid., 128). He adds, however, that we cannot "observe" those mental phenomena. The reason is that when something is observed, it is the object of attention, and when something is the object of attention, it is the primary, and not the secondary, object of that act. But acts cannot be their own primary objects (ibid.).

If every conscious act is essentially conscious, as it is for Brentano, then it follows that every act essentially contains both a primary, object-directed intention and a secondary, self-directed one. As Brentano puts it,

> The presentation of the sound is connected with the presentation of the presentation of the sound in such a peculiarly intimate way that its very existence constitutes an intrinsic prerequisite for the existence of this presentation.
>
> (Brentano 1995, 127)

That is, the primary intention not only requires the secondary intention for its status as conscious, but for its existence. Brentano's theory does a good job, then, of preserving the fact that conscious states are not conscious in virtue of something else, but in virtue of their own nature. As David W. Smith puts it, "Inner awareness is not itself a *separate mental act*, but resides somehow in the conscious experience itself."[38]

It is not clear, however, that a Brentanian theory can do justice to Smith's observation. In order for the theory to work, it must be an essential law that every mental act is equipped with two intentions, one directed outward, the other directed at itself. Furthermore, no other act with a different object could possibly occupy the self-directed intention's position within the structure of the act. This makes it very unlike our inattentive awareness of the background in perceptual experience. If I am inattentively aware of a truck in the background, and the truck drives away to reveal a tree, I am now inattentively aware of a tree. The truck-directed act has given way to a tree-directed act, but both acts occupy the same place in the overall structure of my experience. But nothing could replace the Brentanian secondary intention. Finally, this secondary intention must always be an originary intention. Nothing occupying its place within the structure of an act could possibly be empty.

That Brentanian secondary intentions must have these features is not by itself objectionable. Perhaps they permit of some more primitive explanation. Or maybe that is just how things brutely are. The biggest shortcoming of self-representational views, however, is that they seem, to many at least, to mischaracterize the peculiar nature of the two-sidedness of experience. Here, I believe with some but not complete confidence, that the Husserlian and Sartrean view of self-consciousness as non-objectifying is more faithful to the phenomena. On this view, the structure of pre-reflective self-awareness would look something like this:

$$A \rightarrow O$$

On this model, the self-conscious act A has, in addition to its object-directedness, what Uriah Kriegel—a strong critic of this view—calls an "intrinsic glow," an "unstructured, inexplicable, *sui generis* property" (2009b, 101). Whether or not that's an accurate characterization, the phenomenological case for the Husserlian-Sartrean view is the following. Self-consciousness can and often does take an objectifying form. But we, and most of our conscious experiences, are usually not *objects* at all. The self-consciousness involved in ordinary consciousness is non-reflective or pre-reflective (Sartre 2018, 11; Zahavi 2006, 123). We ourselves are not among those objects, but subjects—those *to* or *for* whom things are present.

Our self-consciousness is two-sided. But the two-*sidedness* of experience must be distinguished from its having two *objects*. When I perceive or think, I am not presented to myself as another object in the field of consciousness (see

Zahavi 1999, 56). I am conscious of myself as the *subject* of the experience (Drummond 2006, 207). I can, under suitable conditions, make myself and my experiences objects. But those would be reflective acts built on the original ones. When I am conscious of an object, the conscious *I* is not on the objective side of the conscious act at all, but on its *subjective* side. John Drummond even argues that I am not even properly conscious of myself as an I; "I am not prereflectively aware that *I* am perceiving an object; I am aware of *my perceiving an object*" (Drummond 2006, 212).

Along with myself as the subject of experience, my lived experiences themselves—the ones I am actually undergoing—reside on the subjective side of consciousness as well. Seeing a car and thinking of a car are two different experiences, and part of that difference lies on the side of the subjective act. In seeing a car, I am not just conscious of the car, and not just conscious that the car is there for me. I am conscious of *seeing*, as opposed to imagining or merely thinking about, the car. Husserl marks this distinction by saying that the object—the car—is *perceived*, but the act itself is *experienced*. He says of sensations, for instance, that

> Sensations, and the acts "interpreting" them or apperceiving them, are alike experienced, but they do not appear as objects: they are not seen, heard, or perceived by any sense. Objects, on the other hand, appear and are perceived, but they are not experienced.
>
> (LI 5 §14, 567)

What is (allegedly) true of sensations is also true of acts of perceiving, thought, and so on. They are experienced, but they are not objects of experience. And this does not just mean that they are not "things." It means that they are not on the object-side of the consciousness-of relation at all. Our original consciousness of ourselves and our experiences is both *pre-reflective* and *non-objectifying*. When I am consciously aware of some object O, my awareness itself is not another object. It is not a *Gegenstand*—that is, something that *stands over against* me (Zahavi 1999, 189).

Sartre is often given credit for emphasizing the peculiar nature of pre-reflective and non-objectifying self-awareness, though as Dan Zahavi demonstrates in detail, Husserl was thoroughly familiar with it, even if not all of his attempts to formulate it were fully satisfactory (see Zahavi 1999, 53ff.). But Sartre does deserve credit for drawing out some of the most interesting and perplexing consequences of this fact. On Sartre's view, "any positional consciousness of an object is at the same time a non-positional consciousness of itself" (Sartre 2018, 11). We can take up a positional—or, as I prefer, *objectifying*—attitude toward ourselves and our experiences. (A positional act is a positing one. But not all objectifying acts are positing. One can have an objectifying but non-positing phantasy experience of oneself, for instance.) But in doing so, the *I* which is experiencing is no longer qualitatively identical with the I which is reflected upon and objectified, nor is the actually experiencing I genuinely experiencing the experiences upon which I reflect, at least not fully. "Thus the consciousness which says *I Think* is precisely not the consciousness which thinks." Well, that consciousness thinks too. The point, Sartre clarifies, is that "it is not its own thought which it posits by this thetic act" (Sartre 1960, 45). Less dramatically, we can say that it is not the same act of consciousness as the one it represents, objectifyingly, as thinking. I can, in an attempt at "sincerity," represent myself as, say, sad.[39] But in doing so, I am already beyond that sadness. I am not simply sad; I am conscious of myself as sad, and this conscious *I* which I now am by virtue of living through this reflective act may or may not be sad. (For Sartre, I am now distressingly free to be either sad or not sad.) Perhaps I find the sadness upon which I reflect to be sentimental, weak, or ungrounded. Of course the reflecting I may itself be sad. But if so, I am not sad for exactly the same reasons and in exactly the same way that I was sad in my unreflective state. Instead of feeling sorry about some state of the world, I may now feel sorry for myself. But here again, I do not *represent* myself as feeling sorry for myself. That would in turn require a new act directed at, and therefore distinct from, my self-sorrow. It is because of this, as Dan Zahavi says, that "there will always remain an unthematized spot in the life of the subject" (1999, 189).

Kriegel objects to the non-objectifying view that it is not only mysterious, but also incoherent.[40] In self-awareness, a subject is "*aware of* her experience" (Kriegel 2009b, 104). But, he says, "it strikes me as conceptually true that, in the relevant sense of 'object,' awareness-of is always awareness-of-object" (2009b, 105). There is no denying the force of Kriegel's charge of mysteriousness. But then, some things are mysterious, especially if they are primitive. It would be hardly less "mysterious" if, as on a Brentanian view, every act of representing an object essentially also represented itself secondarily. The charge of incoherence, however, is not nearly as obvious. An object, for Kriegel, just is "that-which-the-intentional-act-is-about" (ibid., n.8). So construed, it seems that an object is what stands over-against the act itself; its *Gegenstand*. But if that's the case, it does not seem to be "conceptually true" that awareness-of is always awareness of an "object." If that were the structure of self-consciousness, then, again, we are stuck with the position that our experiences, and we ourselves, stand over against us in non-reflective experience. And it seems to me to be close to a phenomenological datum that they do not.

Where does this leave us, besides mystified? The most solid finding is that higher-order views are very unlikely to be true. They must treat consciousness—and with it intuitiveness and emptiness—as both extrinsic and contingent features of an experience, and they cannot account for the originary character of our self-awareness. A self-representational view such as Kriegel's owes us an account of how our experiences could be objects of consciousness without standing over against us in consciousness. And the non-representational views must posit a *sui generis* property or mode of consciousness, probably inseparable from the more familiar object-oriented kind of intentionality. It seems to me that the latter might be the solution. There is, on this view, a mode of consciousness that is not the awareness-of something as an object, but of something as a *subject*. If we cannot understand it in terms of anything else, that may be because it just is its own phenomenon. But it's difficult to be too confident here.

2.2.2 The Temporal Structure of Consciousness

In conscious experience, we frequently apprehend objects that exist in and through time. Conscious experience itself exists in and through time. "Every experience is in itself a flow of becoming," writes Husserl. It is "a constant flow of retentions and protentions mediated by a phase of an originary sort, that is itself flowing" (Ideas I §78, 143). When I see a bat hit a ball and the ball rocket into the air, I am seeing a sequentially ordered series of events. I see the-ball-flying-after-it-has-been-hit. And as I watch the ball fly, I also anticipate which way it will fly. I have a "protention" of the immediate future (PCIT §40, 89). I also have a distinctive consciousness of the immediate past, "retention" (PCIT §12, 34). I am not only conscious of where the ball is, but also of where it has just been.

What makes the perception of temporally extended events and processes possible is the distinctive makeup of consciousness. On Husserl's view, each conscious experience has three components: "primal impression," retention, and protention directed upon the present, the immediate past, and the immediate future, respectively (PCIT §11, 30–31). Suppose we hear a familiar melody ("Twinkle Twinkle") that begins as follows: C-C-G-G-A.[41] We can depict the impressional-retentional structure as follows, with a few arrows indicating the intentional direction of the act-moments:[42]

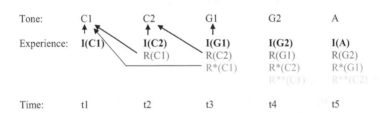

Figure 2.1 Retention

At t1, we have an impression (I) of the first C, C1. At t2, we have an impression of the second C, and at t3 an impression of the first G, and so on. But we could never hear the melody if this is all that happened. At t2, we are impressionally aware of C2, but have a distinctive sort of awareness of the just-past tone, C1. We are aware of it through *retention* (R). The act-moment of retention is present at t2. But the intentional *object* of that act-moment is no longer present; the retention "is retention *of* the tone that has been" (PCIT §11, 31). And it is the consciousness of the tone as having been. As we move from t1 to t2, "The tone-now changes into a tone-having-been" (ibid.). When we move to t3, we find an impression of G1, a retention of C2, and an even deeper retention of C1. Eventually this retentional consciousness dies out, "for a weakening, which finally ends in imperceptibility, goes hand in hand with the [retentional] modification" (ibid., 32).

Retentional consciousness, which Husserl sometimes calls "primary memory" (PCIT §11, 32), is not the same as what we ordinarily think of as episodic memory. Memory is a reproductive form of consciousness. Retention is not, and Husserl argues that it could not be. The reason is that memory already includes retention within itself. If I remember the melody—that is, remember it intuitively and episodically—he says,

> the whole memory-phenomenon has exactly the same constitution, *mutatis mutandis*, as the perception of the melody. Like the perception, it has a privileged point: to the now-point of the perception corresponds the now-point of the memory.
>
> (PCIT §14, 37)

And it also has a retentional and protentional structure. Memory, then, already includes within itself the structure of time consciousness. Memory is "a re-presentational modification of the perceptual process with all of the latter's phases and stages right down to and including the retentions" (PCIT §15, 39).

Unlike memory, retention is an *originary* consciousness of the "just past." In retention, the "being just past is not merely something meant but a given fact, given itself and therefore 'perceived'" (PCIT §14, 38). There's nothing else like it; it is "a unique kind of intentionality" (PCIT §12, 33). And it is necessary for the perception of things like melodies and movement. If the melody above were stretched out so that C2 were played at t5—after C1 has faded from retention—we would not *hear* the melody, though perhaps we could reconstruct it in intuitive memory. Similarly, if an object moves so slowly that there is no discernible change in its position in the time allotted by the scope of retention, we cannot see it move. One consequence of this is that the scope of retentional consciousness plays an important role in determining what sorts of events, processes, and states of affairs we are capable of perceiving. If retention extended further than it does, we could perceive various "slow" events and changes that we cannot perceive now. If it were more limited, our perceptual event-field would shrink.

As mentioned, time-consciousness also involves future-directed protentions. Perhaps after hearing C1, we anticipate that it will be followed by a note, but not any particular note. Hearing C2, along with the tempo, it may begin to sound familiar. With the jump to G1, the melody will sound even more familiar, and the protentions will become more determinate. For instance, at t5 most of us will experience a determinate protention aimed at a repetition of the note A.

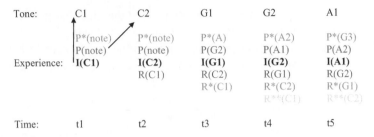

Tone:	C1	C2	G1	G2	A1
	P*(note)	P*(note)	P*(A)	P*(A2)	P*(G3)
	P(note)	P(note)	P(G2)	P(A1)	P(A2)
Experience:	**I(C1)**	**I(C2)**	**I(G1)**	**I(G2)**	**I(A1)**
		R(C1)	R(C2)	R(G1)	R(G2)
			R*(C1)	R*(C2)	R*(G1)
				R**(C1)	R**(C2)
Time:	t1	t2	t3	t4	t5

Figure 2.2 Protention

So, let's consider the structure from t3-t4. The protentional intention at t3 directed toward G2 finds its fulfillment at t4. Because t3 lies within the scope of the retention at t4, we experience a consciousness of fulfillment. But if an experience does not lie within the scope of another experience's retentional horizon, we will not have such an experience. On the diagram above, no anticipations taking place at t1 are fulfilled at t5, since the experience at t5 does not have a retentional horizon that reaches back to it.

Time-consciousness, like all consciousness, exhibits two-sidedness. In his lectures on time consciousness, Husserl discusses the "double intentionality of retention" (PCIT §39, 84). This section is daunting, and I will not try to do it justice. What emerges, though, is a picture of retention as having both a "transverse" and a "horizontal" intentionality (PCIT §39, 86–87). According to John Brough, the transverse intentionality is objectively oriented—it is what accounts for our awareness of temporally extended objects. The horizontal intentionality is what accounts for our consciousness of the "flow" of consciousness itself.[43] When I hear a tone, "I am conscious in retention of both the past tone and my past hearing of that tone; similarly for protention" (D.W. Smith 2007, 212). These two "intentionalities" account for both the *objectifying* consciousness of temporally extended objects, and "the primary self-manifestation of the experiences of these intentional objects" (Zahavi 1999, 75). This latter form of consciousness, however, is not objectifying. For that reason, it is misleading to characterize time-consciousness as having a "double intentionality," at least if by that we mean that it involves an objectifying awareness of the stream of experience.[44] What time-consciousness has is two-*sidedness* in the sense discussed in the previous section. This two-sidedness adheres to all the dimensions of time consciousness and not just to the impressional now-point. My retained experience of the just-past tone does not move into object position for my present consciousness just in virtue of sinking into the past—though of course it *can* be made an object. Rather, it is retained in a non-objectifying way (see Zahavi 1999, 76). Similarly, when I anticipate the note A at t4, I also anticipate my own *hearing of* A, but, again, not in an objectifying manner.

2.2.3 The Attentional Structure of Consciousness

Attention is a vast theme for phenomenological inquiry, and I will simply mention it to round off our discussion of some of the general features of conscious experience. Sebastian Watzl characterizes consciousness's "attentional structure" as what is responsible for "organizing the mind into parts that are central or prioritized and those that are peripheral."[45] When we reflect on paradigmatic conscious experiences, attentive experiences are the first to come to mind. They are the sorts of acts which Husserl calls "cogito" experiences (Ideas I §35, 62). As a moment's reflection will attest, however, not all experiences are attentive, and not all objects within the field of awareness at any given time are attended to. Every perceptual experience, for instance, contains "a halo of *background-intuitions*" (Ideas I §35, 61). For reasons not entirely obvious, Husserl regards a "stream of experiences" consisting solely of "actualizations" or attentive experiences to be an impossibility (Ideas I §35, 62). Of greater interest is his claim that inattentive experiences can become attentive, and vice versa—or, otherwise put, that an object which one is not attending to can become an object of attention. Obviously being attended to is not an intrinsic feature of any object. And while attending to an object nearly always brings further features of it to light, objects do not thereby appear to have changed or acquired those properties just in virtue of being attended to.

Attentive acts of consciousness bear an intimate relation to one's self or ego (see Jacobs 2010, §1). Attentive acts are those in which I pre-eminently live. Husserl even defines attention as "*a tending of the ego toward an intentional object*" (EJ §18, 80). More recently, Carolyn Dicey Jennings (2017) has argued that "the self comes into being with the first act of attention, or the first time attention favours one interest over another." Whatever the precise relation between the self and attention, it is important to emphasize that while the self and its experiences are not typically objects of attention, they are not objects in the halo or margin of consciousness either. As Zahavi (1999,61) puts it, is that "Prior to reflection, consciousness is not given as a marginal *object*," for the simple reason that it is not an object at all.

2.3 Conclusion

In this chapter, we have uncovered a variety of ways in which conscious experiences can differ, even when they have identical or partially identical objects, and we have examined some of the structural features of conscious awareness. In the next chapter, we will take a close look at intentionality and, in particular, at the parts and features of conscious experiences which account for some of the similarities and differences discussed above.

Notes

1 See Romano 2015, Chapter 2.
2 I discuss image consciousness more fully in Hopp 2017.
3 Kurg 2014b.

4 PICM §9, 21. See Dilworth (2005, 113) for a very similar set of distinctions.

5 PICM §12, 27; also Wollheim 1980, 213.

6 James Kinkaid (2020, 5) argues that the relationship between the physical thing and the image object is one of material constitution, a claim with which I agree.

7 Dilworth 2005, 172. Husserl makes a similar point, though not as clearly, in PICM, 586ff. Also see Brough 2012, 547 and Kennedy 1993, 78.

8 See Schneider 2012 for a sophisticated general argument against token physicalism.

9 Ideas I §99, 201; also PCIT §28.

10 PICM, 564; also see Kurg 2014a, 35–36.

11 See Reid 1853, 278, as well as the discussion in Van Cleve 2015, 94ff.

12 LI 6 §47, 790; also Hopp 2011, 69.

13 See Hopp 2012, 339. I am grateful to John Drummond for suggesting "takes ... as" as opposed to my previous formulation, "uses ... as," which wrongly suggests that this must be an action on the part of the subject.

14 Kulvicki 2014, 23; also see Wollheim 1987, 56, whom Kulvicki cites in this connection.

15 See Aldea 2013 and Jansen 2016.

16 See Reinach 1989, 375 and Brough 2005, XXXIV.

17 PICM, 570; Currie 1995, 66; Matthen 2005, 315.

18 Smith & McIntyre 1982, 20 and 355.

19 Compare with the Marvin/Michael example in Dretske 2000a, 105.

20 See A.D. Smith 2002, 75–76. Also see Dretske 1969, Chapter II and Dretske 2000a for many more examples.

21 Searle (1983, 47ff.) is responsible for the insight that the causal relation between the perceived object and the experience itself is built into the perceptual experience's own content. I believe he is right, though the account presented here differs from his in a number of important respects.

22 See Austin 1964, 52 and Travis 2004, §3.

23 See Putnam 1975, 144ff. Husserl discusses what are in effect Twin Earth cases as well in the 1911 Beilage XIX of VB. For helpful discussions, see Beyer 1997, Alweiss 2009, Erhard 2011, and Szanto 2012, 352ff. Beyer's piece contains English translations of sizeable portions of Husserl's text.

24 LI 6 §8, 697. See Strawson 1959, 60. Strawson speaks of the "distinguishing aspect" and the "reidentifying aspect" of identification, but I prefer to couch this in terms of acts. Gareth Evans (1982, 180) makes a similar distinction when he distinguishes between knowledge that is "identification-dependent" and knowledge which is "identification-free."

25 See Romano 2015, 46 for a similar chart, which differs from the present one in some of its particulars. Thanks to Jacob Rump for pointing me to it.

26 Vis-à-vis the image-subject.

27 Vis-à-vis the particulars and states of affairs represented therein. Phantasy is an originary form of intuition with respect to some universals, as is imagination.

28 Ideas I §80, 154. Also see Ideas II §25.

29 Willard 2003b, xix–xx.

30 Thanks to Tarjei Larsen for bringing this point to my attention.

31 See Ideas I §45, 81 for the claim that features of conscious states are presented as having been "already there" when we reflect upon them. Also see §78, 142.

32 Sartre 2018, 64. Also see Willard 1984, 227 and Bernet 2003, 156.

33 Thomasson 2000; Zahavi 2006, 20.

34 For a helpful overview, see Kriegel and Williford 2006. Also see Kriegel 2009b and Montague 2016, especially Chapter 3.

35 See Zahavi 1999, 23 and 2006, 119ff.

36 Strawson 2015, 219. Also see Tye 2009, 117.

37 Lycan 2004, 101–102. Also see Van Gulick 2001, 288–289, whom Lycan also cites in this connection.

38 D.W. Smith 1989, 86. Also see Zahavi 2006, 20.

39 On the impossibility of "sincerity," both with respect to sadness and anything else, see Sartre 2018, 105ff.

40 For a response, and a very sophisticated critique of self-representational views, see Frank 2016, 35ff. At the heart of Frank's criticism is that even if the representing and the represented states

are identical, self-representational accounts cannot explain how they "*know* themselves *as* being the same" (ibid., 35).

41 See Miller 1984, Chapter 6 for, as its title says, "Husserl's Account of Hearing a Melody."

42 See PCIT §10, 29 for Husserl's own time diagram.

43 Brough 1991, LIII. See PCIT §39, 85.

44 Drummond (2006, 217) calls both horizontal and transverse consciousnesses cases of "intentionality," but carefully distinguishes objectifying intentionality from the non-objectifying intentionality proper to self-consciousness.

45 Watzl 2017, 2. See Dicey Jennings 2012, 541–543 for a discussion of Husserl's theory of attention in a contemporary context, and Jacobs 2010 for a very rich discussion of Husserl's theory of attention, wakefulness, and their relation to the self or ego.

Recommended Readings

Dilworth, John. 2005. *The Double Content of Art*. New York: Prometheus Books.

Hopkins, Robert. 1998. *Picture, Image, and Experience*. Cambridge: Cambridge University Press.

Husserl, Edmund. 1991. *On the Phenomenology of the Consciousness of Internal Time (1893–1917)*. John B. Brough, trans. Dordrecht: Kluwer Academic Publishers.

Husserl, Edmund. 2005. *Phantasy, Image Consciousness, and Memory*. John B. Brough, trans. Dordrecht: Springer.

Dretske, Fred I. 1969. *Seeing and Knowing*. Chicago: The University of Chicago Press.

Montague, Michelle. 2016. *The Given: Experience and Its Content*. Oxford: Oxford University Press.

Thomasson, Amie L. 2000. "After Brentano: A One-Level Theory of Consciousness." *European Journal of Philosophy* 8: 190–209.

Zahavi, Dan. 1999. *Self-Awareness and Alterity*. Evanston: Northwestern University Press.

3   Intentionality and Meaning

In the previous chapter we uncovered a number of similarities and differences among conscious experiences, including experiences that shared identical or partly identical objects. In doing so, we also further reinforced the conclusion that consciousness is not transparent in the way that many philosophers suppose. It appears to be a necessary law that one can never provide a complete description of an intentional experience merely by specifying its object, no matter how thoroughly that object's features are described. Knowing that an experience is of a tree, or a tree with such-and-such intrinsic and relational properties, leaves it wide open whether it is intuitive or empty, positing or non-positing, direct or indirect, or originary or not. In this chapter we turn to the nature of meanings and their place within an intentional act.

Before beginning, it is worth repeating what was stated in the Preface regarding the basic subject matter of phenomenology. Husserl writes, we "want to attain clarity about how act, meaning content, objectivity, figure in relation to one another" (ILTK §32b, 169). Again, he says, "To elucidate [the] connections between veritable being and knowing and so in general to investigate the correlations between act, meaning, object is the *task of transcendental phenomenology*" (ILTK, 434). In *The Idea of Phenomenology*, the phenomenological theory of knowledge is charged with uncovering the "correlation between epistemic experience, meaning, and object" (IdPh, 17) or "the correlation of knowledge, its sense, and its object" (IdPh, 18). And in *Ideas I*, Husserl characterizes the subject matter of phenomenology as including the "essential relations that combine the *idea of what truly is* with the ideas of truth, reason, and consciousness."[1]

Furthermore, as he makes clear, studying this threefold correlation is essential to studying consciousness itself. "To the extent ... that every consciousness is 'consciousness-of,' the essential study of consciousness includes also that of consciousness-meaning and consciousness-objectivity as such."[2] In other words: you cannot investigate acts of consciousness without also investigating both their ideal contents and their objects.[3]

Why this should be the case will become increasingly apparent in this chapter. Roughly, ideal meanings—by which Husserl means concepts and propositions—are one important kind of intentional content. And intentional contents are those entities in virtue of which intentional experiences are about the objects that they are about. As we will discover in Chapter 8, meanings are not the only kind of ideal contents. In this chapter, though, we will confine our attention to meanings in order to disclose some aspects of their nature and their place within an intentional experience. We will begin by noting some of the most conspicuous components of an ordinary, unremarkable linguistic act. The purpose here is not to provide a philosophy of language or speech acts, but to isolate meanings from the contexts in which they typically show up and distinguish them from things with which they are easily confused. We will then discuss both the objectivity and the subjectivity of meanings, and then defend Husserl's early view that meanings, and intentional contents in general, are *properties* of intentional acts.

3.1 Some Components of a Linguistic Act

Husserl's First *Logical Investigation* is entitled "Expression and Meaning." It is by no means a complete theory of linguistic acts. It does, however, effectively isolate those things that Husserl calls "meanings"—concepts and propositions—through an extended exercise of what he would later call "eidetic variation."[4] Our task is to run over some highlights of his account in order to get a better sense of what meanings are, what they are not, and how they are related to mental acts.

Suppose that one person, A, turns to another, B, and asserts: "The hood of the car is scratched." The most obvious constituents of this situation are a speaker, an audience, and an "expression" (LI 1 §6, 276). In this case, the expression is a particular token of an English sentence, stated with a certain illocutionary force, namely that of *assertion*. This token utterance can be treated physically as a sound-pattern with a certain volume and lasting a certain duration. It can also be regarded, and by speakers of English will almost always primarily be regarded, as a bearer of meaning or significance. The utterance is a token of a sentence, but is not identical with any sentence. The very same sentence could be uttered numerous times and by different people, whereas A's utterance is a one-time occurrence (see LI 1 §11, 284). Moreover, the very same sentence can be expressed via vastly different physical "marker types," such as the *inscription* "The hood of the car is scratched."[5] Thanks to the conventions governing spelling, this counts as the same signifier or semantic type as the utterance, but it is not the same type of physical marker.

A's utterance is *of* or *about* something, its "objective correlate" or object (LI 1 §12, 286). Because word meanings are public—a fact which Husserl did not, unfortunately, sufficiently emphasize in the first of his *Logical Investigations*—A's token utterance has its objective correlate quite independently of whatever happens to be going on in A's mind when she talks (Evans 1982, 69). But we will assume that A is using this expression responsibly and comprehendingly to talk about the same object that she is thinking about. One thing she is clearly talking about is the hood of the car. But that is not all that she is thinking and talking about in using this expression. That is why the expressions "The hood of the car is red" and "The hood of the car is *not* scratched" are not about exactly the same thing as A's utterance. They do not represent things to be just as A's utterance does. A, rather, is also talking about the property of being scratched, and she is attributing that property to the car's hood. The "full and entire object" of A's utterance and thought is a state of affairs—the being scratched of the car's hood.[6] An obtaining state of affairs is a *fact*. If the state of affairs that A is talking about obtains, then her assertion is true, and otherwise it is false. Note that on this view, facts are *not* true propositions. They are what true propositions are about.

In understanding A's utterance, B's mental life will come to partially resemble A's: he too will now be conscious of the state of affairs of the car's hood's being scratched. B will also likely learn something else, this time about A's mental life, namely that A is carrying out a "meaning intention" or mental act of a certain sort (LI 1 §9, 281). More specifically, B will learn that A believes the car hood to be scratched. Part of what clues B into the status of A's mental life is that A's utterance has a certain illocutionary force, that of *assertion* as opposed to, say, questioning or commanding.[7] Husserl defines meaning intentions, or acts of meaning, as "the determinate manner in which we refer to our object of the moment" (LI 1 §13, 289). Thanks to the sorts of conventions that govern communication in normal circumstances, such as Grice's maxim of quality—which requires us to assert only what we believe on the basis of evidence—B will also assume that A has some evidence for her belief (Grice 1994b, 61). If the tree is nearby, B will likely assume that A has undergone a "meaning-fulfilling act" (LI 1 §13, 289) such as perception, one in which the meant state of affairs is intuitively present.

Despite the information B is situated to gather about A's mental life, A's act of meaning, or meaning intention, is not what A's assertion is about. She is not talking about herself. If A wanted to talk *about* her mental life, she would say something rather different, such as "I believe that the hood of the car is scratched" or "I saw that the hood of the car is scratched." Those sentences are not about the same thing as A's utterance, since they are not even true under the same conditions. The hood could be scratched even if A didn't believe it was, and A could believe it was scratched even if it were not.

A's mental state, her belief, is what her utterance *indicates* or *gives notice* of (LI 1 §7, 277). In roughly the same way that smoke indicates fire and tree rings indicate the age of a tree, A's expression indicates her belief to B. In successful communication, such a giving notice (*Kundgabe*) by the speaker is met with a corresponding taking notice (*Kundnahme*) by the hearer.[8] There is a sense in which A's expression "means" her mental state—it is a case of what Grice would later call "natural" meaning (1994a, 22). In all of these cases, the indicator provides evidence for the existence of what is indicated (Davis 2005, 71). But that is not what A's expression is about, nor what it *means* in the sense in which we are trying to isolate. If it were, then its meaning would shift every time a difference person uttered it, which is not the case. If B were to repeat to C what A said, B would be talking about the same thing A was talking about, and his utterance would mean the same thing that A's does. But B's utterance would give notice of something different to C than A's linguistic act gives notice of to B, namely that *B* believes the car hood to be scratched (see LI 1 §11, 285).

So far, then, we have uncovered the following items and relations:

(1) A Speaker/Thinker
  addresses his or her
(2) Audience
  by producing an
(3) Utterance/Inscription
  which possesses an
(4) Illocutionary Force
  and which is a token of a
(5) Sentence
  which represents an
(6) Objective Correlate
  which is also represented by the
(7) Mental State(s) of the Speaker
  (7a) Meaning intention or act of meaning
  (7b) Meaning fulfillment
  which are in turn given notice to and taken notice of by (2) the audience by (3) the speaker's utterance.
  The meaning intention (7a) is also responsible for *bestowing meaning* on (3) the speaker's utterance.

It would be welcome news to learn that we could assemble a full account of A's utterance and its meaning out of the materials so far uncovered, or at least out of materials not radically different from them. That, however, is not to be. We still have not discovered the

(8) Meaning
of A's utterance, which is *expressed by* A's utterance. Meanings, for Husserl, consist of
  (8a) Propositions
    and
  (8b) Concepts
  out of which propositions are composed, which Husserl defines at one point as "the self-identical meaning of the corresponding expressions" (LI Prol., §59, 217).

Both concepts and propositions can function as the *contents* of mental states. Propositions, in turn, can be systematically ordered into structured wholes, most notably proofs and theories (LI Prol., §67, 237), but also stories, accounts, narratives, reports, contracts, legal codes, and so on. Although every theoretical science owes its unity primarily to the region of reality that it is about, a unity "present in things" (LI Prol., §6, 62), a science is strictly speaking composed of propositions, as opposed to the other entities and connections that help make up a fully realized science. Those include (a) the objects and states of affairs which render those propositions true, (b) the mental acts in which those propositions are known, (c) the signs by whose means those propositions are expressed, and (d) the various material, institutional, sociological, and other "external arrangements" that make the practice of scientific thinking possible.[9]

3.2 What Meanings Aren't

Now we turn to the reasons why meanings are distinct from any of the items (1)–(7) above.

3.2.1 The Meaning of an Utterance is not the Utterance's Object

There are at least five reasons for distinguishing the meaning of A's utterance from its object. First, the most obvious feature of concepts and propositions is the relation they bear to an utterance's objective correlate: they are of it or *represent* it (see Willard 1984, 23–24). Concepts are of or about things, and so are the truth-evaluable wholes that they compose, propositions. This immediately rules out identifying an expression's meaning with its object, at least in most cases. The meaning of A's utterance, the proposition <the hood of the car is scratched>, has an object; it is about the state of affairs or fact of the car's hood's being scratched. But that fact does not have an object. It is not about anything.

Second, the state of affairs and the proposition have different constituents. The proposition is composed of concepts, but the state of affairs is composed of a car hood and the property of being scratched. The concept of being scratched is not, it bears stressing, the same thing as the property of being scratched. The car hood possesses the property, but it does not possess the concept, and I possess the concept, but I do not possess the property (see LI 1 §33).

Third, A's utterance would remain meaningful even if the state of affairs that it represents did not obtain—if the car hood were not scratched, or even if there were no car at all. In those cases A's utterance would be false but still meaningful. This provides an additional reason to distinguish, in almost all cases, the concept of F and the property of F. Some concepts, such as <being equal to the greatest prime number>, are of properties that do not have possible instances. But the concept in question does exist.

A fourth reason for distinguishing meanings from their objects is that the simplicity or complexity of meanings does not necessarily correspond to simplicity or complexity in the objects that they designate. As Husserl notes, the phrase "simple object" expresses a complex meaning, but does not designate a complex object (LI 4 §2, 495). And the meaning of a name, according to Husserl, may be simple even when what it designates is not, for example "Europe" or "Saturn."

A fifth reason for distinguishing between the meaning of an expression and its object is that expressions can share the same object without having the same meaning. Like Frege and Bolzano, Husserl distinguishes between an expression's sense, meaning, or "content" (LI 1 §12, 287) and its "reference" or object.[10] Suppose the car hood had a name, such as "H." Then the expression "H is scratched" would have the same *object* as A's utterance, but would not have the same *meaning*. (I am ignoring for the time the very significant fact that one involves a name and another a definition description). And if A were to point to the car hood and say *"That* car hood is scratched," it would again differ in meaning from the other two despite representing the same state of affairs. In fact a token expression "That car hood is scratched" might differ in sense from a second co-referring token of "That car hood is scratched" if, for instance, various parts of the car are seen from two different windows (see Evans 1982, 84).

The reason for treating these as having distinct meanings is that they do not have the same "cognitive value" (Frege 1946, 209). Whatever cognitive value is, if two expressions have it in common, then someone who understands them will have the same attitudes towards them. In the cases above, this is by no means guaranteed; it is possible for someone who grasps the meaning of each of those expressions to simultaneously hold different attitudes towards any of the others, believing one and disbelieving another, for example. If B doesn't know that *that* car hood = H, then he can coherently believe that *that* car hood is scratched without believing that H is. It is also why someone can believe that gold is heavy without believing that the element with 79 protons in its nucleus is heavy, want to marry Jocasta but not want to marry his own mother, and so on. It is why, to give Frege's example, the proposition expressed by the sentence "The Morning Star is the Evening Star" is informative, while the proposition expressed by the sentence "The Morning Star is the Morning Star" is not. This is not, it should be noted, a mere difference in *signs* or physical markers. The problem of realizing that these terms refer to the same thing is not one of translation. Rather, a difference in cognitive significance "can arise only if the difference between the signs corresponds to a difference in the mode of presentation of that which is designated" (Frege 1946, 210).

3.2.2 Meanings are not Linguistic Types or Tokens

The meaning of A's utterance is also distinct from the utterance itself and the sentence type of which it is a token. This is deeply obvious, but sometimes exploring the obvious has its payoffs. Speaking of "thoughts" or propositions, Wayne Davis observes: "Sentences can be written or spoken, and it is reasonable to identify them with sequences of sounds or letters, or types of such. Thoughts are not composed of sounds or letters" (Davis 2005, 18). So, for instance, utterances have a volume, and inscriptions have a height and length. But meanings cannot be loud or soft, or tall or short. They don't have shapes or volumes. A sentence or a word can be pronounced or spelled correctly or incorrectly. But a meaning or concept cannot. A sentence can be ambiguous, that is, have multiple meanings. But a meaning cannot have multiple meanings (Davis 2005, 19). Words and sentences belong to languages. But meanings do not. There are English and French words, and they can be used to construct English and French sentences, but there is no such thing as an English or a French meaning (ibid.), nor are there French or English theories. If mentalese is a language, there are no mentalese meanings or theories either. It would, like any other language, be a *contingent*, albeit non-conventional or natural, way of expressing or encoding meanings.

A more important reason for not identifying meanings with linguistic types or tokens is that linguistic items only contingently represent what they do (LI 1 §35, 333). This is obvious in the case of markers. Neither the type nor the tokens of the marker "car" bears a necessary relation with its meaning or its object; the marker "car" could have meant something else, or nothing at all, and any other manageable physical inscription, sound-pattern, or marker, such as "shoe" or "blowtorch" or "Socrates," would have done just as well. Many other markers do in fact serve just as well, for instance the German "Wagen." The connections between markers and meanings are forged by conventions, and those conventions can and do vary over places and times.[11]

Conventions are not only responsible for the semantic properties of markers, but for their *syntactic* properties as well. That is, syntactic properties do not supervene on physical ones. As Steven Horst points out, the marker "FOX" can be interpreted as a noun in English, a proposition in the predicate calculus, a line on an eye chart, or countless other syntactically typed signifiers. What syntactic category, if any, it belongs to depends on the conventions operative in the context in which it is used (Horst 1999, 359).

Moreover, as Davis points out, the relation between sentences—which are signifiers and not just markers—and "thoughts" or meanings is many-many. The same sentence, such as "I left my coat at the bank," can be used to mean different things, and different sentences, such as synonymous sentences from different languages, can be used to mean the same thing (Davis 2005, 19). Some words in English have more than one meaning, and some have changed meaning over time. But no meanings have more than one meaning or have changed over time.

Propositions and concepts, by contrast, do not owe their semantic or syntactic features to any conventions. If a word *changes meaning* that does not mean that the concept it expresses is such that *it* changes; rather, it means that the word expresses a different concept than it did before (see LI 1 §28, 322). Similarly, when a person changes their opinion away from liberalism and towards conservativism, liberalism does not change into conservativism. The relation between concepts and their objects is a necessary one. The concept <car> is necessarily of cars. Similarly, the proposition <The hood of the car is scratched> is necessarily of that state of affairs, and its truth value depends *solely* on whether or not the car hood in question really is scratched. It is a *necessary* truth that this proposition is true if, and only if, the hood of the car is scratched. The *sentence* "The hood of the car is scratched," by contrast, is not true solely in virtue of the fact of the hood's being scratched. Its truth also depends on a set of conventions in virtue of which it means what it does. Accordingly, there are two ways it could become false: if the hood were not scratched, or if, by a change in our conventions, the sentence came to express a different, and false, proposition. As Davis puts it, *"sentences have their meaning contingently, by convention or stipulation; thoughts have their content essentially, by nature"* (Davis 2005, 19). Propositions are "what is under-ivatively true or false" (Willard 1972, 97); sentences are true, when they are, in virtue of expressing true propositions (Soames 1999, 106).

One important consequence of this is that the logical positivist strategy of treating analytic, a priori, and necessary propositions as being true in virtue of linguistic conventions does not succeed. Apart from the absurdity of trying to explain necessary truths in terms of something as obviously contingent and changeable as human conventions, it involves a basic confusion between meanings and the vehicles that carry them. As Laurence Bonjour puts it:

> It is, of course, obvious that new conventions could change the meaning of the word "not", or of the words "red" and "green", but there is no plausi-bility at all in the idea that such changes would result in the *falsity* of the principle of non-contradiction or of the proposition that nothing can be red and green all over at the same time, as opposed to merely altering the way in which those propositions are expressed.[12]

Changing the truth value of a *sentence* simply by changing its meaning leaves the truth value of the proposition it formerly expressed, along with the state of affairs that makes that proposition true, untouched. Sometimes it is diffi-cult to determine whether a sentence has changed its meaning or whether we have changed our mind about the proposition it has always expressed. To take a familiar example, has modern physics taught us that the proposition expressed by the sentence "The table is solid" is false? Or has there been a change in the meaning of the word "solid" such that the physicist who claims: "The table is not solid" is not in fact contradicting our commonsense beliefs? Hard to say. But if we did not know the difference between sentences and propositions, or between symbols and meanings, it could not even occur to us to wonder that. If our only access to the world was through words and sentences—which are themselves parts of the public, physical world, inciden-tally—then we would take any change in the truth value of a sentence to be a change in the world. But we, correctly, don't.

We can illustrate this relationship among sentences, propositions, and states of affairs as follows:

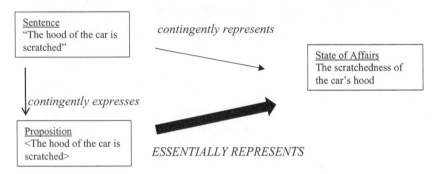

Figure 3.1 Sentences, Propositions, and Facts

Some philosophers are skeptical of the distinction between speech or lan-guage and thought that this account requires. Merleau-Ponty, for instance, protests that accounts of thought and speech such as this one "make anything other than external relations between them inconceivable" (2012, 185). According to him, "The orator does not think prior to speaking, nor even while speaking; his speech is his thought" (ibid.). It's not easy to know what to make of the three claims made in that sentence. The first claim is irrele-vant. The present account does not require that anyone think "prior to" speaking; it's enough that they think *while* they are speaking. The second claim seems clearly false. Or rather: while some orators give every indication of not thinking while they are speaking, others quite clearly do think while speaking. And the third claim, if true, undermines the second one. If the orator doesn't think while speaking, then her speech cannot *be* her thought. In any case, there are lots of types of relations other than merely external, side-by-side relations and necessary relations. As Husserl points out, speech acts and acts of thought do not just co-occur. Word and thing enter into an "intentional unity" thanks to the "interconnection of the corresponding acts to form a single act" (LI 5 §19, 584).

3.2.3 Meanings are not Mental Acts

Perhaps, then, the meaning of A's utterance is (7) A's mental state. This is a more promising proposal in one respect, since mental states are not merely contingently about their objects. The act of thinking that the hood of the car is scratched would be a different act if it were about something else; it could not, for instance, have been an act of thinking that Socrates is snub-nosed or that photons have no rest mass. Those would be different acts of thinking, not the same acts with different contents. Nevertheless, the meaning of A's utterance is not A's or anyone else's mental state.

Earlier we distinguished between the (7a) meaning-fulfillment and (7b) meaning intention. The meaning of A's utterance cannot be the meaning-fulfillment, whether we understand that to be a perceptual experience of the car's hood's being scratched or a presentification of it in imagination or memory. As one might suspect based on the discussion of empty and intuitive presentations from the previous chapter, perceptual experiences can vary while the meaning of an utterance remains identical. Perception of the intended state of affairs can even, and in fact usually does, cease entirely. As Husserl writes,

> If the sense of a statement survives the elimination of perception, and is the same sense as before, we cannot suppose that perception is the act in which the sense of a perceptual statement ... is achieved.

(LI 6 §4, 681)

Exactly the same holds of imagination or any other intuitive act. Despite its critical role in intentionality and knowledge, intuition cannot be identified with linguistic meaning.

Not only do expressions remain significant and comprehensible when we are not perceiving or otherwise intuiting their objects, but many are significant even when their objects do not and could not be intuited. As Husserl notes, "*The realm of meaning is ... much wider than that of intuition*" (LI 6 §63, 824). For instance, there is no fulfilling intuition corresponding to the sentence "the tree is playing a cello sonata," and no metaphysically possible intuition corresponding to "the car's hood is scratched and not scratched." But those are undeniably meaningful sentences. They are absurd or counter-sensical (*widersinnig*) but not meaningless or nonsensical (*unsinnig*) (LI 4 §12, 516–518). Meaninglessness would look more like this: "Car or didn't" or "fawoirhpgn apibnapif." Those markers do not express anything false or absurd, because they do not (in English) express anything at all. The first is what Barry Smith calls a "meaning heap" (2000, 291); the latter doesn't even amount to that.[13]

The meaning of A's utterance is also not identical with A's meaning-intention or act of meaning. First, what A means in uttering "The hood of the car is scratched" is something that can be meant and understood by someone who has no idea that A said it, or even that A exists. In fact it could be meant by someone else even if A did not ever say it or exist. If B were to say to C, "The hood of the car is scratched," his utterance would not only have the same objective correlate as A's, as we have seen, but would also have the same meaning (see LI 1 §11, 285).

Second, A's and B's utterances are two distinct events, and so are the acts of meaning that A and B undergo. But what they mean is the same, and it is not an event of any sort. If a thousand people understand the sentence "The hood of the car is scratched," there would be one thousand meaning intentions or acts of meaning, but only one meaning. If they all knew it, there would be one thousand episodes of knowing, but only one proposition known. "Multiplication of persons and acts does not multiply propositional meanings; the judgment in the ideal, logical sense remains single."[14]

Third, unless an extremely robust form of idealism is true, there are many propositions, including true ones, which are not presently being thought by anyone, and many which have never been thought (much less known) by anyone, or at least by any finite minds or populations thereof. The structure of consciousness itself actually ensures this. When I perceive a scratched car hood and attend to it, I am for that very reason not attending to or making judgments about my own experience of perceiving the car hood (recall Zahavi's "unthematized spot"). In particular, I am not judging that I am perceiving a car hood. But that proposition is true. Because every obtaining state of affairs renders some proposition or set of propositions true, and because there are lots of states of affairs that we do not, have not, and never will think about, propositions can be true whether or not they are grasped, entertained, expressed, or otherwise present in or to any human minds (see Armstrong 2004, 15). Provided the hood of the car is scratched, the proposition <the hood of the car is scratched> is true, whether or not anyone says or thinks it or has said or thought it. Even most idealists and antirealists often present idealism and antirealism as doctrines that were true before anyone thought that they were, and despite anyone's opinion that they are not. Regarding truth and being, Husserl writes,

> These two things are given together a priori, and are mutually inseparable. Nothing can be without being thus or thus determined, and that it is, and that it is thus and thus determined, is the self-subsistent truth which is the necessary correlate of the self-subsistent being.
>
> (LI Prol. §62, 225–226)

Provided anything exists without being the object of a mental act, there are true propositions that are not the contents of any mental acts, much less identical with any mental acts.

Fourth, the identification of meanings with mental acts is a version of psychologism, which I, following Dallas Willard, will understand to be the view that "the non-normative statements made by logicians are about, and draw their evidence from the examination of, the particular conceivings, assertings, and inferrings of particular persons."[15] Psychologism, that is, is the position that psychological facts both make logical laws true and constitute our evidence for them.

Neither position, however, is the case. Concepts and propositions obey formal laws, discoverable a priori, that determine (a) how concepts can be lawfully combined to form meaningful wholes, including propositions, and how atomic propositions can in turn be combined into complex propositions, and (b) how propositions can be assembled to form formally valid or truth-preserving proofs and theories. It is the task of the science of "pure grammar" to discover the first set of laws (LI Prol. §67, 236). And it is the task of "syl-logistics" (LI Prol. §68, 239) or the "theory of validity" (ILTK §18b, 69) to discover the second. Both are parts of pure logic, which Husserl at one point characterizes as "the science of meanings as such."[16]

Concepts belong to syntactic and semantic categories that determine how they can combine with other concepts to compose unified meaningful wholes. These laws are purely formal. To use Husserl's example, in the expression "This tree is green," we can remove all non-logical or materially contentful terms to yield the form "This S is P" (LI 4 §10, 511). We can then replace the variable "S" with any "nominal material" whatsoever, including "this gold" or "this algebraic number" (ibid.) "Where nominal material stands, any nominal material can stand" (ibid.)—and so on for each syntactic and semantic category. If <S is P> is a proposition, any noun can replace <S> and any predicate phrase can replace <is P> to yield another proposition. Such substitutions might yield propositions that are absurd. But they are not *nonsensical* (ibid., 512). These laws, Husserl insists, are purely ideal or neces-sary. That we cannot substitute the variable "S" above with the verb <jumps> or the adverb <happily> and detect any unified sense in the resulting heap of meanings is not "a mere factual incapacity, the compulsion of our mental make-up," but a necessity grounded in the meanings themselves (LI 4 §10, 510–511). No one could find them meaningful, because they are not mean-ingful, quite independently of our factual mental constitution.

The same holds for logical laws. They are true of meanings, but not true in virtue of anything having to do with our minds. If, for instance, the proposi-tions <All As are Bs> and <S is an A> are true, then <S is a B> is also true, whether or not anyone thinks or expresses it, whether or not anyone feels compelled to believe it, and even whether or not there are any speakers, thinkers, or linguistic expressions at all. The science of logic is purely a priori, and like every a priori discipline, its propositions are neither made true by contingent matters of fact nor justified on the basis of our experience of matters of fact. More specifically, logical laws are not laws concerning actual mental states or mental processes.

> No logical law implies a "matter of fact," not even the existence of presenta-tions or judgements or other phenomena of knowledge. No logical law, properly understood, is a law for the facticities of mental life.
>
> (LI Prol. §23, 104)

The meaning of A's utterance could not be his mental state, since the existence of his mental state is not entailed by the existence, the logical properties, or the truth of the proposition that functions as its content. Nor could meanings in general be identical with mental states, since meanings fall under logical laws that are entirely independent of the existence of mental states of any type. This argument, it should be noted, also shows that meanings are not linguistic entities. The laws of pure grammar and logic hold independently of the existence of any languages or linguistic acts.

3.3 The Objectivity of Meanings

It appears that meanings—concepts and propositions—enjoy a rather robust objective existence. They are objective insofar as, first, they can function as the identical contents of numerically distinct meaning intentions and linguistic acts.

Second, meanings are essentially of what they are of. Their aboutness is objective insofar as it is beyond the reach or influence of any individual or collective decisions, conventions, edicts, or pronouncements. Concepts and propositions do not just happen to represent what they represent in the way that words, symbols, signs, and most indicators do. The concept <car> could not have been of something else, and the proposition <The hood of the car is scratched> could not have had truth conditions different from those it has.

Third, propositions owe their truth or falsity solely to the obtaining or nonobtaining of the states of affairs that they represent. A proposition is true, or a "truth in itself," writes Bolzano, "whenever the object with which it deals really has the properties that it ascribes to it" (Bolzano 1972, 32). This is plainly a realist theory of truth. In Husserl's hands, in his early work at least, it is a "correspondence" theory.

> Corresponding to a proposition is a state of affairs, precisely the one that is posited in it as obtaining. If the proposition is true, then the state of affairs actually obtains (and the object-about-which actually exists), and it does not obtain if the proposition is false.[17]

Truth is one kind of accurate representation. And this holds even for purely logical truths. Logic, construed narrowly as a science of meaning and validity, has as *its* objective correlate formal ontology, which specifies the essential formal relations among objects, properties, relations, and states of affairs. This is why:

> just as each law of inference can be viewed as a law of validity for propositions of a certain form, so, in an obvious conversion, it can be viewed as a law for the obtaining and not obtaining of states of affairs.[18]

That any proposition with the form <S is P and Q> entails <S is P> has, as its ontological correlate or truthmaker, that any state of affairs with the form of S's being P and Q necessitates the state of affairs of S's being P. We can, in a logical frame of mind, say that (i) the proposition <If the car hood is scratched and red then it is scratched> is necessarily true. But we can also speak directly of the states of affairs: (ii) necessarily, if the car hood is scratched and red, then it is scratched. Those two claims are necessarily equivalent but not identical (see LI Prol. §62, 226). The first, (i), is a specification of a formal law of meanings, the other, (ii), a specification of a formal law of objects.

Corresponding, then, to logic narrowly construed as the "science of meanings as such" (LI 1 §29, 323) is formal ontology, "*the pure (a priori) theory of objects as such*" (LI 4 Introduction, 435). The pure categories of meaning, such as "Concept, Proposition, Truth, etc." have "married to them by ideal laws" such "correlative concepts such as Object, State of Affairs, Unity, Plurality, Number, Relation, Connection etc." (LI Prol. §67, 237)—not to mention, of course, such categories as Part and Whole. At *all* levels of meaning, then, from that of materially contentful propositions to purely formal ones, there is a correspondence between meanings and their objects. Logic is about something, namely the ontological form of the world. Husserl, therefore, endorses what Michaela McSweeney calls "metaphysical logical realism." As she characterizes it, "for the metaphysical logical realist, logic is certainly not ontologically neutral (our logical commitments either are ontological commitments, or are shaped by our ontological commitments)" (2019, 1). In accepting *logical* laws, one is doing a lot more than agreeing to use symbols in accordance with certain conventions. One is accepting that reality must, could, and could not be certain ways.

Realist theories of truth have not, to say the least, been looked upon favorably by all philosophers, and neither has realism about intentionality in general. In part this is due to the prevalence of naturalism and physicalism—representation, and therefore accurate representation, is not something clearly and obviously physical.[19] In part this is due to "postmodern" worries about truth in general—though, as Greg Jesson once noted in conversation, while plenty of people express skepticism about whether there really is such a thing as truth, no one seems to doubt the existence of lying. My own view is that if a theory cannot accommodate something as obvious as representation, and with it accurate representation, then it is clearly false, not least of all for the familiar reason that a *theory of something* is itself a representation *of* that something. Note, however, and in anticipation of a later discussion of metaphysical realism and idealism, that realism about truth does not rule out idealism about the objects which make true propositions true (Alston 1996, 79). A red, square Berkeleyan idea S might depend on being perceived for its existence. But if it exists, it makes true the proposition <S is square and red>. Furthermore, there are many objects and states of affairs that depend on human intentional acts and conventions. That Colorado's northern border is the 41st parallel obtains thanks, in part, to our decisions and conventions. The boundaries between states are "fiat boundaries" which "owe their existence to acts of human decision or fiat, to laws or political decrees, or to related human cognitive phenomena" (B. Smith 2001a, 133). But the existence of this boundary, once established, nevertheless makes true the corresponding proposition <Colorado's northern border is the 41ˢᵗ parallel> entirely independently of our decisions and conventions. We can, through mental and speech acts, make some objects exist and some states of affairs obtain. What we cannot do is make an existing object or obtaining state of affairs *make true* a corresponding proposition, or prevent it from doing so.

Fourth, meanings are objective insofar as they do not require that anyone think or know them, nor do they need to be expressed or expressible in any factually existing language. As Bolzano puts it, a "proposition in itself" is "any assertion that something is or is not the case, regardless whether or not somebody has put it into words, and regardless either whether or not it has been thought" (Bolzano 1972, 20–21). On this point both Husserl and Frege agree. Not only are propositions distinct from any individual acts of thinking them, but they do not need a "bearer" at all (Frege 1956, 302). Husserl writes that meanings—"concepts, propositions, truths"—"are an ideally set of general objects, to which being thought or being expressed are alike contingent" (LI §35, 333).

Fifth and finally, meanings are objective in a way that many philosophers find more than a little problematic: they are non-real entities, neither physical nor mental. They are not the kind of things that have a velocity or a volume or a rest mass, nor are they real psychological events or processes unfolding in time in this or that mind or community of minds. They do not have any of the familiar "primary" or "secondary" qualities.

From Bolzano through Lotze to Frege and Husserl, we see a series of increasingly straightforward acknowledgements of their existence. According to Bolzano, propositions in themselves do not exist (Bolzano 1972, 21). His reason for saying so, however, is that he confines *existence* to things in time or space: "they are not something that exists at some location, or at some time, or as some other kind of real thing" (Bolzano 1972, 32). But they do have properties, among them truth and falsity.

Hermann Lotze, another important influence on both Frege and Husserl, agrees with Bolzano: propositions do not *exist*. He does maintain, however, that they are *valid* (Lotze 1884, 439). According to Lotze, there are four kinds of "Reality." Real things exist; real events occur; real relations obtain; "lastly, we call a proposition Really true which holds or is valid" (Lotze 1884, 439). Certainly no eliminativist about events or relations would take comfort in Lotze's position. And neither would an eliminativist about (true) propositions upon learning that although they do not "exist," they do have "Reality."

Frege, too, holds that thoughts are neither mental nor physical, but seems to make bolder ontological commitments by concluding that: "A third realm must be recognized" (Frege 1956, 302). Husserl agrees. Meanings are "ideal" rather than "real" entities. Of course, fictional objects are also not real. But this does not mean that ideal objects are similar to them. Fictional objects have no being at all. "Ideal objects, on the other hand, exist genuinely."[20]

It cannot be overemphasized that Husserl is not *identifying* ideal objects such as universals with meanings. Meanings "constitute a class of 'universal objects'," but not all universal objects are meanings (LI 1 §33, 331). The color red is a universal, but it is not a meaning. It is not, for instance, the concept <red>. Unlike that concept or any other concept, the color does not refer to anything. Moreover, the class of things which possess the property of red—the red things—is not the same as the class of things which possess the concept of <red> (see Willard 2000a, §IV). Numbers are also ideal, as are all properties, kinds, and essences. But these are not concepts or meanings, and they certainly aren't "concepts" in the sense of something particular in anyone's mind. As Husserl rather humorously puts it when criticizing empiricism and nominalism, "Certainly essences are 'concepts'—provided one understands by 'concepts' what this polyvalent word permits, namely essences."[21]

It is worth pausing here to clarify Husserl's position, in both the *Logical Investigations* and *Ideas I*, on this topic. Husserl is often described as—or accused of being—a platonist. This is not a small matter. Dallas Willard, for one, writes that: "it is obvious that Ideas (universals, 'species', essences) and the viewing and analyzing thereof form the substance of his entire philosophy."[22] Essences—"Ideas"—comprise the subject matter of phenomenology itself. As Willard was fond of pointing out, *these*, and not individual Lockean mental representations, are what are being referred to in the title of Husserl's work *Ideas* (see Ideas I §18, 34).

Platonism about ideal entities such as numbers, meanings, properties, species, and essences is the view that (a) they exist, that (b) they exist mind- and language-independently, and that (3) they exist independently of having any actual instances falling under them. Husserl endorses all three claims. Regarding their existence, he does not pull his punches:

> In contraposition to nature ... there are ... *ideal* worlds, worlds of ideas, which are non-spatial, non-temporal, and unreal. And yet, they exist indeed, as for example, numbers in a series exist.[23]

Regarding our grounds for asserting their existence, Husserl is again as clear as can be: "If I see the truth that 4 is an even number ... then this object cannot be a mere fiction" (LI 2 §8, 352–353). More generally, we are conscious of universals in acts of fulfillment, and are entitled to take things so given to exist (see LI 2 §1).

As for the *manner* of their existence, Husserl is again clear. First, they do not depend on anyone's consciousness of them. This is true of both non-intentional ideal objects such as numbers and intentional ideal objects such as meanings. As he writes:

As numbers—in the ideal sense that arithmetic presupposes—neither spring forth nor vanish with the act of enumeration, and as the endless number-series thus represents an objectively fixed set of general objects, sharply delimited by an ideal law, which no one can either add to or take away from, so it is with the ideal unities of pure logic, with its concepts, propositions, truths, or in other words, with its meanings.

(LI 1 §35, 333)

Again, discussing numbers, Husserl writes,

A presentation of a number is not a number itself; it is not the *Two*, this sole member of the series of numbers, the member that, like all such members, is a non-temporal being.

(Ideas I §22, 41)

The existence of ideal objects, then, is "non-temporal," and quite independent of whether we turn our mental gaze towards them or not.

Finally, ideal objects do not depend on whether they have actual instances, but only on *possible* instances. As Husserl puts it, "to every ideal object there belongs inseparably an ideal extension, the idea of a totality of conceivable single instances" (PP, 16). As for the universals with which we have been principally concerned, namely meanings and other mental contents, Husserl is quite clear that there are "countless meanings" which are "never expressed" and never will be expressed (LI 1 §35, 333).

If Husserl, at least at the time of these writings, is not a platonist, then it's difficult to identify any philosopher besides Plato who is. Why, then, does Husserl deny that he is a "Platonic realist"? Because "Platonic realism" is not the same thing as platonism. According to "Platonic realism," "the Species really exists *externally* to thought" (LI 2 §7, 350). Reading that sentence out of context, one might think that on Husserl's view the species "really exists" *internally* "to thought." But that interpretation would make complete nonsense of what we've just covered; in fact it is exactly what Husserl refers to as "A deceptive line of thought" in the title of LI 2 §8 (351). To whose "thought," for instance, would the number *Two* exist internally? There is only one number *Two*, sitting over against the countless possible collections of two things and the countless actual and possible acts of counting and thinking of the number *Two* (see Willard 1984, 189ff.).

More importantly, situating universals "in" the mind as *real* things would be absurd as well, as Husserl's criticism of Locke's theory makes clear. In Locke's view, the "general triangle" is an idea with a small "i", a mental entity which represents all triangles. And it is itself a triangle. But in order to fulfill its function of representing all triangles, it "must be neither oblique nor rectangle, neither equilateral, equicrural, nor scalenon; but all and none of these at once" (Locke 1975, 596). Apart from the fact that *your* general triangle and *mine* are alike in kind but differ in number, in which case we only have a reduction of this universal to a mental universal, Husserl diagnoses Locke's error succinctly: "Locke should ... have reminded himself that a triangle is something which has triangularity, but that triangularity is not itself something that has triangularity" (LI 2 §11, 359). That is, triangularity is not itself a triangle. More generally, we cannot treat (most) universals as falling under themselves as instances.

The problem with the view that "the Species really exists *externally* to thought" is identical to the problem with the view that it "really exists" *internally* "to thought." And the problem is that both views treat ideal objects as things which *really* exist—as though they were concrete entities of the same type that they are instantiated in. They involve, respectively, "The metaphysical and psychological hypostatization of the universal" (LI 2 §7, 350). *Real* existence—"*real*" rather than "*wirklich*" or "actual" is Husserl's term—is existence in time, and ideal objects do not exist in time. "What is real is the individual with all its constituents: it is something here and now. For us, temporality is a sufficient mark of reality" (LI 2 §8, 351).

That ideal objects are not *real* does *not*, however, entail that they do not *exist*. The reason is that "existence does not mean the same as real existence" (LI 2 §11, 361). There is, Husserl "emphasizes," "a fundamental categorial split in our unified conception of being," a distinction between "ideal being and real being; between being as Species and being as what is individual" (LI 2, §8, 353). Note, moreover, that both mental and physical entities and processes fall on the "real" side of this divide: "For us, what is 'in' consciousness counts as real just as much as what is 'outside' of it" (LI 2 §8, 351). Ideal objects are not real things in consciousness, nor are they real things outside of consciousness, because they are not real things at all. But they *do*, Husserl says, "exist genuinely [existieren wahrhaft]" (LI 2 §8, 352).

Substantially the same points are made in *Ideas I*, §22. As Husserl makes clear there, he simply doesn't share the view that there is anything *wrong* with ideal entities, and insists that it is a complete falsification of the sense of our consciousness of them to construe them as anything real or mental, such as "concepts" in the sense of real, particular mental representations. "Prejudices," he writes, "make for remarkable smugness in a theoretical respect. There *cannot* be essences; so, too, there *cannot* be intuition of an essence" (Ideas I §22, 41). Against this, Husserl insists that there is and there are. The number *Two* is not my thought about the number *Two*, nor is it any collection of *Two* objects. It is one object, situated between *One* and *Three*, which can not only be emptily thought of but given in suitable acts of intuition. To treat it as something mental, a real "presentation" in my mind or yours, is "absurd, an offense against the completely clear sense of arithmetical discourse" (ibid.).

For what it is worth, much later Husserl was to write:

> Despite all the Platonic turns of phrase by which we have described its relation to the particular, the ideality of the universal must not be understood as if it were a question here of a being-in-itself devoid of reference to any

subject. On the contrary, like *all* objectivities of understanding, it refers essentially *to the processes of productive spontaneity* which belong to it correlatively and in which it comes to original givenness. The *being of the universal* in its different levels is essentially a *being-constituted* in these processes.

(EJ, 330)

Before the nominalist finds consolation in that passage, however, note that if we wish to preserve even the rudiments of the account of meanings presented above, then the only interpretation on which it could be true that ideal objects are essentially related to "processes of productive spontaneity" is one on which the latter are themselves construed as ideal types—that is, an interpretation according to which the being of ideal entities is correlated with the *types* of acts which could possibly disclose or "constitute" them. It bears noting, incidentally, that "constitution" is not a process of making objects, but of carrying out the acts in which they are given. As Husserl puts it, "[S]eeing consciousness ... is just acts of thought formed in certain ways, and things, which are not acts of thought, are nonetheless constituted in them, come to givenness in them."[24] But then we will have explained ideal entities in terms of their relations with other ideal entities. If, on the contrary, ideal entities are essentially correlated with *actual* mental processes and *actual* acts of givenness, or were literally *made by* them, then their existence is a factual matter, and in order to show that they exist we would have to establish empirically just which processes produced them, at what time, and by which subjects. (Whether the subjects or "egos" in question are "empirical" or "transcendental" makes no difference.) For my part, I am strongly inclined to answer Husserl's former rhetorical question affirmatively: "are the numbers not what they are, whether we 'construct' them or not?" (Ideas I §22, 41).

3.4 The Subjectivity of Meanings

Having insisted upon the objectivity and non-mental character of meanings, the fact remains that minds and meanings share an exceptionally close connection with one another—a fact which psychologism, to its credit, accounts for (see Willard 1984, 146). It is thanks to bearing *some* sort of relation with concepts and propositions that particular acts of thinking, meaning, and speaking are about what they are about, are true or false, and so on. A's "belief"—that is, her psychological state of believing—that the hood of the car is scratched is *compatible* with her belief that it will soon rain. This does not merely mean that both *states* can coexist in one human mind, but that their *contents* are *logically* compatible, that is, capable of being *true* together. Her states must bear some relation to those contents if they are to take on this logical relationship.

We have not yet determined what the relation between a psychological state or act and its meaning-content is, however. One possibly tempting answer is that this relation is intentionality, this time between the individual act, on the one hand, and the proposition, on the other. This appears to be a dominant view.[25] Frege, whose views share a number of similarities with Husserl's, does not do much to clarify the relationship between propositions and acts of thinking them, but his language certainly invites an interpretation according to which thoughts and their constituent senses are the objects of our acts of thinking (Willard 1994a, 241–242). Thoughts—propositions—are "grasped," and thinking is the "apprehension of a thought" (Frege 1956, 294). But it's not an appealing view. When I believe there is scratch on a car hood, the object of my belief is a chunk of reality that includes a scratch and a car hood.

There is, it bears pointing out, a trivial sense in which propositions are objects of belief. They are objects of a certain sort—that is, they are some-things that have properties as opposed to nothings which don't—and they are "of belief" insofar as beliefs bear *some* relation to them. But it is a mistake to construe that relation as intentionality. Propositions are not the usual *intended objects*, the *about-whiches*, of acts of believing. A.N. Prior writes that the phrase "object of thought" may be used to designate either "(1) what we think or (2) what we think *about*," and he makes it clear that in thinking a proposition, what we think *about* is not that proposition. Similarly, Prior points out, "what we say" is not "what we are speaking about."[26] We say sentences; we talk about things.

On this point Husserl is in full agreement. When A says to B, "The hood of the car is scratched," she expresses the proposition <The hood of the car is scratched>. But she is not talking about the sentence or the proposition it expresses. She has not said one word about that proposition, nor has she predicated anything of it, including truth. She is talking about a state of affairs—exactly the state of affairs that the proposition itself is about. Her utterance, that is, along with the English sentence of which it is a token, is about the very same thing that the proposition above is about: the being-scratched of the car's hood. "If ... we make a statement, we judge about the thing it concerns, and not about the statement's meaning, about the judgment in the logical sense" (LI 1 §34, 332).

Moreover, what A is *thinking about* in uttering that sentence is the same thing that she is *talking about* in uttering that sentence. And what she is talking about is the car's hood's being scratched, not the proposition. And so, her act of thinking is not *about* the proposition, but bears some other relation to it. "In the act of meaning we are not conscious of meaning as an object."[27]

That propositions are not the objects of all propositional acts of thought is supported by straightforward phenomenological reflection. If propositions were the sole direct objects of belief and other propositional attitudes, then the worldly states of affairs that those propositions are about would have to be indirect objects of thought. But they are not. Indirect intentional acts are perspicuously indirect; it is part of their very phenomenal character to be indirect. In indirect conscious acts, as we saw in the previous chapter, we are conscious of one object in virtue of being conscious of another object, and taking the latter as a representation of the former. For Husserl, this representational character of the directly presented object is "no intrinsic character" of it; "an object is not representative as, e.g., it is red and spherical" (LI 5, Appendix to §11 and §20, 593). What makes an object given to consciousness a representation of another just is the way in which it is taken up.

Husserl may be partially mistaken on this point. There is a sense of "represent," after all, in which plenty of things represent others. A barometer carries information about air pressure, and so represents it, in this sense, regardless of whether anyone is aware of it or not, or even whether there are any people at all. Husserl's point, however, is that an object that happens to represent another thing cannot direct a mind *to* that other thing unless the representation is taken up in consciousness *as* a representation of that other thing. Being aware of a barometer, a sentence, or an ancient rune is not sufficient to be aware of what it represents, whether consciously or unconsciously, directly or indirectly—not even when we know *that* it is a representation of something or other. If propositions or anything else really do function as immediate representational objects of thought and other propositional attitudes, this should be obvious upon reflection (Willard 1967, 515). We should readily find, just as we do in image consciousness, that one thing is standing in for another. But we do not find this. In thinking about a car hood's being scratched, we think directly of the fact that the car hood is scratched.

Another reason for not treating the propositional content as one of the act's objects is that anything whatsoever, including propositions, can be meant or intended in more than one way. What Jerry Fodor says of modes of presentation or "MOPS" holds for concepts, propositions, and other meanings as well: "there are as many ways of thinking about a MOP as there are of thinking about a rock or a number. That is, innumerably many; one for each mode of presentation of the MOP" (Fodor 1998, 18). It is not just objects or properties for which we can draw the distinction between sense and reference, but anything whatsoever, including senses or meanings—concepts and propositions—themselves. For instance, we can think about the proposition expressed by A's utterance in all of the following ways:

a   The proposition that the hood of the car is scratched.
b   The proposition conventionally expressed by the English sentence "The hood of the car is scratched"
c   The proposition conventionally expressed by the German sentence "Die Kühlerhaube des Autos ist zerkratzt."
d   The proposition whose subject term is the complex concept <the hood of the car> and whose predicate term is the concept <is scratched>.

And so on. But if the proposition P itself must be thought of or presented in some way or via some sense, as it must if it is in the object position in the intentional act, then we would need to summon another sense S to serve as the sense of the mental act directed upon P. But this confronts us with a dilemma.

On the one hand, if senses must be objects of consciousness to function in directing a mental act to its terminal object, then we must push this new sense S into object position. But then we will face the same problem all over again, and will need a new sense S* to be about S.

If, on the other hand, senses can function without being objects of consciousness, then there is no reason to have ever put our functioning sense or proposition <The hood of the car is scratched> on the object-side to begin with.[28] Meanings, then, are not only subjective, but when functioning *as contents* reside on the left-hand side of the intentional act.

3.5 Meanings as Intentional Properties

We've landed ourselves in the following paradoxical situation: concepts and propositions appear to be both intimately subjective and radically objective, both woven into the fabric of subjectivity and off somewhere in Plato's heaven. Even if we had an account of how our minds could go beyond themselves and into such a realm, everything they reach would still be on the object-side of the intentional act, which is exactly where the propositional content of an act is not. This is a general version of what Dallas Willard calls "the paradox of logical psychologism."[29] The paradox in question is that the kinds of statements that logicians make about truth, validity, entailment, and so forth both obviously have something important to do with events of thinking, judging, and inferring as carried about by creatures with psychological configurations such as ours, but "do *not* draw their evidence from the examination of such events" (Willard 1972, 94). Another, related version of the paradox is this: there are on the one hand powerful reasons for situating concepts and propositions in the mind, and equally powerful reasons for situating them outside the sphere of real or actual being altogether.

The way to solve this paradox is to consider how something, or rather some things which are very intimately related, can be both in the mind and yet objective and ideal at the same time. Husserl's answer is that the relation between ideal meanings and subjective acts of meaning is that of instantiation: ideal meanings are present in acts, not as *parts*, nor as *objects*, but as *properties*.[30] As Husserl puts it,

> The manifold singulars for the ideal unity Meaning are naturally the corresponding act-moments of meaning, the *meaning-intentions*. Meaning is related to varied acts of meaning... just as Redness *in specie* is to the slips of paper which lie here, and which all "have" the same redness.[31]

And this also provides us with an answer to the question of what meanings are. Meanings, or concepts and propositions, are "more-or-less complex intentional properties of more-or-less complex mental acts" (Willard 1984, 178). They are "natural signs" in Laird Addis's sense. A concept or proposition is an intentional "*property* of the mental act" and "not, in any sense whatsoever, an object of the mental act of which it is a property" (Addis 1989, 70). As a property of an act, its ideal content, its *of-O-ness*, it can be "shared without being divided," to borrow a phrase that C.D. Broad applies, aptly, to knowledge (Broad 2000, 43). Furthermore, such intentional properties do not depend for their existence on being instantiated (Willard 1984, 183). Propositions, as Willard puts it, are "*complex referential qualities*, which may or may not be instanced by minds" (Willard 1984, 183).

This position resolves the paradox, and explains how meanings can be both objective and subjective. A good theory of meaning, including the formal-logical laws that pertain to concepts and propositions, should account both for their objectivity and their subjectivity. Husserl's theory does that.[32] Meanings are objective insofar as they are shareable, mind- and instantiation-independent properties or species that fall under discoverable necessary laws. They have an especially tight connection with our psychologies because they are instantiated in various acts of thought and meaning. As a result, mental states inherit many of the properties of their contents, including their logical relations with other contents and the mental states that instantiate them, their intentional directedness, and, in the case of propositions, their truth or falsity. And this is why "logical laws also apply informatively and normatively to particular acts, and do so precisely because they are about the characters of such acts" (Willard 1984, 185).

So, for instance, when A and B both judge that the car hood is scratched, there is one meaning involved, namely the proposition <The car hood is scratched>. There are two acts of meaning involved. And the proposition is not the object of those acts of meaning. The object of A's and B's act of meaning is the state of affairs of the car hood's being scratched. The proposition is a property of the act; "it *is* the ofness or aboutness, the specific intentionality, of the act for its object, and as a property, it is repeatable in instances and shareable between persons" (Willard 2002, 74).

A position similar in some respects to Husserl's species view has been defended recently and independently by both Scott Soames and Peter Hanks. On Hanks's view, propositions are "abstractions from" such actions as "predicating, asking, and ordering" (Hanks 2015, 25). Scott Soames has defended a related view, arguing that propositions are "act types," namely acts of predicating (Soames 2010, 73). Husserl, however, maintains not that meanings are act- or action-types, but rather that they are types of *moments* or "aspects" of acts (see LI 5, Introduction, 533). Moments, or "abstract parts," are non-separable parts of the wholes to which they belong (see LI 3 §17, 467). For instance, the Great Pyramid has *its* shape-moment, which is inseparable from the Great Pyramid and will go out of existence with it. It is individual and unshareable. So is the color-moment of this table, the particular ache in my stomach, and the surface tension of this particular volume of water in the glass before me. But all of these particular abstract moments are instantiations of properties that can be shared by other individuals. Similarly, A's act of meaning and B's act of meaning are complex entities with a variety of parts and moments, including real contents. Among those moments is a sense-bearing one, its real content, which is an instantiation of its ideal content. As Husserl writes,

> [W]e can mean by "content" … its meaning as an ideal unity … To this corresponds, as a real (*reelles*) moment in the real (*reellen*) content of the presentative act, the intentional essence with its … quality and matter.
>
> (LI 5 §45, 657)

Despite calling this real moment an "intentional *essence*," it is a *real (reeles) part* of the act. It is "The ideational abstraction of this essence"—this complex act-moment, that is, and not the total act itself—which "yields a 'meaning' in our ideal sense" (LI 5 §21, 590). The ideational abstraction of an *act* of predicating or meaning, by contrast, yields the type "act of meaning," just as the ideational abstraction of a red cube yields the type "red cube." This is not fine-grained enough to give us the type "red," and not fine-grained enough to acquire the type "meaning" (see B. Smith 1994, 171).

3.6 Objections to the Species View

The species view is not without its problems. In this section I will examine some of them, and argue that none of them are fatal.

3.6.1 *Thinking of What Does Not Exist*

One might think that there is one thing the object-theory of content—that is, the view that propositions, concepts, and other contents are the immediate objects of consciousness—can explain which the species view cannot. We sometimes talk and think about things that do not have being—objects which do not exist, for instance, and states of affairs that do not obtain. It might seem, however, that if an act is *directly* about an object, that object must exist—that direct consciousness entails existence. If so, the direct object of a false thought must be something whose existence is entailed by the act of thinking itself, and concepts and propositions seem to fit that bill in a way that contingent states of affairs do not.

The most serious problem with treating thoughts of what does not exist as indirect is that it does not help solve the issue at all, as Dallas Willard (1967) has shown. Introducing representations of any sort to serve as the "direct" objects of consciousness, such as propositions in place of non-existent states of affairs, or images or ideas instead of non-existent objects, merely postpones by one step the problem of representing something that does not exist. Suppose the structure of our consciousness of non-existent objects looked like this:

$$\text{Act} \rightarrow R \rightarrow O$$

How is the intervening representation R, whatever it is, supposed to represent some object O which does not exist? Either R represents O directly or it does not. If we insist that it cannot represent O directly, we will have to postulate another representation R* standing between R and O, like this:

$$\text{Act} \rightarrow R \rightarrow R^* \rightarrow O$$

But the same question will arise for R*, and R**, and so on. And if R is *directly* of O, then we have no reason to object to a mental act itself being directly of O without the mediation of R, like this:

$$\text{Act} \rightarrow O$$

No matter which option we choose, R is either insufficient or unnecessary. As Willard puts it, "If the aboutness of a false belief calls for an object, then no less does the aboutness of a false proposition" (Willard 1967, 517).

3.6.2 The Situated Character of Intentionality

Meanings are abstract entities whose instances are abstract parts or moments of mental acts. But these moments are parts of larger wholes, namely conscious experiences, which belong to still larger wholes, namely organisms and, paradigmatically, persons, which in turn reside, as a matter of physical and perhaps metaphysical necessity, in concretely determined physical, ecological and, in our case, historical and social environments (see B. Smith 2001b, 15). These environments play an enormous role in enabling or restricting the kinds of things we can perceive and think.

This point is of course entirely compatible with Husserl's view. As with just about any other kind of property, concrete circumstances greatly restrict or enlarge what sorts of properties can be instantiated at a place and time. The property of being a planet could not have been instantiated in the first year of the universe; the property of being a living organism could not have been instantiated in the first several billion. The property of being a scientific publication requires even more conditions for its instantiation. Meanings are abstract, but many can only be instantiated if an organism, for instance a human person, occupies a very distinctive physical, social, and cultural environment. Not just any mind is appropriately situated to entertain thoughts about Brahms's rhapsodies, the element Einsteinium, or Edmund Husserl. That is compatible with the contents of those thoughts being ideal.

A more serious concern is that there are some intentional contents that, as a matter of necessity, depend for their instantiation on the *actual existence* of actual circumstances and individuals in the world. The proposition we have chosen as the content of A's linguistic act is a case in point. Not just anyone can understand that proposition, since not just anyone is suitably situated to entertain thoughts about A's car's hood and, by extension, the scratch that is on it. And some meanings, including all indexical and demonstrative expressions, are, in Husserl's words, "essentially occasional." In order to understand such expressions, "it is essential to orient actual meaning to the occasion, the speaker and the situation" (LI 1 §26). In order to understand the full content of my expression "I now see that tree in the yard," one has to know that I uttered it, the time at which I uttered it, and the tree to which I am referring. The meaning of indexical and demonstrative expressions such as "I," "here," "now," "that," and others is "in part universal and conceptual"—such expressions have a general meaning—but their referent is also partly determined by the context in which they are uttered.[33]

In the *Investigations*, Husserl maintains, incorrectly, that all such essentially occasional expressions can be eliminated and replaced by "objective" or context-independent expressions (LI 1 §28, 321). It is true that every such expression expresses a proposition that is necessarily equivalent to one containing no indexical or demonstrative expressions. As a matter of necessity, the proposition <I see the tree> is true if and only if <WH sees the tree> is true. But these propositions are not identical, since they do not have the same cognitive value. As John Perry famously argues, it is possible for John Perry to believe the proposition <John Perry is spilling sugar> without believing the proposition <I am spilling sugar>, since he might not know that he is John Perry (Perry 1979).

After the *Logical Investigations*, around 1911 or so, Husserl realizes that many meanings are empirical or *impure*.[34] "This paper is white," for instance, expresses a meaning that refers to this actual piece of paper before me, and can only be understood on the basis of a present or recent perceptual experience of that individual piece of paper (Erhard 2011, 215). A pure or nonempirical meaning, by contrast, is one that can be fulfilled even in empirically nonpositing intuitive experiences such as phantasy. An example is the concept <red>, which can be instantiated in and fulfilled by acts that do not posit anything actual. Husserl concludes that an "empirical meaning" is not an "idea in the sense of an eidos" (VB, 211).

Christopher Erhard (2011, §5) has argued, however, that the fact that some meanings are empirical or impure does not defeat the species view. The conclusion to draw is not that essentially occasional and other empirical expressions do not express ideal contents, but rather that those contents are impure rather than pure species or universals. As Erhard points out, Husserl himself introduces impure universals a couple of decades after abandoning the species view. Consider non-intentional universals such as natural kinds and properties. In the case of empirical universals, such as "dog" or "water," we are conscious of them as "bound to this world" (EJ, 330). That is, in thinking of the type "dog," we posit it as a type of thing whose home is the *actual* world. In the case of pure universals, by contrast, we do not posit any actual world along with them. For instance, "shape" is a pure universal. We can see the difference between them when we realize that merely imagining a new shape is to succeed in discovering one. But in the case of empirical universals this is not so. As David Kasmier puts it, "Imagining talking dogs does not establish another sub-species of dog" (Kasmier 2003, 186). If you want to learn about the various kinds of dogs, the empirical way is the only way.

Husserl does point out, however, that the "copositing of an empirical sphere" in which such impure universals are exemplified is done "without harm to their ideality" (EJ, 330). And that opens up a way of salvaging the species view of meanings, as Christopher Erhard argues. Just as in the case of other universals, some meanings are pure and involve no attachment to what we posit as actual, while others can only be instantiated in and fulfilled by contexts in which the objects are posited as actual. That boundedness does not threaten their status as intentional properties, any more than it threatens the doghood of dogs. The proposition <*that* hood is scratched> might depend for its instantiation on the existence of the hood. Even so, if A and B each think it, they think the same thing. If neither thinks it, it remains true. Just because an intentional property can only be instantiated *at* a time, or even *by* one person, does not mean that it is *in* time or a *part* or moment of that person. As John McDowell points out in relation to Frege's quite similar view, the objectivity of thoughts and senses is not compromised by assigning a distinct sense to each person's "I"-thoughts. There are thoughts "that only I can entertain; but it does not follow that they are not available to be entertained independently of my actually entertaining them" (McDowell 1998c, 223). But if they are "available," that is because those "thoughts"—which Husserl would call "propositions"—exist.

One might object to this version of the species view along the following lines: in phenomenological inquiry, we are supposed to bracket or make no appeal to the actual existence of the world in our phenomenological descriptions. This view, however, seems to require that we do so. Impure meanings are those that are bound up with this world. We cannot investigate those meanings, or the acts in which they are given, without positing the world.

If this were right, it would not by itself constitute an objection to the species view. It could just as well be read as an objection to the phenomenological method here invoked. Methods are ways of knowing objects, in this case a certain class of meanings and their psychological instances. If the objects do not lend themselves to a method, it's the method that is to blame.

However, the objection is not correct in any case. First, this version of the species view need not be committed to the claim that impure meanings and other non-intentional universals are bound up with the *existence* of the actual world. It is rather, as Lilian Alweiss (2009, 70) points out, that they are, as part of their own phenomenological character, bound up with the *positing of* the world *as existing*. If we were deluded or mistaken on this point, if the surrounding world of which we are continually aware did not in fact exist, it would remain the case that we posit it as existing, that it is part of the very sense of what it is to be a dog, or to be *this* car hood, that only acts which are positing with respect to this world count as revealing more about dogs or this car hood, and that certain acts of meaning can only be instantiated when we co-posit an actual world in which they occur and their objects exist. Were we to somehow learn that this world is one enormous hallucination, we would not say, "Well, at least we learned a lot about dogs!" Our dog-beliefs would, in virtue of their own sense, be abandoned in the same stroke that our world-belief is abandoned. Our mathematical and geometrical beliefs would survive.

It may *also* be true that such impure meanings can only be instantiated if the world *in fact* exists, and that we can undergo various experiences of world-bound individuals and kinds on the condition that they exist. But that is perfectly compatible with simply bracketing the question of whether those objects do in fact exist for methodological purposes. It is a misconception to suppose that phenomenological bracketing or disregarding of the question of the existence of an object carries a commitment to the view that an intentional act directed upon that object can exist even if its object does not. Bracketing commits us to no such thing. In geometry we bracket color by disregarding it, by not incorporating any propositions about colors into our proofs. We are not thereby committed one way or the other to the metaphysical possibility of colorless extended objects.

3.7 Conclusion

In this chapter we examined acts of meaning, partly to get some clarity about what meanings are and are not, and to determine how they are related to both the objects that they refer to or are about and the mental acts in which they are thought. Quine regards meanings to be "obscure intermediary entities" (Quine 1961a, 22). On Husserl's view, they are neither obscure nor intermediaries. They are phenomenologically discoverable properties of some of the most familiar things in the world, acts of conscious thought, and they enable us to think of things directly and as they are. In the next chapter, we will examine the parts of mental acts in more detail.

Notes

1 Ideas I §142, 283. Also see LI, Introduction to Volume II, §2, 253–254 and PAS, 643. Also see Rudolf Bernet (2003, 154) on the "interweaving between subject, object and meaning."
2 PRS, 90; also see LI, Appendix, §5, 862.

3 For a good discussion, see Willard 1984, 193ff.
4 For very helpful overviews of Husserl's theory of meaning in the *Investigations*, see Mohanty 1974, Simons 1995, and Benoist 2003.
5 On the distinction between markers and signifiers, see Horst 1999, 356–358.
6 LI 5 §17, 579. Also see Smith and McIntyre 1982, 8–9.
7 Husserl does not say much about illocutionary force as such in the First Investigation, but he does point in its direction in the Fifth when he distinguishes an act's matter or content and its quality, and notes that "To be alike in 'content,' while differing in act-quality has its visible grammatical expression" (LI 5 §20, 587). It shows up in the difference between "The hood of the car is scratched" and "Is the hood of the car scratched?"
8 LI 1 §7, 277. Findlay translates "Kundgabe" as "intimation." I am grateful to Daniel Dahlstrom for providing a more suitable translation.
9 LI Prol. §62, 225. Also see LI Prol. §§6, 48, and 66B., as well as Willard 1984, 169ff., for discussions of the various "interconnections" that constitute a fully realized science.
10 See Frege 1946 and Bolzano 1972, 33. Bolzano's example involves "the concept of a line which is the shortest between two points" and "a line of which all parts are similar to each other." Husserl criticizes Frege's terminological choice, however, of using "Sinn" to designate the meaning of an expression and "Bedeutung" to designate its reference or referent. See LI 1 §15, 292. See Willard 1994a and Rosado Haddock 2000 for helpful discussions.
11 See Aristotle 1941, §4, 42; LI 6 §7, 691; Horst 1999, 353–354; Davis 2005, 19.
12 Bonjour 1998, 53. Also see Davis 2005, 19.
13 In his later work *Formal and Transcendental Logic*, Husserl marks these distinctions differently. See FTL §90 and Benoist 2015, 111–112.
14 LI 1 §31, 329; also see LI Prol. §47, 183.
15 Willard 1972, 94. This needs to be distinguished from "psychologism" in the sense in which Tim Crane means it, according to which psychologism is a rejection of the view that we should investigate intentionality by examining propositional attitudes, and specifically the propositional contents of such attitudes (Crane 2014, 19). On *that* understanding of "psychologism," phenomenology is thoroughly psychologistic.
16 LI 1 §29, 323. This more closely corresponds to our contemporary conception of logic. Husserl also, however, has a broader conception of logic as a "theory of science" (see LI Prol. §6, 60; §11, 70) or, better, as the "*A priori theory of science*" (ILTK §14, 53). Logic so construed also includes formal ontology, or "*the pure (a priori) theory of objects as such*" (LI 4, Introduction, 435).
17 ILTK §14, 52. For more, see Willard 1984, 189.
18 ILTK §14, 52. Also see LI Prol. §67, 237.
19 See David 1994, 55.
20 LI 2 §8, 352.
21 Ideas I §22, 41. See LI 2 §42 for Husserl's discussion of the ambiguity of the word "concept." "General objects and general presentations or meanings ... are alike called concepts, but equivocally so" (ibid., 431). I have, of course, stuck with considering concepts to be meanings.
22 Willard 1984, 187. Also see Moreland 1989.
23 BP §9, 16. Also see LI 2 §8, 352.
24 IdPh, 52. For clear statements that constitution is not construction, see Sokolowski 1964, 54, Mohanty 1989, 151–152, Willard 2006, 597–598, and Poellner 2007, 412.
25 As Willard (1984, 146) points out in his powerful criticism of it.
26 Prior 1971, 3. Also see Crane 2013, 7 and Davis 2003, 317–318.
27 LI 1 §34, 332. Or, as Wayne Davis puts it, when we think about Mary, we exercise the idea of Mary, but do not think about it. "Thinking about the idea of Mary requires the occurrence of a second-order idea, the idea of the idea of Mary" (Davis 2003, 482).
28 Willard 1994a, 242–244. Also see Bell 1979, 122, whom Willard (242) credits with this objection.
29 Willard 1972. Husserl speaks of the "paradox of antipsychologism, according to which a theory of knowledge is not a psychological theory" (PR, 120). See Willard 1984, 147ff.
30 For excellent discussions, see Willard 1972, 99; Willard 1984, 184–185; and B. Smith 2000, §3.
31 LI 1 §31, 330. Also see Fodor 1998, 20, Davis 2005, 324, and see Davis 2003, Ch. 15.
32 See Willard 1972; B. Smith 2000, §3.

33 LI I §26, 317. For an account of Husserl's theory of demonstratives, see D.W. Smith 1982 and Smith and McIntyre 1982, 213ff.
34 VB, 214; also see Erhard 2011, 205–206.

Recommended Readings

Addis, Laird. 1989. *Natural Signs: A Theory of Intentionality.* Philadelphia: Temple University Press.

Davis, Wayne A. 2005. *Nondescriptive Meaning and Reference: An Ideational Semantics.* Oxford: Oxford University Press.

Frege, Gottlob. 1946. "Sense and Reference." *The Philosophical Review* 57: 209–230.

Husserl, Edmund. 1970. *Logical Investigations.* Two volumes. J.N. Findlay, trans. London: Routledge & Kegan Paul. See especially the Prolegomena, the First, Second, and Sixth Investigations.

Husserl, Edmund. 2008. *Introduction to Logic and Theory of Knowledge: Lectures 1906/07.* Claire Ortiz Hill, trans. Dordrecht: Springer.

Smith, Barry ed. 1982. *Parts and Moments: Studies in Logic and Formal Ontology.* Munich: Philosophia Verlag.

Woodruff Smith, David and McIntyre, Ronald. 1982. *Husserl and Intentionality: A Study of Mind, Meaning, and Language.* Dordrecht: D. Reidel.

Willard, Dallas. 1984. *Logic and the Objectivity of Knowledge.* Athens, OH: Ohio University Press.

4   The Mental Act

In the previous chapter meanings emerged as ideal entities that are neither mental nor physical, distinct from any existing linguistic or mental acts. Meanings are intentional properties, whose instances are non-independent parts of mental acts. In this chapter we will examine some of the parts and structures comprising an intentional experience.

The most basic type of intentional act, for Husserl, is an "objectifying act." Despite the centrality of this type of act in the *Logical Investigations*—they take over the function that Brentano ascribed to "presentations," namely being the most basic kind of act on which all others are founded—Husserl never does provide a tidy characterization of them.[1] Following Barry Smith, I will understand an objectifying act as one that is "targeted towards an object" (B. Smith 1990, 34). Another way to put it is that objectifying acts are those in virtue of which we are conscious of objects as being, or not being, some way or other. Some objectifying acts are positing. These include, for Husserl, a wide range of "nominal acts," acts of judgment, and, importantly, acts of perception. Other objectifying acts, such as acts of imagination or phantasy, are not. Objectifying acts stand opposed to acts in which we do *more* than represent objects. For instance, desire, hope, fear, love, and so on are acts in which an object is more than merely represented as being a certain way. All such acts are, according to Husserl, founded on objectifying acts, since the latter provide them with objects.[2] In order to want an apple, one must carry out an objectifying act whose object is the apple.

4.1   The Intentional Essence of an Act

Every intentional act has an *intentional essence*. This means that even the most basic concretizations of intentionality, objectifying acts, have both a *matter* and a *quality* (LI 5 §21, 590). Husserl defines them as follows.

Matter:

[T]hat element in an act which first gives it reference to an object, and reference so wholly definite that it not merely fixes the object meant in a general way, but also the precise way in which it is meant

(LI 5 §20, 589)

[T]hat moment in an objectifying act which makes the act present just this object in just this manner.

(LI 6 §25, 737)

Quality:

[T]he general act-character, which stamps an act as merely presentative, judgemental, emotional, desiderative, etc.

(LI 5 §20, 586)

[T]he modes of believing, entertaining, wishing, doubting, etc.

(LI 6 §27, 743)

As is often the case in phenomenological inquiry, we can achieve a better understanding of the nature of matter and quality by observing how they can be independently varied. Consider the following acts, where "H" designates A's car hood:

  i A judges that *this car's* hood is scratched.
 ii A wonders whether H is scratched.
iii A judges that H is scratched.
 iv A wonders whether her neighbor's car's hood is scratched.

Acts (i) and (ii) refer to the same object, but they do not have the same matter, since they do not refer to that object in the same way. Nor do they have the same quality, since one is an act of judging, the other an act of doubting. Acts (i) and (iii) share the same quality and the same object, but again differ in matter. Acts (ii) and (iv) share the same quality, but (iv) differs in reference, and therefore in matter, from each of (i)-(iii). Acts (ii) and (iii), finally, share the same matter, but differ in quality. Each of these corresponds to different meaning intentions. In the act of expressing any of them, the matter would correspond with an expression's meaning or content, and the quality with a speech act's illocutionary force.

Matter and quality are inseparable "abstract aspects" of acts; no act can consist of merely a quality or a matter (see LI 5 §20, 588). More specifically, they are abstract or non-independent parts or "moments." They are not properties but non-concrete individuals. Two acts can share the same type of matter and quality, but no two acts can share the *very same* matter or quality. Matter and quality are, however, independently variable. Some qualities, such as straightforward belief, are positing; any act with such a quality presents its object as existing or as bearing relations to what exists. On Husserl's view, this quality is not limited to acts with propositional matters. "Nominal acts" such as naming can have a positing character as well (LI 5 §34, 625). Think, for instance, of the act of reading a menu or a list of the world's longest rivers— the referents of the terms are intended as actual. This is different from reading a list of the descendants of Finwë the elf.

Furthermore, an act's positing of existence cannot be reduced to its matter or content. The proposition <The hood of the car most certainly exists> can be the content of the most certain conviction, but it can also be the content of a doubt, a mere act of thinking, a hope, or even an act of phantasy. Similarly, in the case of other qualities, the quality of an act can never be reduced to any part of the matter of the act. To hope that the hood of the car is not scratched is not simply to be in a mental state whose propositional content is <I hope the hood of the car is not scratched>, since being in a state with that content is compatible with having no hopes about the car's hood at all, or even hoping it is scratched all over. Hoping is not the same thing as representing oneself to be hopeful, or of representing something as hoped for by oneself or anyone else. In hope, I am aware of the world hopefully, and only non-positionally aware of my own hope. Furthermore, I can think the proposition <I hope the hood of the car is not scratched>, and also recognize that this thought is false. Even when I recognize that it is true, it is true because I so hope—my hopefulness is the truthmaker for the judgment *about* my hoping.

Husserl holds, as we have seen in §3.5 in the previous chapter, that meanings are "ideational abstractions" from the intentional essence of an act. In one sense this is right: to know what someone means in uttering a sentence, it is crucial to know both the content of the utterance and its force, which give notice of the corresponding act-matter and act-quality, respectively. But meanings as Husserl conceives of them, namely concepts and propositions, are ideational abstractions from the *matter* of an act alone. The reason is that logic, as he conceives of it, is a "science of meanings as such" (LI 1 §29, 323), and the quality of an act is completely irrelevant to both pure grammar and pure logic. Whether or not one believes, doubts, or denies the proposition <The hood of the car is scratched>, it entails <There is something that is scratched>. Furthermore, in anticipation of the discussion in Chapter 8, meanings are not ideational abstractions from the matters of *all* acts, but only from those whose matters instantiate concepts or propositions.

In the case of all matters, however, whether conceptual or not, the matter is responsible for an act's intentional direction or *reference to* its object. Since many matters can refer to the same object, we must distinguish an act's *reference to* an object and its *sense*. Senses are what concepts and propositions are, and what matters are instances of. The instantiation of sense, however, is not a *piece* of the matter; "there is not one piece of matter corresponding to an identical object, another to the differing mode of presenting it" (LI 5 §20, 589). In fact, it is not even a moment or abstract part.

How, then, is the sense related to the *reference to* an object? Husserl's account of this relation answers some pressing questions which Frege's theory leaves unspecified, namely just how senses are related to references to objects, and why exactly the sense of an expression (or act) determines its reference to an object—that is, why acts or expressions with the same sense must be about the same things. On Husserl's view, the relation between senses and references to objects is straightforward: senses are simply *determinate ways* of referring to or being intentionally directed upon an object (LI 5 §20, 589). Just as there is no way of being conscious of something without being conscious of it in some determinate way, in the narrower sphere of meaning there is no such thing as simply referring to something. Every object must be referred to in some manner, that is, using some concept or other intentional content. Senses, or meanings, *are* those manners, "just ways of being directed towards objects," as Barry Smith puts it.[3] This does not mean that we can only refer to things "indirectly." As Gareth Evans puts it,

> The fact that one is thinking about an object in a particular way can no more warrant the conclusion that one is not thinking of the object in the most direct possible fashion, than the fact that one is giving something in a particular way warrants the view that one's giving is somehow indirect.
>
> (Evans 1982, 62)

We will see, however, that there are ways of being conscious of objects in addition to meaning or conceiving of them.

4.2 Quality and Modification-Character

One of the most significant shortcomings of Husserl's characterizations of quality is that he never completely defines it. That is tolerable and perhaps to be expected; it may be primitive. However, a couple of common misconceptions about quality need to be avoided. One might quite reasonably suppose that *thinking* that the tree is in the yard, *perceiving* the tree to be in the yard, *imagining* it to be in the yard, and *remembering* it to be in the yard have the same matter, but differ in quality. There are strong textual and philosophical reasons not to endorse this view, however.

First, the text of the *Logical Investigations* is unambiguous in not treating the distinctions among *intuitive* acts as differences in quality. Not only do no such acts show up on Husserl's (admittedly incomplete) lists of act-qualities, but he insists that "specific differences among intuitive acts do not depend on their intentional essence"—and therefore do not depend on either their matter or their quality (LI 5 §21, 592). This is why he writes that a "percept may ... have the same matter as a flight of fancy" (ibid.) and that "perception can pass over into a corresponding picturing (an act with like 'matter' differently interpreted) yet without change in its positing character" (LI 5 §40, 646). The view in the *Investigations* is the rather obscure one that differences among intuitive acts are due to an act's "interpretive form," which determines how the sensational content in an act is taken up in relation to the act's quality and, primarily, its matter (see LI 6 §27, 743). I will not elaborate on this view here because Husserl later abandons it, and, I think, rightly so. The important point is that Husserl does not differentiate intuitive acts from one another, or any of them from empty thinking, in terms of quality.

Second, Husserl says things about matter and quality which would be both straightforwardly absurd and incompatible with some of his core commitments if perception were an act-quality. He writes, "any objectifying matter can be combined with any quality" (LI 5 §38, 641). But consider an intentional matter such as <round square> or <a square which is not square>, whose object is something impossible. No such matter could be the matter of a possible intuitive act. Not only is that clear, but the whole point of Husserl's crucial distinction between "possible" and "impossible" meanings is that the latter are intuitively unfulfillable—that is, "impossible" meanings are those whose objects cannot in principle be intuited (LI 6 §30). If perception were a quality, Husserl's claim about the limitless combinability of matters and qualities would have to be construed as an incredible oversight.

Third, and more straightforwardly, perception can have the same quality as thought. And memory can have the same quality as both.[4] Nearly two decades after the *Investigations*, Husserl says so clearly: "When we compare a perception... with a predicative claim, there is obviously commonality with respect to quality."[5] Both, that is, have the quality of positing their objects as actual. In the same text, Husserl even uses the English term "belief" to designate that quality. In a still later work, he writes, "Original, normal perception has the primordial mode, 'being valid simpliciter;' this is what we call straightforward, naïve certainty" (PAS, 75)—a "mode" that acts of thought can obviously share. Husserl also writes, this time contrary to some passages in the *Investigations*, that what distinguishes perception from judgment is the *matter* of an act.[6] Comparing a case where an object or state of affairs is judged with a case in which it is perceived, he writes:

> In the one case we have thought-matter, in the other an intuition-matter, and if belief positing (true-opining) takes place, we have with respect to the semantic essence in one case a logical proposition [logischen Satz] ... in the other case so to speak an intuitive proposition [anschaulichen Satz], an intuitively meant-as-such, perception.[7]

The case for that claim will have to wait until Chapter 8. The point for now, however, stands: "perception" does not name an act quality. Rather, perception has a positing quality that can be and often is shared with acts of judging.

Husserl eventually came to see that *phantasy* is not an act quality as well. Acts of phantasy stand apart from all others as essentially non-positing (PICM, 4). This does not, however, mean that phantasy is among the *doxic* qualities. As we saw in §2.1.2 of the present volume, acts of phantasy do not sit anywhere along the continuum from naïve certainty to radical doubt. The reason is that acts of phantasy cannot, like any acts with a positing character, be converted into other types of doxic acts by the availability of evidence concerning what is actual. If I imagine that a dragon is invading Boston, my act cannot be confirmed or refuted by any of my positing experiences or beliefs, but only quasi-confirmed or quasi-refuted by other acts of phantasy.

There is also a more general, and more interesting, reason why phantasy could not be an act quality of any type, whether doxic or otherwise: any positional act whatsoever has a corresponding phantasy-modification, which shares, among other things, its quality.[8] The puzzling nature of the phantasy-modification vis-à-vis the quality of an act is brought out nicely by Husserl's remark that "We say correctly, and yet again incorrectly: In mere phantasy we do not believe" (PICM, 606). What makes this assertion correct is that phantasy is not *really* believing. It is *as-if* or *quasi*-believing. What makes it incorrect is that there is such a thing as phantasy-*believing* as opposed to phantasy-*doubting*, phantasy-*entertaining*, and so on. There is a quasi-counterpart to *every* positional experience, one that preserves that experience's quality. As Husserl puts it, "like all of these characteristics, belief admits of imaginative modification. That is to say, the whole apprehensional nexus with its modal characteristic of certainty admits of imaginative modification" (PICM, 358). Since every single act quality that can show up in positing consciousness can show up in phantasy as well, phantasy cannot be just another quality (see Cairns 2013, 46).

Suppose, for instance, that I construct a world in imagination. In that world some objects are given to me in the mode of simple certainty. I see a mountain; I am certain that it exists. But other act-qualities abound. I am unsure whether a dragon lives there. I hope he doesn't, but fear that he does. Or rather: I *quasi*-see, am *quasi*-certain, *quasi*-doubt, and *quasi*-hope. In phantasy "everything is 'modified' into what is *quasi*," into the as-if (PICM, 263). It is clear, then, that the phantasy-modification is not an alteration of an act's quality, since the phantasy-modification can coexist with any quality whatsoever (see PICM, 106). Note, moreover, that in phantasy, there are *quasi*-originary acts, such as acts of perception, and they automatically carry with them a *quasi*-belief in the existence of what is given.[9] The *quasi*-seeing carries with it a *quasi*-conviction; it is a modification of the *whole act* of perception.

Consider another example: the judgment that the hood of the car is scratched. Letting "<p>" stand for the propositional content (matter) of the act, letting "S" designate the state of affairs that is this judgment's object, and letting "→" stand for the relation of intentionality, we can represent this act as follows:

(1) J<p> → S

When this act is modified into doubt, it becomes

(2) D<p> → S

If the phantasy-modification were one among the intentional qualities, then an act of phantasy would have this structure:

(3) PH<p> → S

That, however, cannot be right. Corresponding to *each* type of act is a possible phantasy act sharing *its* quality. Since that is so, the problem with (3) above is clear: it fails to specify whether the phantasy-act in question is one of judgment, doubt, hope, fear, or any of the other act-qualities that can be conjoined with the content <p>.

Perhaps, then, the phantasy-counterpart of a positional act A is an act of phantasy, with a certain content <p*>, that has A as its *object*. In the present case, that would look like this:

(4) PH<p*> → J<p> → S

That, however, is not right either. When I entertain a phantasy judgment that the car's hood is scratched, the object of my act of phantasy is not an *act of judging* that the car's hood is scratched, but the car's hood's being scratched. As Husserl says, there is a difference between the "imagining of the perception of A" and "the imaginative consciousness of A," where it is A, not the perception of A, which is "on the right side of the 'of'" (PICM, 218), and the same holds in this case. When I am quasi-judgingly conscious of the car's hood's being scratched, I am not directly aware of an experience of judging the hood to be scratched. Rather, I am directly aware of the car's hood's being scratched, but in the mode of as-if.

Phantasy, quite simply, is not an act-quality. It is a different type of *modification* of an act altogether (see Marbach 1993, 61). The phantasy-modification of (1) above is a *phantasy-judgment* that the car's hood is scratched. That is,

(5) J$_{ph}$<p> → S

The phantasy-modification of (2) is a *phantasy-doubt* that the hood is scratched. That is,

(6) D$_{ph}$<p> → S

We can also perform phantasy acts with the content <p> whose total quality lies outside the doxic modifications altogether. I can fear that the car's hood is scratched, for instance, and that act too has its phantasy-modification, an act of phantasy-fear.

If this analysis is correct, then treating intentional experiences in terms of their matter and quality alone is insufficient. What the subscript "$_{ph}$" in (5) and (6) above symbolizes is neither the matter nor the quality of an act. It designates a certain modification that other acts can undergo. As Husserl puts it, "mere phantasy is an ultimate and altogether original modification" (PICM, 468).

Memory is another example. Suppose that I want to re-live a certain experience I had in the past, such as a particularly invigorating and scenic hike in the mountains. In re-living the experience, I undergo an experience that "points back to perception in its own phenomenological essence."[10] And, just as any experience can in principle undergo a phantasy-modification, that is the case with memory as well: "there corresponds to every mental process ... a series of ideally possible memorial modifications" (PICM, 261). Perception, for its part, is unmodified. It is not, as part of its own nature, experienced as a modification of memory, phantasy, or anything else.

4.3 Many-rayed, Compound, and Founded Acts

The life of consciousness, as anyone can attest upon reflection, is almost never a matter of carrying out just one act directed upon one object. Rather, conscious experience as a rule, and perhaps as a matter of necessity, is complex. As I sit here now, I enjoy a complex experience of the words on my screen, the objects that they refer to, the sound of the fan in the background, a desire for more coffee, a slight sense of fatigue, and much else (see LI 5 §38, 640). My experience as a whole is "many-rayed" (LI 5 §38, 640).

This "unity of experience," however, does not add up to a "unity of *act*" (LI 5 §18, 580). When I hear a fan and read the words on the screen, these experiences do not present me with a new unified object. The two experiences are freely variable, and their unity consists of nothing more than their co-occurrence within my field of consciousness. Only *compound* acts can generate a unity of act; they are unified, many-rayed acts which have their own proprietary objects. In a compound act, which is a genuine experiential whole rather than a mere collection of co-occurring acts, an object is intended through the contribution of part-acts, each with its own intentional essence (ibid.).

An example of a compound act is the continuous perceptual experience of an object over time. If B examines the scratch on the car hood for some period of time, looking at it, running his thumbnail across it, and so on, the whole series of acts is "fused" into one continuous and temporally extended act (LI 6 §47, 790). This fusion is not something we actively do or perform; it just happens in a kind of "passive synthesis." The same sort of thing occurs when we hear a melody or a sentence. This unity arises without any super-vision by an "ego," and is one of the most pervasive and important features of conscious life.

Another example of a compound act occurs in the case of linguistic con-sciousness. When, for instance, one reads or hears a sentence about a car hood that is scratched, one is both perceptually conscious of the sentence, emptily conscious of the car hood, and conscious of the sentence *as* a repre-sentation of the car hood. Similarly, when one expresses a judgment or a wish, one is aware of both the sense perceptible signs by which the content is expressed and the objects which the act is about. We can appreciate the complexity of the consciousness involved in a typical linguistic act when we consider that we are typically conscious, in some manner or other, of all of the components discussed in §3.1.

Furthermore, as we saw in the previous chapter, there are some acts which are not only compound, but phenomenologically *founded*—their object is distinct from that of any of the underlying acts. Hearing a melody is one such act—it is a compound act that is also phenomenologically founded insofar as its object, the melody, is distinct from the objects of any of the underlying acts. Image consciousness is arguably a case of such an act as well, since the object of the act is a complicated relational structure of A's depicting of B. Acts of relational identification, again, are phenomenologically founded. The complete object of an act of identifying *a* with *b* is not *a*, or *b*, but the identity of *a* with *b*. Perceiving a tree from a fixed position for ten seconds, however, is not a phenomenologically founded act, since each fused part-act has the same object as the total act (LI 6 §47, 790).

Propositional acts, such as the act of thinking that the car hood is scrat-ched, are also phenomenologically founded acts on Husserl's view. This is because he regards the nominal component of the act as the content of a "nominal act" (LI 5 §38, 638). Whether there are really multiple *acts* taking place in a typical act of propositional thought, belief, or assertion, however, is really not phenomenologically obvious, at least in the case of acts whose contents are atomic propositions. But we can regard such acts as the actuali-zation of multiple distinct abilities, distinct abilities whose exercise results in an act with a phenomenologically founded content. As Gareth Evans puts it when introducing his "Generality Constraint":

> We cannot avoid thinking of a thought about an individual object x, to the effect that it is F, as the exercise of two separable capacities; one being the capacity to think of x, which could be equally exercised in thoughts about x to the effect that it is G or H; and the other being a conception of what it is to be F, which could be equally exercised in thoughts about other individuals, to the effect that they are F.
>
> (Evans 1982, 75)

According to the Generality Constraint, someone who can think that a is F and b is G should have no "conceptual barrier" to thinking that a is G or b is F.[11] The Generality Constraint, and related claims regarding the capacities of *thinkers*, must be distinguished from claims about the systematic and compositional structure of the *contents* of thought, namely concepts and meanings. According to Evans, however, the compositional structure of thought contents and the Generality Constraint are intimately related. As he puts it:

> It is a feature of the thought-content *that John is happy* that to grasp it requires distinguishable skills. In particular, it requires possession of the concept of happiness—knowledge what it is for a person to be happy; and that is something not tied to this or that particular person's happiness.[12]

Even if Evans is wrong about the capacity of all thinkers to dissociate the capacities exercised in judgment as freely as the Generality Constraint requires, and even if we disagree with Husserl that a propositional act is composed of multiple *acts*, it is definitely multi-rayed, and as such requires the exercise or actualization of multiple intentional and conceptual abilities. Furthermore, its *content* is founded because its object, a state of affairs, is distinct from that of any of the objects of its contentful parts. Finally, because the contents of thoughts have a systematic and compositional structure, whatever explains a particular subject's *in*ability to abide by the Generality Constraint is not rooted in the nature of the contents of her thoughts, but in something else. In the same way, it is an empirical question whether or not all humans can appreciate the logical validity or invalidity of arguments. But if some cannot, that fact is not rooted in the nature of the contents of thought.

All of the examples above involve acts whose compound structure is due specifically to the compounding of their intentional *matters*: in each case, the object of the compound act is intended in the manner in which it is intended in virtue of the objects of the underlying acts intending their objects as they are intended. There are, however, also *qualitatively* complex acts. An act of fearing that a lion is nearby or hoping that the car hood is not scratched can be founded on acts of belief with the same intentional matters, for instance. Some act qualities, too, seem to require founding. If I really fear something, I must really posit it as something that exists or could exist or happen, and also desire that it not exist or happen. A wide range of act qualities, in fact, can be constructed out of belief and desire.[13]

4.4 The Intentional Relation

One of the most striking features of Husserl's account of the mental act is that the act's intentional essence, a real part of it, is responsible for its reaching out to an object which is, in most cases, *not* a part of it.[14] "This 'reference to an object' belongs peculiarly and intrinsically to an act-experience."[15] This is true of all acts, whether or not their objects exist. Whether I am conscious of the tree in the yard being in bloom, the god Jupiter, the number 3, or whatever, the matter of the act is a sufficient condition for my being conscious of that object.

If the intentionality of an act is an intrinsic property of it, and if an intrinsic property is one that an entity can have irrespective of the relations it bears to other things, then Husserl is committed to the view that mental acts do not entail the existence of their objects. And there are undoubtedly passages in which he seems committed to such a view.

> If this experience is present, then, *eo ipso* and through its own essence ... the "intentional relation" to an object is achieved ... And of course such an experience may be present in consciousness together with its intention, although its object does not exist at all, and is perhaps incapable of existence.
> (LI 5 §11, 558)

This feature of "existence-independence" is often thought to be a feature of intentionality in general (Smith and McIntyre 1982, 11–12).

One may rightly worry, however, that this view does not do justice to genuinely relational acts, acts which *necessitate* or guarantee the existence of their objects (Mulligan and Smith 1986, 117). And there are such acts. First, "immanent perception," such as the "perception" of ongoing conscious experiences and certain universals, "guarantees necessarily the existence of its object" (Ideas I §46, 82). Later I will argue that ordinary perception is likely relational as well. There is a way of understanding Husserl's position, though, that does not turn at all on the question of whether some acts are relational. Even in the case of relational acts, there is a distinction between the act and its object, and it is the nature of the act that makes the *intentional* relation between them intelligible.

4.4.1 Consciousness and Existence

It is a familiar point that on Husserl's view, not *all* intentional experiences entail the existence of their objects. This position is both phenomenologically obvious and, for what it is worth, necessary for a defense of a commonsense, direct realist account of consciousness.

According to many notable philosophers, the only objects of which we are directly or immediately aware lie within the sphere of consciousness itself. Consciousness is, on this view, "an immanent domain that consist[s] of all of what we are occurrently aware of directly, that is, a mental world closed in upon itself" (Natsoulas 2013, 92). Against this view, as the psychologist Thomas Natsoulas rightly notes, Husserl "maintained it fundamental to consciousness that we manage, as it were, to break out of the subjective realm" (ibid.). That is, against the allegedly Cartesian nature of Husserl's position is a deeply *anti*-Cartesian (and anti-Lockean, anti-Berkeleyan, anti-Humean, etc.) account of intentionality.[16] That we can think about what does *not* exist shows that what we think about is not always a constituent or component of our own minds. It also shows that the Midas touch view of consciousness cannot be true of all acts. As Willard notes, "if it [intentionality] imparted a property to its object, then of course the object would have to exist" (Willard 1995, 156). But not everything we represent does exist—not even "in the mind." So, intentionality or representation does not, in all cases, impart a property to its object.

If one thinks that the object of an intentional act simply must exist, and then notices that a wide variety of intentional acts can occur even when their putative physical or mind-independent objects do *not* exist, one will be compelled to find objects whose existence is entailed by the consciousness of them. Traditionally those objects have turned out to be mental, or at least not physical: ideas, images, representations, sense data, concepts and propositions—sometimes understood as mental particulars rather than ideal species—or something else along these lines (Willard 1967, 515–516; Smith and McIntyre 1982, 42). The result is the familiar picture of us as somehow trapped within the confines of our own minds and its representations.

Whatever metaphysical or epistemological problems such views give rise to, they are objectionable on purely phenomenological grounds. When, to use an example of Husserl's, we think about the god Jupiter, it is self-evident that we are thinking about a god. It is also evident that this god does not exist. There is a standing temptation to treat what doesn't exist as somehow "in the mind." But the god Jupiter is not in anyone's mind. The reason is simple: whatever exists in a mind exists, and the god Jupiter does not exist. Similarly, positive states of affairs involving him do not obtain in the mind. Jupiter does not hurl lightning bolts against enemies in my or anyone else's head. He just doesn't do that at all, since there is no *he* to do the deed. The same holds of lots of things we can think about. Some, such as the greatest prime number or a round square, could not possibly exist, and it is no less absurd to install them in the mind than to suppose they are anywhere else.

This is why, if we are at all clear regarding what we are thinking about when we think about the god Jupiter, we will agree with Husserl that:

> This intentional experience may be dismembered as one chooses in descriptive analysis, but the god Jupiter naturally will not be found in it. The "immanent", "mental object" is not therefore part of the descriptive or real make-up of the experience, it is in truth not really immanent or mental. But it also does not exist extramentally, it does not exist at all.
>
> (LI 5 §11, 558–559)

The same goes for many objects we think about in many different categories: the property of being red and green all over at a time, the state of affairs of Oregon being larger than Siberia, and so on.

Perhaps, then, someone who believes Jupiter exists, wields thunderbolts against foes, and performs other deeds both godly and ungodly, is instead thinking about something else, their *idea of* Jupiter, or some other "immanent object" that falls short of but bears some relation to Jupiter. But this proposal is hardly better than putting Jupiter himself in the mind. That an *idea of* Jupiter zaps foes with lightning, or zaps ideas of foes with ideas of lightning, is not what the believer in Jupiter's mighty powers believes. Any theory according to which our experiences of nonexistent objects are really directed upon existing mental or immanent objects commits the cardinal phenomenological sin of replacing what we are obviously conscious of with something completely different (see, e.g., LI 2 §37, 411–12). Such a theory does "succeed in giving every act an object," but "in most cases it gives acts the wrong objects" (Smith and McIntyre 1982, 52).

The shortcomings of this view are especially obvious in the case of states such as desire, hope, fear, expectation, and other similar attitudes. In the case of desires directed upon nonexistent objects, the relational theory must absurdly treat the object desired as one that the subject already possesses. When, to use a well-worn example, Ponce de León hopes to find the Fountain of Youth and sets about searching for it, the thing he is looking for does not exist. And as Harman points out, "he was not looking for an idea of the Fountain of Youth. He already had the idea."[17] Since the Fountain of Youth in whose existence Ponce de León believes is the very one that he is looking for, it follows that his belief is not directed upon a mental or immanent fountain either.

4.4.2 Immanence and Transcendence

Husserl's position is largely motivated by the fact that objects are "transcendent" to the acts intending them. As he writes,

> In real (*reell*) phenomenological treatment, objectivity counts as nothing: in general, it transcends the act. It makes no difference what sort of being we give our object, or with what sense of justification we do so, whether this being is real (*real*) or ideal, genuine, possible or impossible, the act remains "directed upon" its object.
>
> (LI 5 §20, 587)

The reason that "objectivity counts as nothing," Husserl here writes, is that it "transcends the act." Here, though, it's important to take a closer look at what transcendence amounts to and why it is important.

In his 1907 lectures on *The Idea of Phenomenology*, Husserl distinguishes two senses of the terms "transcendent" and "immanent": an object can be *really* transcendent or *intentionally* transcendent.[18] *Real* (*reell*, not *real*) immanence and transcendence are mereological relations. Something is *really* or *genuinely* transcendent to consciousness if it is not a part or piece of the stream of consciousness itself. Otherwise it is *really* immanent. So, for example, the matter and quality of an intentional experience are really immanent to that experience—though the universals of which they are instances are not. But in many cases, the object of an act is really transcendent to the stream of consciousness. A scratched car hood is not a component of any stream of consciousness. Neither is the god Jupiter.

Intentional immanence and transcendence are not mereological but epistemological relations. Something is *intentionally immanent* when it is totally or adequately given. Intentionally immanent objects are not given from perspectives: "The immanent object has only one possible way to be given in the original in every Now."[19] Adequate or immanent intuition is also a form of consciousness which, according to Husserl, is infallible, one that "guarantees necessarily the existence of its object" (Ideas I §46, 82). So, for instance, conscious sensations are, or are at least nearly, intentionally immanent. For virtually every change in our consciousness of a sensation, there is a change in the sensation of which we are conscious. "There are no perspectives to be had on our sensations."[20] Something is *intentionally transcendent* when it is either not given at all, or only incompletely or inadequately given.

In many cases the distinctions between real and intentional immanence and transcendence coincide. Spatial things and their features are really and intentionally transcendent. And occurrent conscious experiences are both really and intentionally immanent to the subject whose experiences they are. "*An experience does not present itself in profile*" (Ideas I §42, 75).

Nevertheless, real and intentional immanence are distinct features, and they can come apart. For instance, certain essences and essential relations are capable of being given adequately, but essences and essential relations are not really immanent to any stream of consciousness.[21] And some real components of the stream of consciousness can be misapprehended. What Brentano and others call "inner perception" is often fallible (LI 6, Appendix §6, 866) To modify Husserl's example, a pain, which in itself is experienced adequately, also feels as though it is in a hand. But, as phantom limb syndrome demonstrates, one could be wrong about this. It should also be clear that not all mental *states* are intentionally immanent. A person is more than a flow of consciousness. Persons have beliefs, desires, values, priorities, and a life organized around various poles of cognitive, evaluative, volitional, and affective importance. And obviously, in light of what mysteries we are to ourselves, we cannot have an adequate intuition of this complex web of acts and dispositions. Most of us probably cannot, for instance, know with certainty what we regard as most important in human life. That is a question that others may sometimes be better qualified to answer about us than we are (see Dahlstrom 2017, 55–56).

As will become increasingly clear in subsequent chapters, and ought to be borne in mind throughout, the distinction between real immanence and transcendence has no epistemological importance at all, except to the extent that it coincides with intentional immanence and transcendence.[22] If constituents of the stream of consciousness are known better than physical things, it is not because they are "in" the mind as real (reell) constituents. It is because they are given adequately. And if it should turn out that spatial things such as car hoods are, after all, constituents of the stream of consciousness, their *intentional* transcendence would render our perception and knowledge of them identical with what it is at present.

This means that it would be no solution whatsoever to skeptical worries to become an idealist about scratched car hoods. If our knowledge of them is fallible, that is because they are given inadequately, and that fact cannot be changed by installing them in the mind. Even transmuting the car into an array of harmonious experiences or a noematic "correlate" of such experiences would solve nothing. Instead of the skeptical "worry" that the physical car I see doesn't exist, I will have the worry that an indescribably vast array of possible future experiences or noemata would not harmonize with my present one. A great deal would be lost metaphysically, and nothing would be gained epistemologically (see Lyons 2009, 6–7).

We can illustrate the relation between these senses of "immanent" and "transcendent" as follows:

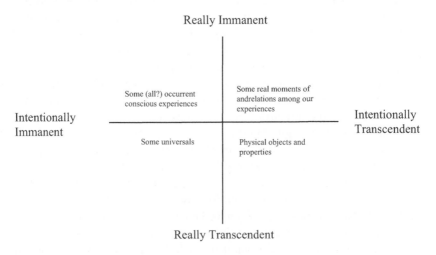

Figure 4.1 Real and Intentional Immanence

This, however, is not enough. We must also distinguish two kinds of *real transcendence* and *real immanence*. First, something might be really immanent to *the same stream of consciousness* as a given act A. Second, something might be really immanent *to act A itself.*

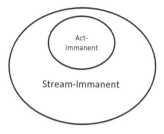

Figure 4.2 Stream- and Act-Immanence

Everything which is act-immanent to A is stream-immanent to A—A's parts are parts of the stream of which A itself is a part. But not everything which belongs to the same stream of consciousness as A is a part of A. So, for instance, if I reflect upon an experience that I just had or am currently undergoing, I carry out a reflective act A, whose object is another intentional act A*, like this:

$$A \rightarrow A^*$$

In this case, A* is stream-immanent to A. But it is not act-immanent to A. It is the intentional object of A, but is not a *constituent* of A. What *is* act-immanent to A is its intentional essence, its matter and quality.

Recall that Husserl writes that when we engage in phenomenology, "objectivity counts as nothing" because "it transcends *the act*" (LI 5 §20, 587, my emphasis). It is *act*-transcendence that is at issue here, namely the act-transcendence of the *object* of that act. And then he writes:

> It makes no difference what sort of being we give our object, or with what sense of justification we do so, whether this being is real (real) or ideal, genuine, possible or impossible, the act remains "directed upon" its object.
>
> (LI 5 §20, 587)

Now if the being of the object "makes no difference," then even the being of what is stream-immanent makes no difference. And if it "makes no difference" what sort of "justification" we have for believing in the object, then even the existence of what is absolutely indubitable makes no difference. If that is right, then it "makes no difference" even in the case of another act A* upon which I am reflecting, an act (a) which is stream-immanent relative to A, (b) which is intentionally immanent and in whose existence I believe with absolute justification, and (c) whose existence is guaranteed by my reflective awareness of it.

To what is it, exactly, that these facts "make[] no difference"? The answer is not that they make no difference to the *existence* of the act. It is not even that they make no difference to the *essence* of the act. It is, rather, that they make no difference to *what it is about the act that makes it intentionally directed upon its object*. To understand *that*, we need to appeal to an act's own proper parts and moments. The central issue of "transcendence" is not how an act reaches beyond the sphere of consciousness, or beyond the sphere of what is indubitable. It is the issue of how an act reaches out beyond *itself*.

The existence of an object might *causally* explain why I am conscious of it and why my conscious act has its parts and properties, and my act might even be *necessarily* related to the object. But it is the *having of* those parts and properties that *constitutively* explains why I am conscious of that object: having an experience with those properties is *what it is to be* conscious of an object in the manner in which I am conscious of it.[23] In Aristotelian terms, the content and structure of an act is the formal cause of its being of its object, a claim which is fully compatible with the claim that the object is part of the efficient cause of the act's having that content, and also fully compatible with the claim that its existence is entailed by that of the act. The properties of the *object* cannot explain that; there is no of-ness to be found in most objects, and even when there is—as in the case of A's being directed upon A*—the of-ness we find *in* the object isn't the of-ness of the act directed *upon* that object. I normally cannot discover the of-ness or aboutness of an act in or among its objects, no matter how intimately they are related to the act itself.

Perhaps an analogy would help. It is part of the nature of volume to exist only if a tone and its other parts and moments exist. But we can still ascribe features to the volume itself, and apprehend *its* distinctive contribution to the overall character of a tone, for instance that the tone's intensity is 100 decibels. The other features of a tone, such as its timbre and pitch, must also be present if the volume is to exist, and something or other must have caused the tone to exist. But it would be wrongheaded to appeal to *them* to apprehend the contribution that the *volume* makes to the tone. No matter how much I examine them, I will be in the dark about why the tone has an intensity of 100 decibels.

In a similar way, it would be wrongheaded to appeal to the object of a conscious state to explain what it is about the act in virtue of which it is of that object. This is true no matter *what* the object is, no matter *where* it is, and no matter *how well* it is known. The intentional direction *upon the object* is not to be found among *its* parts, moments, or properties. For that, we need to appeal to what belongs to the act itself. Even if the act and its object together constitute a genuine whole, one in which the act is a non-separable part, the *intentionality* that takes place within that whole flows from the act to the object, and is to be explained in terms of the nature of that act.

This, if right, has two important consequences. The first is that the reasons for paying attention to the inner character of acts—and, in Husserl's later philosophy, for following his method of "bracketing" what does not belong to them—does not at all constitute a rejection of the genuinely relational character of some acts of consciousness. Nor does it constitute an indifference to the question of whether of those objects must exist *if* certain acts directed upon them exist (see Zahavi 2003a, 63; Alweiss 2013).

The second is that merely appealing to the object of consciousness does not explain why a given act is directed upon it. As important as it is to point out that a certain volume-moment *v* depends for its existence, as a matter of essence, on a timbre-moment *t* and a pitch-moment *p*, that does not disclose the nature of *v* itself or explain its contribution to the whole tone. And pointing out that an act can only exist if its object exists does, while certainly an important observation, does not disclose the *intentional* nature of that act. It only gives the appearance of disclosing it. Saying, for instance, that an object is "immanent" to the stream of consciousness, or that it is "in" the mind as a real part, or endorsing some version of metaphysical idealism according to which objects depend for their existence on the acts which are of them, sheds no light whatsoever on why or how an intentional act is of what it is of.

These comments bear directly on the point and nature of the phenomenological reduction, and I will return to them in §10.5.

4.5 Conclusion

In this chapter we have explored some of most important components of an intentional act, including its quality and matter, the distinction between modified and unmodified acts, the distinctions between many-rayed, compound, and founded acts, and, finally, the reasons for explaining intentionality in terms of the nature of acts themselves and their parts and features. In the next chapter we will turn to the relations between acts of meaning and acts of intuition.

Notes

1 Brentano classifies mental phenomena into "Presentations, Judgments, and Phenomena of Love and Hate" (1995, 194), and maintains that "presentation deserves the primary place, for it is the simplest of the three phenomena, while judgement and love always include a presentation within them" (1995, 266). For a discussion of objectifying acts in Husserl, see LI 5, §37.
2 See LI 5, §41, 648 and Schuhmann and Smith 1987, 354.
3 B. Smith 2000, 294. Also see Benoist 2015, 97ff. and LI 1 §13, 289.
4 See Bernet, Kern, and Marbach 1993, 94.
5 LAW, 72. I am indebted to Daniel Dahlstrom for his assistance in translating this and other passages from this text.
6 In at least some passages in the *Investigations*, Husserl holds that in fulfillment the intuitive and thought act have identical matters. See LI 6 §28, 744 and LI 6 §25, 738. In Chapter 8 I argue that this is not the case.
7 LAW, 73. As D.W. Smith (2007, 290) points out, "the German term 'Satz' is the traditional term for a proposition." However, it includes the "positing character such as judging..."
8 See Ideas 1 §113, 219–220 and PICM, 434. Also see Aldea 2013, 390.
9 Martin 2003, 414. Also see Dorsch 2010, 176.
10 Ideas 1 §99, 201; also PCIT §28.

11 Evans 1982, 102. Also see Fodor's (1987, 151) example involving "John loves Mary" and "Mary loves John."
12 Evans 1982, 102–103. Also see Peacocke 1992, 43–44.
13 See Searle 1983, 31ff.
14 For a discussion of the points that follow, see Willard 1984, 218ff.
15 LI 5 §20, 587. Also see Ideas I §36, 63 and Willard 1984, 221.
16 See Willard 1984, 219ff.; Zahavi 2008, §2.
17 Harman 1990, 36. Chisholm makes the same point regarding Diogenes's search for an honest man. "If the doctrine of intentional inexistence is true, the very fact that Diogenes was looking for an honest man implies that he already had the immanent object; hence *it* could not be the object of his quest" (Chisholm 1967, 11, quoted from Smith and McIntyre 1982, 52).
18 See IdPh, 27–28. I borrow this terminology from Philipse 1995, 258 and Crowell 2008, 345.
19 PAS, 53; also TS §10, 22.
20 A.D. Smith 2002, 135. Also see Hill 2009, 101 for the same claim about qualia.
21 See IdPh, 38–39.
22 LI 5 §5, 543. Also see Crowell 2008, 346.
23 See A.D. Smith 2003, 33. See Dasgupta 2017, 75ff. on constitutive explanations.

Recommended Readings

Brentano, Franz. 1995. *Psychology from an Empirical Standpoint.* Antos C. Rancurello, D. B. Terrell, and Linda L. McAlister, trans. New York: Routledge.
Crane, Tim. 2013. *The Objects of Thought.* Oxford: Oxford University Press.
Husserl, Edmund. 1970. *Logical Investigations.* Two volumes. J.N. Findlay, trans. London: Routledge & Kegan Paul. See especially Investigation V.
Willard, Dallas. 1967. "A Crucial Error in Epistemology." *Mind* 76: 513–523.

5   Meaning and Intuition

In the previous chapter we examined the generic structure of intentional acts. Every conscious intentional act has an intentional essence composed of a matter or content and a quality. The intentional essence is literally a *part* of an intentional experience—its *real* content. Every conscious intentional experience also *instantiates* properties. What is instantiated in the matter of an act is an ideal content. In the case of acts of meaning, the content in question is a concept or a whole composed of concepts, such as a proposition or body of propositions. Finally, every intentional experience directs itself to, or is of, an object.

As before, the interrelations among the intentional triad of *act, content,* and *object* will be our guiding thread throughout what follows. And with good reason. As we will see in the coming chapters, one of the basic principles of phenomenological inquiry, including phenomenology within a realist tradition, is that there is a complex set of essential relations among these items. In his phenomenological study of values and value consciousness, Max Scheler—who is no idealist—writes:

> Our point of departure is the ultimate principle of phenomenology: namely, that there is an interconnection between the essence of an object and the essence of intentional experiencing.
>
> (Scheler 1973a, 265)

Edith Stein, another realist, makes a similar point:

> To every object and to every class of objects there correspond certain adapted coherences of consciousness ... There's an ideal lawfulness that regulates the [reciprocally adapting] coherences of constituting consciousness and constituted objects. The exploration of this lawfulness is the task of pure transcendental phenomenology.
>
> (Stein 2000, 7)

Husserl goes further. According to him, "a correlation of perceivability, intuitability, meanability and knowability, is inseparable from the sense of being in general" (LI 6, §65, 831). Our task is not to take that as a point of departure, but to make it intelligible. After all, it is not an exaggeration to claim, as Husserl did more than three decades after the *Investigations*, that "the essential interrelation between reason and what is in general" is the "enigma of all enigmas" (Crisis §5, 13).

At this point it is not intelligible. Acts of meaning are incredibly powerful cognitive tools. Thanks to the compositional structure of concepts, there are infinitely many thinkable thought contents. A thinker, one who has thoughts, should be able in principle to think about things that she neither perceives, imagines, or otherwise intuitively presents. She should be able to think about, and talk about, the world from an armchair, just as we in fact can and do.[1] It would be impossible to overestimate the importance of that ability for virtually every human achievement of cultural or scientific worth.

The power of conceptual thought to detach itself from what is presently perceived is also its weakness. An armchair is not the best place to acquire knowledge, the best vantage point from which to come into genuine contact with reality. And playing language games is not the preeminent way of learning about the objects of thought and discourse. From the armchair, we are free to weave together all sorts of thoughts for which we have no evidence whatsoever. We are free to think propositions that have no actual or even possible objects corresponding to them. From the comfort of this armchair, I can think about the many moons of Saturn, the weather in Vancouver, and the descendants of Finwë the elf. To actually find things out about the world, though, we need to get out and *experience* it, not emptily in mere thought, or by hashing out our empty thoughts with the empty thoughts of a community of armchair residents, but by encountering in a more genuine way the things and states of affairs that our concepts are about and which make our thoughts true or false.

Equally importantly, it is unclear whether we would be able to even think about most of what we do think about from an armchair if not for a more authentic encounter with those objects. Getting out into the world is not just essential for experientially verifying thoughts we already are capable of entertaining. It is also essential for being able to entertain many of those thoughts in the first place. That's why we cannot form de re thoughts about future individuals or the inhabitants of other planets (Campbell 2002, 122). I can think about the hood of my car when I am far away from the hood of my car. But my ability to do that seems to require that I have had appropriately relevant experiences of a certain type—experiences of cars and car hoods, among other things.

The problem with acts of meaning, then, is that they are "in themselves '*empty*', and ... 'are in *need* of fullness'" (LI 6 §21, 728; Reinach 1982, 327). In order to make sense of knowledge, and even of meaning itself, we must turn to another class of acts that we have only touched upon, namely intuitive acts such as perception, and the relations that such acts can bear to acts of meaning. That is, we must turn to what Husserl generically calls "Evidenz."

Evidenz is "the giving of something itself" (FTL §59, 156). It is the "mode of consciousness ... that offers its intentional objectivity in the mode belonging to the original 'it itself'" (FTL §63, 168). "Evidenz" is a potentially misleading term. It does not mean the same thing as "evidence" (see Heffernan 1998, 7). One reason is that evidence is best construed as something we are conscious *of*, whereas Evidenz is a certain privileged consciousness of it. *Evidenz* is the preeminent consciousness of *evidence*.[2] Evidenz is *givenness*, and it encompasses both originary intuition, such as perception, and acts of fulfillment, which we will discuss momentarily.[3] The importance of Evidenz or givenness for intentionality cannot be exaggerated: "a life of consciousness cannot exist without including evidence" or givenness (FTL §107d, 289). This is, in part, because the intentionality of intrinsically empty contents is ultimately parasitic upon the intentionality of acts of intuition or givenness. As Husserl says in his discussion of our assertions about universal objects, "we seek to clarify their 'true meaning' or significance through plainly establishing their intention in the sense of their *fulfillments*, which are first realized when suitable intuitions are adduced" (LI 2 §6, 348).

5.1 Cognitive Fulfillment

Fulfillment is one of the most important relations in phenomenological philosophy, and it comes in a lot of varieties. In this chapter we will be concerned with cognitive fulfillment, which is a distinctive relation between an act of meaning and an act of intuition. To illustrate a case of fulfillment, let us return to our example from the previous chapter. A, recall, turns to B and says "The hood of the car is scratched." If things go well, her speech act will be met with comprehension. Suppose that B, showing some interest and considerable doubt, responds: "Really? Let me check." What will B likely do?

Here are some things that B will *not* likely do. He will probably not open his mouth, find a piece of spinach lodged between his teeth, and say "Ah yes, you're right!" Nor is he likely to examine Euclid's proof that there is no greatest prime number and say, "I'm afraid you're wrong." Here is something else B is unlikely to do. If B leads A to the driveway and shows him the scratched hood in full daylight, B will not likely respond: "How on Earth does this provide any evidence at all that the hood is scratched?" These reactions are so off that if they happened, it would probably *not* make us first question B's rationality. It would make us doubt, before anything else, whether he even *understands* what A said. This already says a lot about the connection between perceptual experience, evidence, and acts of meaning. It is difficult to credit someone with understanding the meaning of a term or sentence which is about perceptible objects and states of affairs if they simply have no idea what, in the perceptual field, the object meant might be, or whether or not it provided any evidence for what was asserted.

What B would probably do to verify what A said is what most of us would probably do: he would go examine the hood of the car. Upon doing so, he will see and feel it to be scratched, and he will come to believe what A said. That is because, on the assumption that B understands what A said, is not hallucinating or suffering from visual agnosia, and has no overpowering ideological reasons to deny that the hood is scratched, he will *recognize* the thing A's statement is about, namely the car hood, to be just the way A said it was. He will undergo an experience that Husserl calls "recognition" or "fulfillment." He will:

> experience how the same objective item which was "merely thought of" in symbol is now presented in intuition, and that it is intuited as being precisely the determinate so-and-so that it was at first merely thought or meant to be.
> (LI 6 §8, 694)

This is a very familiar kind of experience. Perception is recruited in the service of confirming, disconfirming, and originating beliefs hundreds, thousands of times each day. From finding out where one left one's phone to realizing that it is raining outside, fulfillment is something that, for us, pretty much occurs all the time that we are conscious. If you have ever thought something was a certain way, and also saw, heard, felt, or otherwise perceived that it was that way, you have undergone an experience of fulfillment.

Fulfillment is so pervasive and easy for us that it is easily confused with perception itself. It is not, however, perception.[4] Perceptual consciousness is a proper part of an act of fulfillment. Acts of fulfillment involve the actualization of several distinct abilities, only one of which is the ability to perceive. In order for fulfillment to occur, one must

i   perceive or intuit the intended object,
ii   mean or think about the very same intended object (see LI 6 §14a, 710), and
iii identify the intuited object *as* the meant object.

These three abilities must always be exercised in the case of perceptual judgment. (They are not, however, sufficient for perceptual judgment. One might undergo an experience of fulfillment without judging things to be as they perceptually appear to be.[5]) Moreover, one need not always possess those abilities *before* an actual experience of fulfillment. Like many important abilities, they can also be acquired in the very act—or more likely repeated acts—of exercising them. When those abilities are actualized in the required way, the result is an act of recognition (Erkennen) or knowledge (Erkenntnis). Or, since fulfillment permits of degrees of perfection, the result is at the very least an approach toward the "goal of knowledge" (LI 6 §13, 709).

Note, moreover, that the third requirement is essential. In fulfillment, an object is not just seen and thought of. It "is seen as being exactly the same as it is thought of."[6] In order for that to happen, the intuitive and signitive acts must enter a "phenomenologically peculiar form of unity" or synthesis (LI 6 §8, 694). That unity requires, among other things, that the intuitive experience and the act of meaning occur in the same subject, and simultaneously. Your perceptions cannot fulfill my thoughts, and my perceptions from yesterday cannot fulfill the thoughts I have today (Willard 1984, 225–226).

Furthermore, it is possible for (i) and (ii) to occur, at the same time and for the same subject, without (iii) occurring, and in such cases fulfillment does not take place (see LI 6 §7, 690–691). Those with prosopagnosia, for instance, have functioning vision but cannot recognize faces. It's also a mundane fact of life for most of us. Marginal or inattentive perception occurs without fulfillment quite often. There are numerous features present in one's perceptual field that are not conceptualized. Even *attentive* perception does not entail fulfillment. To recruit an example from Putnam (1975, 143), I can think about beech trees, and I can perceive beech trees, but I cannot recognize a beech tree as a beech tree. If shown an elm and a beech, and asked to match up the concepts <elm> and <beech> correctly, I would simply guess. "In fulfillment," writes Husserl, "our experience is represented by the words: 'This is the thing *itself*'" (LI 6 §16, 720). Since I cannot recognize beech trees, a simultaneous perception and thought of a beech tree will not result in me realizing that *this* is a beech tree *itself*. Or, to give another example, I can think of musical notes, and I can hear them just fine. But I cannot identify them or recognize them on the basis of hearing them. Good hearing is one thing. The capacity to have one's thoughts about notes fulfilled on the basis of good hearing—perfect pitch—is something different, and much rarer (see Peacocke 2001, 240).

Because of the peculiar synthesis holding among an intuitive act and the act of meaning in fulfillment, fulfillment is itself a distinctive third act that is *phenomenologically founded* upon the others (Willard 1995, 150–151). As a phenomenologically founded act, its object is distinct from the objects of either of the underlying acts.

> A more or less complete identity is the objective datum which corresponds to the act of fulfillment, which "appears in it". This means that, not only signification and intuition, but also their mutual adequation ... can be called an act, since it has its own peculiar intentional correlate, an objective something to which it is directed.
>
> (LI 6 §8, 696; also see PAS, 114)

That is, what appears in fulfillment is the identity of what is given with what is meant (see Hardy 2013, 87). That means that acts of fulfillment are acts of relational identification, as discussed in §2.1.4 of the present book. Fulfillment is a double-rayed act in which an object is intended by two different acts.

At one point Husserl denies that fulfillment is an act of relational identification on the grounds that "no intentional consciousness of identity, in which identity, as a unity referred to, first gains objective status" in fulfillment (LI 6 §8, 697). As we will see, this is true of certain kinds of fulfillment, namely purely intuitive fulfillment, which we will discuss when we turn to perception (§6.4). And he is also right that identity, as an equivalence relation that obeys Leibniz's Law, is not objectified as such in each act of fulfillment. But in the examples so far discussed, the identity of the perceived and the meant *is* objectified. In the best cases of fulfillment, "The object is not merely meant, but in the strictest sense *given*, and given as it is meant" (LI 6 §38, 765). But if the object is given *as* it is meant, it is not enough that it is the same object which is given and meant. It must be given as *being identical with* what is meant (see Crowell 2016, 187). Willard's characterization of fulfillment brings this out: it is the "union of the conceptualizing act with the object, on the basis of a corresponding intuition of that object together with a recognition of the identity of the object of the concept and of the perception" (Willard 1995, 152).

What *is* true is that the identity that *appears* in fulfillment is not *conceptualized*. In fulfillment the identity of the meant and the perceived object is *intuited*.[7] It takes a higher order act to bring *that* identity itself to *fulfillment*, one in which not the object, but the identity of the object meant and given, is *itself* both meant and given.[8] Acts of that sort are comparatively rare. But they can occur. They are occurring right now, in fact: we are conceptually thematizing the relation of fulfillment on the basis of exemplary cases of it, bringing fulfillment *itself* to fulfillment.

It is critical to distinguish between fulfillment and other relations with which it may be confused. In particular, fulfillment is not the same thing as the *detection* of individuals or features, nor of the detection of individuals and features together with the formation of thoughts or beliefs about those individuals or features. Suppose that someone, D, is a reliable detector of the surface colors of objects in her vicinity, and that when she does detect the color of something, she immediately forms the belief it is that color. Suppose, however, that what enables D to detect colors so well is not good color vision. Rather, she uses an electronic color sensor, which relays the information to her verbally. This is not fulfillment, since she is not perceptually—that is, originarily—aware of the colors she detects. What she perceives are the readings of her color sensor. She does not genuinely perceive colors, or even intuit them at all, and so is missing one of the components necessary for fulfillment. (If, as some think, the sensuous colors, the ones we see, are mere signs or indications of the "real" colors, then we're in no better position than D.)

5.2 Authentic Intentionality

In an act of fulfillment, two subordinate acts occur, an intuitive act and an act of meaning. Although we have not shown this yet, we will assume that each of those acts has a content. In the case of an act of meaning, that content is a concept or a whole composed of concepts, such as a proposition, an argument, or a proof. We do not yet know what the content of the intuitive act is, but we can at least specify it in functional terms that we touched upon in Chapter 3: it is part of the *fulfilling sense* of the concept or proposition. Husserl defines the fulfilling sense as "the *identical content* which, in perception, pertains to the totality of possible acts of perception which intended the same object perceptually, and intend it actually as the same object" (LI 1 §14, 291). Elsewhere, he writes that:

> the unified sense of one and the same word covers (or, in the case of a non-sense-word, purports to cover) an ideally delimited manifold of possible intuitions, each of which could serve as the basis for an act of recognitive naming endowed with the same sense.
>
> (LI 6 §7, 691–692)

He continues: "To the word 'red', e.g., corresponds the possibility of both knowing as, and calling 'red', all red objects that might be given in possible intuitions" (ibid., 692). What gives rise to such knowings are fulfillments through originary intuitions. The fulfilling sense of a meaning M is *the manifold of contents of possible originary intuitive experiences that could fulfill it.* In the case of some concepts, such as the concept of the exact sensation I am now feeling in my left foot, this is not a very big set of experiences. In the case of others, such as the concept <the human brain> or <The Milky Way>, it is immense, and contains numerous ideally possible experiences that are not factually achievable by us. In general, concepts referring to concrete individuals and natural kinds have very expansive fulfilling senses.

To mean something, to think about it, is obviously not to know it, much less to perceive it. But there is an intimate connection between fulfillment and meaning. If one wants to know what a term means, and thereby "grasp" the concept that it expresses, the single best way is to perceive the object that the term or concept is about—to find the "impression" behind the "idea," in Hume's terminology.[9] As Husserl puts it,

> If we realize, e.g., the meaning of the expression "white surface" on an intuitive basis, we experience the reality of the concept; the intuitive appearance really presents something white and a surface, and precisely as a white surface.
>
> (LI 6 §30, 751)

And that is exactly the same procedure one would select as the first and pre-eminent way of *verifying* a proposition. If B wants to learn *what A means* when she says "The hood of the car is scratched," the best way to start teaching him is to show him the scratched hood. That is also the best way to show B that what A said is *true*. This is what we do.

The reason why seems rather obvious. Thoughts with conceptual and propositional content are directed toward things, as is our speech when we express those thoughts linguistically. Meanings are, to repeat, "ways of being directed towards objects" (B. Smith 2000, 294). When a concept or proposition is the content of our conscious state, what we are conscious of is not, in the first instance, the concept or proposition itself, or a set of rules or moves in a language game, as important as these may be in shedding light on our cognitive abilities. Nor are we normally primarily conscious of another set of words or concepts, or a definition or description that would provide a roadmap to the object. What we are conscious of, in the first instance, is the *object* which the concept or proposition is about.

If one wants a clear sense—that is, *knowledge*—of just *what* meanings are directed upon, or whether those things are the way they are said to be, one should encounter the objects themselves, if possible. This is not possible in an empty act of meaning or in a mere language game. To establish a genuine relation with objects, *perception* or *originary intuition* is required. Empty acts, by contrast, are in a certain way "inauthentic" (LI 6 §63, 825). As Husserl puts it,

> We can say without hesitation that non-intuitive presentations are only called presentations in an inauthentic sense; genuinely speaking they do not actually present anything to us, an objective sense is not constituted in them; nothing is built up in them as the being of this or that content through actual intentional structures such that we could continuously acquire knowledge of it.
>
> (PAS, 113–114)

To authenticate such empty meanings is to bring them into contact with their object through the mediating link of perception in an act of fulfillment. The reason is that "the sense of a thing is determined by the instances of givenness of the perception of it" (Ideas I §44, 78).

5.2.1 Epistemic and Semantic Authenticity

Despite Husserl's characterization of empty intentional acts as inauthentic, there is a danger in identifying empty thinking with inauthentic intentionality. If that is right, then a vast range of known propositions, especially those in the most developed a priori and empirical sciences, would only ever be the contents of inauthentic acts. As Husserl himself points out, the majority of statements comprising the existing sciences "behave meaningfully without any elucidation from intuition, and ... only a vanishing section, even of the true and the proven, are and remain open to complete intuitive illustration" (LI 6 §41, 777).

It may be that those statements are only inauthentically *known*. That appears to be Husserl's own view. And it is not an implausible one. There are better and worse cases of knowing. From the point of view of knowledge, anything that falls short of fulfillment is second best. That is not to say that each case of fulfillment is superior to every case of inferential knowledge in terms of its epistemic status. Mathematical proofs are more certain than immediate empirical knowledge. But it is to say that, with respect to one and the same object or state of affairs, it is better to know *it* through fulfillment than through any other means. It is simply better to verify something through observation than through reasoning or some other source, better to *see* a tornado, or a scratched hood, or Oumuamua, than learn of their existence and nature through inference or testimony. Fulfillment, and the perceptual awareness on which it is based, is, to use Mark Johnston's phrase, "better than mere knowledge."[10] So in that sense, empty acts, even empty knowings, are inauthentic.

Nevertheless, this kind of *epistemic* inauthenticity must be sharply distinguished from another kind of inauthenticity, namely the kind of inauthenticity that comes from not even knowing what would count as perceiving the meant objects at all. Consider an example. I can think, right now, about the weather in Vancouver. But am I really *conscious* of the weather in Vancouver? Well, yes. I am armchair-conscious of it, language-game-conscious of it. But this is hardly a paradigmatic case of consciousness-of, despite the frequency with which such empty acts occur and the attention that they have, rightly, received from philosophers. Vancouver's weather is not given, and givenness or *Evidenz* is, as Husserl puts it, "the universal pre-eminent form of 'intentionality,' of 'consciousness of something'" (FTL §59, 158). The problem with my consciousness of Vancouver's weather is that it does not, by itself, provide me with any reason whatsoever for believing its content. It is not an encounter with reality.

While my thoughts about the weather in Vancouver are inauthentic insofar as they are intuitively empty, there is another way in which they *are* authentic. I at least know in general what sorts of perceptual experiences I *would* have, if appropriately situated, *if* it were raining or sunny in Vancouver. I have been to Vancouver, and can also recognize generic weather conditions. I have the ability to answer the question, on the basis of perceptual experience, whether or not it is sunny or rainy in Vancouver. I have some handle on the *fulfilling sense* of propositions such as <It is sunny in Vancouver>. If perceptually confronted with a sunny Vancouver, I could, given my present abilities, experience the fulfillment of my thought that it is sunny there. And that is, in a certain sense at least, a way of exercising the concept authentically, even if emptily. As Willard puts it, an authentic concept can be *derived* only through an experience with an appropriately "fulfilled" intention; but once obtained it may be *used* without the relevant fulfilment occurring.

(Willard 1984, 91)

To use a concept authentically in this sense is not necessarily to have it fulfilled, but to know the conditions under which it would be fulfilled. I will refer to this as *semantic authenticity*.

Fulfillment, then, sits at the center of both Husserl's theory of knowledge and his theory of meaning. One has a semantically authentic possession of a concept when one knows its fulfilling sense. And to know the fulfilling sense of a concept is to have the capability to experience acts of fulfillment in which that concept is the fulfilled content. *Semantically authentic concept possession is a capacity to recognize or know on the basis of fulfillment.*[11] As Dallas Willard puts it,

The procedures of confirmation or disconfirmation which occur to us may not be ones that we can carry out in actuality, but unless some such general procedure can be brought to mind, there is little point in insisting that our thought is of any definite thing at all, or that it is even a thought.

(Willard 1984, 206)

If this sounds like a form of verificationism about meaning, that is because it is. But, as we will see below, it is quite different from the familiar logical positivist variety.

Because the fulfilling senses of some concepts consist of a vast manifold of possible originary experiences, many of which we have not and cannot undergo, semantically authentic concept possession comes in degrees. Most of us have an authentic possession of the concept <pain>, for instance, but a much less authentic possession of the concepts <photosynthesis> and <uranium>. There are a number of factors that influence the degree to which we authentically possess a concept. One set of factors, obviously, are our sensory and cognitive limitations. Another is context. If an object is one about which one can have thoughts fulfilled, it must have a distinctive way of appearing, at least compared with other things in the same general region as the subject (Evans 1982, §8.3; Millar 2008, 125). Another factor involves the richness of the object's fulfilling sense. There's a lot to a concrete individual or a natural kind of stuff like gold or water that is not evident to the unaided senses or even to technologically unaided experimentation.

Inauthentic intentional experiences are quite common, and providing a full account of just how they work would be a monumental task. For our purposes, it is enough to make two points. First, it seems clear that inauthentic concept possession is parasitic upon authentic concept possession. It's difficult to see how we could possess any concepts at all if we did not have the ability to identify at least some of the objects that they refer to in perceptual and other intuitive experiences. Many of the examples that illustrate inauthentic concept possession still involve some degree of authenticity. Like Putnam, I cannot tell elms from beeches. But I can tell elms and beeches from rowboats and rabbits. That's because I know they are trees, and I have a tolerably authentic grasp of the concept <tree>. If, as far as I knew, the word "elm" referred to rowboats, or if I simply had no idea whether any given item in my perceptual field was or was not an elm, I would not possess the concept <elm> inauthentically. I just wouldn't possess it at all.

The second point is that authentic concept possession is the *preeminent* way of possessing a concept, and ultimately explains how conceptual intentionality works at all. Concepts do not have a fulfilling sense in virtue of their intentionality. They have their intentionality in virtue of having their fulfilling sense. The connection between concepts and their objects, and the power of concepts to confer a specific intentional direction upon the acts in which they are instantiated, is not a brute or primitive connection but rather, at least at some level, an intelligible one. Corresponding to every meaning that could be the content of an authentic act of meaning is a fulfilling sense. And the fulfilling sense of a concept consists of some portion of the contents of the totality of originary experiences of the object that the concept is about. Originary experiences, such as perceptual experiences, are those which reveal the object itself, experiences in which it itself becomes manifest as it itself is. Thanks to perception, "The linkage to reality is thereby established before meaning and language come into play" (B. Smith 1994, 179).

5.3 The Ideal Connections Among Meanings, Fulfilling Senses, and Objects

So far we have discussed authentic concept possession from the perspective of thinkers and their abilities. While instructive in some ways, it threatens to obscure the ideal, necessary relations among the contents involved in the act of fulfillment, and their essential relations to the object given and meant in such an act. Acts enter into intentional relations with their objects and one another in virtue of their contents, and the relations among contents and objects, and contents and contents, are ideal, necessary ones (Willard 1984, 194). *Of all the core commitments of phenomenological philosophy, in both realist and idealist traditions, this might be the single most central and important.*

The first thing to note about the contents of the perceptual experiences comprising the fulfilling sense of a meaning, and also the manifold of an object, is that they are, like the meanings they fulfill, types or universals with possible instances.

The ideal conception of the act which *confers meaning* yields us the Idea of the *intending meaning*, just as the ideal conception of the correlative essence of the act which *fulfills* meaning, yields the *fulfilling meaning*, likewise *qua* Idea.

(LI 1 §14, 291)

Two individuals can have perceptual or intuitive experiences of the same type, experiences whose intentional content is the same. There are many propositions and concepts that will never be thought, and there are many perceptual contents which will never be the contents of experience. To say that such contents exist—to say of any universal that it exists—is just to say that they have corresponding possible instances.[12] Those instances are moments or dependent parts of mental acts—their *matters*.

Just as the logical and grammatical connections among meanings are not merely psychological or conventional but ideal, so it is with the connections between meanings and their fulfilling senses. As Husserl puts it, "it is not possible that a signitive intention with matter M should find a possibility of fulfillment in some intuition, while another signitive intention with the same matter M, should lack this possibility."[13] If A's perceptual experience of the scratch on the hood genuinely fulfills her thought that the car hood is scratched, a thought with the same thought content should be able to be fulfilled by the same type of perceptual experience as A's. A given subject may lack the capacity to bring an intuition and a concept into the unity of fulfillment. That, however, does not impugn the ideality of the connections among them. In the same way, that a subject may lack the capacity to identify logically valid arguments does not call into question the necessary character of the laws of logic.

As we saw in the previous chapter, the connection between concepts and their objects is a necessary one, as is the connection between experiences with conceptual content and their objects. On Husserl's view, in fact, the connection between *any* experience and its object is a necessary one.[14] The reason is that every experience essentially has the content it does, and the content of an experience is essentially of the object that it is of. The concept <car> is essentially of cars, and it is a *necessary* truth that the proposition <The hood of the car is scratched> is true if and only if the hood of the car is scratched.

The connection between fulfilling senses and their objects is equally necessary, and for even more evident reasons. In fact, it is the connection between fulfilling senses and objects that ultimately grounds the connection between concepts and their objects. The fulfilling sense of a meaning consists of at least some portion of the contents of the totality of originary experiences of that meaning's object. We can regard that same totality of originary contents from the side of the object itself: it is part of the object's *perceptual manifold*. Husserl characterizes the *complete* manifold of an object as follows:

Standing across from the unity of the thing is an infinite, ideal manifold of noetic experiences with a quite specific and, despite the infinity, a surveyable essential content, experiences that are all unified in being consciousness of "the same".[15]

What Husserl means by "noetic experiences" are just consciousnesses-of the object. So, for instance, standing over against the state of affairs of the car's hood's being scratched is a set of propositions that it makes true, such as <the hood of the car is scratched>. This proposition is the possible content of an act of consciousness, and those possible acts, with those contents, belong to the object's manifold.

The complete manifold corresponding to this state of affairs does not only include the contents of possible thoughts of the object. It includes the contents of *all* possible "noetic experiences" of it, including acts of fulfillment and perceptual or otherwise originary intuitive experiences. The *perceptual manifold* of an object O is a proper subset of an object's complete manifold, namely the totality of the contents of possible *originary* experiences of O. And the contents of the experiences composing the perceptual manifold—or rather some portion of it— is the very same thing as the fulfilling sense of the concept of O.

Necessarily, if we fix an object's identity and its properties, we fix its perceptual manifold. An object's perceptual manifold will be different across different possible worlds, but only because the object's properties and relations to other things differ across different possible worlds. The essential connection between an object and its perceptual manifold becomes phenomenologically clear when we keep firmly in mind that perception is an act in which an object is present, manifest as what *it itself* is. Perception is "the act that places something before our eyes as the thing itself, the act that *originally constitutes* the object" (PCIT §17, 43). Any act, or total manifold of acts, which brings an object to our awareness "as the thing itself" could not present some other thing, on pain of that object *being* some other thing. A perceptual experience of spinach lodged between someone's teeth could quite conceivably function as a *sign* or *indication* that the hood of the car is scratched. It could quite conceivably carry *information* about the hood's being scratched. It could be *caused by* scratched car hoods. It could be tightly *associated with* thoughts about car hoods. But it could under no possible circumstances be an *originary intuition* of any car's hood's being scratched (see Fasching 2012, 127). And since meanings can only be fulfilled by experiences which present their objects, such an experience could not possibly *fulfill* the proposition <The hood of the car is scratched>. It just makes no sense to say that an experience of spinach lodged between teeth is a manifestation of a scratched car hood as it itself is.

A perceptual experience of the scratched hood, by contrast, does not just happen to fulfill that proposition. The reason is that the perceptual experience does not just happen to be of the same thing the proposition is of. What is given in the flesh when B perceives the hood to be scratched is not a *clue* or a *sign* that the hood is scratched, something that contingently or even necessarily *indicates* or "represents" it. It *is* the hood's being scratched.[16] Again, a perceptual experience of an itching sensation on one's arm could not possibly be an originary experience of the color red. It could indicate to one that one's arm is red. It could carry information about the redness of one's arm. In fact it often does. But it couldn't be a *perception* of the color red. Therefore it could not possibly fulfill the concept <red>. The only experiences that could fulfill a meaning are those that *present* that meaning's object, those belonging to the object's perceptual manifold.

5.3.1 Categorial Meaning and Intuition

The essential relations among meanings, their fulfilling senses, and objects extends to every kind of objectifying act, including "categorial" acts.[17] Husserl goes to great lengths to explain how we can perceive not just sense-perceptible things such as individuals and their individual property instances, but such things as *"aggregates, indefinite pluralities, totalities, numbers, disjunctions, predicates* (right-ness), *states of affairs"* (LI 6 §45, 785). Not only can we perceive a tree on one side and a house on the other, but we can perceive the complex state of affairs of a tree's standing to the right of a house. And not only can we perceive a tree and the color green, but we can perceive the tree's-being-green.[18] Not only can we see objects juxtaposed in space and succeeding one another in time, but we can perceive interactions among them. To see someone dribbling a basketball, turning a screw with a screwdriver, or smashing a hole in a wall with a sledgehammer is to see various objects and events standing in causal relations with one another. Furthermore, we can not only perceive this green moment or property instance of the tree, but the color itself, Green, as something instantiable in multiple objects (see LI 6 §52). One can, for instance, see the *same color* when one looks at three different tree leaves in succession, even though there is no individual thing such that it was seen in each of those three experiences.

Husserl's account of just *how* categorial intuition works is rather complicated. But the evidence *that* it is possible is straightforward (see LI 6 §45): just as there is a distinction between merely thinking of individuals or qualities and having them present in the flesh, so there is a distinction between merely thinking of categorial objects such as states of affairs and universals and having them given in the flesh. The empty meaning intention whose content is <The hood of the car is scratched> or <Dan is in his office> can be fulfilled by a corresponding perceptual encounter with the state of affairs and events those propositions are about. The importance of complex and founded acts discussed in the previous chapter is evident here. When it comes to states of affairs and universals, "We are dealing with a sphere of objects, *which can only show themselves 'in person' in such founded acts"* (LI 6 §46, 788).

It is in the sphere of categorial acts that we find some of the clearest examples of meanings which are fulfillable or unfulfillable, not in virtue of some psychological capacity or incapacity on our part, but in virtue of ideal relations among the *contents* of the fulfilling and fulfilled acts. As Husserl notes, not every "signitive intention" can "fit" with a corresponding intuition. Some meanings are "impossible" or "internally inconsistent," while others are "possible" or "internally consistent" (LI 6 §30, 749). Because intuitions present us with objects themselves in an authentic and originary way, and because there are categorial meaning formations which are absurd, such as:

(a) <This car is red and green all over right now>

we should expect there to be meanings that have no fulfilling sense at all. And that is the case. My inability to recognize elms and beeches is due to a psychological shortcoming of my own, not because the concepts <elm> and <beech> lack a fulfilling sense. My inability to attach a fulfilling sense to (a) above, by contrast, is not. Objectively, quite independently of my or anyone's psychological constitution, that is a proposition that could not possibly be fulfilled in an act of recognition (Erkennen) or knowledge (Erkenntnis).

The proposition (a) above is unfulfillable in virtue of its material content. Other meanings are unfulfillable in virtue of their *form* alone, such as:

(b) <This car is red and not red all over right now>

This proposition is necessarily unfulfillable no matter what we substitute for the material concepts <car> and <red> (see LI 6 §63, 825). Again, whatever the material content in question, we cannot at one and the same time intuit w to be a proper part of W, and also intuit W to be a proper part of w (see LI 6 §62, 821). The laws determining what sorts of meaning *forms* are fulfillable and which are not are the pure "laws of authentic thinking" (LI 6 §62, 820). They are *"laws of categorial intuitions in virtue of their purely categorial forms"* (ibid., 823). They are, moreover, purely formal or "analytic"—that is, they "contain no reference to material species" (ibid., 822).

One thing worth noting here is that while formal contradictions and materially absurd propositions have no fulfilling sense, and so cannot even in principle be thought authentically, many are such that their negations do have a fulfilling sense. One can not only think, but see, that nothing can be red and green all over at the same time. When we try to unite those colors in a unified whole, we find ourselves incapable of doing so. This, however, is not the intuition we are looking for. As Husserl puts it, "the *factual failure* does not establish a *necessary failure*. Possibly greater power could ultimately overcome the resistance" (LI 6 §32, 753). We do not discover that, as a matter of necessity, nothing can be red and green all over at the same time by introspectively discovering some psychological resistance within ourselves. Even if that could establish such a necessity—it cannot—it would still not be an *intuition* of the incompatibility of those properties. The relevant intuition, rather, is one of "*the relationship of conflict*" (ibid.). That is, we have a direct, though founded, insight into the fact that red and green cannot be united into the very same parts of the very same whole.[19]

In the case of some meanings, then, our thinking is essentially inauthentic. We cannot have a capacity to know the fulfilling sense of the proposition <The car is red and green all over right now> because it has no fulfilling sense. Each time we try to clarify the sense of that thought for ourselves, to bring its object before us in imagination for instance, we find that there is a conflict—the two properties cannot be united in that fashion in a possible whole. Still, it is important to recognize that the proposition is meaningful. It has an object toward which it is directed, an object distinct from the objects of other absurd propositions, such as <1 = 2>. What it does not have is an object that could possibly exist or possibly be exhibited in perception.

Authentic acts of meaning, then, have two distinct sets of requirements. On the one hand, there must exist ideal relationships among the (i) the act's meaning content, (ii) its fulfilling sense, and (iii) its object. Its meaning content must have a fulfilling sense, and its fulfilling sense must belong to an object. On the other hand, the subject of that act must have the ability to synthesize the meaning content and the fulfilling sense into a unity of fulfillment, to be able to recognize or know the object on the basis of an intuition of it.

5.3.2 Manifolds and Fulfilling Senses

If appealing to fulfilling senses is a promising way to understand the nature of empty intentionality or acts of meaning, at least with respect to a wide range of meanings, then we should expect there to be similarities and differences in fulfilling sense corresponding to similarities and differences in meaning.[20] Establishing a thesis like that across all types of meaning is far beyond the scope of this work. Nevertheless, we do find this to be the case in a number of important cases.

When we turn to examples involving names and attributive definite descriptions, for instance, the differences in their meanings is stark, as is familiar.[21] So are the differences in their fulfilling senses. To use an example from Smith and McIntyre (1982, 210), consider the shop owner who expects the first customer of the day. And suppose that Mrs. White is the first customer. The description "the first customer of the day" does not have the same fulfilling sense as the name "Mrs. White." Someone can grasp the concept <the first customer of the day> authentically without having any idea who Mrs. White is. To fulfill it, one would wait until the store opens and then find the person who is both a customer and the first one. It is fulfilled, not by the perception of that person *per se*, but by the perception of that person satisfying certain conditions. The identity of the person is irrelevant. That is why the meaning of the description does not vary when we vary which individual satisfies the description, as it would have to if it were genuinely *of* an individual.

To fulfill the concept <Mrs. White>, by contrast, one would have to perceive Mrs. White—that individual and no other, whether or not she was the first customer, the last customer, or no customer at all. Here the identity of the person, far from being irrelevant, is all-important. In the actual world, we will find that Mrs. White does instantiate the relevant properties specified in the definite description. In other possible worlds, we will find someone else who does. The *one* fulfilling sense of that definite description encompasses all of those possible experiences. And that is not because is meaning is vague. Its meaning is perfectly precise. The reason different individuals can figure in its fulfilling sense is because it does not mean *any* of them. That is also why one can know exactly what the definite description means while having no idea who satisfies it. Finding out who a name *refers to* is finding out what the name *means*. Finding out who satisfies a description, however, is *not* a matter of finding out what it means. In fact one must already know what an attributive definition description means to inquire into who or what satisfies it. I can, to use Donnellan's example, know the meaning of "Smith's murderer is insane" without knowing who Smith's murderer is (Donnellan 1966, 285). But I must know the meaning of the definition description "Smith's murderer" in order to find out who that might be. The definite description is not a particular way of *referring* to who satisfies it, not even indirectly.[22] Names, by contrast, are typically used as referring expressions. As Husserl puts it, "a proper name … names an object 'directly'. It refers to it, not attributively, as the bearer of these or those properties, but without such 'conceptual' mediation, as what it *itself* is."[23] A name's content is therefore fulfilled by the referent showing up as what it itself is—though, as we will see momentarily, this is only part of the story.

We can make similar distinctions with respect to states of affairs. The proposition <The car hood is scratched> can be fulfilled by an experience of seeing the one, deep scratch on its surface. But it could also be fulfilled by an experience of a different scratch on the hood, or a multitude of scratches on the hood. The proposition <*That* scratch is on the hood>, by contrast, can only be fulfilled by an experience of that very scratch on the hood. Their differing senses correspond to differing fulfilling senses.

One challenge, though, is to explain how co-referential names or referring expressions can differ in sense. Because the perceptual manifold of an object is the totality of the contents of all possible originary experiences of it, identical objects have identical perceptual manifolds. That means that the perceptual manifolds associated with co-referential concepts are identical. If we identify a concept's fulfilling sense with its object's manifold, then all co-referential concepts will have identical fulfilling senses. But if all co-referential concepts have the same fulfilling sense, then the fulfilling sense cannot fix a concept's identity. If it did, then all co-referential concepts would be identical, which is not the case.[24]

We can put this more simply in the following inconsistent triad, where "FS" stands for "fulfilling sense":

1   If two concepts <a> and <b> are co-referential, then FS<a> = FS<b>.
2   If FS<a> = FS<b>, then <a> = <b>.
3   It is not the case that if <a> and <b> are co-referential, then <a> = <b>.

Proposition (3) is true. Co-referential terms do not all have the same sense, which means that they express concepts that are co-referential but not identical. The concepts expressed by "water" and "H_2O" are not identical. It is possible to possess one authentically without possessing the other authentically. Nor are the concepts expressed by "Hesperus" and "Phosphorus." Or, to take an example from John Campbell (2002, 84–85), the two contents expressed by two utterances of "that wire is live," said by someone pointing first to a wire coming out of the ceiling and second to a wire coming out of the floor, do not have the same sense, even if the wire coming out of the ceiling is the same wire as the one coming out of the floor. In each of these cases, someone who is fully rational might possess the relevant concepts, and possess them authentically, and still fail to realize they refer to the same thing. If (1) and (2) are true, however, (3) is false. Either (1) or (2), therefore, is false.

It's possible that both are. But even if (2) is false—I suspect it is not—(1) is independently problematic. There are differences and similarities in sense among concepts that are best explained by differences in their fulfilling sense. We can make sense of this on Husserl's view, according to which there are better and worse experiences of objects, and that what counts as better or worse is in some cases relative to interests. If, for instance, one wants to determine whether a car is scratched, or which steps must be taken to repair it, looking at it from a considerable distance in dim light is not an optimal experience, for obvious reasons. It is not the type of experience in which the object is given clearly and distinctly, nor is it the type of experience which best fulfills a thought about it. If we want to know more about the scratch, our perceptual experience will be oriented toward a "circle of maximum givenness" (TS §36, 106).

What lies within this circle is in part determined by the nature of the object itself. But it is often determined, in part, by our interests, on which features or relations of the thing we want to discover, or which of the manifold of perceptual appearances of the object most frequently confront us. As Husserl says,

> The natural interest in a flower is different than the botanist's interest, and thus in the two cases the best appearances are different, and the full givenness, in which the interest is satisfied, is essentially very different in each case.[25]

Furthermore, Husserl argues, some concepts are related, not just to any set of appearances of their objects, but to certain *privileged* appearances (see TS §37). The appearances that are optimal relative to the "natural interest" in the flower are those that fulfill the ordinary concept <flower>. Those that fulfill the botanist's concept <Pelargonium>, however, are different. We can think of other cases. If the concept <Hesperus> is optimally fulfilled by perceptual experiences of an individual with a certain characteristic appearance, and the concept <Phosphorus> is fulfilled by perceptual experiences of an individual with a different characteristic appearance, then it is natural that the concepts <Hesperus> and <Phosphorus> will differ in their fulfilling sense. What counts as the circle of optimal fulfilling or recognition-enabling appearances differs in each case.

The fact that some concepts are tailored to various interests and perspectives does not entail that they are not objective in all of the ways discussed in §3.3. The reason is that interests and perspectives themselves are types that are multiply instantiable. Many people can have the *same interest* in the flower and employ the same interest-relative concept of the flower, or have the *same perspective* on Venus every morning and employ the same perspective-relative concept.

If that is right, then the fulfilling sense of a concept is not, in many cases at least, the content of the *entire* perceptual manifold of its object, but a certain preferred subset of the contents of perceptual experiences composing that manifold. What explains why someone who possesses the concepts <Hesperus> and <Phosphorus> authentically, and yet does not know that Hesperus = Phosphorus, is that this person does not realize that the two fulfilling senses belonging to each are parts of the same object's manifold. Nevertheless, if two concepts are of the same thing, then there should either be an overlap in their manifolds, or there should be some other manifold or set of manifolds linking them together. It should be possible in principle to discover that they refer to the same object by pursuing the fulfilling sense of one and winding up having experiences belonging to the fulfilling sense of the other through a continuous series of experiences (see Kinkaid 2020, §2.5).

One benefit of this account of concepts or senses, including those expressed by proper names, demonstratives, and other directly referential expressions, is that it presents us with a tolerably clear and fairly attractive alternative to what Wayne Davis calls the "Frege-Mill Dichotomy," according to which "proper names must have descriptive meanings or no senses at all" (Davis 2005, 320). Davis rejects such a view. So does Husserl. Despite the fact that proper names refer "directly" and not "attributively" (LI 6 §5, 684), each expresses a sense or meaning, one that is determined by its fulfilling sense. A further benefit is that it goes some way toward explaining how it is that we can know what we mean, and which objects our acts of meaning are about, without having definitions of them or knowing much in the way of definite descriptions of their objects. Knowing definitions or definite descriptions is neither necessary nor sufficient to have an authentic understanding of the meaning of a term or to authentically possess a concept. For instance, we can see and recognize faces very well. But trying to define a face is futile, and trying to provide uniquely identifying definite descriptions is usually both very difficult and completely unnecessary. In experience the relevant objects are given, not defined or described, and given in such a way that what and how they are becomes manifest in the experience itself. Of course, as we will see, experiences are inadequate to their objects, and in many cases experience fails to reveal a number of their properties and powers. But these too, in many cases, are also disclosed by more searching experiences.

5.3.3 Meaning Beyond Possible Originary Intuition

The precise details of the dependence of intentionality on originary givenness are not entirely clear. Husserl sometimes writes as though having a fulfilling sense is necessary for intentionality and meaning. In his lectures on *Passive and Active Synthesis*, for instance, he says:

> we would not be able to speak at all of empty presentations and to attribute to them the character of having a relation to an object if it did not belong essentially to each empty presentation ... that it could enter into a synthesis with a corresponding intuition.

(PAS, 113)

On one interpretation this is simply false. As we have seen, there are many undeniably meaningful "empty presentations" which cannot be fulfilled. But as a claim about primitive or simple contents, it may be true.

According to Husserl, many unfulfillable acts have contents that are semantically complex. Their ultimate meaning components, however, do have a fulfilling sense. Thanks to the purely formal, compositional structure of meanings, there is "an endless host of *complex meanings*" that can be generated which "lack 'reality' or 'possibility'," meanings "to which ... *no possible unitary correlate of fulfillment can correspond*" (LI 6 §63, 824). It is because of this that there is not a "*complete parallelism*" between "types of categorial intuition and *types of meaning*" (ibid.). Husserl continues: "Only in connection with primitive types can and must such parallelism obtain, since all primitive meanings 'originate' in the fullness of correlated intuition" (ibid., 825). This is true, Husserl argues, of all primitive meanings and all primitive meaning *forms*, such as <S is P>. What enables us to understand a proposition such as <There is a round square> is that we do have an authentic grasp of its constituent concepts, <round> and <square>. The idea, then, is that every primitive meaning and every primitive logical form has a fulfilling sense. Intentionality that exceeds the bounds of possible fulfillment is possible because there are various complex meaning-forms that are largely indifferent to material content.

Unfulfillable propositions, then, retain a link to intuition insofar as their simple constituents have a fulfilling sense. They also retain a link to intuition in a second way. That is because, despite being intuitively unfulfillable, they are intuitively *verifiable*, at least in principle. A necessarily false proposition represents how the world necessarily is not, and has a contradictory proposition that represents how things necessarily are. <Something is red and green all over at the same time> has as its contradictory the proposition <Nothing is red and green all over at the same time>, and that is something that can be verified intuitively. According to Husserl, "*every* judgment can be brought to either a positive or a negative adequation" (FTL §90, 220). So while absurd and contradictory propositions have no fulfilling sense, their contradictories do.

One challenge for this view, however, is that even some syntactically simple meanings appear to have no fulfilling sense, such as names that have no referent. Names that refer to what is actual, according to Husserl, have a certain kind of "generality." More specifically, to each term, including names, belongs "an ideally delimited manifold of possible intuitions, each of which could serve as the basis for an act of recognitive naming endowed with the same sense" (LI 6 §7, 692). This is just to say that each term has a fulfilling sense composed of multiple possible originary experiences of the referent of that term. What, however, of "imaginary" names, such as "Sherlock Holmes"? Husserl says that they "may be names, but they cannot *actually* be used to name anything, they have, properly speaking, no extension, they are *without generality in the sense of the possible and the true.* Their generality is *empty pretension*" (LI 6 §7, 692).

On one understanding, empty or "imaginary" names have no fulfilling sense, and so are not really names. After all, they do not *name* anything. Such names are, as Barry Smith puts it, "mere pieces of language masquerading as names" (1987, 196). That is very likely true of some putative names, such as "Prester John" or "Vulcan." However, this position does not seem to capture the sense of all fictional names. The name "Santa Claus" has a meaning, and it also has a fulfilling sense. It makes perfectly good sense to ask "What does Santa Claus look like?" and there are correct and incorrect answers to that question. If someone were to ask it, it would be a slightly entertaining joke to draw a picture of a void. But it wouldn't be the right answer.

Because acts of phantasy, of which fiction-consciousness is a species, is a phenomenological modification of worldly, positing consciousness, we should expect there to be parallel acts not only of thought, but of perception and fulfillment—acts of quasi-thought, quasi-perception, and quasi-fulfillment.[26] And that does seem to be the case. We can see, without being *told*, that Bilbo is putting on a ring. That we can attach a fulfilling sense of sorts to names of fictional objects is due, in part, to the fact that there can be intuitive presentations of what does not exist. Intuition, or at least non-originary intuition, is no guarantee of existence. In many cases of image consciousness, and in all cases of phantasy, existence is not even a condition on their success. Phantasy acts are not nonveridical experiences of the world, but quasi-veridical experiences of quasi-objects (EJ §87d, 344). Furthermore, unlike standard names of actual individuals, fictional names seem by and large to be introduced by description. As David Liebesman puts it, "Sherlock Holmes" designates the person who is "Holmesesque," that is, the person who possesses the "conjunction of all of the properties that Holmes has according to the fiction."[27] If the name just picks out whoever has those properties, then its fulfilling sense will be that of a definite description. And definite descriptions have senses even when nothing satisfies them.

Whatever the correct theory of fictional names, the place to start in constructing one is to do what we would do in any other case of meaning: turn to the experiences of intending them and see what, if anything, fulfills those intentions, and how those fulfilling experiences resemble and differ from those directed at other kinds of objects, such as actual individuals. And it does appear that at least some fictional names have a fulfilling sense. In their case, however, the fulfilling sense is not the totality of the contents of possible originary intuitions, since there cannot be originary intuitions of fictional objects. But there can be *quasi-originary* experiences of them, the kind we can carry out in phantasy or in image-consciousness.[28]

Furthermore, the quasi-originary character of such intuitive experiences is something that marks these experiences and their fulfillments themselves. The fulfilling sense of a fictional name behaves very differently from the fulfilling sense of the name of something actual. Our concept of an actual individual may be largely general and indeterminate, but we will also intend that individual *as being* fully determined with respect to its properties (see Casey 2001, 106). When we actually perceive that individual, details will be filled in—there will be an "overabundance that intuition supplies" beyond what was emptily meant (PAS, 122)—and this overabundance *always* count as revealing more of the individual. I can think that Dan is in his office. When I walk in, however, I will see him to be in his office in a determinate way—seated in his chair, wearing a particular tie, drinking tea, eager to talk philosophy, and so on. All of those experiences count as revealing more about Dan. They enlarge my knowledge of him.

There is, to be sure, a similar "overabundance" of intuition in the case of our consciousness of many fictional and imaginary entities. Roman Ingarden points out that in all merely "represented objects," including those in fiction, there are "spots of indeterminacy" (1973, 246ff.). As Ingarden writes, "every literary work is in principle incomplete and always in need of further supplementation" (ibid., 251). One consequence of these "spots of indeterminacy" that essentially cling to any fictional work is that they "preclude[] a strictly accurate realization ... of the represented world—for example, in the stage play," or in cinema (ibid., 251). Ingarden is aware that we are, when absorbed in a fiction, largely unaware of these indeterminacies. One reason that is especially relevant is that "during his reading and his aesthetic apprehension of the work, the reader usually *goes beyond* what is simply presented by the text ... and in various respects *completes* the represented objectivities" (ibid., 252). Any intuitively contentful "concretization" of a fictional world, such as on the stage or in cinema, is bound to go beyond and "complete" the work. And because of this, there is always the aforementioned "overabundance" of intuition that exceeds the meaning-content of our consciousness of a work.

To give an example, suppose that, in watching Martin Freeman play Bilbo Baggins, we see him smoke a pipe or cast a worried look in a certain wizard's direction. This counts as *seeing* that *Bilbo*, and not Martin Freeman, smokes and was looking to Gandalf for assurance. No one *told* us he did these things; we saw them. Here we intuit something integral to the cinematic work, even if it qualifies as an enlargement of what is strictly stated in the text from which it is adapted.

Despite the fact that both perception and our intuition of fictional entities involve a surplus of intuition over and above the meaning-content, in the case of fiction, some intuitions will not be integrated into our overall intuition of the fictional world or update and enlarge our conception of it. The reason is that much of what we experience intuitively in fiction is "mere filling" (PAS, 122) with no world-disclosing function. For instance, Ian Holm does not resemble Martin Freeman too closely, but this does not interfere with our Bilbo-consciousness as we see those two actors play him in different productions. They look different, but we do not regard the two series as providing conflicting narratives on account of *that*. The reason is that we do not learn at any point that *Bilbo* looks exactly like Freeman or Holm. There is no one he looks exactly like, because there is no determinate way that he looks at all.[29] The precise look of either actor, that which in intuition exceeds the rather general and vague meaning-content associated with Bilbo, is "mere filling"—something that has to be there if we are to have any intuition at all, but does not provide additional knowledge of that world. In the case of real people, however, this would be a massive conflict. If you were promised an opportunity to meet Ian Holm, and somebody who looks exactly like Martin Freeman showed up instead, you may and should still be happy, but your expectation would not have been met.

One of the virtues of this account is that our puzzlement about the status of non-existent objects, the content of our concepts of such objects, and the fulfilling senses of those concepts, nicely line up. Consider, for instance, acts of phantasy and their corresponding objects. "In the actual world nothing remains open; it is what it is. The world of imagination 'is,' and is such and such, by grace of the imagination which has imagined it" (EJ §40, 173). This is why so much of the intuitive content that goes beyond the narrative content counts as "mere filling," and why in a retelling of a story, one taking place in one and the same imagined world, that filling can vary widely without bringing the two tellings into conflict. It is also why the worlds of imagination, unlike the world of perception and positing belief, do not constitute one unified world. Real things and events bear, and we are conscious of them as bearing, real spatiotemporal relations to one another, and it always makes sense to ask whether or not an individual of which we are conscious at one time is or is not identical with an individual of which we are conscious at another (see EJ §§39–40; Marbach 2013, 440, 443). But in the world of imagination, these questions do not make clear sense when asked across worlds, provided we simply stick to the narrative descriptions of those worlds and do not avail ourselves of any real-world, external information about authorial intentions. "It makes no sense, e.g., to ask whether the Gretel of one fairy tale and the Gretel of another are the same Gretel" (EJ §40, 173). What does make sense is simply to stipulate that they are or are not (ibid.).

One way, then, that all meanings may be grounded in intuition is that each either has a fulfilling sense, or is composed of items that do. The fulfilling sense in the case of fictional objects cannot be composed solely of possible contents of *originary* intuitions. But non-originary intuitions are, ultimately, parasitic upon originary ones.

5.4 Ideal Verificationism

That every proposition or its contradictory has a fulfilling sense means that, ideally speaking, every proposition can in principle be verified through fulfillment. A.D. Smith characterizes Husserl's position as "ideal verificationism," according to which "There is nothing, no possible entity, that is not in principle experienceable."[30] Husserl is explicit in his endorsement of ideal verificationism:

> To each object "that truly is," there corresponds in principle ... the idea of a possible consciousness in which the object itself can be apprehended *in an originary* and thereby *perfectly adequate manner.*
>
> (Ideas I §142, 283)

Since anything that is "experienceable"—that is, capable of being originarily given—can be meant as it is given, this entails that everything can in principle be recognized or known in fulfillment. Husserl writes,

> Every possible object is ... the subject of certain predicates. To each belongs an ideally closed body of true propositions in which what the object is is thought. To the possibility of each true proposition belongs *a priori* the possibility of a demonstration, and this requires an originary giving intuition of the intended state of affairs and therefore also of the object-about-which, i.e. the object to be determined. An object is without doubt possible without me or anyone else actually thinking of it ... But an object is in principle unthinkable that would lack the ideal possibility of being experienced, and with it also the possibility of a subject experiencing it.[31]

Here we have one of the clearest expressions of the core of Husserl's transcendental idealism, according to which there are complex essential connections between being, meaning, intuition, and consciousness. The claim that there are things, or a world, beyond the scope of all possible intuition and knowledge is not logically impossible, but it is a "material absurdity," according to Husserl (Ideas I §48, 87). It itself is a claim with no possible fulfilling sense.

In §3.3 I noted that, for Husserl, every logical law has an equivalent but non-identical formal ontological law corresponding to it, and that logical concepts and propositions have formal-ontological correlates. The correlate of the logical concept <truth> is *being*, for instance: to say that the proposition <the hood of the car is scratched> and that the state of affairs of the hood's being scratched obtains are equivalent (but, again, not identical). To this correlation Husserl adds a third: the *epistemological* correlate of truth, and with it being, is Evidenz or givenness, understood as an ideal rather than an empirical possibility. "There are," he writes, "decimal numbers with trillions of places, and there are truths relating to them. No one, however, can actually imagine such numbers, nor do the additions, multiplications, etc., relating to them." Nevertheless, "inward evidence" with respect to them is "*ideally* speaking" a "possible state of mind" (LI Prol., §50, 191). Because of this, Husserl writes, "every proposition of pure mathematics tells us something about possible and impossible happenings in the mental realm" (ibid.). Indeed *all* propositions "tell" us, once we grasp the essential correlations in question, something about such possible and impossible mental happenings. What is the case makes propositions true. And true propositions are, ideally speaking, the kinds of things that can in principle be verified on the basis of originary acts of intuition.

The term "verificationism" is not likely to evoke supportive sentiments from many readers; the verificationism of the logical positivists is supposed to have been refuted long ago. But Husserl's verificationism differs from theirs in a number of ways. First, it is an ideal form of verificationism (see Hardy 2013, 100). It is not the absurd position that everything is such that we, given our evident limitations, can verify it. "Obviously there are things and worlds of things that cannot be demonstrated in a definite way in any human experience" (Ideas I §48, 88). It is that every thing that is can be intuited in principle, and that, with respect to the sphere of real being, that every real thing can in principle be *perceived*, that "whatever really is, but is currently not yet experienced, can come to be given" (Ideas I §48, 87), if not to us, "then [to] other egos who are superior and more discerning."[32] What Husserl is claiming, on the weakest interpretation at least, is that every real entity is the *kind of thing* which is possible, in principle, to perceive, that manifest-ability to consciousness is an ideal possibility for any real object.[33] And that really is not an outrageous claim. If it were false, there would have to be something that, as a matter of metaphysical necessity, could not be given in an originary way to any possible mind whatsoever.

The second difference is that Husserl does not confine intuition, or "experience," to sense experience. There are similarities, to be sure, between Husserl, on the one hand, and empiricists and positivists, on the other. Husserl approves of "empiricist naturalism" for its "radicalism in the practice of knowing, aimed at establishing the legitimacy of autonomous reason as the sole authority in questions of truth" (Ideas I §19, 34). For Husserl, the empiricist's mistake consists in thinking that only sense experience and empirical reflection are originary, and that, correspondingly, the only things that show up in an originary way are things of nature (Ideas I §19, 35). Husserl and other phenomenologists, by contrast, maintain that not only sense-perceptible objects are given directly in experience, but so are states of affairs, essences, values, norms, and meanings, among other things. No phenomenologist confines the intuitively "given" to physical objects and properties, much less to "sensations" or "ideas" or "sense data." In fact many phenomenologists deny that sensations are ever given at all, except perhaps in an artificial attitude.[34]

In any case, if we confine our attention to the sphere of real being for the time, the claim that all real entities are in principle capable of being perceived is not an outrageous one. The most worrisome counterexamples are various "theoretical" entities posited or appealed to by the advanced sciences. One class includes such things as:

(A) quarks, photons, black holes, and so on.

Another includes such things as:

(B) frictionless planes, perfectly elliptical orbits, objects which are not acted upon by any other objects, and centers of gravity.

These two classes, respectively, embrace what Lee Hardy (2013, 199) calls "real" and "ideal" unobservables. The former are, at least according to a natural, realist construal, real things—things which materially compose, constitute, and/or causally interact with other real things, including the sense perceptible things that we manage to perceive (Hardy 2013, 144). While these are unobservable by us, it is not at all clear that they are unobservable in principle (ibid., 199). And it does seem that if we take a realist, non-instrumentalist attitude towards the theoretical entities postulated by our best sciences, we at least often conceive of them as being in principle the kinds of things that can appear in person to an appropriately sensitive conscious mind. We strive to make unperceived things intuitable in some manner through the use of models and diagrams. Most of us have encountered Bohr's model of the atom, for instance, and have profited from models showing the inner workings of a living cell or the solar system. While such models do not provide us with genuine fulfillment, they do provide us with a certain kind of illustrative fulfillment, one that does not provide "genuine confirmation," but is "merely clarifying, merely disclosive" (PAS, 122). But the fact that we make such models not only speaks in favor of the felt need to clarify our concepts by resorting to the intuitions that present those objects, but also suggests that we place those modeled objects within the sphere of what is in principle perceivable, despite our inability to perceive them.

Gareth Evans, who is not immune to the attractiveness of ideal verification-ism—and especially its allure to *realists*—objects that extending the theory to include such objects is a case of "extreme artificiality" (Evans 1982, 96).

> To apply the model to ... microscopic objects would force us to try to make sense of a possible encounter with one of these objects—if not by ourselves, then be a being either very much smaller or very much more sharp-sighted than we are.
>
> (ibid.)

Somehow, though, making sense of that possibility does not seem terribly difficult. Exactly what is the problem with very small beings encountering very small things? Arguably microscopes themselves are a means we ourselves have devised to "encounter" many of those very entities. When we see through a microscope, what we see are microscopic entities under the lens. We do not see an image, nor is seeing through a microscope a case of image consciousness. And in any case, it is by no means obvious that the claim that microscopic entities are in principle perceivable is less plausible than the claim that they could not, as a matter of metaphysical necessity, be perceived by any mind of any possible type.

What about the unobservable entities in the second category, the ideal unobservables? These help make up the "garb of ideas" (Crisis §9h, 51) that, according to Husserl, is methodologically indispensable for exact science. They are also, according to Husserl, regarded by one influential interpretation of science as constituting the "real" world. On this conception, "the 'objec-tive-true' world" is "in principle not perceivable" (Crisis §34d, 127). It is a "mathematical manifold" (Crisis §9, 23). Or, in the language of *Ideas I*, the "real" thing is the "unknown cause of appearances" (Ideas I §52, 94), some-thing which cannot itself possibly be intuited, "a reality that *itself* can never be grasped" (ibid., 98).

Husserl, quite plausibly, rejects this view. More specifically, he accepts that ideal unobservables are incapable in principle of being perceived, but denies that they are real. Such entities and the laws governing them, while exact, are "idealizing fictions with a *fundamentum in re*" (LI Prol., §23, 106). But, as Lee Hardy argues, since they are "idealizing fictions," their unobservability does not contradict Husserl's ideal verificationism (see Hardy 2013, 161). And for what it is worth, it seems to be well-recognized, or at least easy to recognize, that these idealized models are *just* models, and that their utility consists in being simplified and idealized substitutes for the real thing, not the real things lying behind appearances. As Gary Gutting points out, "Idealizations are of interest to the scientist only insofar as they provide a convenient way of approaching the complexities of empirical reality. It is the ideal models that are regarded as imperfect approximations to the concrete phenomena, not vice versa" (Gutting 1978, 44).

5.4.1 Ideal Verificationism and Realism

The question of realism will be dealt with more fully in the final chapter. One point that bears stressing before moving on, however, is that ideal ver-ificationism does not entail idealism or any other form of anti-realism. I will understand *metaphysical realism* with respect to some class of entities to be the position that those entities exist, and that neither their existence nor their nature is *grounded in* their being the actual or possible objects of objectifying acts of thought, perception, or discourse carried out by finite minds. As Michael Devitt puts it, an object has "objective existence" or is metaphysi-cally real just in case "it is not constituted by our knowledge, by our epistemic values, by our capacity to refer to it, by the synthesizing power of the mind, by our imposition of concepts, theories, or languages" (Devitt 1997, 15). So, for instance, metaphysical realism with respect to planets is the position that planets exist, and that they do not owe their existence or natures to what we or any other finite minds perceive, think, feel, or say about them. Metaphysi-cal antirealism is the negation of metaphysical realism. There are lots of ways to be a metaphysical antirealist (ibid.). One may be an eliminativist. One may be an absolute idealist. One may hold that planets exist, but are certain pat-terns of experiences or sense data. Kant, on many interpretations at least, is not a metaphysical realist about phenomena, holding that they owe many of their features and possibly even their existence to our faculties of sensibility and understanding.

Metaphysical realism regarding a class of objects is not the view that they exist independently of minds or language, though obviously that would be a sufficient condition for metaphysical realism. One can be a metaphysical rea-list, or not, about minds, mental acts, meanings, and language themselves (Vinueza 2001, 51–52). Provided one does not hold that their being is groun-ded in their being the objects of objectifying acts, one is a realist about them.

Epistemic realism is metaphysical realism with respect to the objects of veridical perception and true thought, including knowledge.[35] It is not, how-ever, entailed by metaphysical realism (Drummond 1990, 254). On one inter-pretation of Kant, for instance, he is a metaphysical realist about things in themselves, but is not an epistemic realist about them because he holds that they are unknowable. An epistemic realist about things in themselves, by contrast, would maintain that not only are they metaphysically real, but we can entertain true thoughts and possess knowledge of them. On the assumption that many of the objects investigated in mathematics and science are known to exist and have the properties they are represented as having, a rather sweeping version of epistemic realism is summed up in Edwin Holt's first two theses in his contribution to the New Realist program of the early twentieth century:

1   The entities (objects, facts, etc.) under study in logic, mathematics, and the physical sciences are not mental in any usual or proper meaning of the word "mental".
2   The being and nature of these entities are in no sense conditioned by their being known

(Holt et al. 1912, 472).

The denial of epistemic realism is often, though not always, based on some version of what Dallas Willard calls the "Midas touch" account of consciousness, which we have already encountered (§2.2.1), according to which "to take something as our 'object' automatically transforms it in some essential way" (Willard 2000b, 38). Consider, for instance, Hilary Putnam's contention that "'Objects' do not exist independently of conceptual schemes. *We* cut up the world into objects when we introduce one or another scheme of description" (Putnam 1981, 52). On this view *something*—"the world"—is transformed into a domain of "objects" by our "scheme[s] of description." This is quite clearly just the kind of view that epistemic realism rules out. For the epistemic realist, Jupiter is there no matter what our conceptual scheme happens to be. But provided our conceptual scheme contains the concept "Jupiter," we can think and even know about it.

To see that ideal verificationism does not entail any form of antirealism, consider the case of the planet Jupiter. Ideal verificationism about Jupiter is true, since not only is Jupiter the kind of thing that could possibly be perceived and known by some mind of some type, but it is actually perceived and actually known by minds of the human type. But this does not entail that Jupiter's existence or nature is in any way whatsoever grounded in its being the object of thought, talk, experience, or knowledge. To get from the premise "Jupiter is a possible object of knowledge" to the conclusion "Jupiter is not metaphysically real," at least another premise needs to be added, and whatever that premise is—most likely one that entails radical skepticism about the possibility of knowing independently real things—it will certainly itself require extensive philosophical support. Nothing changes, in this respect, if we begin to add to the list. Not only is ideal verificationism true of Jupiter, but it's true of its moons Ganymede and Io. It's true of badgers, the Horstman Glacier, and a mole on someone's arm. It's also true of things which are not presently objects of anyone's consciousness or knowledge, such as any one of the probably billions of remote uninhabited exoplanets (and pebbles and water molecules on those planets) in this galaxy alone. It's unclear, then, why the claim that *everything* is such that it could, as an ideal possibility, be an object of perception and knowledge would rule out metaphysical realism.

What ideal verificationism rules out are *Kantian* things-in-themselves, that is, entities that are essentially unknowable. But it does not rule out the existence of things which exist in themselves, that is, whose existence and nature is not grounded in their being possible objects of experience and knowledge. The identification of things in themselves with Kantian things-in-themselves is the result of a radical skepticism about the possibility of knowing anything whose existence and nature are not grounded in the nature or activities of the mind. But obviously that kind of skepticism cannot simply be assumed, and is certainly not a commitment shared by all metaphysical realists.

5.4.2 Yoshimi's Objection

Ideal verificationism is not obvious. There are, moreover, some rather strong arguments directed against Husserl's idealism that target his ideal verificationism more directly. Consider Jeff Yoshimi's recent appeal to Edwin Abbott's "flatlanders," who live in a 2d world. As Yoshimi shows, the flatlanders would have no possibility of intuiting our 3d world. And their resident transcendental idealist, Husserl2d, would be required to claim that an intuitable 3d world is "a kind of material nonsense" (Yoshimi 2015, 8). But, Yoshimi points out, we know that Husserl2d is wrong; such a world is given to *us* constantly. Something real clearly lies outside of the world the flatlanders have "constituted." Yoshimi further invites us to consider our inability, whose roots might run to metaphysical bedrock, to know what it is like to be a bat (Yoshimi 2015, 8; Nagel 1974).

I think Yoshimi's arguments demonstrate quite conclusively that there may be and are minds for whom various regions of reality are inaccessible in principle. In the case of the flatlanders, Yoshimi depicts Husserl2d as maintaining that 3d objects are countersensical because they are unperceivable by flatlanders (Yoshimi 2015, 8). I'm not sure that would be the response. Perhaps we, and even Husserl2d, can conceive of some possible modification to the flatlanders perceptual apparatus whereby 3d objects come into view—a sort of radical version of the transformation experienced by "Stereo Sue" when she gained stereoscopic vision, a transformation that far exceeded what she had imagined it would be (Sacks 2010, 124). Husserl is aware that we are constrained by "factual limits" (Ideas I §48, 88).

Nevertheless, Yoshimi has a strong case against Husserl's particular view. The reason is that for Husserl, "one can see that what is recognizable by one ego must be recognizable *in principle* by *every* ego" (Ideas I §48, 87). Yoshimi's and Nagel's example of knowing what it's like to be a bat seems to be a fairly decisive counterexample to this claim. I could not know what it's like to be a bat without being a bat, and I cannot be a bat (Nagel 1974, 439–440).

But ideal verificationism as formulated here does not require the strong thesis that everything can in principle be recognized or known by every mind. It is that everything can be known by some possible mind—or, even more weakly, that every possible thing is the kind of thing which could in principle be known by some possible mind. And even knowing what it's like to be a bat is known by one kind of mind, namely bat minds.

Yoshimi's examples above involve entities which cannot possibly be known—or authentically represented—by one type of mind, but can be by another. What we need to really sink ideal verificationism is a type of object that cannot be known, or authentically represented, by any possible mind of any type. Yoshimi mentions Kantian things in themselves as candidates (2015, 10). But it seems that this confronts Yoshimi with a dilemma.[36] On the one hand, the more thoroughly and authentically we represent something as having properties, functioning as a constituent of various states of affairs, standing in relations to other things, and making various propositions true, the less it appears to be unknowable in principle. On the other hand, the less thoroughly and authentically we represent a Kantian thing in itself, the less of a grip we have on what we might even mean in saying that such a thing possibly exists at all. Merely understanding, in a completely inauthentic way, the sentence "Unknowable things in themselves possibly exist" is not a way of establishing that they possibly exist.

I feel the pull of both Yoshimi's arguments and Husserl's, and despite my sympathies for ideal verificationism, I certainly don't have anything like a refutation of Yoshimi's position. I am obviously limited to conceiving of what I can conceive, and feel uneasy about passing those limitations on to reality. On the other hand, however, the connections Husserl draws among being, meaning, and experienceability seem compelling as well. But even if global ideal verificationism is false, it is a rather big deal, philosophically, that ideal verificationism is true of the kind of objects that we can authentically represent, given what those objects in fact are. Finally, it is philosophically noteworthy that no form of ideal verificationism, whether global or restricted, entails or even motivates idealism or antirealism.

5.5 Conclusion

This chapter began modestly and ended ambitiously. The central modest claims of the chapter are, first, that each concept that refers to something has a fulfilling sense, and that authentic concept possession is a matter of knowing some portion of a concept's fulfilling sense or, equivalently, having a capacity to undergo an experience of fulfillment directed at that object. The main ambitious claim, of course, is that every actual and possible being that we can think about is the kind of thing that can in principle be known on the basis of fulfillment. Since we think and talk about physical objects, and have authentic concepts of them, the account given here entails that they can be perceived by us. In the following chapters, we will take a closer look at perceptual experiences, how they manage to present us with an objective world, and their distinctive kinds of intentional content.

Notes

1 See EJ, 80, 319 and Camp 2009, 289.
2 See A.D. Smith 2003, 50.
3 Husserl writes: "I often used 'evidence' in a sense equivalent to the givenness of something itself. But surely we must distinguish: evidence as insight that belongs to judgment, <to the> judgment that <something> is there itself that exists and that is given again <as> that—and, on the other hand, the being-given itself" (PCIT, 305).
4 See Miller 1984, 34–35, who makes this point by distinguishing perception from perceptual judgment, which is what fulfillment is. Also see Dretske 2000a, 102.
5 Thanks to Søren Overgaard for pointing this out.
6 LI 6 §8, 696. Also see Dahlstrom 2001, 64–65.
7 This point depends on the results of Chapter 8, in which it is argued that intuition is not a kind of conceptualization.
8 See Dahlstrom 2001, 67 and Crowell 2016, 188–189.
9 See Willard 1984, 17 and 207. Also see Moran 2007.
10 Johnston 2006. Also see Siegel 2010, 27.
11 Husserl's account of authentic concept possession bears some similarities to Russell's "principle of acquaintance (1999, 40) and, even more to Evans's modified version of it on which "a subject cannot make a judgement about something unless he knows which object his judgment is about," where the sort of knowledge in question is "discriminating knowledge: the subject must have a capacity to distinguish the object of his judgement from all others" (Evans 1982, 89).
12 See LI 6 §30, 749–750 and PP, 16. Also see Cairns 2013, 253. Thanks to David Kasmier for drawing this to my attention.
13 LI 6 §30, 749. Also see LI 6 §39, 766 and Willard 1984, 232.
14 Ideas I §36, 63. Also see A.D. Smith 2008, section III for a very helpful discussion.
15 Ideas I §135, 268; also see Smith and McIntyre 1982, 244, where the manifold is defined as "the set of all possible acts of consciousness that are co-directed with the given act".
16 See Hardy 2013, 182 and A.D. Smith 2003, 164.
17 For an excellent overview, see Lohmar 2002.
18 LI 6 §44, 783. Husserl's example is "gold-being-yellow."
19 Thanks to Guy Schuh for his insights on this topic. For a good discussion, see Benoist 2015, 107ff.
20 Husserl himself appeals to differences in fulfilling sense when defending the claim that "Naming and asserting do not merely differ grammatically, but 'in essence', which means that the acts which confer or fulfill meaning for each, differ in *intentional essence*" (LI 5 §37, 636).
21 Kripke 1972. On the distinction between attributive and referential descriptions, see Donnellan 1966.
22 See Bach 2008, 19. Donnellan (1966, 281–282) distinguishes between denoting and referring. Both attributive and referential descriptions denote their objects, but only the latter refer.
23 LI 6 §5, 684. See Beyer 2001, 282. This article identifies a number of interesting anticipations, on Husserl's part, of developments in the anglophone philosophy of language.
24 This issue is raised and discussed in Kinkaid 2020, §2.4. I am grateful for conversations with him on this topic.
25 TS §36, 107. For a rich discussion, also see Doyon 2018, 175ff.
26 For two very rich discussions of these and related issues, see Jansen 2013 and Marbach 2013.
27 Liebesman 2014, 307. Note that Liebesman does not argue that the name "Holmes" is in fact introduced by description—it could be the name of an "actual abstract object" picked out by ostension, for instance (311).
28 See Kurg 2014a, §2.4 for an outstanding discussion.

29 As Gregory Currie points out, "Fictional worlds are indeterminate because there are questions about fictions that have no determinate answer" (1990, 54). Precisely how Bilbo looks is one such question. For an outstanding treatment, see Casey 2001, Chapter 5.
30 A.D. Smith 2003, 186. Also see Hardy 2013, 92 and 100. For a couple of arguments for ideal verificationism, see Kasmier 2015.
31 TI, 146. Thanks to Daniel Dahlstrom for assistance in translating this passage.
32 Ideas I §52, 95. For discussions, see A.D. Smith 2003, 188–191 and Wiltsche 2012, 118–120.
33 See Willard 1984, 237, Wiltsche 2012, 109, and Hardy 2013, 93 and 167.
34 Scheler 1973a, 55–56; Scheler 1973b, 203; Merleau-Ponty 2012, 236.
35 See Willard 2002, 69 and Willard 2003a, 163. Also see Drummond 1990, 253.
36 I owe this objection to David Kasmier. Also see D.W. Smith 1982a, 48.

Recommended Readings

Evans, Gareth. 1982. *The Varieties of Reference*. Oxford: Oxford University Press.
Hardy, Lee. 2013. *Nature's Suit: Husserl's Phenomenological Philosophy of the Physical Sciences*. Athens: Ohio University Press.
Husserl, Edmund. 1970. *Logical Investigations*. Two volumes. J.N. Findlay, trans. London: Routledge & Kegan Paul. See especially Investigations I and VI.
Husserl, Edmund. 1999. *The Idea of Phenomenology*. Lee Hardy, trans. Boston: Kluwer Academic Publishers.
Ingarden, Roman. 1973. *The Literary Work of Art*. George G. Grabowicz, trans. Evanston: Northwestern University Press.
Sartre, Jean-Paul. 2010. *The Imaginary*. Jonathan Webber, trans. New York: Routledge.

6 Perception

As much as phenomenologists differ regarding the nature of perception, Kevin Mulligan nicely sums up two points of widespread agreement when he writes that "perception is entirely direct and necessarily incomplete" (1995, 194). Over the next two chapters those claims will be defended. In this chapter I will defend the claims that perception *can be* incomplete or inadequate, and that it is always direct. In the next chapter I will defend the much more ambitious claim that it is "necessarily incomplete" or inadequate. The upshot of all of this is that (a) ordinary objects which transcend our perceptual consciousness of them can be perceived, (b) they can be perceived directly despite being perceived inadequately, (c) perceiving them in something like the way we do—inadequately—is as good as the perception of them gets, and (d) there is no other class of sense-perceptible entities that we perceive adequately against which our perception of ordinary things can be unfavorably compared.

Perception, as we saw in Chapter 2, is a type of intentional experience with at least four basic features. First, it is an *intuitive* experience. In perception objects are presented and not merely meant or thought of. Second, perception is a *positing* sort of experience. Unlike phantasy, the objects of perception are presented as real fixtures of the one actual world. Third, perception is intentionally *direct*. Though there is such a thing as perceiving one thing in virtue of perceiving something else, and while image-consciousness is an indirect *intuitive* experience, there is no such thing as indirect *perception*. This chapter will provide reasons for thinking so. Finally, and most importantly, perception is an *originary* experience. In veridical perception, we encounter the thing itself, as what it itself is.

Perception also, as we saw in the last chapter, plays a central role in conceptual acts. Meanings, and the acts in which they function as contents, are intrinsically empty. They derive their sense, and with it their reference to the world, from their fulfilling sense. As Husserl writes,

What things are—the only things that we make assertions about, the only things whose being or nonbeing, whose being in a certain way or being otherwise we dispute and can rationally decide—they are as things of experience.

(Ideas I §47, 85)

Perception does not just provide us with evidence for our empirical judgments. It is what determines what they even mean. This is why, as we saw, perceiving the state of affairs that a proposition is about is both the best way to verify that proposition and to determine what it means.

Finally, every other form of intuition is, as part of its own phenomenological character, a modification of perception. "Perception is the primordial mode of intuitiveness."[1] Intuitive memories are re-livings of perception, and are experienced as such. As Husserl puts it, "a remembering in itself manifests itself as a presentification of a perception."[2] Image-consciousness is a modification of perception as well. Intuitive acts of phantasy are modifications of the positing character of perception; they are "as-if" acts of perception. In phantasy, "One is conscious of what is phantasied 'as if [it were] existing'."[3]

It would be fantastic if perception, which plays so many fundamental roles in the life of consciousness, were susceptible to a quick and easy phenomenological treatment. Sadly, it is in many ways the most difficult thing to describe, and a topic concerning which there is a depressing lack of consensus. The disagreements among philosophers regarding perception are not slight, and many of the positions that have historically been widely adopted diverge far from common sense.

Before seeing how, it is important to remind ourselves of some ordinary commonsense truisms. People sometimes talk and think about things such as scratches on car hoods. Moreover, we think and talk about those things directly. Furthermore, there are people who know how to repair scratches on car hoods. And, again as far as we can tell, those knowledgeable individuals, along with their customers, sometimes actually see and feel scratches on car hoods. That appears to be a pretty basic condition of repairing them, as well as the most typical way of discovering that they need to be repaired. To use the jargon from the last chapter, sometimes people's thoughts about scratches on car hoods are *fulfilled*. When B goes to check the hood of the car and discovers that it is scratched, when he sees the gouge running through the paint and feels it catch his thumbnail, the thing he directly sees and feels is identical with one of the objects of his thought, namely the scratch on the hood. He can say things like "Oh, there it is," and mean by "it" the very same thing he sees, the scratch, and not, say, a diagonal patch of color in a two-dimensional visual field.

In the lifeworld, these are trivialities. In philosophy, they ought to be but are not. Many philosophers have been firmly persuaded that things like cars and scratches on cars cannot be perceived, at least not "directly" or "immediately," and that the proper objects of perceptual consciousness are not the familiar things of ordinary life, but something else entirely. Hume, discussing our belief in the externality and independence of the objects of perception, writes:

> But this universal and primary opinion of all men is soon destroyed by the slightest philosophy, which teaches us, that nothing can ever be present to the mind but an image or perception, and that the senses are only the inlets, through which these images are conveyed, without being able to produce any immediate intercourse between the mind and the object.
>
> (Hume 1993, 104)

Hume may be right that the "slightest philosophy" destroys this "opinion." But perhaps slightly more philosophy can restore it.

In this chapter I will defend the claim that things like scratches on car hoods can be perceived directly. Before beginning, though, it is important to distinguish this claim from others with which it is often tied up. To that end, let us put aside, as much as possible, any worries about whether we can represent mind-independent objects as they really are, or whether reality is in some measure a reflection of our conceptual schemes, or whether we can really reach "outside" the mind. Those questions come later. The next two chapters are not a defense of direct realism. Direct realism makes definite claims about the metaphysical status of the objects of perception: they are "real" not only in the sense of existing in time, but insofar as they do not depend, for their existence or natures, on being represented. The task here is more modest: to determine whether or not a thing like a scratched car hood—never mind its metaphysical status—is the kind of thing that can be perceived.

The reason for holding back on the metaphysical question is not grounded in any skeptical worries. In fact our knowledge of car hoods would be identical in status whether they are real or ideal. Even if car hoods are in the mind or immanent, they are *intentionally* transcendent, and that's what explains why our knowledge of them could never be as secure as our knowledge of our own experiences. The reason for postponing the metaphysical question, rather, is so we do not confuse it with the related, but distinct, phenomenological question. The most interesting phenomenological and epistemological feature of such things as scratches on car hoods is not that they are "external" or independent of our minds. It is, rather, that they cannot be perceived completely, or adequately, in any single experience of them. Whatever a scratch on a car hood is, whether it exists as a constituent of minds, whether our minds prescribe laws to it, whether it is the product of our conceptualizing the world, or whatever other relation it does or does not bear to minds, it is essentially the kind of thing which, if given, is only given from a perspective. Without making sense of how we can perceive things like that, there is no making sense of direct realism.

6.1 Adequate and Inadequate Intuition

Earlier (§1.5) it was stated that the single most important distinction among intentional acts is that between those that are intuitive and those that are empty. Husserl, in one of his most significant contributions to human thought, introduces and develops a further cardinal distinction among intuitive acts themselves: the distinction between those that are *adequate* to their objects, and those which are not. The distinction between adequate and inadequate ideas and knowledge is not new. Locke writes that "Ideas" are adequate "which perfectly represent those Archetypes, which the Mind supposes them taken from" and inadequate when they "are but a partial, or incomplete representation of those Archetypes to which they are referred" (Locke 1975, 375). Leibniz characterizes knowledge as adequate when "everything that enters into a distinct definition or distinct knowledge is known distinctly, down to the primitive notions" (1989, §24, 56).

What Husserl makes clear, however, is that an act can be *intuitive* and *inadequate*. In *Thing and Space*, where Husserl calls adequate intuitions "self-posing," he writes that "What differentiates them resides in what is given in them" (TS §9, 21). He explains this as follows: "the identity of the object and the identity of the perception are one and the same; I mean different perceptions have different objects" (TS §10, 22). A good example of such objects are sense data. Sense data have traditionally been regarded as *objects* of consciousness that may or may not be really immanent to the stream which really contains the experiences of them. But almost everyone seems to agree that a sense datum is *intentionally* immanent. "Its goods, so to speak, are entirely in the shop-window" (Price 1950, 145). Speaking of his knowledge of color by acquaintance, Russell writes, "I know the colour perfectly and completely when I see it, and no further knowledge of it itself is even theoretically possible" (Russell 1999, 32). Because they are given adequately, one cannot view a sense datum from any other perspective, or get a better or worse look at one. That is why "it has been said to exist only from a place" (Price 1950, 145). They are, furthermore, typically regarded as being such that their existence is entailed by our awareness of them (ibid., 19).

Because sense data are given adequately, every difference between two experiences is a difference in the sense datum that is perceived in those experiences. As a consequence of that, two experiences of a sense datum cannot differ insofar as one reveals more parts, moments, features, or relations of the sense datum than another. There is nothing more to discover, perceptually, about them. I cannot view a sense datum from closer up or from another angle, for instance, because in doing so I will either change the features or the identity of the sense datum. I cannot touch a sense datum that I see, because if I did that would acquaint me with a further property of it that was not there before, contrary to the claim that it was perceived adequately.

In the case of physical objects, things are different. We can take a closer look at a physical thing without it changing or appearing to change, much less appearing to go out of existence and be replaced by something else. We can explore physical objects and find out more about them. The very same one can be perceived by more than one sense. In perception, objects are seen from perspectives. And often when an object is seen from a perspective, some of its parts and features are intuitively present, while others are not. One cannot see the underside of an opaque and closed car hood while looking at it from above. And even when all of the parts and features of a car hood are intuitively present, there are other perspectives from which it can be given. Because of this, our individual experiences of car hoods are incomplete or inadequate.

Note, moreover, that in saying that a car hood is seen from perspectives, I am not saying that we see a partially subject-dependent object, a car-hood-from-a-perspective. Such a thing—H-from-P—could not be seen from another perspective. But the car hood, H, can. Furthermore, if we see H-from-P and then move to see H-from-P*, we would not have any consciousness of seeing the same thing. But we do see the same thing in such a transition. What we see is H, from P, and then that very same thing, H, from P*. In fact if all we perceived were objects-from-perspectives, perception would not even be perspectival, since objects-from-perspectives are not themselves given from perspectives. The claim that we see an object O from a perspective does not entail that we perceive some perspective-dependent object, O-from-a-perspective, but is arguably incompatible with it.

To say that an experience of an object is inadequate is to express, from the side of the experience, the very same thing that we express by saying that the object is *intentionally transcendent* to the *intuitive* content of the act. We have already discussed intentional transcendence in §4.4.2. Something is *intentionally transcendent* when it is either not given at all, or only incompletely or inadequately given. A car is intentionally transcendent to any act of perceiving it. No matter the conditions under which we perceive it, there will always be parts or features that are out of view. This is grounded in the nature of what spatial things are. "Inadequate modes of givenness belong essentially to the spatial structure of things; any other way of givenness is simply absurd."[4]

Furthermore, even the parts of a car that are in view are intentionally transcendent. The scratch on the hood is something whose appearance changes with variations in our perspective. And some perspectives enable us to perceive more of a thing, or to see it more clearly or in richer detail, than others. A person examining a scratched car hood will look at it from a variety of perspectives, and in lighting conditions that render its features visible. She will aim to get a "maximal grip" on it (Kelly 2010, 152; also Merleau-Ponty 2012, 315–316), the perspective from which it is perceived with just the right balance of "richness and clarity" (ibid., 332). If she succeeds, she will arrive at the "optimal givenness" of the thing (TS §36, 104). But even this is not an *adequate* perception of the scratch. It is just one of many possible experiences that belongs to a "circle of maximum givenness" (ibid., 106). And even if it is the most rich and clear experience from among that circle, the manifold of experiences within that circle are superior to that experience alone.

The same holds of its properties. The shape and size of the car do not have one way of looking, but look differently depending on one's perspective. This is also true of its color. An experience of a color is never adequate, since the color "appears but while it appears, the appearance can and *must* continuously change in the course of ostensive experience of it" (Ideas I §41, 72). Colors are normally perceived to be the same across different conditions of illumination. If you want to change the color of your car, moving to a cloudy city will not do the trick, nor will it seem to do the trick. There is no shape, size, color, or any other property that can possibly be instantiated in a transcendent object, which can be given adequately (Noë 2004, 193). It is an essential property of each that they are given from perspectives, and therefore given inadequately from any one of them.

That spatial things cannot be adequately presented in any single experience is a phenomenological point. They not only *are* intentionally transcendent, but they *appear to be* intentionally transcendent. "Physical objects appear like that—i.e. as having more to them than is revealed in one glance—and we take them to be like that."[5] As Husserl puts it,

> If an experience is *imperfect*, if it makes the intrinsically existent object appear only one-sidedly … then the experience itself … is that which, on being consulted, tells me so; it tells me: Here, in this consciousness, something is given as it itself; but it is more than what is actually itself grasped; there is more of the same object to be experienced.
>
> (FTL §94, 233)

To see something from a perspective is to perceive it *as from* a perspective. And to see something as from a perspective is to see it as something that can, in principle (stars) and often in practice (cars), be seen from other ones (see Wiesing 2014, 41). In the perception of a car, the car is not only objectively intentionally transcendent to my experience; it is *phenomenologically* intentionally transcendent to my experience. The perception of physical objects involves, to use D.W. Smith's phrase (1989, 185), a "sense of transcendence." We perceive things like cars as being more than what we perceive of them at a time, and we discover, repeatedly, that they really are.

6.2 Transcendence and Constancy

There is an intimate relation between the sense of transcendence and perceptual constancies. Tyler Burge defines perceptual constancies as "capacities to represent environmental attributes, or environmental particulars, as the same, despite radically different proximal stimulations" (Burge 2010, 114). However, perceptual constancy is straightforwardly discoverable phenomenologically, while the sameness or difference of "proximal stimulations" is not (see Madary 2010, 145–146). A better characterization for phenomenological purposes is that perceptual constancy occurs when "we experience a property to remain constant even though our experience of that object undergoes variation" (Madary 2010, 146). Any object or feature that exhibits constancy is one that is given from perspectives (Burge 2010, 385). And any object that is given from perspectives is one that is given inadequately or incompletely from any one of them. Finally, any object that is given inadequately is intentionally transcendent to our consciousness of it. As Burge puts it, "A perceptual system achieves objectification by...exercising *perceptual constancies*" (Burge 2010, 408). It is thanks to them that a world of things and features rises up over against us as something "outside" of us, something whose *esse* is not its *percipi*.

The term "inadequacy" has a negative connotation. In this context, it should not. If perception were always adequate, we could not perceive what we do. We would not have any "sense of transcendence." We would not perceive objects and their properties as constant across changing experiences of them. We would instead regard every change in our experience as a change in the objects of our experience. If we took what we see when we see a car to be the kind of thing that goes out of existence or changes as soon as we approach, circle, or explore it, we would not even be conscious of the car, or even any of its sides, parts, or properties (Gallagher and Zahavi 2012, 108). As Husserl writes,

> It is clear that a non-intuitive pointing beyond or indicating is what characterizes the side actually seen as a mere side, and what provides for the fact that the side is not taken for the thing, but rather, that something transcending the side is intended in consciousness as perceived, by which precisely *that* is actually seen.
>
> (PAS, 41)

A being who, with eyes pointed in the direction of a car, takes every change in its visual experience to be a change in the *things* (rather than just the circumstances) which it sees, would not be misperceiving the car. It would fail to be perceptually aware of the car at all. It is only in virtue of its inadequacy that perception can present us with objects (Madary 2017, 74).

6.3 Transcendence and Horizons

Because characterizing the objects of perception as transcendent is a phenomenological claim about the way objects manifest themselves to us, there must be something on the side of the *act* in virtue of which objects appear transcendent. Husserl's answer is that every perceptual experience is "a mixture of fulfilled and unfulfilled intentions."[6] When B looks at the car from the front, he has an intuitive or fulfilled intention toward the parts facing him. He has an empty consciousness of the back of the car, the inside of the car, what is under the scratched hood, and so on. This empty consciousness can be more or less determinate in content. If the visible portions of the car are red, B will likely emptily intend the unseen parts of the car to be red as well. He will likely emptily intend it to have tires and a trunk. But B will probably not have an empty intention about the precise position of the valve stem on the driver's side rear tire, or the exact contents of the trunk (see Gurwitsch 1964, 236–237).

It is important to note that the intentions towards the unperceived portions of the car are *empty*. Another proposal, after all, is that the unperceived parts of an object are the objects of other, nonperceptual *intuitive* acts. "How," asks Wilfrid Sellars, "can a volume of white apple flesh be present *as actuality* in the visual experience if it is not seen? The answer should be obvious. It is present by virtue of being *imagined*."[7] But this "obvious" answer, as Husserl pointed out nearly three quarters of a century earlier, does not work. As he writes, "even appearance in phantasy ... brings some thing to appearance only by presenting it ... one-sidedly, exactly as does *perceptual* appearance."[8] That is, imaginative acts also consist of empty and filled intentions. He continues: "even in phantasy we cannot represent a house from the front and the back at the same time; if the front side stands before our eyes, then the back side does not, and vice versa" (ibid.). Just as we cannot perceive an object from multiple perspectives at once, we cannot imagine one from multiple perspectives at once.

In the *Logical Investigations,* Husserl identifies empty intentions with "signitive" intentions, and signitive intentions with *meanings* (see LI 6 §14a, 710). As we will see, however, this is a serious mistake, both in its own right and in its consequences, and one that Husserl progressively abandons. In his middle and later work, Husserl characterizes perceptual experiences as consisting of intuitive content and a *horizon*.[9] The concept of the horizon is one of the most important in phenomenology. Actually, Husserl often means slightly different, but clearly related, things by the term "horizon" (see Hopp 2011, 54):

a   Sometimes he uses the term to refer to the *unperceived or undetermined parts and properties of the object*. He writes, for instance, that a perceived object "has an empty horizon of yet unknown features."[10]

b   Sometimes Husserl uses "horizon" to designate the *possible intuitive experiences* of those unperceived or undetermined parts and properties of the object. The "individual thing in perception," he writes, "has meaning only through an open horizon of 'possible perceptions'" (Crisis §47, 162).

c   Elsewhere he characterizes the horizon as a feature of the act of perceiving itself, namely *the actual empty or partially empty intentions* that
intend the unperceived or undetermined parts and properties of the thing.
"The 'horizons' of perceptions are another name for empty intentions …
that are integrally cohesive and that are actualized in the progression of
perception in and through different orientations" (PAS, 144). The horizon
"itself has the fundamental trait of consciousness as the consciousness of
something" (PAS, 42).

This last conception will be the operative concept of the act's horizon hence-
forth. Horizons include both the empty and indeterminate intentions (those
are not the same) in virtue of which we are conscious of the unperceived or
indeterminately perceived features of the object, as well as the intentions
towards the surrounding environment in which the object is situated—the
internal and external horizons of the act, respectively. It is because of them
that our perceptual experiences are inadequate to their objects. That is, the
reason that a perceived object is intentionally transcendent is because it
appears to be more than what we perceive of it. And it appears to be more
than what we perceive of it because there is a consciousness of that "more," a
consciousness brought about through the act's intentional horizon. And, of
course, the horizon does not just specify that the object has further sides and
properties; "the intentional horizon cannot be filled out in just any manner"
(PAS, 42). The horizon specifies how the object is, could be, or, in rare cases,
must be, and with varying degrees of determinacy. As Husserl puts it,

> The particular perceptions, which fill the empty horizon which the table has
> for me in a perception, can not be inserted in the seeing of the horse and
> further determine the horse.
>
> (PP §35, 139)

That is why it would be shocking to discover that a horse's hind legs are table
legs. More extreme examples become absurdities. A piano sonata cannot,
upon further examination, have most of the properties of an omelet. A
material thing in space cannot, upon closer inspection, turn out to have most
of the features of an event. And we implicitly understand this in perception.
The open possibilities of horizonal fulfillment simply do not include these.

    We can understand the nature of the horizon better when we see how it gets
filled in, how the intentions contained in it reach their fulfillment. If you view
a car from the front and then circle around it, empty intentions directed
toward unseen parts of the car find their intuitive fulfillment, while those that
were intuitive become empty. "Gain and loss are balanced at every step: a
new act has richer fullness in regard to certain properties, for whose sake it
has lost fullness in regard to others" (LI 6 §16, 721). At no point is the entire
car given intuitively. Unless an object is completely unfamiliar, or one is in a

very unusual state of consciousness, the filling in of an empty horizon is not motivated by "mere blind strivings," but informed by "protentional anticipations which refer to what will attain givenness" (EJ §21, 87). If things go smoothly, not only do emptily intended and anticipated features come to givenness, but new and unanticipated features also come into view (PAS, 46). Some of those features will not have been emptily intended at all. As this occurs, and we become increasingly familiar with objects and types of objects, the horizonal intentions become more determinate. There is a typical way living rooms appear, but the horizonal anticipations of one's own living room are much more determinate than those of an unfamiliar one. Horizonal intentions are even present with respect to parts and features that are in view (PAS, 43). The precise contours and depth of the scratch can be determined more closely. The color of the hood, and of the scratch on it, may be present with a certain indeterminacy that can come to fulfillment via "specification" (PAS, 45). But while all acts of specification via intuition are acts of intuitive fulfillment, the converse is not true. Seeing the determinate color of one's car hood yet again is not a process of specification, but it is a process of fulfillment (see PAS, 48).

Things do not always proceed as anticipated, of course. An object can turn out to be other than we anticipated it to be. In that case we experience "disappointment."[11] Not all cases of disappointment entail that the initial experience was illusory or hallucinatory. If B anticipates that the car is uniformly red, but discovers that the rear of the car is covered with primer, his anticipation will be disappointed, but this is not a perceptual illusion. If, however, the car initially looks red to B, but further investigation and specification reveals it to be orange, his initial experience will prove to have been illusory. And if he walks toward the car and it disappears, his experience may prove to have been hallucinatory.

Finally, we must distinguish between the internal and the external horizon of perceptual experience. The internal horizon specifies both (a) unperceived sides and properties of a thing and (b) the further determinations of those sides and properties which are perceived (see PAS, 44). When one looks at a car, for instance, the internal horizon contains intentions towards the unseen parts of the car. But it also contains unfulfilled intentions towards the seen parts. The hood may look smooth from ten feet away, but it is part of the experience's own character that this feature would be better perceived by taking a closer look and by touching it. Its color may be in full view, but further experience may be required to determine its exact shade.

The external horizon is what accounts for the thing's situatedness "within a *field of things*" (Crisis §47, 162). It is the consciousness we have of the surrounding environment, and ultimately of the surrounding world, and it can be empty or intuitive. Both the external and internal horizon are essential for the sense of transcendence. Without an internal horizon, the object would not appear to be a complete object given incompletely, but an incomplete object given completely—not like a book that is half-read, but like a book that is half-written. And without the external horizon, our experience could not even have an internal horizon. The reason is that the further parts and features of a thing are those that could be perceived from other perspectives. But those perspectives are from places in the environment of the thing, not, in most cases, from parts of the thing itself. And these are places where one could in principle be located. The external horizon does not just consist of the consciousness of other, unthematized objects, but of other places from which the thematic object itself can be perceived.

6.4 Intuitive Fulfillment

As has been stated already, perception involves a process of fulfillment, a process that depends on the presence of horizons (PAS, 108). The intuitive fulfillment taking place in perception is, however, distinct from the kind of cognitive fulfillment discussed in §5.1 (see Bernet, Kern, and Marbach 1993, 128). One major difference is structural. In the case of cognitive fulfillment, the fulfilling and fulfilled acts *must* take place at the same time. In the case of intuitive fulfillment, however, they *cannot* take place at the same time. I cannot anticipate a note and hear that note at the very same time, or experience an empty horizonal intention toward the trunk of the car and its fulfillment at the same time. Rather, the anticipatory empty intention must precede the intuitive, fulfilling intention. A further difference, which will be defended in §8.3.5, is that in cognitive fulfillment, an intuitive act and a conceptual act enter into a synthesis. In the case of intuitive fulfillment, by contrast, what gets fulfilled is not a conceptual act or an act with conceptual content. Horizons, as we will later see (§8.2.4), are not concepts.

6.5 Manifolds and Objects

In §5.2 we discussed the perceptual manifold that belongs to each thing. The perceptual manifold of a thing is "the ideal total content of 'possible perceptions' of the same object" (TS §11, 26–27). To say that something is intentionally transcendent to a given possible perceptual experience, then, is to say that the object's perceptual manifold contains more contents than the content of that one experience. And to explore an object further, to perceive it from other sides and to determine its features and properties more clearly, is, on the side of the act, to actualize more and more of its perceptual manifold, to transform the "possible perceptions" making it up into *actual* perceptions.

In the best case, the exploration of the object will occur in a temporally extended "continuous synthesis of manifold perceptions."[12] As A takes a closer look at the scratched car hood, she will undergo a sequence of experiences in which the scratch is not only given, but given as the same thing that was given previously—an "identity-consciousness" (TS §10, 24). This is an act—and, as Husserl points out, the only type of act—in which we have "pure evidence" or an originary intuition of the identity of the thing across different experiences and over time.[13] In determining the scratch more closely, feeling it and seeing it through a multi-modal experience of it, A will experience the scratch *as* the same thing.

This is, in part, because the horizonal intentions themselves point toward possible fulfilling experiences, and those experiences occur. Each phase of the continuous perception of the thing is not only intuitively full to some extent, but emptily points towards both (a) further features of the scratch and (b) further *experiences* in which those features will be given in the flesh. This last point is important. The empty or indeterminate experience of a part or feature carries with it an anticipation of how that part or feature will manifest itself in intuition. As Husserl says, "what is actually perceived 'points' to a systematic multiplicity of all possible perceptual exhibitings belonging to it harmoniously" (Crisis §47, 162). That might be an exaggeration. What we have in experience, as Merleau-Ponty puts it, is a "presumptive synthesis" which "only operates with certainty and precision within the object's immediate surroundings" (Merleau-Ponty 2012, 72). Nevertheless, horizonal consciousness involves a consciousness of both the objective properties of a thing and the *experiences* in which they would be given. And the structure of intentionality itself might provide an answer why (see §2.2.2). Horizonal consciousness involves both an objectifying awareness of the intended features, and a non-objectifying awareness of the actual past and possible future *experiences* in which they have been or would be given. Because those acts are not occurring now, they must sit within the retentional or protentional scope of the act in question, but on the act- rather than the object-side.

The continuity of this synthesis of experiences is important in the case of real individuals. Keeping track of an object through a temporally extended continuum of experiences is completely different from perceiving that object one day and then again on the next. In the latter sort of case, the *identity* of the object perceived on Tuesday and again on Wednesday is not itself given. We may have exceedingly good reasons for thinking it is the same thing. What, after all, would be the thing we mistake for the Matterhorn, or our own house? But we can see the difference when we turn to other sorts of objects. Socks look a lot like other socks, and the identity of the sock you see on Tuesday and the sock that looks just like it on Wednesday is not itself given. But if you keep track of the sock in a continuous series of perceptual experiences from t1 to t2, the identity of the sock across time is itself given and not merely surmised or inferred.

Each object has its own manifold, but the manifold of every object overlaps with those of others. In thought we can direct our minds to isolated objects. In perception this is a rarity. Perception occurs within a field. The total perceptual field, according to Gurwitsch, has the following invariant structure:

Theme: the object of "focus".

(Gurwitsch 1964, 55)

Thematic Field: everything that is "experienced as" relevant to the theme.
Margin: everything given with the theme, but which has "no material relevancy to it".

(ibid., 56)

When A examines the scratch on the hood of the car, she is also aware of the hood of the car and the car itself. They both belong to the thematic field. The sound of traffic, the feel of the breeze on her neck, and so on belong to the margin. Because of this overlapping of objects in perceptual experience, there is an overlapping of manifolds belonging to each. The manifold belonging to the car overlaps with the manifolds belonging to the car hood and the scratch on the car hood. It is not obvious, however, whether or not it includes them as proper parts. Examining the scratch through a microscope is a way of determining the scratch more closely, but it is unclear whether that experience belongs to the manifold of the car. On the one hand, such an experience on its own would not count as a consciousness of the car. On the other, it could be connected through a synthesis of identification with perceptual experiences of the car, by zooming out or zooming in. It is, in short, unclear whether the manifold of a proper part of W is a proper part of the manifold of W. Note, moreover, that these distinctions are each orthogonal to the distinction between intuitive and empty intentions. In a normal case, some aspects of *each* of the theme, thematic field, and margin will be intuited, and others will be empty. What these correspond to, on the side of the act, are not differences in intuitive content, but differences in the structure of attention (see D.W. Smith 2004b, 184).

What is clear is that different objects have different total manifolds. Exploring the trunk of a car does not count as perceiving more of the hood; the manifold of experiences of the inside of the trunk and the manifold of experiences of the hood share few if any parts in common. And while some perceptual illusions and errors are possible, some are not. Synthesizing the perceptual experience of a car hood with the experience of the interior of a trunk into one continuous experience *of the hood* is not a possible error. This is grounded in the nature of those experiences' contents themselves. As Husserl puts it, "A perception or representation of an elephant and that of a stone can not be fit, according to their essence, into an identification" (TS §10, 24).

Because every object has a different total manifold from every other, different total sets of possible experiences that could be woven together via identity-consciousness, we can say why, when B points his eyes in a certain direction in space, his experience is pre-eminently an experience of the *scratch* rather than everything else co-given with the scratch, such as the car, the car hood, the color of the car hood, and so on. If he is attending to the scratch, there is a manifold of possible experiences that will count as perceiving that thing more closely or determinately. If he is attending to the car hood, or the car, or the color of the car, or even the top half of the scratch—that is, *any-thing* else—a different manifold of possible experiences will count as perceptions of the same thing. From his present experience of the scratch, B can continue to perceive the scratch from other sides and angles. If his theme is the scratch, then in moving his field of view to, say, the side door of the car, he will experience a "difference-consciousness" (see TS §10, 25), a consciousness that what he sees is not the theme of his previous experience.

Because objects are given inadequately, and because they are always co-given with other objects, no *single* experience's *intuitive* content could ever decisively determine what is thematic in an experience. Every experience of a shape is also an experience of a color, for instance, and every experience of a river is also an experience of a part of the river. But we are not stuck with single, punctual intuitive experiences. Experiences are woven together in the temporal flow of both identity- and difference-consciousness. And they are capable of being so unified in virtue of their horizons. What in an experience is thematic, along with its horizons, determines which courses of experience will count as a consciousness of the same thing. If the shape-moment of an object is the theme, then changing its color will not affect the identity-consciousness of that shape-moment over time. If the theme is the color-moment, however, it will. If our thematic object is the river, then we will see more of the same thing as we sail down it. If it is a river-stage, we will not. Again, the perceptual manifold of a statue differs from that of the matter that constitutes it.

Moreover, the manifolds of highly resembling objects will themselves resemble one another highly. A sock and its partner look a lot alike. But they do not have identical manifolds. If I put sock 1 on my left foot and sock 2 on my right, they plainly have different perceptual manifolds. If I were to track the career of sock 1 after taking it off of my foot, I would have a different set of experiences than if I were to track sock 2. Similar remarks go for any two individuals. Once sock 1 and sock 2 go into and emerge from the laundry, I will not be able to tell which is sock 1 and which is sock 2. But my inability to *recognize* the individual I see as sock 1 does not mean I do not *see* sock 1 when I do. We must, again, be mindful of P.F. Strawson's (1959, 60) distinction between relational identification and distinguishing identification. Relational identification—identifying *that* with *sock 1*, say—involves two intentional acts, with two distinct intentional contents. When successful, those contents are of the same object; otherwise not. But merely distinguishing sock 1 from everything else—that is, perceiving it as a distinct and unified spatial object—does not require that I carry out an act of relational identification. And neither does tracking sock 1 through a continuous series of experiences of it. Continuously perceptually tracking an object through space and time is an act of distinguishing identification, not relational identification.

Similar remarks go for properties and natural kinds.[14] The totality of experiential contents that are originary with respect to the color red—the perceptual manifold belonging to it—could not belong to any other color. Nor could the totality of possible experiential contents that are originary with respect to water be of some other stuff. Of course, it is compatible with Husserl's view that some things may superficially resemble others. An orange patch might appear red under certain lights, and pyrite might look like gold under some conditions. And it is compatible with Husserl's view that there are more ways that the color red—to say nothing of water or gold—could possibly present itself to conscious creatures over and above the ways that it presents itself to us.

However, the *totality* of possible ways in which the color red, water, or gold presents itself could not present something else. Something might resemble water in wide variety of ways and contexts. But there is no possible stuff, distinct from water, *all* of whose actual and possible ways of manifesting itself to *any* possible consciousness are identical with those of water. Not only could there be no rational motivation for believing in such stuff—to what could one possibly appeal as evidence?—but we cannot form any contentful conception of such stuff. Just what would it be? In such a case it would not only have all of the same properties as water, but also the same causal powers, since a difference in causal powers would be a way of distinguishing it from water. If such stuff existed, God could be tricked into confusing it with water—though no possible mind of any possible type could possibly set up the trick, or discover that God had been tricked. Such a supposition is as incoherent as supposing that something could feel exactly like pain but not be pain. But as Kripke points out, "To be in the same epistemic situation that would obtain if one had a pain *is* to have a pain" (Kripke 1972, 152; also Chalmers 1996, 147).

Thought experiments involving "Twin Earth" do not put pressure on this position. In Putnam's famous example involving Earth and Twin Earth—one in which the term "water" refers to H_2O, and another just like it except that "water" refers to a different clear liquid XYZ (see Putnam 1975, 139ff.)—water and twin-water plainly have different manifolds. They resemble one another superficially. Far from presenting us with cases of distinct objects whose manifolds are identical, Twin Earth cases presuppose for their intelligibility that the objects are distinguishable, and are in fact distinguished by the person performing the thought experiment and anyone who understands it.[15] Putnam, for instance, writes, "My concept of an elm tree is exactly the same as my concept of a beech tree" (Putnam 1975, 143). But as Searle (1983, 202) points out, as inauthentic as his and Putnam's concepts of elms and a beeches are, it is not true that his, or Putnam's, concept of an elm is the same as his concept of a beech, since one thing they each know about elms is that they are not beeches. Putnam has forgotten how much he knows. It's always good, in cases like this, to remind oneself that we really are conscious of all the things we are conscious of. Every time we successfully contrast something that is "internal" with something that is "external," we are conscious of both of them, and conscious that they are different. And if we are conscious of them as different, then we are carrying out acts that are different, acts with different matters or contents.

That of course doesn't directly address what is genuinely interesting about Twin Earth cases. They aren't designed to show that any two things are absolutely indistinguishable. What they are designed to show is that for some subjects, in some contexts, subjects in indistinguishable mental states can be aware of different objects. The minimal conditions of all Twin Earth thought experiments are these: (a) things on Twin Earth are apprehended in mental states that are subjectively indistinguishable from those which occur on Earth, but (b) those things on Twin Earth are different from the ones on Earth. The subject's mental states are indistinguishable, moreover, because as far as the subjects are concerned their *objects* are indistinguishable. So, for instance, prior to around 1750 Earthlings and Twin-Earthlings did not know that water is H_2O and that twin-water is XYZ. Nevertheless, argues Putnam, their terms "water" referred even then to H_2O and XYZ, respectively.

I think Putnam is right, and that Husserl would agree (see Kroon 2013, 138). The case is similar in a number of relevant respects to the Dan/Stan example from §2.1.4 of the present work. It is similar to all sorts of real-world examples too. To repeat, lots of things look like other things and are easily mistaken for them. In the Dan/Stan case, as we saw, that I mistook Stan for Dan when seeing him does not entail that my perceptual experience was of Dan. It was not: I had a veridical perceptual experience of Stan. My problem was not perceptual. It was a problem of fulfillment: I misidentified Stan, given to me in perception, as Dan.

If we ask why, in this case or in the water/twin-water case, very different things are indistinguishable to the subjects in question, there is a straightforward phenomenological answer. Either (i) the objects are given inadequately, (ii) the subject has a partly or completely inauthentic possession of the relevant concept of that object, or (iii) both. Twin Earth thought experiments don't work in cases where those conditions aren't met. As Kripke's earlier point makes clear, twin pain is just pain—that is, there's no sense of talking about a "twin" in this case. And it's also why the things which work best for Twin Earth thought experiments are individuals and natural kinds, those things with the richest manifolds and which, accordingly, are given the least adequately.

As Steven Crowell (2008, 346–347) points out, in the water/twin-water case, the local liquid is given inadequately to everyone, at least prior to 1750. It has an invisible structure that is responsible for its various properties and causal powers. But it is not just the brute fact that water and twin-water have an invisible structure that explains why the two community's terms refer to different things. In order for the term "water" and its associated concepts

<water> and <twin-water> to pick out different stuffs, the local liquids must be *intended as having further properties* to be discovered. And water likely was so intended, since people bothered examining it further. They wanted to know more about water, which only makes sense on the condition that they intended it as having a nature to be discovered. On Earth, those empty horizons are filled in in a different way than they would be on Twin-Earth. We owe *that* fact to differences between the two environments. But a necessary condition of the fact that the two communities' terms "water" diverge in reference, even prior to the discovery of the nature of water and twin-water, is that the term "water" expresses two concepts that are inauthentically possessed by those communities. Not only are they ignorant of water and twin-water, but they also understand themselves to be ignorant of water and twin-water. Both are intended via empty horizons that specify further features and further possibilities of disclosing them.

6.6 Why Perception is Direct

We have examined the claim that perception can be inadequate. But what of Kevin Mulligan's claim that perception is "entirely direct" (1995, 194)? One reason one might have for *denying* that it is direct is the very fact that it is incomplete or inadequate.[16] That, however, is a mistake. As we saw in §2.1.3, an act A is indirectly of an object O if and only if

(a) A is of O in virtue of being of some other object O*, and
(b) the subject of A takes O* as a representation of O.

An experience can be inadequate and direct. In fact an experience can be completely empty and direct.

Furthermore, to repeat, indirectness is not the same thing as *foundedness* or dependence. Hearing a melody depends on hearing its notes, but we do not necessarily indirectly hear melodies. The individual notes are not, and are not taken to be, *representations* of the melody. More generally, parts of wholes are, except in exceptional cases, not representations of those wholes. Nor is it indirect awareness when the perception of one property depends on that of another. The perception of an object's shape depends upon the perception of its orientation. And the perception of its orientation in turn depends on the perception of its shape. But we perceive both directly, since neither is a representation of the other, and there is nothing else functioning as a representation of either of them. And if there were, say, perspectival properties given in perception along with the intrinsic ones, our consciousness of the intrinsic ones would not thereby be indirect. For that to occur, the perspectival properties would have to be taken as *representations* of the intrinsic properties.

Let's take as our example, again, the scratched car hood. If our perception of it were indirect, then there would have to be some perceived object R that we take to represent it. R either resembles the scratch or it does not. If it does not, then it must function as some sort of *sign* of the scratch, since sign-consciousness is a kind of act in which the relation between the representation and the represented is "contingent" and "external" (LI 6 §26, 741). Even if a sign happens to resemble what it represents—Husserl gives the example of "*A* is a letter of the Latin written alphabet"—that resemblance is not the feature in virtue of which it is a sign (LI 6 §14a, 711).

There are two problems with this proposal. The first is that being aware of an object O by means of intuiting a sign of it, whether that sign is an indication or an expression, is not even a way of intuiting O. We do not intuit, much less perceive, a car just by being aware of a sign of it, whether it's a conventional sign such as the word "car" or a natural sign such as the impression of its tire tracks in fresh snow.

A second problem is that if there were something functioning as a sign, this should be evident. As we saw in §2.1.3, if something functions as a representation of something else for a subject, that is because of the manner in which it is taken up by the subject (see LI 5, Appendix to §11 and §20, 593). For a sign to direct a consciousness to a designated object, it must be taken as a sign of that object. But when we see a scratched car hood, we do not see something that we take as a sign of something else (see Ideas I §43, 76).

This objection holds equally well for the claim that R *does* resemble the scratch on the car. If we are aware of something that does resemble the scratch on the car, and use it as a representation of the scratch on the car, this should be evident. The acts in which we do this are cases of image consciousness. In such acts, as Husserl notes, "the image is immediately felt to be an image" (PICM §12, 28). The reason is that a necessary condition of its functioning as an image is, as in sign consciousness, that it be taken up as an image. As Husserl writes, "Only a presenting ego's power to use a similar as an image-representative of a similar ... makes the image *be* an image" (LI 5, Appendix to §11 and §20, 594). If something does function as an image of the scratch, we should be conscious of it as an image of the scratch. But there does not seem to be any such item in the field of consciousness when we see a scratched hood.

If there were something functioning in that way, moreover, then the familiar rupture of space that occurs in image consciousness *would* occur. The image subject, the thing allegedly perceived, would be located in a space different from, or at least bearing no perceived spatial relations with, the one that we occupy. Note that this rupture even occurs if an image subject is simultaneously intuited in an image and in person. If you are image-conscious of a car hood while also perceiving the car hood itself, it will not appear to you that you are perceiving two car hoods, nor will there be any question which one of the two is genuinely perceived and which is given in an image.

But when B perceives the car hood, no such rupture of space will take place. The car hood is right there, in front of him, in the same general region of space he himself occupies.

What, however, about the emptily and indeterminately intended parts and features of a perceived object? Are they indirectly perceived? It is difficult to see how they could be. Apart from the fact that, once again, there is no directly perceived item in the field of consciousness that is taken to be a representation of them, the more obvious problem with this proposal is that those parts and features are not perceived at all. And so they are not indirectly perceived.

One noteworthy consequence of this position is that any view according to which we only perceive worldly objects indirectly is really a view on which we do not perceive them at all. And that seems to be exactly right. The traditional theory of ideas, and the sense datum theories that succeeded them, never do seem to give us any *perceptual* access to the world at all.

6.7 Qualia and Separatism

On the view presented over the past two chapters, intuitive experiences are essentially of their objects, and it is in virtue of them that empty, conceptual acts are of theirs. That is, the intentional relations that hold among acts and their objects are not contingent. A visual perceptual experience of a car hood, complete with its phenomenal character, doesn't just happen to be of a car hood. It could not have been a perceptual experience of a mountain, a piano sonata, or sandpaper, any more than a thought about a car hood could be of those things. Furthermore, perceptual experiences are both originary and direct. When we perceive an object, something genuinely shows up in our field of consciousness, and what shows up is that very object, not something else that indicates or represents it.

There is a prominent view regarding the nature of perception—and of consciousness generally—which is difficult to reconcile with these claims. According to *separatism*, an experience's phenomenal character and its intentionality are "mutually independent of one another" (Graham, Horgan, and Tienson 2009, 514). Separatism, if true, potentially spells trouble for the account given here. The reason is that if it is true, there does not seem to be any essential connection between what one would consider the most important phenomenological feature of perceptual experience, namely its phenomenal character, and its intentional content.

One common argument in favor of separatism is the argument from the inverted spectrum (Shoemaker 1982). Suppose A and B are qualia-inverted with respect to one another. Red objects look to A the way green objects look to B, and vice versa. This difference makes no difference in their behavior. They both call red things "red" and green things "green." They both obey traffic laws. The story, by now, is familiar.

There is no good reason I can discover to deny that this is possible. But what does it show? According to separatists, it shows that intentionality and phenomenal character can come apart. When A and B say "raspberries are red," they both express the same thought. When they look at a ripe raspberry, they each *veridically* perceive the raspberry to be red. As far as *intentionality* goes, there is no difference. But there is a difference in their experiences, and it's in their qualia or sensations (see Huemer 2001, 67 ff.; Lyons 2009, 50–51). Following Michael Tye, I will understand qualia to be "intrinsic, consciously accessible features that are non-representational and that are solely responsible for [experiences'] phenomenal character" (Tye 2018, §1).

Should we accept that? It is not clear that we should. First, the fact that A and B both agree to the same *sentences* by no means entails that they use those sentences to express the same *propositions*.[17] It is consistent with the thought experiment that when A says "Raspberries are red" she means what B would mean were he to say "Raspberries are green." If they say the same things in the presence of the same things, that could be because they use the same words to express different concepts.

It is also consistent with the thought experiment that instead of A and B having phenomenally different but *veridical* perceptions of the *same* color, A and B have phenomenally different experiences of *different* colors, at least one of which may be *nonveridical*. And there are strong reasons for thinking that they do *not* see the same colors. Suppose A looks at a ripe raspberry and exclaims, "That's my favorite color!" "Mine too," B replies. "And that," A says while pointing to some freshly mown grass, "is my least favorite." "Same here," says B. And so A and B verbally agree: "red is the best, and green is the worst." Do they have the same taste in colors? If the separatist picture above is correct, they do. But they undoubtedly have opposing tastes in *something*, and it seems to me rather obvious that this something is color.

This example is inspired by the following example from Ned Block. He, however, draws the opposite conclusion: "And my daughter at age 7 commented on first hearing the inverted spectrum hypothesis that it explained why some people didn't have purple as their favorite color" (Block 2013, 288). But if it turned out that each of us called our favorite color whatever produced purple* qualia (if such exist) in us, I think it would be more natural to claim that we all have the same favorite color, namely purple. The reason people wouldn't *say* so would be because our respective color terms do not mean the same thing, that is, have the same fulfilling sense.

A and B have different tastes in something. And what they have different tastes in is something that each is aware of intuitively. This means that if we understand colors to be theoretical or unobservable features of objects, they do not have differing tastes in colors. That is probably not the best way to think of colors, however. On the terms of our own experience, colors are given in the flesh. John Campbell, I think, gets it right:

> When you manipulate the color of part of a painting, in order to affect the perceptions of people who look at it, you do not seem to be acting in a hit-or-miss way on some hidden variable or other—a presumed underlying molecular structure, for example. The variable on which you are acting, in order to affect those perceptions, is staring you in the face—it is the manifest color of the thing.[18]

We may be wrong about there even being such properties, or about their being intrinsic properties of objects. But whatever we are conscious of in color consciousness, it is something that shows up in *propria persona* in the experience of color, not a "hidden variable" merely reliably indicated by a quale or sensation. Color is not an unknown something-or-other on the far side of our intuitive experience (see Quilty-Dunn 2013, 305). It shows up in person.

It is open for the separatist to claim that what A and B really have different tastes in are *color sensations* or *qualia*. I find that rather implausible. What A likes is what covers the surface of a raspberry, five feet in front of her. But her sensations don't cover surfaces five feet in front of her. Even if that were right, however, A's and B's experiences still differ intentionally and not *just* phenomenally. The reason is that A and B have different tastes in *what they see*. And since *what they see* sits on the object or right-hand side of the consciousness-of relation, it follows that even if they have different tastes in color sensations or qualia or something besides color, then those things, whatever they are, are *objects* of consciousness. This is a point which at least one defender of qualia, Sydney Shoemaker, acknowledges and adopts. For Shoemaker, both A and B perceive the same color, but they do so in virtue of *perceiving* different "phenomenal properties." "The idea," he writes, "is that we perceive the colors and other secondary qualities of things by perceiving phenomenal properties that are associated with them."[19] But in that case, as Shoemaker acknowledges, their experiences differ intentionally: they have at least partly different objects. If what they like = what they see, and they don't like the same things, then they don't see the same things.

If we ask what cognitive work non-intentional qualia are doing on a separatist theory, beyond imparting a certain glow to experience, then it seems that the *most* they could be doing is serving as signs or indications of something else, presumably in virtue of standing in causal relations to them.[20] As Ned Block puts it,

> An experience has the intentional content of looking red if it functions in the right way—if it is caused by red things in the right circumstances, and used in thought about red things and action with respect to red things rightly.
>
> (Block 1990, 58)

At best, on this conception, qualia are indices of right functioning.

This leads to a further objection. A green* quale can undeniably be caused by, and thereby reliably *indicate,* the color red or the fact that one is causally responding to something that is red. It could carry information that something is red. It could enable one to detect red things. And by the lights of many causal or informational theories of intentionality, such as Block's, that would make the experience itself *of red*. But if a green* quale, or a green* experience, were to count as a *perception* of the color red in virtue of *indicating* it or being caused by it, then it is unclear why *any* experience with any qualitative character whatsoever could not also possibly count as a perception of the color red.[21] There are lots and lots of ways one might detect the color red. Not only could red be detected greenly, it could be detected with the help of an appropriately configured alarm, or a friend bellowing "red" every time something red is nearby. It could be detected by means of experiences with nearly any phenomenal character you choose—the phenomenal character of an experience of hearing a middle C played on a harp, or having an intense itch on one's arm, for example. Similarly, it is conceivable that spinach-between-the-teeth qualia could indicate a scratched car hood.

This, however, seems clearly mistaken. In originary intuition, the object itself is given, and given as what it itself is. This is why, as Husserl writes,

> It is … a fundamental mistake to suppose that perception … does not get at the thing itself, or to suppose that the thing is not given to us in itself and in its being-in-itself.
>
> (Ideas I §43, 76)

The separatist qualia theory commits just this mistake. It takes us to perceive something that differs radically from what is given in the flesh. But when we treat perception as being of something which does not even appear, something hiding behind any possible number of indicators or signs, we are violating "the sense that lies in the very essence of experience and is proper to it, namely the sense of a thing's being given" (Ideas I §52, 94–95). If the color red could be the object of experiences as different as those with red* or green* or itchy* or spinach-between-teeth* qualia, then the color red is precisely not "given to us in itself and in its being-in-itself." Only the qualia are. But in that case *they* are perceived, and the color red is not. If this brand of separatism is true, we detect colors, but we don't see them.

This leads to one final objection to separatism, and that is that it could not possibly be true of intentionality all the way down. According to the separatist, the phenomenal character of our experience of colors can come apart from the intentionality of such experiences. We can perceive the color red while experiencing red* or green* qualia. But what are we to say of our consciousness of those qualia themselves? Could the intentionality of our originary consciousness of *them* come apart from the phenomenal character of that consciousness? Could we be originarily, intuitively conscious of a red* quale by means of green** quale? How about a pleasurable quale by means of an agonizing one? It is hard to see how that would be possible. At some point, intentionality has to involve things showing up as they themselves are, and not just as signs or indications of something else. If something does show up as an indication or sign of something else—such as the words on this page—it itself must *also* show up as what *it* is. And something's showing up as what it is is just what perception itself is.

6.8 Conclusion

In this chapter we explored the distinction between adequate and inadequate intuition, and tried to make sense of the intentional structure of perceptual acts in virtue of which inadequate intuition is possible. I have also argued that perception is, despite its inadequacy, intentionally direct, and argued against separatism regarding perceptual experience. In the next chapter, I will argue that the perception of worldly objects is not only sometimes inadequate, but that it is essentially inadequate.

Notes

1 PAS, 110; also see FTL §86, 209.
2 PAS, 110; also see FTL §59, 158.
3 PICM, 546; also see Brough 2005, LV.
4 PAS, 58; also Ideas I §42, 75.
5 A.D. Smith 2008, 324; also see Kelly 2008, 684; Cairns 2013, 124; Jansen 2015, 62.
6 LI 6 §14b, 714; also see TS §18, 48 and PAS, 44. For an alternative to the traditional horizontal account offered here, see Bower 2014.
7 See Sellars 1978, §16. Thanks to Jake Quilty-Dunn for making me aware of this passage.
8 TS §18, 47; also Mulligan 1995, 194.
9 As Matthew Bower (2017, 1773) notes, the horizon is also a kind of "sense" or content. We will examine reasons in Chapter 8 to deny that it is *conceptual* content.
10 PP §35, 139. Also see Smith & McIntyre 1982, 240 and Christensen 1993, 760. For a good discussion of the horizon, see Christensen 2013, section III. For two recent phenomenological works that discuss horizons in detail and rightly place them center-stage in understanding intentionality, see Yoshimi 2016 and Madary 2017.
11 EJ §21a, 88; also Reinach 1982, 326–327.
12 TS §30, 83. Also see A.D. Smith 2008, 326ff. for an excellent discussion.
13 TS §10, 24. Also see A.D. Smith 2008, 326.
14 I am indebted to David Kasmier for his insights on this. See Kasmier 2015.
15 See Searle 1983, 202–203.
16 See Noë 2004, 85 and Schellenberg 2008, 58, for what seems to be the view that we perceive intrinsic properties indirectly.
17 See Harman 1990, 47ff. for a discussion of some of the possibilities here.
18 Campbell 2005, 107; also see Johnston 2006, 264.
19 Shoemaker 2000, 251. Shoemaker's view is an attempt to reconcile intentionalism and the qualia view.
20 A possibility noted by C.I. Lewis (1929, 75). If they do less than that, then they are simply irrelevant to perception or to knowledge. See Johnston 2006, 242 on the "Wallpaper View" and Lyons 2009, 51.
21 See A.D. Smith 2002, 74 for related worries.

Recommended Readings

Burge, Tyler. 2010. *Origins of Objectivity.* Oxford: Oxford University Press.

Husserl, Edmund. 1997. *Thing and Space.* Richard Rojcewicz, trans. Boston: Kluwer Academic Publishers.

Husserl, Edmund. 2014. *Ideas I: Ideas for a Pure Phenomenology and Phenomenological Philosophy.* Daniel O. Dahlstrom, trans. Indianapolis: Hackett. Especially relevant is the Second Chapter of the Second Section (§§33–46).

Gurwitsch, Aron. 1964. *The Field of Consciousness.* Pittsburgh: Duquesne University Press.

Madary, Michael. 2017. *Visual Phenomenology.* Cambridge: The MIT Press.

Merleau-Ponty, Maurice. 2012. *Phenomenology of Perception.* Donald A. Landes, trans. New York: Routledge.

Smith, A.D. 2002. *The Problem of Perception.* Cambridge: Harvard University Press.

Yoshimi, Jeffrey. 2016. *Husserlian Phenomenology: A Unifying Interpretation.* Cham, Switzerland: Springer.

7 The Essential Inadequacy of Perception

In the previous chapter, I argued that perception is direct, and that it can be and often is inadequate. In this chapter I will argue that it is *essentially* inadequate.[1] As Husserl puts it,

> it is already evident that we cannot speak of an adequate perception of a thing in the sense of an appearance of it which, as absolute givenness, would leave nothing more open, no possibilities of re-determination, enrichment, or more precise determination.

> (TS §37, 108)

As we will see, however, the issue is complicated by Husserl's inclusion of sensations and/or "profiles" in the perceptual act. Similarly, Alva Noë maintains that perception is *"virtual all the way in"* (Noë 2004, 193), essentially involving both presence and absence. But his position regarding perspectival properties, discussed in §7.2 below, seems to stand in tension with that claim.

It might seem incredible that perception is essentially inadequate. We've already seen how perception can, thanks to the contribution of empty and indeterminate horizons, be inadequate. What's puzzling, though, is that it could be essentially inadequate, inadequate through and through. How can something be perceived inadequately unless something else is perceived *adequately*? Let us call the view that this must occur the Principle of Adequacy:

PA: If S perceives O, then S perceives something adequately.[2]

Is this right? One way to find out is to go on a hunt for the adequately given.

This hunt will be rather involved. The payoff, though, is that in addition to having further opportunities to explore the character of perceptual experience, we will undermine the invidious contrast between our perception of ordinary objects, on the one hand, and the allegedly superior perception of something else, on the other. A quite natural thought is that if our perception of ordinary things is inadequate, and our perception of something else is adequate, then the former kind of perception is not *really* perception in the strict sense, but at best is only called "perception" in a metaphorical or extended sense.

Perhaps what we perceive in the strict sense is an appearance, or a two-dimensional colored patch, or a profile. This, however, is likely a mistake. The inadequate perception of worldly objects is as good as worldly perception gets. There are not adequate givens that are perceived in a more genuine or authentic manner.

7.1 The Sense Datum Theory

One theory that definitely conforms to the Principle of Adequacy is the sense datum theory, discussed already in §6.1. I will understand the sense datum theory to encompass most versions of the theory of ideas, according to which the objects of perception are mental particulars or mental images of some sort. I take the theory of ideas to simply provide an answer to the question of precisely what sense data are (see Price 1950, 19 on the neutrality of the term "sense-datum").

One of the better known arguments for sense data is the argument from perceptual relativity, an argument which, as Berkeley points out, applies to both "secondary" qualities such as color and sound and "primary" qualities such as shape and motion (Berkeley 1975b, §§11–15). I will focus on Bertrand Russell's presentation of the argument.[3] Russell asks us to consider the appearance of a table and its properties from different perspectives. Beginning with its color, he writes,

> Although I believe that the table is "really" of the same colour all over, the parts that reflect the light look much brighter than the other parts, and some parts look white because of reflected light. I know that, if I move, the parts that reflect the light will be different, so that the apparent distribution of colours on the table will change.
>
> (Russell 1999, 2)

Concerning its shape, Russell makes the following observations:

> If our table is "really" rectangular, it will look, from almost all points of view, as if it had two acute angles and two obtuse angles. If opposite sides are parallel, they will look as if they converged to a point away from the specta-tor; if they are of equal length, they will look as if the nearer side were longer.
>
> (Russell 1999, 3–4)

Since, Russell argues, the table appears to be all of these different and incompatible colors and shapes, and since it is arbitrary to pick any one of them as the "real" one, none of them can claim to be the real one (ibid., 2).

To get a better handle on Russell's argument regarding the shape of the table, consider this reconstruction:

1   The way a table looks to be shaped changes with changes in my perspective.
2   If the way a table looks to be shaped changes with changes in my perspective, then the shapes I see change with changes in my perspective.
3   Therefore, the shapes I see change with changes in my perspective.
4   If any shape I see is the shape of the real table, then all of the shapes I see are shapes of the real table.
5   Not all of the shapes I see are shapes of the real table.
6   Therefore, none of the shapes I see is the shape of the real table.

This argument has one rather odd feature. If it were really true that the *real* table appears to have different shapes from different perspectives, then (a) the real table would appear, and (b) our experience of *it* would be nonveridical. But Russell does not adopt this view. Instead of saying that we see the real table nonveridically, he concludes that we see something else, a sense datum or collection of sense data, veridically. In fact, it's clear on Russell's view that we do not see the real table *at all*. On his view, perceptual experience not only *includes* something adequately given. It is *confined to* the adequately given. But then it is false that the real table appears to be different in shape, since *it* does not appear at all.[4] And so, as so often happens in discussions of perception, what would on Russell's terms have to be a set of nonveridical experiences of one thing (the real table) is replaced with a set of completely veridical experiences directed upon something totally different (a collection of sense data).

The undeniable fact to which Russell draws our attention is that something or other appears differently under different conditions. What he says, though is that this something "appears to be of different colours from different points of view" (Russell 1999, 2), and that "what we see is constantly changing in shape as we move about the room" (ibid., 4). That is, Russell goes beyond the obvious claim that the color and shape appear differently to the claim that they *appear to be different* (see Allen 2016, 32 and Hopp 2011, 79).

Do they? Is the first premise correct? Do the parallel sides of a table appear to converge, as Russell says? To many, the sides look to be parallel and receding into the distance, to be *"parallel in depth"* (Merleau-Ponty 2012, 272), just as they in fact are. What appears to change is not the shape or size of the table, but my distance from and orientation to the table.

Russell claims that the change in shape is a discovery we will make if "we try to draw" (Russell 1999, 3). If a skilled artist manages to depict how the table appears from the point of view of someone sitting at its end, she will draw converging lines to represent its parallel sides. She will draw a regular trapezoid on a two-dimensional surface. Does it follow that the table looks trapezoidal and two-dimensional? It does not. The fact that the table looks like something which *is* trapezoidal and two-dimensional does not mean that it *looks* trapezoidal and two-dimensional. In order to get that conclusion, the table would have to look like something that *looks* trapezoidal and two-dimensional (Hopp 2013, 820). And when a skilled artist manages to produce something that does look like a table whose sides recede into the distance, the shape she produces does *not* look trapezoidal and two-dimensional, even though it is.[5] A convincing depiction of a table, despite being trapezoidal, looks similar to the way a rectangular table looks—that is, like an "oriented rectangular surface," some of whose parts are closer to the viewer than others (Jagnow 2008, 62). The image would most closely resemble the table if it were a trompe l'oeil image. But the reason such images look so realistic is not because they make things appear two-dimensional. That's what art lacking in verisimilitude does. It consists, rather, in the fact that they do *not* look two-dimensional. As A.D. Smith puts it, "to say of a painting that it is *trompe l'oeil* is to say that it *looks* three-dimensional."[6]

7.2 Perspectival Properties

The position that things look flat makes the wrong predictions about the visual look of things, including realistic two-dimensional images (see Siewert 1998, 229ff.). Many of the criticisms of the sense datum view therefore apply to a more recent family of views that partly endorse the sense datum theory's phenomenological descriptions of experience, but also maintain that we can perceive real tables and their intrinsic properties. Alva Noë, for instance, writes that a plate tilted away "looks to be circular," but adds, "*and* it looks elliptical from here (it really does)."[7] Its ellipticality (from here) is a perspectival property, or "P-property," which Noë characterizes as "the apparent shape and size of objects" (Noë 2004, 83). Perception involves both intrinsic and perspectival properties showing up.

This position is certainly an improvement over the sense datum theory, which cannot make sense of our perceiving ordinary physical objects at all. However, it inherits many of the same problems. One problem with the view that the plate has an elliptical P-shape, or looks "elliptical from here," is that the plate also appears to be round *from here*. As Charles Siewert puts it, "If I experience the plate as constant in shape as it turns, surely it is still 'from here' that I thus experience it" (Siewert 2006, 7). If that's right, then "round" is a perfectly good answer to the question how the plate looks *from here*.

Further problems arise when we ask how we are to determine which P-shape is presented in visual perception. The answer, according to Noë, is that "The P-shape is the shape of the patch needed to occlude the object on a plane perpendicular to the line of sight" (2004, 83). So, a round plate tilted away will have an elliptical P-shape because it would require an ellipse to occlude it on a plane perpendicular to the line of sight. As Søren Overgaard points out, there is obviously something "uniquely important" about planes perpendicular to the line of sight. But once the perception of depth is recognized, it's not easy to see what that might be (Overgaard 2010, 282, n. 22).

And depth perception must be recognized even by someone who endorses this view. The claim that things look flat is by no means equivalent to the claim that they do not appear to be in depth, for two reasons.

First, and most obviously, flat things, such as walls and mirrors and properly hung paintings, are seen to be some distance away. Even if the space within an image does not appear to contain depth, the image-object itself is seen to be some distance away from you, the viewer. Second, when objects appear to be located on planes, their parts will appear to be *different* distances away. If everything looks the *same* distance away, then everything must appear to be on the inside of a sphere centered on the eye(s), as Thomas Reid holds regarding "visible figure."[8] And if we cannot perceive distance at all, then what appears would have to appear to be on the eye. But things do not appear to be either on the inside of a sphere or on our eye.

It might be responded that there is something distinctive about seeing a shape from head-on rather than obliquely. That is the point of view from which a shape achieves its optimal appearance, where we get the "maximal grip" on it.[9] It is the point of view in which the shape of a thing is most clearly distinguished from other shapes.[10] That is correct. But things present their optimal appearances from optimal perspectives, and an optimal perspective is still a perspective. Or rather: when perception is veridical and an object is given from an optimal perspective, it is given *as from* an optimal perspective. When we say a round thing tilted away looks elliptical, what we mean is that it looks the way ellipses do when seen from head on, that is, from an optimal perspective. But P-properties, like sense-data, do not present themselves as from perspectives. They have only one way of appearing. If you try to get a closer look at the plate's P-shape by rotating it, or its P-size by stepping closer, you will thereby be confronted with a different P-shape and P-size. Furthermore, there is no reason to think that when a round thing is presented from a non-optimal perspective, it looks like an ellipse presented from an optimal perspective. On the contrary, it is part of the phenomenological character of a veridical experience of a round plate tilted away that its shape is seen from a non-optimal perspective, and that it could be seen better from head-on (Kelly 2010).

7.3 The Perception of Depth

We might chalk up the errors above to the view that we either cannot perceive depth, or that we only perceive depth indirectly or inauthentically. For some time, many philosophers and psychologists believed, in the face of what one would have thought is empirical and phenomenological evidence about as conclusive as any to be found, that we cannot see depth. The reasons for this are almost always non-phenomenological. Berkeley, for instance, argues that we cannot see depth because a line of light projects only a point on our eye, and we cannot gather how long that line might be based on such a stimulus

(Berkeley 1975a, §2, 7). In the same way, A.D. Smith (2000, 488) points out, you cannot tell how long a sharp stick is if someone pokes you with it. But, as Smith explains at length, seeing is not like getting poked with a stick. We have two eyes, for starters, and they manage to cooperate with one another. We can also move. And it turns out that there are numerous visible objects and visual features of our experience that enable us to determine both the relative and the absolute distance of things. And while it may or may not be true that newborns and the newly sighted do not see depth, that would not entail that we do not, any more than the inability of a newborn to digest honey or read the paper entails that we do not.

Some of the factors that make depth perception possible are not in the field of consciousness. We are not, for instance, normally consciously aware of the disparity in retinal stimulation ("images") that makes stereoscopic vision possible (see A.D. Smith 2000, 492). Many factors involved in depth perception, however, are in plain view and play a role in depth perception because they are—though we often do not attend to them or conceptualize them. There is, for instance, the visible angle of the object, how many degrees of your visual field it takes up. That is not nearly sufficient to tell how large or how far away something is, of course—visual angles are determined by size and distance together, not one alone—but there are others.

For instance, sometimes a portion of one object occludes the parts of another. If you look at the scene in front of you, hold up your hand in front of your eyes, and then move it slowly to the left, it will not look like a two-dimensional sense datum is being erased. It will look like a hand is situated *between* you and the scene. As the hand marches out of the left of your visual field, the scene behind it will gradually come back into view. This is texture deletion and accretion (Palmer 1999, 229). Textures also become, as a rule, denser with distance (Gibson 1986, 164–165). The horizon intersects objects at the height of one's eye, ensuring that an object cut in half by the horizon for a person whose eyes are six feet high is 12 feet tall, no matter how large or small the angle it subtends in one's visual field (Chemero 2009, 108).

Motion expands the field of what we can perceive dramatically. Motion parallax ensures that nearby objects move more rapidly through the visual field than distant ones (Palmer 1999, 225). Thanks to visual parallax, objects closer than where we fix our gaze will move in the opposite lateral direction as our heads in our visual field, while objects farther away will move in the *same* lateral direction as our head (Shapiro 2011, 64)—a powerful way of telling what is in front of what. As we learn to see, we also learn how the appearances of things vary with movement (Noë 2004). A solitary, stationary eye getting jabbed by rays of light might not be able to see depth, especially if it is united to a consciousness unable to synthesize appreciable fragments of time into one ongoing present and is instead stuck with punctual atoms of sensation. But, as J.J. Gibson's work makes clear, an eye that belongs to a moving organism, which has another eye as its partner, who lives in and through time and not merely at points of time, and which is responsive to variant and invariant features of its environment, is not similarly compromised.[11]

Sometimes the features discussed above are called "cues" to depth. Gibson rightly opposes this term, since it suggests that we originally perceive in two dimensions and require *further* information for the third, that the perception of depth is something over and above direct perception itself (see A.D. Smith 2001, 504). "If *depth* means the dimension of an object that goes with height and width, there is nothing special about it" (Gibson 1986, 148). And it does go with height and width. Look at two objects on opposite sides of your visual field. Now walk over to the one on the right, and take a look at the one that was on the left. It will, if all goes normally, appear to be about the same distance in front of you that it previously appeared to be to the left of the other object. "Height becomes depth when the object is seen from the top, and width becomes depth when the object is seen from the side" (Gibson 1986, 148). Merleau-Ponty (2012, 268) adds that something can only function as a "sign" of depth if we already know what depth, and with it space, is. But since perception is the original way of finding out what space and depth are in the first place, it must already have been given without the aid of signs.

Depth perception is the great enemy of adequate givenness (see Siewert 1998, 231). There is a certain plausibility to the idea that two dimensional objects can be given adequately—provided we neglect that they can be seen upside down, and also neglect that there is a space between us and the surfaces on which they are located, a space that can in principle be occupied and afford closer or further views of things. As Merleau-Ponty puts it, "breadth can, at first glance, pass for a relation between things themselves in which the perceiving subject is not implicated" (2012, 267). But there considerably less plausibility in the idea that something given in depth can be given adequately. Depth is "the most 'existential'" of dimensions because "it clearly belongs to perspective and not to things" (ibid.). It shows, to use Merleau-Ponty's language, that I am an inhabitant of space in addition to being a perceiver of space (see 2012, 140). And as an inhabitant of the same space that contains the objects I see, I can move in it and see those things from other perspectives (ibid., 141). If the table is presented as having a far side, it could be perceived from that side rather than this one. And it will appear differently, because that perspective will bring different features and relations to givenness.

7.4 Sensations

Let us turn back to the quest for the adequately given component of perception. Neither sense data nor P-properties fit the bill. Perhaps, then, we should turn to something else, *sensations*. Treating perception as a process of doing something or other with sensations is a time-honored strategy, one that Husserl takes over and makes his own. Perception, on Husserl's "Auffassung-Inhalt" account, consists of the interpretation (Auffassung) of intrinsically non-intentional sensory or "hyletic" content (Inhalt).[12] In perceptual experience, sensuous material is "in a certain manner 'interpreted' or 'apperceived', and ... it is in the phenomenological character of such an animating interpretation of sensation that what we call the appearing of the object consists."[13] In Husserl's view, especially in his early work, sensations are involved in every act of sensory perception. Sensations, moreover, are supposed to be adequately given. If that is right, then it seems that the Principle of Adequacy must be correct.

The problem with this reasoning, however, is that it confronts us with a dilemma. On the one hand, sensations are not among the objects of perception.

> Sensations, and the acts "interpreting" them or apperceiving them, are alike experienced, but they do not appear as objects: they are not seen, heard, or perceived by any sense. Objects, on the other hand, appear and are perceived, but they are not experienced.
>
> (LI 5 §14, 567)

What is *experienced*, on Husserl's view, sits on the left-hand side of the consciousness-of relation. And that's where sensations are. But since sensations are not *perceived*, they are not perceived adequately.

On the other hand, much of what Husserl says about sensations commits him to placing them on the right-hand side of consciousness. The problem in that case, however, is that what he calls "sensations" are not adequately given. In either case, the presence of sensations in perception does not support the Principle of Adequacy. Moreover, there are good reasons to reject Husserl's account of sensations and their role in perception entirely.

We can get a better sense of what Husserlian sensations are by looking at the work they are supposed to perform. Consider the case of color perception. According to Husserl, we must distinguish "the colour-sensation and the object's objective colouring" (LI 5 §2, 537). To convince us of the difference, he reminds us of "the readily grasped difference between the red of this ball, objectively seen as uniform, and the indubitable, unavoidable projective differences among the subjective colour-sensations in our percept." He then adds that this is "a difference repeated in *all* sorts of objective properties and the sense-complexes which correspond to them."[14] So, we should expect to find size-and shape-sensations, texture-sensations, tone-sensations, and so on for each property in each sense modality.

What is being explained here is clearly perceptual constancy: in constancy something changes, and that is sensation, and something remains constant, and that is the transcendent property, present to us courtesy of interpretation (see Mulligan 1995, 182). This, however, does not square with some phenomenologically patent features of perception. In perceptual constancy, both what changes *and* what remains constant are among the *objects* of perception. Or rather, it is not that we have constancy on the object-side and change on the act-side of the intentional relation. We have both on both. The act of perceiving a shape from head on and from an angle differ because the intrinsic shape is constant and the orientation is different. Both of those features are *perceived*, and there are corresponding *experienced* similarities and differences on the side of the perceptual act. The differences in the appearance of the uniformly colored surface are in our field of vision, among the things that we see. The reason is that we see the light and the shadow. And when we attend to them, it is clear that they were there, in the field of vision, all along. If sensations are in consciousness, then these manners of appearing are *not* sensations. As Herman Philipse puts it, "adumbrations of spatial objects in this sense are spatial themselves. They may be painted or photographed."[15]

The problem with Husserl's account of perception is that it involves a confused conception of sensation. On the one hand, sensations are supposed to resemble the properties that they help present.[16] On the other hand, sensations are constituents of experiences, and experiences are not even spatially extended (Ideas I §41, 73). Husserl is quite clear that the experience's "sensed color" could not be identical with the object's "perceived color" (TS §14, 37). But nowhere is it made clear why the former is not just another *color*, something perceptible by sight. On the contrary, Husserl routinely says things that invite us to treat sensed and perceived colors as the same in generic kind.

A good example of the confusion between objective qualities and sensations is Husserl's claim that "*The same* color appears 'in' continuous manifolds of *shades* of color" (Ideas I §41, 72). Here Husserl appears to identify the sensations that vary with shades of color. But the relation between a color and a shade of that color is the relation of determinable to determinate. A shade of a color is itself a color, a lowest species of it. Its home is not in the act but in the object. And it can only belong to a whole that is extended. Furthermore, determinate shades can *themselves* appear differently while appearing to be the same: not only can a ball look red, it can look to be a determinate shade of red, even when parts of it are in the light and others in the shade. If it appeared to be of different shades, it would appear to be of different colors.

Another example comes from Carleton Christensen, who claims, quite rightly I think, that an "elliptical appearance of a circular plate I am perceiving from the side" is another good example of a Husserlian sensation (Christensen 2013, 112). But, first, anything elliptical is extended in space, and experiences are not. Furthermore, as in the color case, ellipses themselves are given inadequately, since it is possible to see any ellipse from a different perspective. If these are good examples of Husserlian sensations—and they are—then such sensations are both objects of perception and not adequately given.

There are further problems with construing what varies in cases of perceptual constancy as sensations on the side of the act of perceiving. P.M.S.

Hacker provides a nice list of *"sensations proper."* They include "such things as aches, pains, tickles, tingles, twinges, nausea, heartburn, erotic sensations, itches, and prickles" (Hacker 1987, 68). Max Scheler agrees. Sensations "in the strict philosophical sense," he writes, "are only those contents whose appearance or disappearance makes for some kind of variation in our own bodily condition, for example, hunger, thirst, fatigue, etc." (Scheler 1973b, 203). Hacker goes on to note a number of their salient features. Here's a partial list:

- They have a felt bodily location (1987, 68).
- There is no organ of sensation (ibid., 69).
- They have "degrees of intensity" (ibid.).
- They "belong to the category of the hedonic," and can be pleasant, unpleasant, or somewhere in between (ibid., 70).
- They "are had or felt, but not *perceived*" (ibid.).

Husserl's perceptual sensations have *none* of these features, not even the last. Neither do "profiles" or adumbrations of spatial objects, which Husserl identifies with the "data of sensation" (Ideas I §41, 73). Such things do not have a felt bodily location, a degree of (felt) intensity, a hedonic character, and they are perceived visually rather than felt.

In light of all of this, it is not surprising that so many phenomenologists repudiate Husserl's Auffassung-Inhalt theory of perception. Johannes Daubert locates hyletic data "in the transcendent sphere of objects" (Schuhmann and Smith 1985, 776). Scheler, anticipating Merleau-Ponty, writes:

> It would be basically erroneous to answer that the perspectival side of the cube is given, or even that "sensations" of it are given. The "given" is the cube as a whole—as a material thing of a certain spatioformal unity that is not split up into "sides" or "perspectival aspects".
>
> (Scheler 1973a, 55–56)

Roman Ingarden (1976, 45 and 62) prefers the view that only the ego and its experiences are really immanent to consciousness, and that sensations and profiles are transcendent. Merleau-Ponty begins the main text of *Phenomenology of Perception* with an attack on sensations (2012, Introduction, Chapter I). Among other things, he points out that "The determinate quality by which empiricism wanted to define sensation is an object for, not an element of, consciousness" (ibid., 7). Gurwitsch rejects the sensation-interpretation theory entirely in favor a Gestalt-theoretic account (Gurwitsch 1964, 265–267). And Sartre famously writes:

> By endowing the hyle with the characteristics of a thing and the character-istics of consciousness, Husserl believed he could facilitate the passage from

one to the other, but he succeeded only in creating a hybrid being that consciousness rejects, and which cannot be part of the world.

(2018, 20)

We can see Husserl give them both characteristics when he speaks of "immanently sensed colors" which, despite varying, allow us to perceive "an identical spatially extended body-color" (PAS, 54). Colors, somehow, exist on both sides of an act of perceiving colors. And therein lies the problem. Husserl's hyletic data or sensations cannot be "part of the world" because they are supposed to be adequately given, intentionally immanent, and nothing in the world has that character. And they cannot be part of consciousness because the things Husserl actually cites as examples of sensations, at least in the case of visual perception, are not constituents of acts at all. They are objects of our awareness, features of spatial things and their environments. And they are both really and intentionally transcendent.[17]

7.5 Profiles

Perhaps, though, some sense perceptible properties and objects *can* be intentionally immanent. If so, then perhaps the Principle of Adequacy is correct after all. We could attempt to develop such an account on the basis of a remark made by Hermann Philipse. After pointing out, quite rightly, that the things Husserl identifies as profiles or "adumbrations" are not experiences, but are, on the contrary, extended and can be photographed, Philipse suggests that "photographs are essentially of adumbrations" (1995, 259). To pursue a line of reasoning that Philipse does not: if adumbrations or profiles are *intentionally* immanent, and since photographs are both of spatial objects and spatial themselves, this would be a counterexample to the claim that all spatial properties are intentionally transcendent. Perhaps we should think of what is adequately given in perception along the lines of what is given in a photograph. Photographs, one might think, capture how things look, at a time, in perception. If what is given in photographs is adequately given, then how things look in perception at a time is adequately given as well.

In Chapter 2, §2.1.1, as we saw, there were three items which must be intuitively present in order for image consciousness to occur: the physical thing (Dingbild), the image object, and the image subject. The physical thing is not given adequately. What about the image subject and image object? Let's suppose that after hearing A's report that there's a scratch on the car hood, B requests evidence but refuses to leave his armchair. A instead hands him a photograph of the hood.

Because B is interested in the car's scratch rather than the photographic medium, he will likely attend to the image subject. But is the image subject an adequately given profile? There are some good reasons to think so. The image subject cannot be explored or seen from other points of view. If B turns the photograph to the side, he will not thereby see the hood from a different perspective, nor will A and B see it from different perspectives when they simultaneously look at the photograph from different angles or distances.[18]

The fact that other sides of the image subject cannot be seen does not entail that it is not intended as having them, however. One of the interesting features of image consciousness, as many have noted, is that the image subject is cast into a space that bears no perceived relations with one's own. "The real world of present experience is torn open and an other world comes to the fore."[19] And that "other world" encompasses a space that is not occupied by you, the perceiver (Wiesing 2011, 245). This severing of spaces comes about through a kind of conflict (PICM, 51). The conflict consists, most basically, in the fact that the image subject does not fit with the surroundings. A picture of Pike's Peak fits on a wall. Pike's Peak does not. So when you see Pike's Peak on a wall, something's got to give.

If the image subject were adequately given, it would not be the thing that has to give. The conflict that sets it in another space would either not occur at all, or, it if did, would be resolved in its favor. Whatever is adequately perceived is either compatible with whatever else you perceive, or, if not, would win in a conflict with it. If you have a ferocious headache and also see a car in front of you, but somehow learn that only one of those experiences is veridical, there's no question which one has to go. In image consciousness there is conflict over a piece of perceived space. The image subject loses. If it were adequately given, it would win.

Part of what generates the conflict between image object and image subject is that there are divergent horizonal intentions belonging to each. The latter can be fulfilled. The former cannot. A car is not a star; there is no good reason why a really present one couldn't be examined and explored from other perspectives. But the imaged car cannot (Madary 2017, 69). Instead of being presented as an originarily and adequately perceived car-profile, the image subject is instead presented as a non-originarily and inadequately intuited *car*. Image consciousness does not provide a non-perspectival perception of a profile. Rather, it freezes us in a perspective on a transcendent thing that we have no power to alter. The reason one cannot view the image subject from other perspectives is not because it is adequately given. It is, rather, because the inadequacy of the experience is so severe that it cannot be overcome, or not much, by anything one can do in the space one occupies. To see more of the thing, one would have to enter the other space of the picture.

Of all the components of image consciousness, it is the *image object* that has the best claim to be adequately given. John Brough writes that the image object is "exhausted in its appearance" (Brough 2012, 548)—a view that Husserl appears to share. There is no doubt that the image object is given more adequately than a typical image subject. But even it is not given adequately. If it were, then I would take any change in my intuitive consciousness of an image-object to constitute a change in the image-object of which I am conscious. That, however, does not seem to be the case. A detective closely examining a photograph for clues is examining an image-object, hoping and possibly managing to discover features of it that did not appear initially. If a knife is discovered in the image *subject*, that is, the crime scene, that will be because an *image of* a knife is discovered in the image *object*. But if that happens, then the image object was not fully given before the knife-image was discovered. Finally, the image object is not adequately given because its appearance can change with changes in distance and, even more profoundly, with orientation. If you move ten feet away from an image on a wall, or turn it upside down, it will appear differently. But it will not necessarily appear to be different (Dilworth 2005, 172).

If this is right, then the "profiles" which allegedly function in perception cannot be modeled on anything given in image consciousness. Profiles are supposed to be adequately given. But nothing given in image consciousness is adequately given. And of even greater phenomenological interest is that the more adequately an object is given, the *less* it is capable of being an image subject in the first place. There is no possible way to be image conscious of a sensation, for instance, or an experience. Very simple qualities that are barely given from perspectives, such as flavors and odors, are hardly better off.

The reason is that there are two competing demands on image consciousness. One is that the image subject and the image object must be experienced as resembling one another.[20] The other is that they be discernibly different. As Husserl puts it,

> If the appearing image were absolutely identical phenomenally with the object meant, or, better, if the image appearance showed no difference whatsoever from the perceptual appearance of the object itself, a depictive consciousness could scarcely come about. This is certain: A consciousness of the difference must be there.[21]

Suppose, for instance, that A constructs an exact replica of the scratched car hood and brings it into the room. In such a case B might be brought to think about the car hood. At first he may think it *is* the car hood. After learning the provenance of this strange object he might come to know that the hood is scratched. But he will not be image conscious of the car hood. In image consciousness, as we have seen, we undergo a two-pronged experience in which an image-object is intuited directly, and an image-subject is seen in the image object.[22] But B will not see the original car hood *in* the replica, any more than perceiving a sock is a case of image consciousness of its partner.

One reason for thinking so is that the replica will look exactly the same whether or not one knows anything about the original or has any consciousness of it at all. Having one's intentional act terminate in the replica will not affect the way the replica looks. But in the case of genuine images, it does. As we saw in §2.1.3, the consciousness of the image-subject and the image-object are mutually founding. If I am image conscious of a car, the car would not appear to me as it does if the image object did not appear as it does. But the image object would not look the way it does if I did not see a car in it. After all, it *looks like* an image of a car.

Image consciousness necessarily involves a conflict among the horizons of the acts directed upon the image object and the image subject. The only way such a conflict can occur is if those acts are inadequate to their objects. We cannot, therefore, explain inadequate perception in terms of the adequate perception of something like an image plus something else. Rather, image consciousness itself is only possible on the basis of inadequate intuition. *If perception were always adequate, image consciousness would be impossible.* This strikes me as a strong additional reason to reject any theory that treats perceptual experience as always adequate.

7.6 Explaining the Disagreement

Why do an appreciable number of people claim that a tilted plate does looks elliptical, or, in general, that objects somehow look to be two-dimensional and adequately given? As phenomenologists, this should be a question that concerns us. There are a number of possible answers. Part of the explanation might just be that people are reporting what a theory—that what is given in vision are "retinal images," or that it must be impossible to perceive depth, for instance—says must be true rather than what they discover experientially to be the case. This is Gibson's take: "No one ever saw the world as a flat patchwork of colors—no infant, no cataract patient, and not even Bishop Berkeley or Baron von Helmholtz" (Gibson 1986, 286).

Eric Schwitzgebel, while characteristically cautious about reporting on the phenomenological character of his own experiences, definitely inclines toward the view that things neither look flat nor concave (2006, 592). He offers the following hypothesis about why anyone would say otherwise. It is, he ventures, "due to *over-analogizing* visual experiences to flat media such as such as paintings and snapshots" (ibid., 593; also see Gibson 1986, 285), and presents some admittedly inconclusive but certainly suggestive historical evidence for his hypothesis.

Both Gibson's and Schwitzgebel's proposals are likely part of the story. The problem with all of those proposals as complete explanations, however, is that each denies or downplays the actual experiences that many people sincerely report having. The evidence is that some people do, at least some of the time, see round things tilted away as elliptical and things of the same size as looking different in size when they are placed at different distances.

One promising explanation for this is Robert Briscoe's "make-perceive" view. On this view, we sometimes *imagine* or form a mental image of the plate while seeing it. We "imagine its P-shape while viewing the object at the same time" (Briscoe 2008, 479). We perceive the plate as elliptical when "attention is directed to properties of an internally constructed mental image superimposed on the region occupied by the object in one's field of view" (ibid., 480).

Another explanation is that we sometimes suffer, or are able voluntarily to induce, a misperception of the relative depth of the parts of the plate and to visually represent them as being the same distance away. That is, the awareness of ellipticality is brought about through an *illusion* of the relative distance of the plate's parts, bringing in its wake an illusion regarding the intrinsic shape of the plate. This appears to be Merleau-Ponty's view: "When the painter squints, he destroys the organization of the field according to depth" (2014, 321).

Both the make-perceive and illusionist accounts preserve an important phenomenological fact pointed out by Sean Kelly, and that is that we are unable to perceive a plate as elliptical and round at the same time (Kelly 2008, 686). There is one final possible explanation, though, which is compatible with and complementary to those above. Merleau-Ponty claims that a common mistake consists in "deducing the given from what can be provided by the sense organs" rather than describing what is in fact given (Merleau-Ponty 2012, 22; also 33). And one prominent way in which this occurs is that we, and especially philosophers and psychologists, are explicitly or implicitly committed to the "constancy hypothesis," and even engineer our experiences, in the special circumstances of introspection or phenomenological reflection, along make-perceive or illusionist lines to conform to it. Aron Gurwitsch defines the constancy hypothesis as the position that "sense-data depend entirely upon, and are determined exclusively by, the corresponding physical stimuli" (Gurwitsch 1964, 90). According to the advocate of the constancy hypothesis, as Köhler says in his attack on "introspection," "Visual size ... should be proportional to retinal size; changes in retinal shape should be followed by changes in seen shape ... and visual brightness with retinal intensity" (Köhler 1947, 55).

The existence of perceptual constancies is exactly what the constancy hypothesis does not predict. (It is unfortunate that "constancy" is used for both. Perceptual constancies are constancies of the perceived objects and properties across experiences and "stimulations" that vary. The constancies posited by the constancy hypothesis are constant correlations between stimuli and phenomenal experiences. See Mulligan 1995, 191.) But the introspectionist is, according to Köhler, undaunted: constancies are the result of learning, judgment, interpretation, or something else that has polluted the perceptual experience. On this view, normal cognitive maturation is not a matter of learning to perceive better, but of forgetting how to perceive purely. The task of discovering the "true sensory facts" can only take place in a "special attitude," an attitude designed to remove the effects of learning (Köhler 1947, 51). This is the attitude that Merleau-Ponty (2012, 235) calls the "analytic attitude," and it sometimes requires special instruments and laboratory conditions to enact. As he points out, "A white wall that is weakly illuminated, which appears in spontaneous vision as white ... appears gray-blue if we see it through the window of a screen that hides the light source from us" (2012, 320). For the analytic attitude, in this process we recover the "pure" experience we had all along in "spontaneous vision." All along the dimly illuminated white wall looked gray-blue, just as the constancy hypothesis predicts. Similarly, a round plate tilted away will look elliptical if we remove every "cue" for depth—something that can be done by viewing things through tubes, squinting, or even by a concentrated effort to disregard them.[23] And that, according to the introspectionists, is how these things really looked all along.

But, as many have emphasized, there is no reason to think that. Just because an object appears to be F in the special analytic attitude or when conditions have altered, it does not follow that it looked that way all along.[24] Nor does it follow that this is the way it ought to look, or the way it has ever before looked. Instead of discovering through analysis what was lying there the whole time, the introspectionists have produced "rare facts" by means of "an artificial procedure" (Köhler 1947, 51; also 52). And the artificial procedure in question can only discount the role of perceived illumination, distance, orientation, and other contextual and "learned" factors by assuming in advance that they do not play a constitutive role in natural perception. The alleged "sensations" discovered in this process may, instead of being constituents of the original experience, be products of this attitude. As William James puts it, "Consciousness, from our natal day, is of a teeming multiplicity of objects and relations, and what we call simple sensations are results of discriminative attention, pushed often to a very high degree" (James 1952, 146).

The constancy hypothesis, according to Köhler, fails to predict the character of almost all of our natural experiences. The way to save it is to ignore or discount those experiences, and instead appeal to a very special class of experiences whose production requires "attention, more precise instructions, rest, and extended practice" (Merleau-Ponty 2012, 8). The constancy hypothesis can then be vindicated by pointing out that it does correctly predict the character of *those* experiences (Köhler 1947, 45). Apart from the fact that these experiences are clearly not the natural ones, the whole procedure begs the question. The experiences not predicted by the constancy hypothesis are exactly the ones which will be thrown into the pile of experimentally irrelevant experiences, and exactly because they do not verify the principle. An a priori decision in favor of the constancy hypothesis is used as a criterion for admissible experiences, effectively shielding the "hypothesis" from any conceivable empirical or phenomenological refutation. As Köhler puts it,

> Introspectionism follows the orders of an authority to whom the testimony of experience as such means little. This authority subjects direct experience to a screening process, finds most of it defective, and condemns it to corrective measures.
>
> (Köhler 1947, 57)

To top it off, the experiences purified by "corrective measures" are over-whelmingly nonveridical. If a round thing tilted away looks elliptical, or the two portions of the red carpet look different in color, then they do not look to be the way they are.

The constancy hypothesis is very likely false. Whether adherence to it, or something like it, explains the disagreements about how things look is another matter. But I suspect that it likely plays some role.

7.7 Perception without Immanence

As Kevin Mulligan (1995, 190–191) points out, Husserl has sometimes been accused, quite wrongly, of endorsing the constancy hypothesis. Aron Gur-witsch also realizes that Husserl could not, as a phenomenologist, expressly endorse the constancy hypothesis. Phenomenological reflection brackets sti-muli, retinal images, visual systems, and other causal factors that are not given in experience. That is, it does not posit them or appeal to them in its descriptions. But, says Gurwitsch, there are aspects of Husserl's theory that reveal a similar commitment. "It is as though the constancy-hypothesis sur-reptitiously intervenes in phenomenological investigations" (Gurwitsch 1964, 271). The tacitly assumed principle, perhaps, is the Principle of Adequacy or something similar to it (see Philipse 1995, 258)—the view that something must be adequately given and then operated upon by acts or processes of "interpretation." The two are likely not wholly unrelated. Retinal stimulation changes with every change in perspective. If what we perceive or any portion thereof is fixed by that, then it is something that can only be perceived from one perspective. The adequately given, then, corresponds with what changes whenever stimulation changes. It is quite possible to bracket all stimuli but retain their alleged phenomenological correlates, sensations, profiles, or per-spectival properties.

What is common to the sense datum theory, the theory of perspectival properties, and Husserl's theory of sensations is that they all account for the constancy of color, shape, and other sense perceptible properties by appealing to more colors, shapes, and other sense perceptible properties. This strategy is not necessary. There is a difference between the way shapes look from differ-ent perspectives. But, as René Jagnow points out, "this difference is not a difference in perceived shape" (Jagnow 2008, 63). We can specify how a shape appears by saying that it looks round from an angle, or large and at a dis-tance, or by appealing to a number of other features disclosed in the percep-tual field. We can specify how the portions of the red rug look the same insofar as each looks to be the same shade of red, but different insofar as one appears to be in the light and the other in the shade (ibid.).

The Gestalt psychologists, and the phenomenologists most heavily influ-enced by them, including Merleau-Ponty and Gurwitsch, reject the constancy hypothesis along with the phenomenological correlates of stimulations,

Husserl's sensations and hyletic data. On their view, the appearance of a thing is radically underdetermined by punctual retinal stimuli, sensations, or anything else that might be thought to be or correspond to anything adequately given. Instead, the appearance of each sense perceptible thing and property is partly determined by its place within a perceptual field. Shape is the kind of thing which not only exists at a distance and from and an orientation to any other point in space, but can only manifest itself if it is perceived *as at* a distance and *as from* an orientation. And colors are the kinds of things which, if they appear, not only do so under conditions of illumination, but *as of* under conditions of illumination. As Merleau-Ponty puts it,

> The red patch I see on the rug is only red if the shadow that lies across it is taken into account; its quality only appears in relation to the play of light, and thus only as an element in a spatial configuration.[25]

As I open the curtains and the colors appear differently, what changes lies within the field of *what I see*.[26] The same colors appear, but appear differently, because they appear to be under brighter light. We can explain constancy by appealing to the fact that properties such as shape and color always appear in a context, and we are able to keep track of changes in the property and changes in the context in which it appears (Kelly 2001, 606). Even the "special attitude" in which we attempt to isolate these factors does not succeed in doing so. It merely replaces one perceived distance, orientation, or condition of illumination with another. Trying to rid the perception of shape of the perception of distance and orientation is as hopeless as trying to purify the perception of a volume of the perception of timbre and pitch.

What accounts for perceptual constancy, on this view, is not that perception involves "interpreting" adequate givens, whether they are sense data, P-properties, sensations, or profiles. Rather, it is that we are capable of keeping track of changes in the intrinsic properties of things and changes in the circumstances or field in which they are perceived, including the circumstances of our own bodies. We can see how objects and their intrinsic properties remain constant across variations in their environment and variations in us. When one portion of a red carpet is seen under a shadow and another under the light, something is the same and something is different. What is the same is its color. What is different is the perceived presence and absence of the shadow. When a plate is seen from head on and then tilted away, something is constant and something changes. What remains the same is its seen shape, its roundness. What changes is its perceived orientation. Notice that we must appeal, not (just) to the objective illumination or the objective orientation, but to the *perceived* illumination and orientation (see Briscoe 2008, §3). Realistic images induce illusory experiences of depth and color constancy because of the *perceived* orientation and illumination of the figures in them. But there is no need in either case to appeal to any colors or shapes beyond the ones that remain constant, no need to appeal to another kind of color or shape, and no need to appeal to visual sensations or profiles.

Husserl himself emphasizes the holistic character of perceptual experience, especially in his later writings. "For consciousness the individual thing is not alone; the perception of a thing is perception of it within a perceptual field" (Crisis §47, 162). That field consists, most basically, of figures against a comparatively undifferentiated and generally unshaped ground (Merleau-Ponty 2012, 4). "Look at any landscape photo. You see the shape of the things, the mountains, and trees and buildings, but not of the sky."[27] Things, material objects with boundaries, are the principal bearers of shape. And the perception of shape is inseparable from the perception of distance and orientation. "All factors ... which determine orientation must *pari passu* determine perceived shape."[28]

Equally importantly, the perceptual field consists not only of what we consciously apprehend that is in plain view, but what we emptily apprehend that is not. That is, the Gurwitschean distinction between the theme, thematic field, and margin does not identify three items each of which is adequately given. Nor does the field consist of one big adequately given Gestalt, a theme-thematic field-margin configuration. If it did, we could not see how those items can independently vary. Rather, it also involves both an internal and external horizon (Gurwitsch 1964, 237 and 369). The presence of surrounding objects such as trees and houses, the ground and the horizon, the rate at which objects move through your visual field, and so on all contribute to the way a thing looks. And the nonintuitively intended features play a critical role in the structure of this Gestalt-contexture. The car looks like something that has a back, an inside, something that can be entered, explored, looked over. And we repeatedly find that looks are not deceiving in this respect: cars really can be entered, explored, and so on.

Thanks to that, the parts and sides that we see present themselves as parts and sides rather than a complete object, a car-from-here or a car-profile. As Merleau-Ponty writes,

> If the subject moves, these are not signs, but rather sides of the die that appear; he does not perceive projections or even profiles of the die; rather, he sees the die itself sometimes from here, and sometimes from over there.[29]

Just as the car and its properties appear the way they do because of their place within a perceptual field that can be surveyed, navigated, and explored, they appear the way they do thanks to the *non-intuitive* consciousness of their hidden parts and unactualized modes of appearing. As Gurwitsch puts it, "the perceptual presentation cannot be the appearance of a sphere, unless it contains references to the unseen interior" (Gurwitsch 1964, 229). Husserl, despite his doctrine of sensations, clearly agrees, especially in his later works. The various "aspects" that are intuitively given "are nothing for themselves;

they are appearances-of only through the intentional horizons that are inseparable from them" (PAS, 43). Or, as Husserl puts it elsewhere, "What 'authentically' appears is not hereby to be separated from the thing somehow as a thing for itself." What authentically appears, he goes on, "forms a *non-self-sufficient part*, a part that can only have a sensible unity and self-sufficiency in a whole that *necessarily* contains in itself empty components and components of indeterminacy" (Ideas I §138, 274–275).

7.8 Kinesthetic Sensations and Motor Intentionality

If the considerations above are correct, the Principle of Adequacy is false: inadequate perception is not founded on adequate perception. There may be one more role for non-intentional sensations to play in the perceptual process, however. Among the various factors and conditions that enable us to perceive physical things and properties as constant across experiences that differ from one another is the existence and the determinate condition of our own bodies. As I move my head to the right or left while looking at a stationary car, I do not take the car to be moving to the left and to the right (see TS §50, 148). Similarly, we can tell the difference, most of the time, between our hand moving over a stationary object, and that same object moving under our stationary hand. This is possible, in part, because of the awareness we have of our own bodies. Objects are always perceived as being some distance away, up or down, to the left or right or straight ahead—that is, in some portion of an egocentrically oriented space. And they aren't in a space relative to a disembodied mind or to an ego outside the world. Rather, they are perceived by me, the embodied human person, who occupies the very same spatial world that I perceive. "The 'far' is far from me, from my Body; the 'to the right' refers back to the right side of my Body, e.g., to my right hand" (Ideas II §41a, 166).

In his 1907 lectures collected in the volume *Thing and Space*, Husserl distinguishes two kinds of sensations: "presentational" and "kinaesthetic" (TS §46, 135). The presentational sensations are those which we have already discussed. They somehow come to present objective features of things by means of interpretation or apprehension. Kinaesthetic sensations, by contrast, do not undergo any such objective apprehension. They do, nevertheless, "play an essential role in the apprehension of every external thing" (ibid., 136).

Take a case of viewing a stationary object and doing nothing more than moving one's eyes. If, says Husserl, the "kinaesthetic ocular sensation K_1 is at first also constant ... then the visual image i_1 is also constant" (TS §51, 149). If we move our eyes, thereby experiencing a different sensation K_2, the "image" will change to $i2$. For instance, if we move our eyes to the right, the object we see will now be in the left of our visual field. And "If K_2 reverts back to K_1, then so does i_2 into i_1" (ibid.). However, as Husserl notes, individual kinaesthetic sensations and "images" do not bear any necessary connection with one another; they are related "functionally but not essentially" (TS §49, 143). Rather, our eyes, and our whole bodies, are often in the very same positions while our perceptual experience of our environment changes—this happens, for instance, as you drive a car. If I keep my eyes in condition K_1, and the object I perceive moves, I will have K_1 but with a different visual experience. And if the object I see starts to move while I follow it with my eyes, I can have the same visual experience across a sequence of different kinaesthetic experiences K_1, K_2, ...K_n.

It is thanks to such systems of kinaesthetic sensations, and their functional interdependence with other kinds of perception, that objects show up to us at in motion or at rest, and therefore show up as in space and as having determinate spatial features. And while the relation between particular kinaesthetic sensations and particular types of perceptual experiences is non-essential, the relation between kinaesthetic sensations and perceptual experience as a whole is essential. As John Drummond puts it, "Every phase of the perceptual process is correlated to both an appearance of the object and a kinaesthetic situation, i.e., a definite position of the body and the bodily sense organs" (Drummond 1979, 23). Changes in one's visual, auditory, or haptic fields, then, can be due to either changes in the world, or changes in one's own bodily position. Without kinaesthetic sensations, we would be unable to tell which.

Mere oculomotor sensations and the kinesthesis involved in moving one's head are, of course, only the beginning of the story when it comes to our bodily interactions with things. We can also move around a stationary thing, approach it or move away from it, and so on. Husserl offers detailed and ingenious analyses of these and other phenomena. What concerns us, however, is the connection between the K-system and the contents of visual perception. That connection, as we have seen, is a contingent connection among kinesthetic sensations and "images." Regarding its nature, Husserl writes, "we cannot see how contents that possess no unity of foundation stemming from their own proper character could be unified except through association" (TS §51, 149). Husserl then defines association as follows: "the phenomenological fact of a certain appurtenance and of a certain reference of the one to the other, such that the positing or belief in the one motivates belief in the other" (ibid., 150). It's similar to the phenomenological unity we find between a certain sound-pattern and a meaning when we understand words (LI 5 §19, 584).

There is no doubt that felt, motivating connections can be forged among items that do not bear any nomic relation to one another, as the case of words and their referents shows. But there are reasons to doubt that this is how things work in the present case.[30] On this analysis, kinaesthetic sensations are, like all sensations, devoid of any intentionality of their own. Furthermore, they do not undergo the kind of apprehension or interpretation that allegedly endows "presentational" sensations with significance. They are, accordingly, devoid of all reference to anything, any proper meaning or sense or significance. Thanks to association, however, changes in them motivate various changes in visual experience.

This view, however, does not seem to capture the phenomenon. We can conceive of any meaning whatsoever being united to just about any manageable physical marker whatsoever. But we cannot, I think, so easily conceive of any kinaesthetic experience being united with any object-directed perceptual experience. When I move my head to the left, what occurs is a self-initiated movement in and through *space*. I don't just have sensations which are merely contingently connected with how the world shows up for me and which, through association, have been united with visual "images." Turning my head to the left *means* that, in most cases, stationary objects move to the right of my visual field. It is not just as easily conceivable that this same kinaesthetic experience would be associated with objects staying put, or moving to the left, or up or down. Rather, these are relations inscribed in the very sense of these movements. The act of moving one's head may involve various sensations, but is not reducible to any sensation or complex thereof. The movement of my eyes, head, or body is *movement*, and it is through its own meaning as movement that it motivates other ways of appearing.

If what is experienced in kinaesthetic "sensation" is experienced as movement in space, then it is difficult to see how it does not bear within itself a certain significance, one that helps ground an intelligible rather than brute relationship among bodily comportments and exteroceptive experiences. Of course Husserl is correct that moving my head to the left does not imply that I will experience any *particular* "image." But it does make it highly likely, for reasons far deeper than any that could be accounted for in terms of association, that *whatever* is stationary will be displaced to the right in my visual field, that *whatever* is moving to the left in objective space at the appropriate speed will remain centered in my visual field, and so on. These connections between visual experiences and movements *do* seem to "stem[] from their own proper character."

It appears, then, that even kinaesthetic sensations involve intentionality. More specifically, they involve what Merleau-Ponty calls "motor intentionality" (Merleau-Ponty 2012, 112). Changes in kinaesthetic sensations involve changes in one's "body schema," which Merleau-Ponty characterizes as "the global awareness of my posture in the inter-sensory world" (ibid., 102). This awareness is not, Merleau-Ponty stresses, a "positional" one (ibid.). My awareness of my body in perception is not that of one object among others, a spatial object that I can't get away from. Rather, we experience our body as a *subject*, and our awareness of it is non-positional (Thompson 2007, 249–250). That is why, to return to the preface, Gallagher's insight is true: the parts of my body are not close to or far from me, and one reason is that they are parts of *me*. Nevertheless, our bodies are spatial and apprehended as spatial, and changes in our body schema are changes in its spatial configuration. When I move my hand to grab a cup or walk towards the door, these movements are not objects in the field of perception. Nevertheless, these actions have intrinsic and immediate spatial significance. It is part of their sense to be movements in space.

It is because they are bearers of significance that kinaesthetic, bodily experiences such as movement belong to the body schema, and why the body schema is not an awareness of the body as "a system of current positions, but also … as an open system of an infinity of equivalent positions in different orientations" (Merleau-Ponty 2012, 142). Movements as physically different as moving one's eyes to the left, one's head to the left, one's torso to the left, and rotating one's whole body to the left are, with respect to certain tasks such as keeping visual track of a moving object, equivalent, despite the radical difference in bodily sensations that each involves.[31] And they are equivalent because they bear, relative to that task, the same generic *intentional* significance, namely the significance of keeping track of a moving object in space

7.9 Conclusion

If the foregoing is correct, we can directly perceive objects and properties that are intentionally transcendent to the stream of consciousness. It is possible not only to think about, but also to perceive things like scratches on car hoods. And since all perception is intentionally direct, that means it is possible to *directly* perceive things like scratches on car hoods. The fact that they are given from perspectives does not render our experience of them indirect, nor does it mean that we are more intimately aware of something else instead. We see car hoods from perspectives inadequately, not car-hoods-from-perspectives, sense data, P-properties, sensations, profiles, or the ineffable given adequately.

Notes

1 See TS §35, 101, whose title is "The field as finite means of presentation. The perception of things as necessarily inadequate." Also see Mulligan 1995, 194; Noë 2004, 193, A.D. Smith 2008, 324, Jansen 2015, 62, and Madary 2017, 71.

2 This is closely related to what Hermann Philipse calls the "principle of immanence," according to which "the primary data of outer perception are really immanent in consciousness" (1995, 258), except that his principle pertains to real rather than intentional immanence. It is very distinct from what Daniel Dahlstrom (2018, 225) calls Husserl's "principle of adequate givenness" (see Ideas I §142, 283).

3 See J. Smith 2016, 68–70 for a good discussion.

4 See Somerville 2006, 49, who presents a much more sophisticated version of the same objection to Hume's famous presentation of the argument from perceptual relativity (Hume 1993, 161).

5 See Jagnow 2008, 62 and Overgaard 2010, 275–276.

6 A.D. Smith 2000, 487. Also see Merleau-Ponty 2012, 274: "The perspectival drawing is not at first seen as a sketch on a plane, and subsequently arranged in depth."

7 Noë 2004, 164. Also see Tye 2000, 79.

8 Reid 1997, 103ff. Also see Schwitzgebel 2006, 592.
9 Kelly 2010, 152; also Merleau-Ponty 2012, 315–316.
10 See Koffka 1935, 231.
11 For a very helpful overview of Gibson's work, see Käufer and Chemero 2015, Chapter 7.
12 "Hyletic data" is the preferred term by the time of *Ideas I*. See §97. I discuss some of the problems with Husserl's theory in Hopp 2008a.
13 LI 5 §2, 539. Also see LI 5 §14 and LI 6 §6, 688.
14 LI 5 §2, 538. For a recent excellent discussion, see Marchesi 2015.
15 Philipse 1995, 258. Mohanty (1997, 42) discusses Roman Ingarden's objections to similar effect. See Ingarden 1976, 40–41, 45. For a sophisticated defense of Husserl's hyletic data, on the other hand, see Williford 2013.
16 LI 6 §26, 741; Willard 1984, 224.
17 See Ingarden 1976, 40–41, 45 for a similar criticism.
18 Wiesing 2014, 148. Also see Wollheim 1980, 215–216; Noë 2012, 84; Madary 2017, 69.
19 Aldea 2013, 378. Also see PICM, 570; Currie 1995, 66; Cohen and Meskin 2004, 198; Matthen 2005, 315; Brough 2012, 560–561.
20 PICM, 31; Hopkins 1998, 48.
21 PICM, 22. Also see Hopkins 2010, 152; Brough 2012, 557–558; Cobos 2013, 149; Kurg 2014a, 67–68.
22 See PICM §12, 27: "*in the image* one sees the *subject*." The language of "seeing in" is due to Wollheim (see 1980, 213). Also see Brough 2012, 550–551.
23 Merleau-Ponty discusses the use of a "cardboard tube" with respect to the moon illusion (2012, 30).
24 Köhler 1947, 52. Also see Merleau-Ponty 2012, 33 and 253, and Overgaard 2010, 278.
25 Merleau-Ponty 2012, 5. Also see Kelly 2010, 148.
26 See Bower 2019 for a detailed discussion.
27 Koffka 1935, 209. Also see Merleau-Ponty 2012, 275.
28 Koffka 1935, 235. And again: "Apparent size ... cannot be defined independently of distance: apparent size is implied by distance just as much as it implies distance" (Merleau-Ponty 2012, 272–273).
29 Merleau-Ponty 2012, 339; also see Scheler 1973a, 55–56.
30 See Carman 1999, 212–213.
31 See Shim 2011, 204–205.

Recommended Readings

Austin, J.L. 1964. *Sense and Sensibilia*. Oxford: Oxford University Press.

Gibson, James J. 1986. *The Ecological Approach to Visual Perception*. Hillsdale, NJ: Lawrence Erlbaum Associates, Publishers.

Husserl, Edmund. 2001. *Analyses Concerning Passive and Active Synthesis*. Anthony J. Steinbock, trans. Boston: Kluwer Academic Publishers.

Koffka, K. 1935. *Principles of Gestalt Psychology*. London: Kegan Paul, Trench, Trubner & Co.

Köhler, Wolfgang. 1947. *Gestalt Psychology*. New York: New American Library.

Noë, Alva. 2004. *Action in Perception*. Cambridge: The MIT Press.

Price, H.H. 1950. *Perception*, 2nd Edition. London: Methuen & Co. Ltd.

Russell, Bertrand. 1999. *The Problems of Philosophy*. Mineola, New York: Dover Publications, Inc.

8   The Content of Perception

In the previous two chapters I defended the view that perceptual experience is both intentionally direct and inadequate to its objects. Defending the inadequacy and directness of experience is an essential step in defending direct realism, since on any plausible version of direct realism, the objects of direct perception are things that could only be perceived inadequately—spatio-temporal objects and their features, for starters. If perception were adequate, we could not perceive any of those things. Furthermore, by establishing the essential inadequacy of all perceptual experience, we also remove any temptation to suppose that our perception of such things is in any way mediated by the perception of something else.

In this chapter we will take a closer look at whether perception has intentional content at all, and, if so, what sort of content it has. I will argue that perceptual experience has two kinds of content: intuitive content and empty horizonal content, and that neither kind of content is conceptual.

8.1 Conceptualism

As we have seen in Chapter 3, the contents of mental acts are intentional properties. Meanings are one type of intentional content. One complex unit of meaning that is of enormous philosophical and logical interest is the proposition. Propositions can function as parts of larger meaningful wholes, including complex propositions, stories, narratives, and theories. And propositions are themselves composed of parts. Those parts are concepts. In what follows, I will understand a state with "conceptual content" to be a state whose intentional content is either a concept or a whole composed of concepts. It is worth recalling from §3.5 that the content of an act is not among its objects. Concepts, when functioning as the contents of mental states, are on the side of the act of consciousness, not among its objects. When I *use* the concept <car hood>, I think *about* car hoods, not any concept.

Conceptualism about perceptual experience is the position that perceptual experiences have intentional content, and that their content is conceptual content. On this view, the matters or real contents of perceptual experiences are instances of meaning-properties; perceptual experiences have the same kind of matter or content as acts of thinking and judging. There are a number of powerful considerations in favor of experiential conceptualism, and its acceptance can seem virtually mandatory if we proceed from a certain historically prominent vision of how the mind works, one based on the "dualism of organizing system and something waiting to be organized," which Donald Davidson calls the "third dogma" of empiricism (Davidson 1984, 189).

According to this picture, there is, on the one hand, what Kant calls "the raw material of the sensible impressions" (Kant 1965, B1). Just how "raw" this material must be is a matter of considerable disagreement. For the classical empiricists, it includes sensations of color, of heat, of sound, and so on. For others, such as C.I. Lewis, it is significantly more raw than this—so raw that it cannot even be spoken of as such (Lewis 1929, 52–53). On the other hand, the understanding, by means of concepts, "work[s] up" this raw material into "that knowledge of objects which is entitled experience" (ibid.). As Kant says later, "experience contains two very dissimilar elements, namely, the matter of knowledge [obtained] from the senses, and a certain form for the ordering of this matter, [obtained] from the inner source of the pure intuition and thought" (Kant 1965, A86/B118). The basic idea, then, central to all "dual component" theories of perception, is that perception contains both sensation and "*thought*, or the employment of *concepts*" (A.D. Smith 2002, 67). That is one way of understanding Kant's famous remark that "intuitions without concepts are blind" (Kant 1965, A51/B75).

It is not difficult to see the attraction of conceptualism in general and the dual component theory in particular. Even if we start with a relatively robust view of what sensation can deliver, it very obviously falls far short of the world we effortlessly and continually encounter in perception. When Hume, whose sensations are by no means just "raw material," asks whether we have an impression of substance from which to derive the idea of it, he writes, "If it be perceiv'd by the eyes, it must be a color; if by the ears, a sound; if by the palate, a taste; and so of the other senses" (Hume 1978, 16). But Hume is mistaken here. Tables, trees, and scratches on car hoods are not colors, and yet they can be "perceiv'd by the eyes." Neither are football games, weddings, or ballets. Yet these can be seen. It is not even true that everything perceived by sight must *have* a color. One can see, and not just judge or infer, that A is to the left of B, but that relation does not have a color. We can also see, and not merely judge or infer, that orange is similar to red, but the similarity between orange and red is not another color. And if Hume's sensations fall short of the world of perception, then so, *a forteriori*, do Lewis's ineffable givens—as Lewis himself insists in his own defense of a conceptualist position (Lewis 1929, 54). In light of this, it is difficult not to be sympathetic with Hilary Putnam when he writes "It is because it fails to take account of how much of our perceptual experience is conceptualized ... that the empiricist view that what we see is simply an array of color patches is such a distortion" (Putnam 1999, 158).

A further point in favor of conceptualism, and probably the single most important in recent philosophy, is that perceptual experiences can stand in epistemic relations with our beliefs. A perceptual experience of a scratched car hood provides evidence for the proposition <the hood of the car is scratched>, and thereby provides justification for one's belief in that proposition. And it is widely thought that mere sensations could never function that way. Davidson goes so far as to say that "nothing can count as a reason for holding a belief except another belief."[1] The problem, though, is that since perceptual experiences are not beliefs, they cannot provide reasons for belief either. And that has no plausibility at all. Nevertheless, others, such as John McDowell (1994) and Bill Brewer (1999), have modified Davidson's point in a much more promising direction: only states with propositional content can provide reasons for belief, and so perceptual states, which obviously do make a contribution to knowledge, must have such content.

Finally—and this might explain many of the alleged differences between sensation and perception—it is doubtful whether sensations exhibit intentionality at all. Reid writes,

> The form of the expression, *I feel pain*, might seem to imply, that the feeling is something distinct from the pain felt; yet, in reality, there is no distinction. As *thinking a thought* is an expression which could signify no more than *thinking*, so *feeling a pain* signifies no more than *being pained*.[2]

Husserl also maintains that sensations are non-intentional. In the case of "tactual sensations," for example, there is a certain kind of reference to an object. There is a reference to two objects, in fact: "the bodily member which touches, and ... the external body which is touched" (LI 5 §15b, 573). But, writes Husserl,

> though this reference is realized in intentional experiences, no one would think of calling the referred sensations intentional. It is rather the case that our sensations are here functioning as presentative contents in perceptual acts, or ... that our sensations here receive an objective "interpretation" or "taking-up".
>
> (ibid.)

That is, the sensations themselves are not intrinsically intentional, but only become so when interpreted. If that is right, a natural conclusion to draw is that in perception, concepts are responsible for the *intentionality* of perception, while sensations are responsible for many of the salient features that make perception so obviously different from empty thought—its intuitive character, most obviously.

Putting all of this together, then, conceptualism promises to account for the intentionality of perception, its objectivity, its intuitive inadequacy, its capacity to lay hold of public objects of diverse ontological types, including categorically structured objects such as states of affairs, and its evidential role in the generation of knowledge and evidentially grounded ("justified") belief. In other words, it's a promising theory.

8.2 Against Conceptualism

There is a lot of controversy about whether Husserl himself endorsed a conceptualist position at various points in his career.[3] In my view the evidence is unclear, and it would be massive undertaking to try to clear up that interpretive issue. What does seem rather clear, though, is that conceptualism is not entailed by what has so far been said about the nature of perception, and that there are rather strong arguments against it. More specifically, conceptualism (1) does not account for the fundamentality of perception, (2) does not account for the intentionality of perception, (3) cannot satisfactorily account for the distinction between perception and cognitive fulfillment, (4) cannot account for the distinctive nature of horizonal content and intuitive fulfillment, and (5) cannot account for the distinctive role perception plays in knowledge.[4] Contrary to Kant, intuitions without concepts are the furthest thing from "blind." They are what grounds the entire edifice of intentionality.

8.2.1 Conceptualism and the Fundamentality of Perception

The first problem with conceptualist accounts of perception is that they cannot explain the originary role of perceptual experience. Conceptual intentionality is an empty mode of intentionality. But, as we have seen in Chapter 5, empty intentionality is grounded in intuitive intentionality. The relation between a concept and its object, while necessary, is not a brute or ultimate connection. It obtains thanks to the necessary relation each concept has to its fulfilling sense, and the necessary relation each fulfilling sense—whose contents belong to an object's manifold—has to its object. The reason "signitive acts" are "in themselves '*empty*'" (LI 6 §21, 728) is because their *contents*, meanings, are in themselves empty. "Conceptual content has a decompositional structure that is not context-bound" (Hurley 1998, 137–138). One reason why is that it is intuitively empty and non-originary. A view that equips perception with its own distinctive kind of intentionality can readily make sense of why and how it is capable of grounding the intentionality of empty, conceptual acts. It is because the objects that conceptual acts merely aim at and inauthentically grasp are genuinely and authentically *given* in perceptual acts and other acts of originary intuition. Perceptual experiences give us the "things themselves" that conceptual acts merely aim at.

For the conceptualist, by contrast, it is extraordinarily difficult to explain the fundamental role of perception. There are no concepts that are proprietary to perceptual experience—any concept can in principle be entertained across perceptual experiences that differ. If perceptual experiences have conceptual content, then they must have some additional part, feature, or content that distinguishes them from mere thought. Perception, on any viable conceptualist view, involves the "shapings of sensory consciousness by the understanding" (McDowell 1998b, 452), rather than mere acts of "the understanding" alone.

The most promising account of what this "sensory consciousness" is probably comes from the dual component theory: it consists in non-intentional qualia or sensations. The problem with them, though, is that they can only "say" what has been dictated to and through them by acts of interpretation. This consequence is even more obvious if "sensory consciousness" consists of something even more rudimentary than sensations and qualia, and perhaps especially if the sensory moments could not even exist independently of being "shaped." On any such view, the intentionality of perception is grounded in the intentionality of concepts. But this gets things the wrong way around.[5]

There are a several strong arguments in favor of the grounding role of perceptual experience. For one thing, perceiving something often explains why, on a particular occasion, we entertain a fitting concept. To use Alan Millar's example, I don't see a cat curled up on a sofa because I exercise the concept <cat>, but exercise the concept in virtue of seeing the cat.[6]

An even stronger argument is John Campbell's "argument from the explanatory role of experience" (Campbell 2002, 120). Campbell's target is the view that perceptual experiences have intentional content. But what he really attacks is the view that they have *conceptual* content, the kind of content characteristic of thought. His argument is simple and powerful:

> [E]xperience of objects has to be what explains our ability to think about objects. That means that we cannot view experience of objects as a way of grasping thoughts about objects. Experience of objects has to be something more primitive than the ability to think about objects, in terms of which the ability to think about objects can be explained.
>
> (Campbell 2002, 122)

Mark Johnston makes a similar point: "veridical sensing is an original source of knowledge of external particulars. Sensing continually expands the topics of our thought and talk" (Johnston 2004, 113). Perceptual experience is not one intentional state among others; there is, as Bill Brewer puts it, a "fundamental *difference* between perception and thought," a difference which is "crucial to our capacity for any genuine thought about particular such things and to our growing empirical knowledge about them" (Brewer 2011, 56). It is fundamentally different from any other kind of conscious experience, both in its capacity to verify our thoughts, and in its capacity to furnish them with semantically authentic content.

8.2.2 Conceptualism and Intentionality

There are additional difficulties for a conceptualist view of perception. Among the most widely discussed is that perception is more fine-grained or rich in content than states with (only) conceptual content. We have encountered this thesis already (see Chapter 1, §1.5). Here are some of the phenomena that have been adduced to support this family of arguments against conceptualism. Richard Heck, for instance, writes,

> The leaves on the trees outside my window are fluttering back and forth, randomly, as it seems to me, as the wind passes over them. Yet my experience of these things represents them far more precisely than that, far more distinctively, it would seem, than any characterization I could hope to formulate, for myself or for others, in terms of the concepts I presently possess.
>
> (Heck 2000, 490)

Gareth Evans (1982, 229) asks rhetorically, "Do we really understand the proposal that we have as many colour concepts as there are shades of colour that we can sensibly discriminate?" Christopher Peacocke has a wealth of examples. We can hear tones and distinguish them from other tones without being able to classify them (Peacocke 2001, 240). We can see the very same shape as a square or a regular diamond (ibid., 240–241), and for perception, these are vastly different encounters. As Merleau-Ponty puts it,

> In front of the understanding, a square is always a square, whether it rests on one of its sides or on one of its corners. In the latter case, however, perception hardly even recognizes the square.
>
> (Merleau-Ponty 2012, 47)

Adrian Cussins (2003, 149–150) uses the example of riding his motorcycle, and the difference between the way in which his speed is experienced while actually riding and the way it is represented conceptually in speech and thought. Apprehending his speed conceptually is one thing. Apprehending it through skillful perception and action is something totally different.

What the examples of the fine-grained and rich character of perception show is *not* that perception lays hold of a different range of intentional objects than does thought. The distinction between fine-grained and indeterminate acts is orthogonal to the distinction between perceptual and cognitive acts (see Chapter 1, §1.5). Nevertheless, the examples do cause trouble for conceptualism. What they show is that it is possible to be conscious of something, to have it as an intentional object, without exercising or even having a concept of it. One can see colors and hear sounds for which one does not have concepts, or for which one does not have concepts of the appropriate level of granularity. One can see a screwdriver or a teacup without having a concept of one (Dretske 1969, 7; Campbell 2002, 71). That is why one can learn, of the thing one sees—not the thing one just happens to see, but one's *intentional* object, an object one is attending to and tracking through space and time—that *it* is a screwdriver or a teacup (ibid.). It is also why showing someone a teacup or a screwdriver is one way, and possibly the best way, of leading them to acquire the relevant concept. But if one can be perceptually conscious of an object without having or using a concept of it, then using that concept cannot be a necessary condition of perceiving it.

One widely discussed response to these sorts of cases is that we can think of such things demonstratively. According to McDowell, we can in cases such as these "give linguistic expression to a concept that is exactly as fine-grained as the experience, by uttering a phrase like 'that shade,' in which the demonstrative exploits the presence of the sample" (McDowell 1994, 57). There are a number of problems with this proposal, however, problems explored in detail by Richard Heck (2000, 492–498). Here the most obvious objection will suffice: in order to "exploit[] the presence of the sample" in demonstrative thought, the sample must be present. And it must be present *to* the person who refers to it demonstratively; she must be conscious of it as present. She must perceive it. But in that case, the capacity to entertain the demonstrative thought will presuppose that the perceptual experience of the object has already been constituted.[7]

8.2.3 Conceptualism, Perception, and Fulfillment

A further deficiency of the conceptualist view, especially in its dual component form, is that it collapses the distinction between perception and cognitive fulfillment, as Ka-Wing Leung recognizes (2011, 140). Or rather, it requires us to radically reconceive the structure of cognitive fulfillment. On the account presented in §5.1, which corresponds to the account given in Chapter 1 (§§1–12) of Husserl's Sixth *Logical Investigation*, what provides fullness to the intrinsically empty acts of meaning is *another act*, an intuitive act. Its *content* is not a meaning or an instantiation of a meaning, and therefore is not identical with the content of the conceptual act that it fulfills. What is identical is the *object* of the two acts. Fulfillment, on this *two-act view*, is a higher order act which contains a perceptual act and a thought as proper parts, each directed upon the same object and synthesized in the required way.

On the dual component view, however, what fulfills an intrinsically empty act is not another intentional act with its own, underived intentionality, but a sensation or complex of sensations which, apart from its unity with a conceptual act, has no intentionality at all. On this *one-act view*, sensation is what fulfills, and far from being an independent *act*, it is "a characteristic *moment* of presentations alongside of quality and matter" (LI 6 §21, 729, my emphasis). Despite Husserl's claim while developing this account of fulfillment, principally in Chapter 3 of the Sixth Logical Investigation (§§16–29), that fulfillment involves both an intuitive and a signitive act (LI 6 §24, 735), it is hard to see why the intuitive act itself is not an act of fulfillment. If sensations provide fullness, and if fullness is what fulfills (why wouldn't it be?), then perceptual acts are acts of fulfillment, which share the same matter as a possible signitive act and differ only in having sensation-content of the right sort.[8]

This claim needs to be treated carefully. There *is* a kind of fulfillment—intuitive fulfillment—that occurs purely on the level of perception itself, as we have seen (Chapter 6, §6.4). Empty, horizonal intentions are routinely fulfilled in the course of perceptual experience. For instance, the empty protentional anticipation of the note G is fulfilled by the actual occurrence of that note. The problem with conceptualism is not that it confuses perception with *that* kind of *intuitive* fulfillment. The problem, rather, is that it conflates perception, and with it intuitive fulfillment, with *cognitive* fulfillment, an act which contains the whole perceptual act—including its intuitive and horizonal components—as a proper part.[9]

The main problem with treating perception as cognitive fulfillment is that it does not allow us to distinguish between veridical and nonveridical perception, on the one hand, and correct and incorrect acts of fulfillment, on the other. There are lots of reasons why someone's perceptual judgment might be incorrect, and only some of them are attributable to failures of perception. A. D. Smith (2002, 75–76) makes just this objection to dual component theories, though without using the language of "fulfillment." A snooker referee, to use Smith's example, might veridically perceive that the cue ball hit the yellow ball just before hitting the green ball. She might, nevertheless, judge that it hit the green ball first. She is making a mistake. But the mistake does not lie at the level of perception, but of perceptual judgment—that is, fulfillment. Similarly, when I see Stan but misidentify him as Dan, my mistake is not a perceptual one.

We can also think of cases in which the perceptual experience is illusory, but the judgment is fitting. If the referee suffers an illusion and perceives the cue ball to hit the green ball first, but then forms the judgment that it hit the green ball first, she makes a "correct perceptual judgment about it, and yet misperceive[s] it" (A.D. Smith 2002, 76). The judgment of course is not "correct" in the sense of being *true*. But it is a *fitting* conceptualization of how things show up to her in perceptual experience.

Plenty of other examples along these lines can be produced.[10] Suppose I hear the note C, and then the note F#, but classify or conceptualize the first as an F# and the second as a C. This is not an illusion. This is a mistaken judgment, a mistake at the level of fulfillment. It is perfectly possible to hear a note just as it is, and misclassify it as some other note or, as in the case of most of us, not classify it as any specific note at all. Contrast this with a case in which I misperceive the C as an F#, and fittingly conceptualize it as an F#. Here the error is at the level of perception. We could also, of course, have errors at both levels. I might hear a C as an F# and conceptualize it as a C#.

For conceptualism, perception is constantly on the verge of collapsing into perceptual judgment. The only difference between a perceptual judgment and a non-perceptual judgment is the presence of non-intentional sensations or qualia. Their function, as Mark Johnston nicely puts it, is as unimportant to the intentionality of perception as the wallpaper in a restaurant is to the taste of the food. "The Wallpaper View," as he calls it, "of the deliverances of sensory awareness makes sensory awareness a curious sideshow, a mere provider of sensation alongside the epistemically interesting perceptual act" (Johnston 2006, 242).

8.2.4 Perception and Empty Horizons

The conceptualist need not give up. One of the strongest arguments in favor of conceptualism is that we can only explain the inadequacy of perception by appealing to some admixture of conceptual content in its make-up. We can put the argument as follows:

1   Perceptual experiences are inadequate.
2   If perceptual experiences are inadequate, they have empty content.
3   If an experience has empty content, it has conceptual content.
4   So, perceptual experiences have conceptual content.

We have already noted that, in the *Logical Investigations* at least, Husserl identifies empty content with "signitive" content, and signitive content with meaning-content (LI 6 §14a, 710). If that's right, then premise (3) is true because empty content just is conceptual content.

But is that right? Numerous thinkers have independently cast doubt on the identification of the empty content present in perceptual experience with conceptual contents or meanings.[11] The first to my knowledge was Adolf Reinach. In his rejection of the identification of empty acts with acts of meaning, he writes,

> A presentation which lacks intuition is by no means thereby turned into an act of meaning, and nor, conversely, is an act of meaning which is enlivened by intuition at all to be conceived as a presentation.
>
> (Reinach 1982, 326)

Regarding the second point, we have already seen that this is the case. An act of meaning can be fulfilled by a corresponding intuition, but it does not thereby itself *become* an intuition, but instead enters into a distinctive kind of unity with the intuition. In doing so, it remains an act of meaning, and its content remains intrinsically empty. Regarding the first point, Reinach points out that even if we choose to call the unintuited side of a perceived object "co-meant," we can still distinguish this sort of act of "meaning" from a paradigmatic act of meaning. The reason is that both can occur at the same time, and they are obviously different. Suppose that I judge that the unseen portion of an object—a book, in his example—is such-and-such. Reinach writes,

> Here there appears alongside the enduring non-intuitive presentation a quite different type of act of meaning or intending, one which is linguistically clothed, temporally punctual, self-contained.
>
> (ibid., 327)

The act of meaning or conceiving of the other side is distinct from the perceptual act in which it is, in the language of the last chapter, horizonally intended.

One objection to Reinach's argument is this: the fact that the act of meaning is distinct from the perceptual act in which the hidden side is co-intended by no means entails that they have different *contents*.[12]

Nevertheless, Reinach's intuition is right, and there are two additional and related arguments to bolster his claim. One of the strongest is due to Robert Sokolowski (2000, 79), Daniel Dahlstrom (2006), and Jeff Yoshimi (2009, 125). All three emphasize the very specific dependence of horizonal contents on intuitive contents and concrete circumstances of perception. As Dahlstrom puts it, "there is a new horizon for every appearing-of-a-thing at every phase of perception" (Dahlstrom 2006, 209). And, as Husserl himself says, the "horizon is constantly in motion; with every new step of intuitive apprehension, new delineations of the object result, more precise determinations and corrections of what was anticipated" (EJ §25, 122). In perception, the horizon changes with every change in the intuitive content of the act. Conceptual content, however, does not. There is no conceptual content that changes with every alteration in an act's intuitive content. Not even demonstratives are that dependent upon the specific intuitive character of an experience.

A second and related argument against the view that horizonal contents are concepts is this: for any concept whatsoever, it is possible to entertain that concept while enjoying an intuitive and originary experience of any arbitrary object whatsoever. No matter what the intuitive content of an experience, it is possible in principle to entertain any concept whatsoever. For instance, one can entertain the concept <car hood> while perceiving a chair, the sky, a symphony—or a car's hood. The empty horizonal intentions in perception, however, cannot be the contents of acts with just any arbitrary intuitive content. If I see a car from the back and experience empty horizonal intentions directed towards its unseen hood, those horizonal contents cannot be instantiated in just any act. They cannot be instantiated in intuitive acts directed at chairs, the sky, or symphonies. And, most importantly, *they cannot be instantiated in acts in which the hood itself is given in the flesh.* If the hood comes into view as I walk towards the car, the empty horizonal intention is *replaced* by an intuitive, fulfilling one. In cognitive fulfillment, by contrast, a conceptual content is never replaced with an intuitive one, but enters into a *simultaneous synthesis* with it.

This again points to an important difference between cognitive fulfillment, in which a conceptual content is fulfilled, and intuitive fulfillment, in which an empty horizonal content comes to be fulfilled. In the former case the concept and the intuition *must* be instantiated together. In intuitive fulfillment they *cannot* be. And the reason hinges on the nature of the contents involved. An empty *horizonal* content cannot be instantiated in an act in which that content's object is given in the flesh. An empty *conceptual* content can.

8.2.5 Conceptualism and Knowledge

This brings us to one of the most widely invoked arguments for conceptualism in recent philosophy. Thanks in part, but not entirely, to Wilfrid Sellars's epochal *Empiricism and the Philosophy of Mind*, many philosophers have maintained that mental states and experiences must have conceptual content if they are to justify our beliefs. John McDowell's (1994) defense of conceptualism against the twin threats of the "myth of the given" and coherentism is the most well-known defense. Bill Brewer presents the core argument as follows:

1   Sense experiential states provide reasons for empirical beliefs.
2   Sense experiential states provide reasons for empirical beliefs only if they have conceptual content.
(CC)   Therefore, sense experiential states have conceptual content.[13]

The critical premise of this argument is the second one, which relies on what James Pryor calls the "Premise Principle," according to which only states with propositional content can justify beliefs.[14]

The main problem with this view is that it cannot explain why and how experiences behave so very differently from beliefs in justification and knowledge.[15] Having something given originarily in conscious perception is evidentially relevant. It is a form of consciousness in which we are originarily confronted with the objects and states of affairs that make our judgments true or false, and it typically makes a massive difference in how justified we are in believing what we believe. Husserl, as we have seen, simply calls such experiences acts of *Evidenz*. But undergoing an experience with conceptual content does not, by itself, ensure originary givenness.

More generally, for any conceptually contentful mental state M in which an object is originarily given—this would have to be an act of cognitive fulfillment—there is a possible mental state M* with the same *conceptual* content as M in which that object is *not* originarily given. And all else being equal, the subject of M will have better evidence than the subject of M*. There must be something in addition to conceptual content, then, in virtue of which perceptual experiences and other originary intuitions are evidentially relevant. So, to take an example, let M be an act of fulfillment in which B thinks the proposition <the hood of the car is scratched> and also perceives the hood to be scratched. And let M* be his state before perceiving the hood, in which he emptily thinks the proposition <the hood of the car is scratched>. B is better off, epistemically, in state M than in state M*, and not by just a little bit. Before, he does not know. Afterward, he knows.

The reason B is better off in M than in M* is not because he is entertaining more propositions. For any proposition P we can think of adding to M to explain its epistemic superiority to M*, P can be emptily entertained as well, and we can move it right over to M*. He can emptily think, for instance, that he is being appeared-to in a certain way, or that the car hood is originarily given, or that he is experiencing sensations that reliably indicate scratched car hoods. He can emptily think very sophisticated thoughts to the effect that his experience satisfies various epistemological criteria for knowing that the car hood is scratched. But none of those empty thoughts has any epistemic credentials at all.

The conceptualist about perception can attempt to expand the range of evidentially relevant factors to accommodate the special epistemic role of perception. Dialectically this is a risky move. If something besides conceptual contents can play an evidentially relevant role in knowledge, then those things are either intentional or they are not. If they are, then we must acknowledge a form of intentionality which is not conceptual, and which is evidentially relevant. But if we acknowledge that, then the door is wide open to admitting that perception is its own way of accessing the world, different in kind from conceptual thought. In fact perception would be the most obvious and prominent candidate of just that kind of act. And if the additional factor is not intentional, then the challenge is to provide an explanation of how it can do any evidential work.

For the dual component theorist, it may seem unavoidable to drag sensations or something qualitative but non-intentional in to explain the epistemic power of perception. The problem, though, is that it is not at all clear how sensations, being non-intentional, could possibly perform the epistemic work required of them. This is not, as is often thought, because they are not *propositional*. It's because they are not even *intentional* (Johnston 2006, 242). Sensations only "say" what they've been told to say by conceptual acts of "interpretation." Learning something about the world from sensation, on this view, would be like a ventriloquist learning something from his dummy.

It is no help to say that in having sensations, we are conscious of having them, and this consciousness provides a reason for thinking that the world is as it seems to be. In the first place, that is not our evidential basis for empirical beliefs about the world (see Searle 1983, 73). If we perceive a scratched car hood, we do not, and are not required, to *infer* that a car hood is scratched by examining our own bodily or perceptual sensations and treating them as clues that the hood is scratched. We do not need clues, because we have the thing itself there before us (A.D. Smith 2002, 77).

Second, even if sensations were clues or signs, there remains the question of the manner in which we are conscious of *them*. It is not enough to be "conscious of" sensations to explain their evidential role. We can be conscious of sensations we had last year, or the sensations of other people. What is required is that we be intuitively and *originarily* conscious of sensations. But to explain the difference between the empty and the originary consciousness of sensations, we cannot again invoke more sensations, on pain of infinite regress. But if we are prepared, as we should be, to affirm that there is both a conceptual, empty way of being conscious of sensations and an intuitive, nonconceptual way of being conscious of sensations, it is unclear what stands in the way of saying just the same thing about such things as scratches on car hoods.

However, rejecting conceptualism does not yet answer the challenge: just how is it that experiences justify when they do not have propositional content? The answer, I believe, is not that difficult. What makes propositions compatible or incompatible with one another, and so capable of supporting or defeating one another, is not that they are *propositions*, but that they are *of states of affairs*. As we saw in Chapter 3, §3.3, logical relations correspond to ontological relations. Consistency and inconsistency among propositions correspond to and are parasitic upon the compossibility and incompossibility of the states of affairs, whether material or formal, that they are about. And propositions are just *one* way of representing states of affairs. Other representations can also do so. Sentences do so by expressing propositions. But pictures and maps also represent states of affairs, and they do not express propositions (see Crane 2009, 458). And perceptual experiences are of states of affairs without having propositional content as well. An experience of the car hood's being scratched can obviously be compatible with one's belief that the hood of the car is scratched, since both are about the very same state of affairs. This is one place where the distinction between contents and objects really pays off, and where neglecting it can have significant costs.

For a variety of reasons, some of them having to do with the last century's "linguistic turn," conceptually contentful states such as judgment, thought, and belief have come to be regarded as the paradigms of intentional states.[16] They aren't (Fasching 2012). Armchair or language-game intentionality is a secondary mode of intentionality. And the ability of armchair-acts to lay hold of their objects, while real, is much more difficult to understand than is perceptual experience, and ultimately must be understood in terms of possibilities of suitable perceptual experiences. Husserl, who in the *Logical Investigations* makes the fateful error of maintaining that in fulfillment the intentional matter of intuition is identical with that of an act of meaning, ultimately comes to see this:

> Everything puzzling, everything problematic, lies on the side of the mere meaning. To treat the intuitive self-grasping (*Selbsterfassen*), self-possessing (*Selbsthaben*), as a puzzle...means to philosophize about evidence from top-down (*von oben her*) instead of looking at evidence itself, of bringing it itself to evidence.[17]

And it is in these same lectures of 1917/18 that Husserl correctly locates the difference between perception and judgment in their intentional matters or contents (ibid., 73–74).

8.3 Naïve Realism

A very attractive alternative to conceptualism is naïve realism, also sometimes called the "relational view" (Campbell 2002, Ch. 6) and the "object view" (Brewer 2011, Ch. 5).[18] I will understand naïve realism to have the following commitments, in order of what I take to be their centrality. First, as M.G.F. Martin puts it, "The Naïve Realist thinks that some at least of our sensory episodes are presentations of an experience independent reality" (2009, 272). Second, perceptual experience is relational: it is such that, necessarily, the experience in question could not exist if its object did not. Third, the phenomenal character of a perceptual experience is partly or wholly constituted by the perceived object itself, rather than non-intentional qualia or (re)presentational contents. Fourth, perceptual experience is not representational, or at least not representational in the way that other intentional states, such as thoughts, are. On some naïve realist views, perceptual experiences do not have intentional contents (see Travis 2004; Brewer 2011). These commitments are often summed up in the claim that "the external object, in cases of veridical perception, [is] a constituent of the experience."[19]

After the results of the two previous chapters, there is little point in emphasizing the fact that there is much to like about naïve realism. Perceptual experiences are, to repeat, intuitive, direct, positing, and, most importantly, originary. Moreover, the objects of perceptual experience are intentionally and really transcendent or "external" to them. They include such things as rocks, trees, the sun and the moon, and familiar denizens of the human life world such as tables, dollar bills, and restaurants. And though we have not yet attempted to establish the truth of realism about such things, there's no point in being secretive about where things are heading: it is overwhelmingly plausible that the *intentionally* transcendent items that show up in perceptual experience are also *really* transcendent, that they exist and have at least many of their apparent properties independently of our experience, our language games, our conceptual schemes, or whatever else philosophers have tried to install between us and the in-itself. Naïve realism has no difficulty accounting for the originary character of perception. In fact that's exactly what it best accounts for.

Naïve realism's other commitments are more controversial. So far we have said very little about the nature of perceptual hallucinations and illusions. One reason is so that we could provide a description of a certain class of experiences without regard to their veridicality. If naïve realism is correct, however, we cannot "bracket" the question of veridicality when it comes to perceptual experience. The reason is that if it is true, perceptual experiences differ radically from hallucinations, and possibly from illusions as well, however similar they may seem to their subjects.

Let us start with naïve realism's second commitment, namely that perception is "a relation between the perceiver and the scene observed" (Campbell 2016, 106). In perception, the existence of the act guarantees that of the object. This is not just the claim that, necessarily, if E is a *perceptual* experience, then its object O exists. That is compatible with E's having been, in some possible world, an illusion or a hallucination, since this claim leaves it open that E might only contingently be a *perceptual* experience. Rather, naïve realism is the view that it is part of E's nature, an essential feature of it, that it is a *perceptual*, and therefore relational, experience. There is no possible world, on this view, in which E exists and O does not.

On the assumption that hallucinations are not themselves perceptual experiences, naïve realism likely entails a *disjunctive* treatment of perceptual and hallucinatory experiences, a position first formulated by J.M. Hinton.[20] According to Heather Logue, disjunctive theories of perception maintain that perceptual and hallucinatory experiences are "radically unalike in some respect" (Logue 2015, 198). Since it is hard to determine how unalike two mental states must be to be *radically* unalike, I will regard any account of perception as disjunctive if it is *not* conjunctive. The downside of this is that on this way of understanding things, disjunctivism and conjunctivism are mutually exclusive and exhaustive, which means that some thinkers who endorse neither will wind up classified as disjunctivists (e.g. Johnston 2006, 121). And I will understand a conjunctive account of perception and hallucination to be the position which is committed to what M.G.F. Martin (2006, 357) calls the "Common Kind Assumption," according to which "whatever kind of mental ... event occurs when one perceives, the very same kind of event could occur were one hallucinating." In light of our previous discussions of the structure and content of the mental act, we can state this as follows:

> Conjunctivism: for any possible veridical perceptual experience directed upon a contingently obtaining state of affairs, there is an ideally possible

hallucinatory counterpart to it, where a hallucinatory counterpart is (a) a nonveridical experience which has the same (b) phenomenal character, and (c) intentional essence (content + quality, if any) as the veridical experience.

As Søren Overgaard puts it, on most versions of the conjunctive view "the perceptual experience one enjoys when actually perceiving is of the very same type as the experience one may have when hallucinating—the two only differ with respect to aetiology" (Overgaard 2013, 52).

Given this way of understanding things, disjunctive views come in a variety of possible flavors.[21] Naïve realism, however, is committed to an especially strong version of disjunctivism. In Campbell's relational view, for instance, one radical difference between perception and hallucination consists in the fact that when we perceive, the object is a constituent of our experience (Campbell 2002, 118). But in the case of hallucination, even hallucination "of" a car hood, no car hood is a constituent of one's experience. After all, in hallucination, "there is no object to be a constituent of your experience" (Campbell 2002, 117).

Naïve realism is also committed to rejecting the view that perceptual experiences and hallucinations have the same phenomenal character. It seems like they should share a phenomenal character. After all, what it is like to undergo a perceptual experience is supposed to be just what it's like to undergo a hallucination—this, in fact, is the clearest sense to be made of the notion of a hallucination's "matching" the veridical experience. On a naïve realist view, however, the phenomenal character of a perceptual experience is just as object-dependent as the experience itself. As Campbell puts it, "the qualitative character of the experience is constituted by the qualitative character of the scene perceived" (Campbell 2002, 114–115). But in hallucination there is no "scene perceived," and so *that* cannot constitute its qualitative character.

What about the proposal that perceptual experiences and matching hallucinations share intentional *contents*? This does not work either, according to the naïve realist. The main reason is that according to many advocates of naïve realism, perceptual experiences do not have intentional content at all. Perception is not "representational," as Campbell (2002, 117) says. And Bill Brewer develops what he calls the "Object View" in opposition to the "Content View." According to Brewer (2011, 93), "the most fundamental characterization of perceptual experience is to be given in terms of a relation of conscious acquaintance with certain direct objects of perception," a position that he quite correctly ascribes to early modern thinkers such as Berkeley. It "retains the early modern conviction that the core subjective character of perceptual experience is to be given simply by citing its direct object" (Brewer 2008, 17). The main difference is that for those early moderns, the objects in question were ideas or sense data. For today's naïve realists, they are ordinary physical things. But neither position requires us to invoke intentional contents.

8.3.1 Hallucination

Naïve realism seems to leave us very little to say about the nature of hallucinations. And some naïve realists are quite explicit about this. M.G.F. Martin
writes that

> while there is a positive specific nature to the veridical perception, there is
> *nothing more* to the character of the (causally matching) hallucination than
> that it can't, through reflection, be told apart from the veridical perception.
>
> (Martin 2006, 370, my emphasis)

William Fish holds that hallucinations are simply experiences with the same
set of cognitive effects as perceptions: "a hallucination is a mental event
that, while lacking phenomenal character, produces the same cognitive
effects in the hallucinator that a veridical perception of a certain kind would
have produced in a rational subject in the same overall doxastic setting"
(Fish 2009, 114).

These positions strike me as phenomenologically problematic. Among
other things, they appear to entail that hallucinations are not even intentional, that they are not even of anything. That, however, is at odds with two
things that a successful account of hallucinations ought to explain.

The first is that hallucinations are nonveridical experiences. In hallucination, things go wrong, and go wrong in quite specific ways. The second is that
hallucinations are not *wholly* nonveridical. They can be a source of knowledge. Since knowledge by acquaintance is knowledge (see Chapter 9, §9.5),
they can even be *cases* of knowledge. What each of those claims entails is that
hallucinations are *of* something. They are intentional experiences. You cannot
have a nonveridical experience of something if it is not of anything. In fact,
you cannot have a nonveridical experience of O unless your experience is *of*
O. And an experience cannot count as a case of knowing about something if
it is not even about something.

Let's take a closer look, starting with the second, and more surprising,
feature of hallucination. Mark Johnston points out that hallucination is not
"an original source of *de re* thought about ... particular things or people"
(Johnston 2004, 129). You cannot acquire an authentic concept of an existing
individual on the basis of a hallucination alone, no matter how similar the
thing presented to you in it is to an existing thing. The case is quite otherwise
with respect to properties. As Johnston writes, "I can secure my *first* singular
reference to the quality cherry red or to the structural property C major by
way of hallucinating a scene or a tune." The reason is that hallucination can
provide "*de re* knowledge of quality."[22] And it can do that because qualities
can show up in an *originary* way in hallucination.

Hallucination can provide us with knowledge, and not only originary
knowledge of qualities, but knowledge of various relations and possible states

of affairs. Suppose that, while looking at an 8x8 tile floor, I suddenly hallucinate chess pieces configured in a certain manner. They begin to move on
their own, and black forces checkmate in four moves. If I am attentive, I will
thereby learn how to force checkmate in any similar situation. I will learn
that, moreover, on the basis of what I *intuited*. That is, I undergo an experience of fulfilment, which results in a true belief on the basis of an intuition.

According to Johnston, the "primary objects of hallucination" are "sensible
profiles" (2004, 156). Johnston regards sensible profiles as *"sensory manners of
presentation of particulars"* (2004, 149). For our purposes, I will treat sensible
profiles as composed of sense-perceptible qualities and relations—colors and
shapes, say, rather than modes of presentation of color and shape, which are
not colors or shapes. What I gain knowledge of in hallucination is not just
modes of presentation of sensible properties, but the sensible properties
themselves. In the case of hallucination these sensible profiles are not instantiated. Hallucination, that is, is primarily the awareness of uninstantiated
sensible profiles (ibid.).

That cannot, however, be the whole story about hallucination, for two reasons. First, phantasy is also an experience in which we are intuitively aware of
uninstantiated sensible profiles. We can even have, as we can in hallucination,
originary and positing knowledge of them: *"Positing* and apprehending *essences* by way of initially intuiting them *does not in the least imply a positing of any
kind of individual existence"* (Ideas I §4, 14–15). Nevertheless, phantasy and
hallucination are very different experiences. Phantasy is not failed perception.
Hallucination, by contrast, is a defective and nonveridical mode of consciousness, and its shortcomings are far more conspicuous than its achievements.
Whatever it is, then, that makes hallucination such a clear failure (to those
reflecting on its nature, of course, not to a subject undergoing one) and phantasy perfectly all right cannot be the intuitive presence of uninstantiated sensible profiles that they share in common with one another.

A second reason that hallucination is not just the awareness of uninstantiated sensible profiles is that hallucination is nonveridical, and the
awareness of uninstantiated sensible profiles need not be nonveridical. As
Johnston points out, sensible profiles exist (2004, 158). But the veridical
experience of things that exist is not what hallucination is. That is the very
opposite of what hallucination is. If the presence of sensible profiles were the
end of the story regarding hallucination, we would fail to account for the fact
that it is a failure.

The intentionality of hallucination, then, is rich. It can be both veridical
with respect to one set of its objects, and nonveridical with respect to another.
So what, then, is it nonveridical with respect to, and why? The answer seems
to be that it is nonveridical with respect to the world. It presents the world as
other than it is. And it does so in a particularly egregious way: the objects
that it is of are not, as in illusion, perceived but presented as having properties
that they do not have. In hallucination those objects are not perceived at all.

They either do not exist, or do not exist in the time and place of the halluci-natory experience. And this sets hallucination apart from phantasy. Phantasy also presents us with more than sensible profiles or properties. It too presents us with individuals as having those properties. The difference is that phantasy has no pretensions to present us with the world. It is not positing with respect to actuality. Hallucination, like perception, is.

Moreover, hallucination is a *perceptual* error, not just a mistake in judg-ment (A.D. Smith 2002, 76). And it can remain a positing experience even when one knows, cognitively, that one is hallucinating. If I believe that the hallucinated chess pieces are moving, then I believe things are the way they are presented to be. If I do not believe they are moving, then I do not believe things are the way they are presented to be. But in both cases, the world is presented to be a certain way. And it is presented to be that way in a positing fashion by my hallucinatory experience, quite independently of whether "I"—I the judger, that is—accept its deliverances.[23]

A.D. Smith rightly points out that hallucinations have a *"de re character"* (2002, 252). To appreciate the *de re* character of hallucination, take a look at the scene before you right now. It (I will assume) *intuitively* appears to you that there are physical individuals bearing properties and standing in rela-tions. It does not *just* cognitively seem that way. You are, to use Susanna Schellenberg's terminology, exercising a perceptual capacity, namely the per-ceptual capacity to single out particular objects and property-instances (see Schellenberg 2014, 211). Were you to judge that you see individuals arrayed in space, bearing qualities and relations, your judgment would *fit* what is presented intuitively. It seems to follow from this that you are intuitively conscious of individuals bearing properties and standing in relations. If you were to discover later that you are hallucinating, would it follow that you do not *now* have a consciousness of individuals? That would mean that it would not appear to you now that there are individuals bearing properties. But it does. Granted, in that case you would not have singled out any actual parti-culars—your experience would merely "purport to single out a particular" or be "as of" a particular (Schellenberg 2014, 211). But whatever we say about this "as of" consciousness of particulars in the hallucinatory case, it must be a robust enough form of object-directed intentionality to explain the fact that hallucinations are nonveridical experiences of the world. And in order to be a nonveridical experience of something, one's experience must be of that some-thing. A false thought about the world has to be about the world, and so does a nonveridical experience. If you are hallucinating, you are aware of unin-stantiated profiles as though they were instantiated. And if they appear to be instantiated, then they appear to be instantiated in and among physical objects. As A.D. Smith puts it, hallucination "presents us ... with *normal objects*: normal *physical* objects, to boot, in the sense that they are presented in three-dimensional space" (2002, 234). What makes them nonveridical is that those objects do not exist (ibid.).

Hallucination, like false empirical belief, is a defective way of being conscious of the world. It is the consciousness of what is not as though it is. In it, we are aware of physical things that appear to exist, but do not (see Reinach 1989, 378). Whatever else we say about the debate between disjunctivists and conjunctivists, then, we can see that perceptual experiences and hallucinations share a great deal in common. Contrary to many versions of disjunctivism, hallucination and perception share at least some of the same intentional directedness and phenomenal character, namely whatever phenomenal character is determined by the sensible profiles and de re character common to each (see Schellenberg 2014, 213).

It is difficult to say whether perception and hallucination could, as conjunctivists maintain, completely overlap and, in particular, whether the same *individuals* which we perceive can also be hallucinated. It could undoubtedly seem to us that we are having an experience of an actual individual in a hallucinatory experience. If a hallucinated individual looks just like my friend Dan, I would take myself to have an experience of Dan. However, the fact that what I am conscious of "strikes" me as Dan, or that my experience strikes me as being *of* Dan, does not make it so.[24] Recalling the earlier discussion of the *de re* character of perceptual experience (see Chapter 2, §2.1.4), consider the case in which I *perceive* Stan instead of Dan, but take myself to perceive Dan. The fact that my experiences strikes me as being of Dan does not make it of Dan. It's of Stan. Similarly, the fact that a hallucinated individual strikes me as being Dan does not make my hallucinatory experience of Dan either. It might, as in the Dan/Stan case, be another case of misrecognition, and misrecognition is not hallucination (A.D. Smith 2002, 76).

I am not entirely confident that the conjunctive analysis of perception is false. But I suspect it is, and that naïve realists are right about the relational character of perception. There is an incredibly plausible claim about intentionality, which Jeff Speaks calls the "Perception/Availability Principle." According to it, "If two experiences differ in which thoughts they make available to the subject of the perception, then they differ in content."[25] In our terms: if two experiences fulfill different propositions, they differ in content. And if two experiences differ in which individuals they enable a subject to have de re knowledge of, then they differ in their *objects*. And as we have seen in our discussion of Johnston's position, perception can be an originary source of de re or authentic knowledge of individuals. No matter how many times I have seen Dan, *each* seeing is the kind of experience which could have originated a de re consciousness of Dan, and could have made available de re thoughts about Dan to me. But the hallucination of a Dan-like individual could not make such thoughts available to me. A hallucination's of-Dan-ness would be, on any credible account, parasitic upon previous veridical experiences of Dan. This is not true of veridical experiences of Dan; they do not depend for their originary of-Dan-ness on previous experiences of Dan. But if the veridical experience can be an originary source of knowledge of Dan, while the hallucination cannot, then the two are not identical, as they would have to be if conjunctivism were true. Rather, by the Perception/Availability principle, they differ in content. And by the revised version of that principle, they also differ in their objects. The perception is of Dan. The hallucination is not. This gives us a good reason to agree with A.D. Smith that a properly worked out Husserlian theory of perception is disjunctivist, that perceptual experiences "differ intrinsically, essentially and as a kind from any hallucinatory experiences" (A.D. Smith 2008, 313).

8.3.2 Naïve Realism and the Inadequacy of Perception

This admittedly inconclusive discussion of hallucination need not spell deep troubles for naïve realism. It is compatible with the claim that perceptual experiences acquaint us with independent, worldly objects. It is compatible with the view that they are relational. Those are the two most important commitments of naïve realism. The account of hallucination above is, finally, also compatible with the view that perceptual experiences do not have intentional content. That, however, is the most problematic component of naïve realism.

When it comes to the *structure* of the perceptual act, naïve realism is most similar to the sense datum theory (see Brewer 2011, 138–139; Logue 2014, 225). On most versions of the sense datum theory, as we have seen, the apprehension of a sense datum is to be treated along the lines of the object-theory of intentionality: different acts of apprehension are distinguished by their (direct) objects. That analysis works well for sense data, since, if they exist, they are the kinds of things that can be given adequately. We run into trouble when we try to apply that analysis to physical objects, events, situations, and properties, however. The most obvious difference between the two types of cases is that physical objects are intentionally transcendent. We perceive them partially and from perspectives. The defenders of naïve realism know this (Overgaard 2013, 57). And they have ways of accounting for the perspectival character of our experience. Brewer, for instance, writes that

> perceptual experience is a matter of a person's conscious acquaintance with various mind-independent physical objects *from a given spatiotemporal point of view, in a particular sense modality, and in certain specific circumstances of perception (such as lighting conditions in the case of vision).*
>
> (Brewer 2011, 96)

And Campbell writes that his relational view is compatible with the claim that "hidden characteristics of the objects will play no role in constituting one's experience of them." What might instead "constitute the content" of one's experience is one's "view" or the "egocentric layout of the scene" before one (Campbell 2002, 120). William Fish discusses a number of factors beyond the mere identity of the object that influence our experience (Fish 2009, Chapter 3).

There still remains the question, though, of how effectively this captures the *phenomenological* dimension of inadequacy. I see an object, as Brewer says, "from a given spatiotemporal point of view" (2011, 96). But this is not enough, as we have seen. We do not just see things from points of view. We see things *as from* points of view. And that means that we see them *as* having further features, parts, and manners of givenness. But this raises a challenge: how could the unperceived parts of the object be among the co-determining factors of our present experience on a naïve realist model? There must be some consciousness *of* them. But it's highly unclear how that is supposed to work. To say that the object becomes a constituent of the act of perceiving does not, without further elaboration, illuminate anything. First, putting an object "in" an act as a real constituent sheds no light on the intentionality of the act. Why should a perceptual experience be "of" something just because the object is a constituent of the act, especially when the parts of other acts— their matters and qualities—are almost never those acts' objects?

Second, if A is a part of some whole W, then we can find out more about A by examining W. After all, A is *part* of W. If you examine a car thoroughly, you will eventually encounter its hood, and if you examine a sphere thoroughly, you will eventually encounter its interior. But it's not clear that I would discover the back or inside of an apple, and have it presented in the flesh, if I were to further investigate my present *experience* of its front. To see the back of the apple, I need to investigate the apple by seeing it from other points of view. But in that case I'm not investigating my original experience, but having *more* experiences. This is even true when some of the apple's features are in plain view but, as they always are, susceptible to closer determination. If the apple, or even its facing side, were constituents of my experience, I should be able to find out more about them by examining my experience.

In his discussion of naïve realism, Boyd Millar writes,

> According to the naïve realist, your perceptual experience consists in your standing in the relation of acquaintance to the particular book in front of you and the blueness of its cover. As the particular book and its blueness are constituents of this relational state of affairs, they are constituents of your perceptual experience.

(Millar 2014, 628–629)

There are two ways of taking this passage.[26] On one reading, the experience and the book together constitute a relational state of affairs. But in that case, it does not follow that the book and its blueness are constituents of the *experience*. The fact that X and Y are both constituents of a relational state of affairs S does not entail that either is a constituent of the other. It entails that they are parts of the relational state of affairs.

On another reading, the perceptual experience *is* the relational state of affairs. In that case it does follow that the book and its blueness are constituents of the experience. So which view should we prefer—that the experience is a *constituent* of a relational state of affairs, or that it *is* the relational state of affairs? Either is compatible with the view that experiences are relational, since on the first view the experience might be a non-separable part of the relational state of affairs, with the experience-independent object as a separable part (see Mulligan and Smith 1986).

One reason to prefer the first view is that the relational state of affairs involves (a) a book and (b) something that is *of* or about the book. It seems to me that (b) is not the whole state of affairs, but the experience. The state of affairs of my perceiving the book does not itself seem to be of the book. It does not seem to be *of* anything. Similarly, in the state of affairs of A's-being-to-the-left-of-B, A is to the left of B, but the state of affairs is not to the left of B.

It also seems fairly clear, though admittedly by no means self-evident, that what accounts for the fact that things are seen *as from* perspectives, and as having further parts and features, is that the experience itself contains empty or indeterminate horizonal *content* on the side of the perceptual act in virtue of which those unperceived or indeterminate features are intended. And since our perception of everything is inadequate essentially, there is no part, side, or property of any physical thing that could function in anything like the way sense data do on the sense datum model.

As attractive as naïve realism is, then, it is difficult to see how we can avoid treating perceptual experiences as bearers of intentional content, and specifically intuitive content and empty horizonal content. While this issue could hardly be said to be settled by the considerations here, it is worth noting that there is no reason to think that this opens up a problematic gap between the experience and its object. If the content of perception were conceptual or propositional, it surely would. Naïve realists are right that perception does not have conceptual content. The problem is, their objections to content views seem to apply principally to conceptualist views, as Susanna Siegel points out (2010, 73). But conceptual content is not the only kind. Intuitive content and horizonal contents are also of objects, and, as Michael Madary argues at length (2017, Chapter 4), equipping experiences with that kind of content ("Anticipation-Fulfillment" or "AF" content) handles many of the objections that naïve realists lodge against content views. As Susanna Schellenberg (2014) argues at length, the mere fact that experiences have content is not problematic, provided the instantiation of those contents is appropriately related to reality. After all, a mental content is an intentional property of an act, and "does not encapsulate the mind or its contents, any more than the properties of other things or events encapsulate them" (Willard 2002, 74).

8.4 Perceiving Universals

In several places in this work, I have alluded to the fact that individuals and their property-instances, parts, and moments are not the only kinds of objects that can show up in originary intuition, and that, accordingly, sense-perception is not the only kind of originary intuition. The same contrast between mere thinking and seeing, perceiving, or originarily intuiting something is present in the case of universals as well. This should be clear from the fact that in at least some hallucinatory experiences, we are originarily and veridically aware of something, even though there is no existing individual of which we are veridically aware.

As we have seen, Husserl believes in universals or essences, and regards phenomenology itself as one discipline—but by no means the sole discipline—concerned exclusively with them. On Husserl's view, in fact, *all* sciences contain an a priori component consisting of propositions about essences (see Ideas I §8, 20). Husserl also, as we have seen, maintains that universals can be intuited in an originary way. While defending those claims in detail, and providing a full description of Husserl's rather complicated theory of ideation and "eidetic variation" lies outside the scope of this work, it is worth examining his phenomenological argument for their existence.[27]

Husserl's argument is simple: we sometimes think about or mean universals, and in at least some cases those acts of meaning are fulfilled in corresponding acts of intuition.[28] The best reason to think the first claim is true is actually the second one: universals show up in intuition, and we can and do mean them rather than their instances or anything else that is real and individual.[29]

The evidence for the *givenness* of universals is that we can be intuitively, and not merely emptily, aware of something identical in experiences where there is nothing individual that is identical. This happens in perception all the time. I examine my two volumes of Husserl's *Logical Investigations*, each of which has a distinctive red color. As I look at Vol. 1 and then at Vol. 2, I am aware of the *same* color. Despite the fact that each volume has its *own* individual color-moment, its own "attributive aspect" which is as individual as each book itself, my consciousness of the universal Red is not a matter of simply attending to each of their individual color moments (see LI 2 §19, 376–77). Attending to their individual red color-moments is merely the foundation on which the seeing of Red itself is founded in an act of categorial intuition. What I intuit, on the basis of these two individual books, is Red itself. In such a case "the universal *itself is given to us*; we do not think of it merely in significative fashion as when we merely understand general names, but we apprehend it, *behold* it" (LI 6 §52, 800).

That I *behold* a universal in this case is clear from two considerations. The first is that what I perceive when I move from a visual perception of Vol. 1 to a visual perception of Vol. 2 is the *same* thing, but there is no individual that is the same in those two experiences. I could also examine other copies of these volumes, or other books, or other objects entirely. I could see the very same color in a Munsell chip. We could replace all of the red individuals in the world with other ones, and I could continue to see the same color. If we turn to the concept <Red> that is fulfilled by these experiences, we can see that it does not refer to any individual red color moment. If, when looking at Vol. 1 and its individual red moment, I move to examine the color moment of Vol. 2, my concept <Vol. 1's red color moment> will *not* be fulfilled. I will not experience myself to be seeing the same thing. If, however, I exercise the concept <Red>, it will be fulfilled, no matter which red thing I see or imagine.

The second consideration in favor of the claim that I see something Ideal is that my experience of the color is veridical, and would remain veridical even if my experience of everything individual and actual turned out to be non-veridical. Another way to put this is that the concept <Red>, and my meaning-intention which has that concept as its content, can be fulfilled in acts that are nonveridical with respect to everything actual. If I were hallucinating right now as I behold these books, my experience of the individual color moments would be nonveridical; they would not exist. And if that were all I were aware of, then my experience would be nonveridical through and through. But it is not.

Hallucination, as we have seen, can be a source of knowledge. I can acquire an authentic concept of this shade of Red through a hallucinatory experience, and recognize further instances of it across perceptual, hallucinatory, and phantasy experiences. That is why, as Husserl writes,

> The *eidos*, the *pure essence*, can be exemplified intuitively in instances of givenness in experience, in such instances in perception, memory, and so forth but *also in those in mere phantasy* just as well.
>
> (Ideas I §4, 14)

In such experiences, I do not have an originary consciousness of anything individual. But I do have an originary experience of something, namely a property or universal that could possibly be exemplified in many individuals. As Husserl puts it, "*The discernment of the essence is also precisely an intuition*, just as the eidetic object is precisely an object" (Ideas I, §3, 12). And because they are Ideal objects, "In a consideration of essence, perception and imaginative representation are entirely equivalent—the same essence can be seen in both" (IdPh, 50). Because of this, the intuition of essences and the knowledge that we derive from it can survive the discovery that our experiences are nonveridical with respect to all matters of fact. Whether I see, hallucinate, or vividly imagine a chess game in which black forces checkmate in three moves, I will be in a position to acquire knowledge of how any game of that same type could be won.

Seeing essences or properties and the relations among them also extends to other acts which do not deal with sense-perceptible entities at all. That is, there are cases in which we have genuine insight, and not mere thoughts, about necessary states of affairs, quite independently of the question of whether they are actualized. This becomes especially clear when we consider that this quality of insight can be present or absent even in cases of knowing which are equally *reliable*. Consider the following example from the mathematician Paul Halmos, as related by James Robert Brown (2014, 66–67), appropriately modified. Suppose the population of Boston is 685,096 people, and that we were to organize a single elimination arm wrestling tournament involving every inhabitant of the city. How many matches would there be? Well, in the first round there will be (685,096 ÷ 2) matches, in the second [(685,096 ÷2) ÷ 2], and so on, adjusting appropriately for cases involving odd numbers of remaining competitors. The number of matches is the sum of this series down until there is one person left.

But there's a much easier way to solve this problem. Just consider: how many people lose? Everyone but one. And how many times does each loser lose? Once. So the number of matches is 685,096–1. That's insight. "Simple, elegant, breathtaking," as Brown aptly describes it (2014, 67). The two processes yield the same correct result, and each process is, in principle and even in practice, equally reliable. But the second way is just better. In this case we *see* why it must be so.

In the face of examples like this, philosophers with empiricist and nominalist sympathies typically appeal to "language" or "concepts" to explain how we could have this kind of insight. Perhaps, in A.J. Ayer's words, the examples above simply "enlighten us by illustrating the way in which we use certain symbols" (1952, 79). But *any* strategy along these lines is problematic for numerous reasons. First, despite the allegedly naturalistic credentials of nominalism, it is not at all clear that there is any empirical support for it, at least not if empirical support is supposed to derive from the most successful empirical sciences. Physicists, for example, do not seem to have established that there is no such multiply instantiable property as mass or charge, much less that there are no multiply instantiable properties at all. On the contrary: physics seems to have established beyond reasonable doubt that there are such properties, along with many others, and appears to have been quite successful in telling us about them through both real experiments and thought experiments.

Einstein's general theory, for instance, says that gravitational and inertial mass are equivalent. As part of his argument for that conclusion, Einstein does not posit the existence of any individuals. Rather, he asks us to "Imagine a large portion of empty space," and to "imagine a spacious chest resembling a room" (Einstein 1961, 75). He then asks us to imagine a "being" pulling on a string attached to the lid of this chest with constant force. To the individual inside the chest, this constant acceleration will be just what gravity is, and every experiment that individual performs within the chest will confirm it (ibid., 76). If our "being" causes the chest to accelerate at 9.8 m/s^2, every experience had and experiment conducted by the individual in the chest will be just as if he were in Earth's gravitational field. The person in the chest can rightly regard the chest as being at rest. If he suspends a body from a rope, he can treat the resulting tension in the rope as the result of the presence of a gravitational field (ibid., 77). An outside observer, meanwhile, can rightly regard the chest as accelerating and the tension in the rope as a result of the suspended object's inertial mass. Einstein concludes: "we see that our extension of the principle of relativity implies the *necessity* of the law of the equality of inertial and gravitational mass" (ibid., 78). Is this the thinking of a nominalist or an empiricist? Or is perhaps Husserl, along with James Brown, right in thinking that in this and countless other cases, we are capable of seeing properties and relations among them, not only in perception but also in acts of imagination and phantasy?[30]

Einstein is often regarded as a kind of verificationist or positivist. He also clearly appears to be a realist about properties. Brown rightly points out that there is no tension between these positions:

> Einstein's brand of verificationism is not like any other; it gives special status to the intuitively obvious. His positivism is more an impulse to assign the self-evident a special role than to eliminate unobservable entities.
>
> (Brown 1991, 114)

The only point on which this is mistaken is that Einstein's brand of verificationism, far from being idiosyncratic, is *exactly* like that of the early phenomenologists.

> If "positivism" means nothing less than an absolutely unprejudiced grounding of all sciences on the "positive," that is, on what is to be apprehended in an originary way, then *we* are the genuine positivists.
>
> (Ideas I §20, 38)

And Einstein's thought experiment is just the sort of "originary" apprehension that Husserl has in mind.

A further problem with the linguistic or conceptual approach is that in each of the examples above, the last thing before our mind is language or concepts. Einstein got us to think about mass, not the English word "mass" or the concept <mass>, and clearly took himself to have established a *necessary* truth, on the basis of a thought experiment, about mass. But even if symbols and concepts were the real topics of our and Einstein's thought and insight, the result would still be favorable to Husserl's claim that we both mean and intuit universals. The reason is that our allegedly linguistic or conceptual insights would on any credible account themselves be insights into universals, this time linguistic or conceptual universals. As Reinhardt Grossman notes, "concepts themselves are universals (just like words...)" and "we must distinguish between the concept whiteness* and its many individual occurrences in a given mind" (Grossman 1992, 37). Allowing that we have insight into concepts or words is no better, from a nominalist point of view, than allowing that we have insights into any other kind of universal (see Willard 1983).

On any understanding of what we learn when we learn that red excludes green, or that the number of matches in a single elimination tournament with n contestants is n-1, these truths do not entail the existence of any individual objects with color properties, any actual single elimination tournaments, any particular utterances or inscriptions in any actual language, or any mental acts or other psychological states. As an exercise, try to deduce that we use symbols in a certain way, or that we or any symbols or languages even exist, from the actual content of any of the examples above (see Bonjour 1998, 52).

It would be beyond the scope of this work to try to solve the problem of universals—a problem that we are still debating after 2,500 years (Loux 2006, 71). But it is worth at least drawing our attention to the phenomenological dimension of our consciousness of them.[31] Somehow in phantasy, in thought experiments, and even in hallucination, we acquire knowledge of something on the basis of intuition. Something besides particulars and their individual property instances is not only meant, but given. And, as we will see in our discussion of Husserl's "Principle of All Principles" in §9.4 later, that provides us with defeasible but nevertheless real justification for taking them to exist.

8.5 Conclusion

This chapter has focused principally on the content of perception. I have argued that perception does not have conceptual content. I have also argued that while naïve realism is right that perceptual experiences are genuinely relational acts, it is likely mistaken in its contention that perceptual experiences do not have intentional content. On the view defended here, they have both intuitive content and horizonal content. Finally, I have briefly defended the view that we can "perceive" or have originary intuitions of universals.

Notes

1 Davidson 2001, 141. See Van Cleve 1985 for a very helpful critical discussion of the view that only beliefs can justify beliefs.
2 Reid 1997, 168. See Van Cleve 2015, 25–33 for a good discussion of whether, on Reid's view, sensations have no objects, or whether they have themselves as their objects. Van Cleve defends the former view.
3 See, for instance, Miller 1984, Cobb-Stevens 1990, Mulligan 1995, Kjosavik 2003, Shim 2005, Dahlstrom 2007, Barber 2008, Mooney 2010, Leung 2011, Hopp 2011, Christensen 2013, van Mazijk 2014, 2016, 2017a, 2017b, Zheng 2019, and Kidd (2019). For an excellent and detailed discussion of the evolution of Husserl's views from a conceptualist to an increasingly nonconceptualist position, see Welton 2000, esp. 174–197.

4 Some of these arguments are discussed in Hopp 2011.

5 For a criticism that Husserl is susceptible to this objection, see Bell 1990, 143–144.

6 Millar 1991, 36–37. Also see Roessler 2009, 1028.

7 See O'Shaughnessy 2000, 327; Millikan 1990, 728; and LI 6 §5, 683.

8 Hubert Dreyfus, discussing what is in effect a hybrid of the two-act and one-act views, points out that if we treat the intuitive fulfilling act as having a matter which can be drained of fullness, as it must if conceptualism is true, a vicious regress ensues: "The intuitive act will indeed have its own intentional content, which can be entertained independently of whether this content is fulfilled or not, but then an act having this content is not necessarily a fulfilling act. And we will have to seek again for an act which necessarily supplies the filling" (Dreyfus 1982, 105). The one-act view can stop this regress by no longer looking for a fulfilling *act*, but a fulfilling *sensation*. But that, as the argument of this section attempts to establish, does not succeed either.

9 See Bernet, Kern, and Marbach (1992, 128): "It is important ... not to confuse the cognitive form of fulfillment with the fulfillment of the mere expectation of the further course of experience."

10 The example that follows is inspired by Peacocke 2001, 241.

11 See Reinach 1982, §3; DuBois 1995, 18–20; Sokolowski 2000, 79; Dahlstrom 2006, 209; Williford 2006, 121; and Yoshimi 2009, 124–125.

12 This objection is inspired by Ka-Wing Leung's objection to Husserl's argument in LI 6 §§4–5, that perception does not have meaning content. See Leung 2011, 136.

13 Brewer 2005, 218. Note that Brewer no longer endorses conceptualism, but has moved on to a naïve realist position regarding perception. See Brewer 2011, especially Chapter 5.

14 See Pryor 2013, 210.

15 See Pollock and Oved 2005, 311 and Lyons 2009, 30–31. Lyons does, however, thoroughly reject the kind of theory of experiential justification that will be defended in the next chapter in favor of a reliabilist theory.

16 A fact noted even by defenders of "phenomenal intentionality." See, for instance, Graham, Horgan, & Tienson 2009, 523.

17 LAW, 326–327. This translation is a slight modification of one due to Julia Jansen (2015, 60). Also see Heffernan 1998, 2.

18 See Fish 2009, Ch. 1 and Crane and French 2015, §3.4 for very helpful discussions.

19 Campbell 2002, 118. Also see Brewer 2008, 171 and Martin 2009, 273.

20 See Hinton 1967 and 1973. For some recent phenomenological work on disjunctivism, see A.D. Smith 2008, Hopp 2011, Romano 2012, Overgaard 2013, Staiti 2015, and Overgaard 2018. Not everyone agrees that hallucinations are not perceptual experiences, however. Rami Ali (2018) argues that there are good reasons to endorse an illusionist theory of hallucination, according to which, roughly speaking, hallucinations are misperceptions of worldly things, not experiences of non-existent things. Thanks to Søren Overgaard for pointing this out.

21 See Byrne and Logue 2009, §2.

22 ibid., 130. Also see McGinn 2008, 242.

23 Jake Quilty-Dunn has recently defended the view that perception involves belief. However, contrary to the view defended here, but certainly more in accord with what I take to be the dominant philosophical view, he maintains that beliefs are propositional attitudes (2015, 553–554).

24 Dretske 2000a. According to Johnston (2004, 156), in this case Dan would the "secondary object" of my hallucination, in virtue of the fact that the profile strikes me as being Dan.

25 Speaks 2009, 560. Also see Schellenberg 2014, 212.

26 Thanks to Søren Overgaard for pressing me on the proper construal of the relational view, though I am not confident that I have settled all of his worries.

27 Husserl's most complete accounts of eidetic variation occur in PP §9 and EJ §87. Also see Kasmier 2003, Chapter 6 and Tieszen 2005, Chapter 3.

28 See §1 of the Second Logical Investigation, whose title is "We are conscious of universal objects in acts which differ essentially from those in which we are conscious of individual objects" (LI, 339).

29 "We need only refer to cases where individual or specific presentations are intuitively 'fulfilled', to be utterly clear as to the sorts of objects 'meant' by such presentations" (LI 2 §1, 339).

30 John Burgess issues the following challenge to nominalists: "if they think their versions of gravitational theory or whatever are superior scientifically to standard versions, then one might expect

them to publish their work in theoretical physics journals" (Burgess, 2008, 88). But, Burgess points out, this has not to his knowledge been done, and there's no reason to expect that any such attempt would be successful.

31 For two excellent treatments of Husserl's account of a priori knowledge, see Kasmier 2003 and Piazza 2007.

Recommended Readings

Campbell, John. 2002. *Reference and Consciousness*. Oxford: Clarendon Press.

Husserl, Edmund. 1977. *Phenomenological Psychology*. John Scanlon, trans. The Hague: Martinus Nijhoff.

Huserl, Edmund. 1973. *Experience and Judgment*. Ludwig Landgrebe, ed. James S. Churchill and Karl Ameriks, trans. Evanston: Northwestern University Press.

Husserl, Edmund. 1989. *Ideas Pertaining to a Pure Phenomenology and to a Phenomenological Philosophy. Second Book. Studies in the Phenomenology of Constitution*. Richard Rojcewicz and André Schuwer, trans. Dordrecht: Kluwer Academic Publishers.

Johnston, Mark. 2004. "The Obscure Object of Hallucination." *Philosophical Studies* 120: 113–183.

McDowell, John. 1994. *Mind and World*. Cambridge: Harvard University Press.

Siegel, Susanna. 2010. *The Contents of Visual Experience*. Oxford: Oxford University Press.

Smith, A.D. 2002. *The Problem of Perception*. Cambridge: Harvard University Press.

9 Knowledge

Over the past three chapters we have focused on the nature of originary intuition and, especially, perception. Perception is inadequate to its objects, is intentionally direct, has both intuitive and horizonal content, neither of which is conceptual, and is very probably relational. The task now is to characterize knowledge, the indispensable role that originary intuition plays in its production, and its own indispensable role in all intentional acts.

9.1 Phenomenology and the Problem of Skepticism

Probably no topic was of deeper concern to Husserl than knowledge (Willard 1995, 138). In the natural, day-to-day attitude characteristic of ordinary and scientific life, we take knowledge and our capacity to know for granted. Ordinary consciousness "takes possession ... of a reality that simply exists and is given as a matter of course" (IdPh, 16). Errors occur and disagreements arise. But they are often settled, and are presented to us as matters that can in principle be settled, by the appeal to further evidence or more rigorous reasoning. We correct others and ourselves by producing further evidence, shaping more rigorous arguments, or both.

When, however, we reflect philosophically on knowledge, we find that we do not genuinely understand how it works. Knowledge "belongs to a knowing subject," and yet "The known object stands over against it" (IdPh, 17). In light of this, the question emerges: "How, then, can knowledge be sure of its agreement with the known objects? How can knowledge go beyond itself and reach its objects reliably?" (IdPh, 17)

The answer to this question is to be found by inquiring into the "correlation between epistemic experience, meaning, and object" (IdPh, 17). This should look familiar. It is the intentional triad introduced in the Preface, the examination of which provides the main task of transcendental phenomenology. And, happily, exploring some of the salient features of the items making up that correlation has been the main task of the work thus far. In examining how ideal contents, including meanings, are related to acts of thought and perception, and how intuitions relate to meanings, on the one hand, and objects, on the other, we have covered much of the basic groundwork of a phenomenological account of knowledge.

Before we attempt to say more about knowledge, however, a few important clarifications are in order. It may seem that when Husserl outlines the task of epistemology, he is concerned with overcoming skepticism. Skepticism with respect to some subject matter is the view that we cannot *know about* it. Thanks to the essential correlation between states of affairs and propositions, it is also the view with respect to some body of propositions that we cannot *know* them. Skepticism comes in a number of varieties. Global skepticism maintains that we cannot have knowledge of anything. Local skepticisms target some domain, such as the external world, and hold that we cannot know anything about it. Skepticism can be radical or moderate. The moderate skeptic holds that we have evidence for various beliefs, but that this evidence falls short of whatever is necessary for knowledge. The radical skeptic, by contrast, maintains that we do not even have evidence, and that none of our beliefs about the subject matter in question are even epistemically justified (Huemer 2001, 20). So, for instance, the line of reasoning in Descartes's First *Meditation*, in which he first questions the reliability of experience, then proposes that he may be dreaming, and finally introduces the hypothesis of an all-deceiving evil demon, can be read as an argument for global, radical skepticism (which Descartes then progressively attempts to overcome in the subsequent *Meditations*).

Husserl does take skepticism seriously in *some* fashion. In phenomenology, we take up an "epistemological" or "*purely philosophical attitude*" that "pursues the skeptical problems regarding the possibility of knowledge" (Ideas I §26, 46). In his 1907 lectures *The Idea of Phenomenology*, in which he takes skepticism more seriously than in most other works, he claims that "If I do not understand *how* it is possible for knowledge to make contact with something transcendent to it, then I also do not know *whether* it is possible" (IdPh, 28). That, however, is not true. As a general rule, it is quite easy to know that something is the case without knowing how or why it is the case. People have known that the sun shines for a very long time. We have only recently discovered why, and not many people even now (myself included) could provide more than a rough approximation of the explanation.

The same may well be true in the case of knowledge. Not only do most people know they have hands, know their address, know that apples are not persons, and so on, but they know that they know it. We know that quite independently of knowing any philosophical or psychological account of *how* it's possible, just as we know that we see without knowing an account of seeing and know that we speak without knowing linguistics. And we cannot shed our knowledge even if we try. We can *pretend* to not know that there are trees, just as Descartes pretends for part of his *Meditations* that he doesn't know that he has a body. But he knows, even while insisting that he does not know, and so do we. Possessing a true phenomenological or epistemological theory is not a condition on knowing or even knowing that you know.

The best response to the skeptic is not to produce new reasons to believe in trees and tables and other people. It is to show that the reasons we have always had have always been good enough.[1] Fortunately, Husserl's remark above does not seem to be a view that he consistently endorses. That he addresses "skeptical problems" in the "philosophical attitude" does not mean that in that attitude skepticism is treated as a live threat to our everyday knowledge, or that the latter's status as knowledge depends on a philosophical refutation of skepticism. As Dallas Willard describes Husserl's view,

> When he asks how a certain type of knowledge is possible, the "how" is not a skeptical "how," and does not mean "whether." Rather, he is inquiring only about the means, or the nature of the specific structures and processes, through which subjective experiences succeed in cognitively grasping independent and publicly accessible objects.
>
> (Willard 1984, 5)

Sonja Rinofner-Kreidl agrees: "From a phenomenological point of view, global skepticism represents an arbitrary suspicion that does not call for refutation in any substantial fashion."[2] There is good reason to think that this view is not only true, but that it is Husserl's. In the same section in which he discusses the "epistemological attitude," Husserl congratulates "natural science" for "discarding without further ado the smug and rampant ancient skepticism, and *abandoning* the [project of] overcoming it" (Ideas I §26, 45). Natural scientists should, Husserl continues, be dogmatic "in a good sense" and "accept the kinds of objects of knowledge wherever one actually encounters them" (Ideas I §26, 46).

Similarly, in his essay "Philosophy as a Rigorous Science," Husserl writes, "No reasonable person will doubt the objective truth or the objectively grounded probability of the wonderful theories of mathematics and the natural sciences" (PRS, 74). Over two decades later, Husserl says of the sciences that "The scientific rigor of all these disciplines, the convincingness of their theoretical accomplishments, and their enduring compelling successes are unquestionable" (Crisis §1, 4). And in *Formal and Transcendental Logic*, Husserl writes, "that there are indeed truths in themselves, which one can seek, and also find, by avenues already predelineated in themselves, is surely one of life's unquestioned truisms" (FTL §80, 198), and one on which the sciences depend (ibid., 199). He continues: "We do not intend to give up any of these truisms; they surely rank as evidences" (ibid.). Husserl *never* appears to have genuinely doubted that we have knowledge of the world and of ideal objects as well, and generally treats any theory that results in skepticism about these manifest accomplishments as absurd.[3] The usual targets are naturalism (IdPh, 18) and empiricism (Ideas I §20), which in spite of their professed allegiance to "science" cannot make sense of it as a rational achievement.

What reason is there, then, to address "skeptical problems" at all? One of Husserl's main motivations is that "natural reflection" on knowledge almost invariably winds up there. As he writes, among the tasks of epistemology are to:

> expose and reject the mistakes that natural reflection upon the relation between knowledge, its sense, and its object almost inevitably makes; and it must thereby refute the explicit or implicit skeptical theories concerning the essence of knowledge by demonstrating their absurdity.[4]

The chief of those mistakes is failing to recognize the *essential* relationships among the items making up the intentional triad, and, more generally, the distinctive (and difficult or even impossible to "naturalize") features of intentionality. Psychologism, a natural outcome of an empiricistic naturalism that only recognizes real items given in sensation or reflection or whatever real entities must be posited to most economically explain them, is a prime example. Aided and abetted by systematic ambiguities in language, it confuses the real, temporally located acts and states of judging, believing, and inferring ("judgments," "beliefs," "inferences"), which *are* suitable objects of empirical inquiry, with the ideal contents of those acts—propositions and the ideal relations, such as entailment and implication, that hold among them.[5] As a consequence, psychologism treats logic as a science primarily concerned with mental acts. The skeptical consequence is that the accomplishments of rational consciousness "will be interpreted merely psychologically as 'what humans do'" (Moran 2008, 413). In that case, we should be skeptical whether the various mental transitions from one state to the next that we call "inferring" or "proving" really do match up with any necessary and objective interconnections among the things that those states take as their objects. Perhaps *modus ponens* is nothing more than a natural transition from two psychological acts of judging to a third, one that happens to generate a certain feeling, "belief," in a certain biological species—just "what humans do." Had we *just done* something different, our "insights" would have had different contents but would have felt just as convincing.

While Husserl thinks that phenomenological-epistemological inquiries can "refute" skepticism, he is not committed to the view that this constitutes *rescuing* ordinary knowledge from an existing threat, or of providing, for the first time, its true foundations. And it would be an extremely objectionable epistemology if that were its task, as we will see. Like just about everything else, knowledge exists prior to and independently of there being any branch of knowledge dedicated to studying it—that is, prior to and independently of epistemology and phenomenology.

9.2 A Characterization of Knowledge

Knowledge, according to one prominent tradition, is *justified true belief*.[6] Thanks to the work of Edmund Gettier (1963), we know that this definition is false. To give one of his examples (1963, 122), Smith might be justified in thinking that Jones will get the job to which each of them has applied, and that Jones has ten coins in his pocket. He is justified in believing that the person who gets the job has ten coins in his pocket. But suppose that Smith himself gets the job rather than Jones, and, by sheer chance, Smith has ten coins in his pocket. Then his belief in that proposition is true and justified, but he does not know it. Philosophers have tried to find a fourth condition, typically some sort of tracking or anti-luck requirement, that will rule out such cases.[7] That is not the task of this chapter.

In what follows, I will not attempt to define knowledge. I suspect it is indefinable (see Williamson 2000, Chapter 3). I also suspect that, in the vast majority of real-world cases, we know clear cases of it when we encounter them. In that respect knowledge is a lot like just about everything else: we don't know definitions of almost any important concept, and yet we are capable of identifying what lies within their extensions. Knowledge is itself among the things given to us in the lifeworld, a human achievement with which we become familiar at a very young age. Nevertheless, there is a helpful characterization of what a wide number of paradigmatic cases of knowledge have in common, and one that I think is rather superior to the traditional definition above. According to Dallas Willard, knowledge is "the capacity to represent a respective subject matter as it is, on an appropriate basis of thought and/or experience" (Willard 2000b, 31). Willard is careful to claim that this is not an *analysis* or *definition* of knowledge, but "an initial description of cases which count as knowledge or knowing" (ibid.). That is, it is a characterization of a broad class of paradigmatic cases of knowing, one probably susceptible to some outlying counterexamples, and certainly in need of refinement.

Willard is also explicit that "It is, no doubt, impossible to define 'appropriate basis' in any perfectly general way" (Willard 2000b, 31–32). There are many appropriate bases of knowledge, including, in many cases, the testimony of authorities (Willard 1998). But at least two gold standards for Willard, as for Husserl, are (a) proof and (b) fulfillment or immediate verification. Proof, or "argument," is the process by which we determine that a proposition is true on the basis of other propositions that we know to be true. The best arguments are not merely valid or even sound; they are those whose premises are *known*. Proof is one way, but not the best or the foundational way, of coming to know. The single best way to verify a proposition, and the one we will principally focus on in this chapter, is through *experience* or originary intuition.

9.3 Fulfillment Revisited

In Chapter 5, §5.1, we discussed cognitive fulfillment. Our focus there was the role that fulfillment plays in providing empty conceptual contents with an authentic relation to their objects by means of intuitions. We only touched on its role in knowledge. It was, however, impossible to miss. Suppose, to recall our example, that A tells our recumbent friend B that the hood of the car is scratched. B, for whatever reason, is skeptical. He wants more evidence. There are lots of ways that B could try to go about determining whether what A says is true, many of which are compatible with his remaining in his armchair. B could comb through his beliefs to see how well A's assertion coheres with the rest of them. B could confer with the brightest people he knows to see what they think about the matter. B might, in the course of doing these things, encounter some apparently unimpeachable reasons to believe that it is or is not scratched. Perhaps these reasons contradict A's testimony. Should A pull up an armchair next to B and contend with B's beliefs and the enlightened musings of B's brightest friends? Should she enter the "logical space of reasons, of justifying and being able to justify what one says" (Sellars 1997, 76)? Should she "articulate" her "reasons" (Brandom 2001)?

Probably not. She should leave the space of reasons and turn to reality—that is, what our reasons are *about*—by leading B to the driveway and having him examine the car hood for himself. She does not need to say a word. When B does examine the hood, something fundamentally different happens. When B, who knows perfectly well the meaning of A's assertion, perceives the scratched car hood, B will undergo an experience of fulfillment. The car hood, under these conditions, "is seen as being exactly the same as it is thought of" (LI 6 §8, 696). B is not evaluating a proposition by weighing it up against other propositions, beliefs, or assertions. He is evaluating the proposition by measuring it up against the state of affairs that it is about, verifying that the hood of the car is scratched by appealing to the *fact* that it is scratched.

A sufficiently clear and distinct experience like that—that is, a completely ordinary one similar to thousands we have each day—would simply obliterate almost any countervailing considerations of coherence and the testimony and arguments of peers. "Fulfillment through a primordial impression is the force that mows everything down" (PAS, 76). It would also render almost any additional considerations superfluous. Far from becoming more confident in the scratchedness of the hood because of A's testimony, it is the scratchedness of the hood that makes B more confident in A. As P.M.S. Hacker (1987, 119) puts it, "finding a dozen people to whom this tomato looks red, as it does to me, is not adding to my *evidence* for its redness—I can *see* that it is red; rather, is it collecting witnesses to its redness!"

Perception, when clear and distinct, is powerful enough to normally override highly credible countervailing considerations, and to do so decisively.

Trustworthy testimony, a consensus among the best and brightest, eloquence and erudition, and seemingly ironclad arguments can be overthrown by the simple act of looking. And, it is worth noting, skeptical worries also weigh next to nothing against perception. Here, I think, it is good to pause and remind oneself just how extremely powerful perception and fulfillment are, to put on the hat of "common sense" and recall how things stand in the lifeworld. Many of us—here I speak for myself and on the basis of my impressions of others— feel as though we have a philosophical, or at least a professional, obligation to treat our contact with reality as a matter of grave doubt, to treat skepticism as a live worry rather than a mere puzzle. But as a matter of descriptive fact, clear and distinct perceptual experience enjoys almost total immunity from the kinds of imagined catastrophes which skeptics invoke to undermine it (see FTL §58, 156). This isn't just because these skeptical worries don't arise in ordinary life or that the context of ordinary life has less demanding evidential standards than philosophical ones, as contextualists claim (DeRose 1995). Many ordinary activities, such as the construction of a bridge, a moon landing, or a complicated heart surgery, probably involve considerably higher evidential standards than most philosophers (present company included) are accustomed to observe. That these experts don't worry about whether an evil demon will demolish the bridge, blow up the moon, or damage the patient's stents is not a sign that their thinking is less rigorous or rational, or that they are less serious about knowledge and justification.

Nor is it the case that we lose evidence when we engage in philosophical reflection. Skeptical philosophical reflection does not transform our naïve perceptual confidence in the world into a hunch. It is, for instance, quite *conceivable* that there is a ravenous and irate polar bear in the room with you that you do not, for whatever reason, perceive. After appreciating this genuine metaphysical possibility and bearing it firmly in mind, does your total evidence after thoroughly surveying the room, together with a presumably strong desire not to be a bear's next meal, give you *some reason* to leave the room? It's hard to see how it does. It's hard to see how a whole mountain of merely conceivable disasters—and there are *infinitely* many of them—gives you *any* reason whatsoever to leave the room. Despite the calamitous consequences of your being in the same room as a polar bear, this merely conceivable state of affairs is not a real or live possibility. The proposition that there is a polar bear in the room has not been overridden by perception. It is not a defeated reason. Rather, it doesn't seem to rise to the level of being a reason at all, not even in the abnormal context of philosophical inquiry. It is completely unmotivated by anything that has even the superficial trappings of evidence. As Michael Huemer puts it, "You would not let the mere possibility that *P* is *true* suffice for you to accept it, so why let the mere possibility that *P* is false suffice for you not to accept it?" (Huemer 2001, 105). Our experience is fallible, it can be overridden and crossed out. But this can only occur on the basis of real evidence, not imagined evidence.[8]

9.4 The Principle of All Principles

In light of the tremendous epistemic power of originary intuition, it is no surprise that the centerpiece of Husserl's theory of knowledge is the "Principle of All Principles" (POP), which claims:

> *that each intuition affording [something] in an originary way is a legitimate source of knowledge*, that *whatever presents itself to us in "Intuition" in an originary way* (so to speak, in its actuality in person) *is to be taken simply as what it affords itself as*, but *only within the limitations in which it affords itself there.*
>
> (Ideas I §24, 43)

This is not an entirely fortunate formulation, however. First, this "principle" is really two principles. According to the second, weaker version, we are rationally entitled to take things presented in originary intuition as they are presented to be. So, the second version of the principle entitles us to take an object to be red provided it appears red in an originary intuition, even if we are under an illusion and it is in fact yellow. As Husserl says in an earlier formulation, "whatever is given through clear and distinct perception ... we are entitled to accept" (IdPh, 37).

The first formulation, however, entails that originary intuition is a source of *knowledge* (see Berghofer 2018, 10–11). Now it may be that it is. As we have seen, even hallucination can be a source of knowledge of properties. But illusion is *not* a source of knowledge regarding those putatively real states of affairs that we are conscious of when undergoing one.

There is a way of understanding the two formulations that makes them compatible. The second, weaker formulation is that originary intuition is the preeminent consciousness of evidence, a type of consciousness that provides or can provide prima facie, defeasible *justification* for taking things to be as they are presented in it.[9] The first formulation can be understood as saying that *veridical* originary intuition is (nearly) sufficient for *knowledge*. So understood, and assuming for now that justification is essential for knowledge, it's a special case subsumed under the second, broader formulation. Granted, Husserl does not say this. Nevertheless, I suggest that so construed, the two formulations are both quite close to the truth. In what follows, "POP" will refer to the weaker formulation, unless otherwise noted.

POP is an epistemic principle that specifies sufficient conditions for epistemic justification. Moreover, it is quite clearly a principle of *propositional* epistemic justification. It concerns intuition as a "source" of knowledge and justification, and the legitimacy of "taking" something to be a certain way on the basis of such an originary intuition. It should not be read as saying that originary intuition is *itself* a case of knowledge, or that it is justified. Furthermore, insofar as originary intuition always has a positing quality—perception, as we have seen, presents its objects as actual—originary intuition is *already* a matter of "taking" something to be a certain way. I will argue below that veridical originary intuition is itself a kind of knowledge. But it's not the kind of knowledge at stake in POP.

This creates a difficulty, however. Having an originary, veridical intuition of O's being F is not sufficient for just any subject to justifiably believe every proposition that this state of affairs makes true and which this intuition fulfills. In fact it is not even sufficient to justifiably believe *any* proposition that it makes true. I cannot, for instance, have propositional knowledge that the tree out front is a beech tree on the basis of an originary intuition of that tree. The reason is that I do not possess the concept <beech tree> authentically, and so cannot undergo the appropriate synthesis required for cognitive fulfillment. Again, the state of affairs that makes true the proposition <The Morning Star is in the sky> also makes true the proposition <The Evening Star is in the sky>, but a given subject who sees Venus in the morning sky might only have propositional knowledge of the first of those propositions.

The reason originary intuition is not itself sufficient for propositional justification, then, is that in order for one's belief that P to be justified on the basis of intuition, one must (a) be able to think the proposition P, and (b) do so authentically. In order to know that P on the basis of originary intuition, it is not enough that the content of your intuition fulfills P. Your originary intuition must actually fulfill your thought that P.

POP, then, is best understood as a principle according to which *originary cognitive fulfillment* is a source of justification and knowledge. We should also add that this justification can only occur in the absence of *defeaters*. The most relevant kinds of defeaters are those originally discovered by John Pollock: rebutting defeaters and undercutting defeaters.[10] A rebutting defeater for one's belief that P is evidence that P is false. An undercutting defeater is anything that casts doubt on the manner in which one comes to believe that P.[11] So, for instance, A will have a rebutting defeater to her belief that the car hood is scratched if she discovers that it is tree sap on the hood—this gives her reason to think that her belief is false. She will have an undercutting defeater if she suddenly wakes up to find herself in an armchair, realizing she had an especially vivid dream. This would not by itself give her a reason to think that the hood is not scratched. But it would defeat the connection between originary intuition and belief that must occur if genuine fulfillment is to take place. Notice, too, that what defeats A's justification here is the *discovery* that she was dreaming. The mere unmotivated and empty *thought* that she *could conceivably* be dreaming does not defeat anything.

The Principle of All Principles, then, can be understood as follows:

> POP: If S's belief that P is fulfilled on the basis of an originary intuition, and if S's belief is undefeated, then S is justified in believing that P. If, in addition, that originary intuition is veridical, then S *knows* that P.

There is an even stronger way of understanding the principle, according to which a subject is not only permitted to believe that P in such circumstances, but is rationally obligated to do so. That seems to be Husserl's understanding. What is given *"is to be taken simply as what it affords itself as"* (Ideas I §24, 43). So, for instance, if B were to examine the scratch on the hood of the car, to see it, touch it, try fruitlessly to rub it away with some sap remover and a cloth, and so on, he would be positively irrational not to believe that the car hood is scratched. He is not only permitted or allowed to believe; rational norms obligate him to do so. To see this more clearly: if your thought that a ravenous polar bear is in the room with you and your dear ones was fulfilled, and if the best "evidence" you had against it is the undercutting defeater that an evil demon *might conceivably* be deceiving you, it would be profoundly irrational not to believe it and act on that belief.

Now we turn to some clarifications of the Principle.

9.4.1 The Scope of the Principle of All Principles

Husserl, quite rightly, understands the Principle of All Principles as a perfectly general principle. It is not a principle that is only operative when doing phenomenology, or confined to the field of subjectivity and consciousness with which transcendental phenomenology is concerned. It applies to any mind of any appropriate type regarding any field of possible objects that can be given originarily.

> In regard to every domain of objects and the positings related to them, the *original source of all legitimacy* lies in the immediate evidence for them, and, more narrowly defined, in the *originary evidence* or in the originary givenness motivating those positings.
>
> (Ideas I §141, 280–281)

If it is possible to have an originary intuition of a car's hood as being scratched and have the thought that it is scratched fulfilled by that intuition, then it is possible to satisfy the Principle. Both A and B, in our example, do satisfy the Principle. They know that the hood is scratched on the basis of its originary givenness in perception.

Furthermore, it is important to pay attention to Husserl's claim that we are to take what is given as it is given, *"but only within the limitations in which it affords itself there"* (Ideas I §24, 43). It may be tempting to think that when we perceive a car, the Principle only entitles us to take there to be a car-appearance or car-profile present, since we do not see the car's back or interior. This, however, is a mistake. The "limitations" are not those of *adequate* intuition, but of *originary* intuition. And ordinary perception, which is essentially inadequate, is nevertheless originary. Husserl claims that: "It is …

a fundamental mistake to suppose that perception ... does not get at the thing itself, or to suppose that the thing is not given to us in itself and in its being-in-itself."[12] He says this, moreover, in the very same breath that he denies that the things of perception are adequately given:

> So, too, it is fundamentally mistaken to suppose that it is possible in principle to intuit every entity simply as what it is, and, specifically, to perceive it in an adequate perception affording the thing itself in person *without the mediation through "appearances."*
>
> (ibid.)

Husserl's claim regarding our access to things "through 'appearances'" is susceptible to misinterpretation, as though there are images or representations standing between us and the things we perceive. That's a position Husserl consistently dismisses. All that Husserl means is that we see transcendent things from perspectives. They *themselves* appear, but appear in one of countless ways. And that is why he denies that we can perceive everything "simply as what it is"—the "simply" here means *adequately*. He is not denying that inadequately given objects are given to us as they are— as though they were given as they *aren't*, or not given at all. That is why, after disposing of views that treat perception as a form of image- or sign-consciousness in the next paragraph, he writes, "The spatial thing that we see is, along with all its transcendence, something perceived, *as it is in person*" (ibid.). The perception of a car, then, is not an originary perception of an adequately given sign, clue, image, or profile of a car. It is an originary perception of the car, "along with all its transcendence." What is not given, and so lies outside of the "limitations" above, is that, say, the car belongs to Dan, or that it was manufactured in Detroit, or that it is exactly 1,068 days old.

9.4.2 *The Necessity of the Principle of All Principles*

The Principle of All Principles is, if true, necessarily true. It is true in virtue of a fairly simple set of relations among reality, originary intuition, meaning, justification, and knowledge, relations that are not mere matters of psychological fact. For any mind of any kind, undefeated veridical originary intuition is a source of knowledge.

Originary intuitive contents essentially fulfill the meanings that they fulfill. But fulfillment, when accomplished through an originary intuition, is essentially reason-giving. To undergo an experience of fulfillment is to be in possession of evidence for the content of a proposition—or rather a whole lot of propositions, insofar as every concrete experience fulfills numerous propositions. In fulfillment, we:

experience how the same objective item which was "merely thought of" in symbol is now presented in intuition, and that it is intuited as being precisely the determinate so-and-so that it was at first merely thought or meant to be.

(LI 6 §8, 694)

And if, as Husserl no doubt has in mind in this passage, the intuition is an originary one, then the act will be positing, and the object will show up as *being* the way it presents itself. In such acts it is a matter of *being presented with* the object, of *finding*, of *discovering*, it to be as thought or meant (Willard 2002, 75). It is not just a psychological fact that experiences of this type motivate or cause belief in the fulfilled propositions, as if we simply found ourselves caused to endorse propositions for no intelligible reason. It is, rather, that the contents and qualities of the relevant acts, as a matter of necessity completely unalterable by changes in our conventions, our customs, our language-games, or our psychologies, add up to the preeminent consciousness of evidence. It is contingent that we can appreciate evidence (just as it is contingent that we can appreciate logical relations). What is not contingent is that the perceptual states we enjoy do provide us with evidence for the propositions that they fulfill.

The *epistemological* interconnections here are just as ideal and objective as the interconnections found in the *logical* sphere among propositions and in the *ontological* sphere among states of affairs. It is principally because it deals with these essential connections, and not because of its alleged normativity, that epistemology is not a branch of empirical psychology (Willard 2000b, 25–27). The Principle of All Principles is not only a necessary and universal *normative* requirement on rational belief formation. It is a normative requirement grounded in the essential evidential relations among the acts and objects composing an experience of fulfillment. We ought to take things as they appear to be in intuition because (a) we ought to believe what is evident, and (b) fulfilled propositions are evident. There is nothing normative about (b). When B's thought about the scratched car hood is fulfilled, the proposition is not evident because he ought to believe it. He ought to believe it because it is evident.[13] And it would remain evident even if (a) were false and some other norms determined our belief-forming obligations. If we had a duty to believe what best promotes our happiness, that would very likely change what we ought to believe, but would have no effect on the evidential character of fulfillment.

9.4.3 The Principle of All Principles Is a Source, not a Ground, of Knowledge

Suppose that S knows that P in virtue of undergoing an experience of fulfillment. We can then ask the following question: what is the reason S justifiably believes that P? This sort of question is, as Jack Lyons points out, "notoriously ambiguous."[14] Among the things we could mean in asking it are:

(1) What (if anything) makes it rational or reasonable for S to believe that P?

or

(2) What is S's evidence E for P?

The answer to (1) is bound to be complicated. To answer it, we need to appeal to some salient features of S's mental life, along with some principles in virtue of which those features of S's mental life make it rational for her to believe that P. In our example, the answer to (1) might look something like this:

(1A) S has undergone an undefeated experience of veridical, originary cognitive fulfillment which constitutes an awareness of evidence E for P, and (according to POP) undergoing experiences of this type is sufficient for knowledge.

That answer, however, is not at all what we would expect in response to (2). S's evidence E for P is not *that S has evidence E for P* or any variant thereof. Rather, S's evidence for P, and the answer to (2), is just this:

(2A): E

To make sense of these very different answers, we need to distinguish what Jack Lyons (2009, §2.1) calls "evidential" and "non-evidential justifiers"—or, more simply, *grounds* and *sources* of justification and knowledge (Van Cleve 1979, 69). An evidential justifier or *ground* is one's *evidence* for the propositional *content* of one's belief.[15] Grounds are not grounds for "beliefs," in the sense of acts of believing, but of their contents. When someone believes that the hood of the car is scratched, her evidence is what supports the proposition <the hood of the car is scratched>. This explains why two people can have evidence for the same thing, which would not be the case if the evidence were for their acts of believing.

A non-evidential justifier or *source* is any factor that contributes to the justificatory or epistemic status of a belief that is *not* an evidential justifier (Lyons 2009, 24). Non-evidential justifiers relate, not to propositional contents of belief, but to acts of believing. In the example above, answer (1A) is a specification of some of the *sources* of S's knowledge, while (2A) is a specification of the *grounds* of S's knowledge.

In general, our experiences themselves are sources rather than grounds of knowledge. It is very tempting, when citing our *evidence* for perceptual beliefs, to cite our experiences. As Gianfranco Soldati puts it,

If you ask me why I believe that it is raining, what *my* reason is for believing that it is raining, I may fittingly say, "Because I see *it!*" The perceptual experience justifies my belief *because* it provides *me* with a reason for believing that it is raining.

(Soldati 2012, 31)

It's clear that what Soldati has in mind is his *evidence* that it is raining. But the answer he provides is not, I think, what his evidence is. That is, "Because I see it" is not the evidence that Soldati himself has for the proposition that it is raining. That's the evidence that he will provide you or me, because our asking for evidence indicates that we don't have the same access that he does to the rain (see Alston 1989a, 163). He does not, however, first look at his experience and reason to the claim that the world is a certain way (see Pryor 2000, 519). Rather, as the second sentence makes clear, his perceptual experience *"provides"* him with evidence. It is not *itself* his evidence. It is what makes him *aware of* the evidence. His act of seeing is a source (or provider), not a ground, of his knowledge.

Any theory of knowledge and justification that requires there to be evidential justifiers or grounds is one kind of "internalist" theory. "For something to be the ground of a belief, it must be the sort of thing that the believer can take into account" (Lyons 2009, 23). When A and B come to know that the car hood is scratched, they are definitely taking something of which they are conscious "into account." There is much, however, that they do *not* need to take into account. Among them are the facts that the Principle of All Principles is true, and that their mental states fall under it. That is why the Principle is a source, not a ground, of knowledge. As James Van Cleve puts it with respect to Descartes's principle of clarity and distinctness, this "is not a principle I have to *apply* in order to gain knowledge; I need only *fall under* it" (1979, 70).

Another thing that does not need to be taken into account, perhaps surprisingly, is the relational character of perception. That perception is a relational act may very well be a source of knowledge, since it secures a non-accidental connection with reality. But it is not a ground of most ordinary perceptual knowledge. I can justifiably believe that my perceptual experience bears a real relation to its object only if I am already perceptually aware of its object. It is the relation that makes me aware of the object, but it is my awareness of the object that makes me aware of the relation.

So, in our example above, the reason that A and B each know that the car hood is scratched is that each has experienced a veridical, undefeated originary cognitive fulfillment directed upon the state of affairs of the car's hood's being scratched, and, by POP, that is sufficient for knowledge. But that complicated fact is not their *evidence* that the car hood is scratched. They do not need to infer that the car hood is scratched by (a) learning enough epistemology to know an epistemic principle such as POP, (b) recognizing their own experiences as instances of it, and then (c) concluding that the car hood is scratched. They know that it is scratched just by *undergoing* those experiences, and in virtue of the *truth* of POP, not by *reflecting* on their experiences or *knowing* POP. As Husserl puts it, "If I call this intuited object a 'watch', I complete, in naming it, an act of thought and knowledge, but I know the watch, and not my knowledge."[16] Even when one knows that one knows that P—and I take this to be a normal condition of most human adults—one knows that one knows only if and in virtue of the fact that one knows that P. In knowing that P, one normally does not make it the case that P. Knowledge of knowing is not an exception: in knowing that one knows that P, one does not normally make it the case that one knows that P.

The Principle of All Principles, then, is a source rather than a ground of knowledge. And it would be false if it were not. On the terms of the Principle itself, veridical undefeated originary fulfillment is sufficient for knowledge. Because knowing the Principle is by no means a necessary condition for undergoing such experiences—people, including the very young and unsophisticated, can discover that the hood of the car is scratched without knowing or even being able to know the Principle of All Principles—knowing the principle itself cannot be a further necessary condition for knowledge.[17] What Husserl rather clearly endorses, then, is a version of internalism about grounds or evidence—since *evidence* is an intrinsically internalist notion—but externalism about at least some of the *sources* of knowledge. A very similar view is held by Earl Conee:

> What can be external to the mind of a person whose belief is justified … are epistemological facts about what evidence provides the person's justification and about the nature of the epistemic link of the belief to its justifying evidence. What must be internal, i.e., accessible to the person by reflection, is evidence that does in fact suffice to justify the belief.[18]

One important difference between this view and Husserl's (and Willard's), however, is that one's evidence is typically available, and available as evidence, independently of any act of reflection. As Husserl says, "the subjective act must harbor within it what pleads and warrants its claim to legitimacy."[19]

One of the advantages of this sort of view is that it enables us to know quite a lot without knowing any true epistemic principles, without reflecting on our own mental lives and determining that our psychological states satisfy the antecedents of any true epistemic principles, and without necessarily having the ability to justify the claim that we know what we do to the satisfaction of an epistemologist (or a skeptic). Knowledge is ubiquitous. A fairly young child can have evidence just as strong as a philosopher can have for a vast number of propositions, including the proposition that the hood of the car is scratched, despite the fact that they cannot perform as well as a silver-tongued adult in the "logical space of reasons" (Sellars 1997, 76). Knowledge of knowledge, and especially knowledge of the complicated array of non-evidential factors involved in it, is not at all common. It's an open question whether anyone has much of it. On some versions of internalism, *all* of the "justificatory 'factors' … must be 'accessible' to the person" (Bonjour 2010, 34). But, as Alvin Goldman points out, if that were the case, the result would be "large-scale skepticism" (Goldman 1999, 286). Only a few epistemologists would know anything. And maybe even they wouldn't. As Goldman points out, epistemic principles (such as the Principle of All Principles) are among the factors involved in justification, but are themselves far less certain than many other propositions (ibid., 287). No epistemic principle, for instance, is as certain as an ordinary perceptual judgment, to say nothing of an obvious mathematical or logical proposition.

One additional, and attractive, consequence of this view is that it does not require us to conceive of phenomenology as a discipline that provides the epistemic foundations for the rest of our knowledge.[20] As we have seen in §9.1 above, Husserl knows the sciences produce knowledge, and that they do so quite independently of any help from phenomenology or epistemology. "The existing sciences are essentially neither enhanced nor downgraded by the truths of critique of knowledge" (ILTK, 186). Of course, Husserl does think that such sciences are only "one-sided" (FTL, 16). In particular, they do not thematize their own rational achievements. They are in the business of investigating the nature of their respective subject matters, not their own cognitive relation to those subject matters. To become fully complete and rationally comprehensible two-sided sciences, phenomenological inquiry into their rational achievements is required (see FTL §9).

That, however, is compatible with the claim that they *produce* knowledge of their respective fields of inquiry. It would be an absurd consequence of phenomenological philosophy if it maintained that people do not know their names or know whether they exist, or know that there are apples, or even know geometry and the age of the universe, unless and until they study phenomenology. In fact it would be an absurd consequence of any epistemology if it were not in a position to accommodate the fact that the most developed sciences are vastly more impressive epistemic achievements than anything epistemologists, phenomenologists, or philosophers of any stripe have managed to produce. One does not have to wait until one studies phenomenology to have things given in an originary way and to think of them as they are given. It happens all the time. Knowledge, far from being a far-off goal of intentionality or something only achievable through critical philosophical reflection, is coeval with intentionality, and a condition for much of it even to occur. One could not even conceive of embarking upon philosophical or phenomenological inquiries themselves unless one had a considerable body of knowledge already at hand. As we will see in Chapter 11, however, Husserl does think that no naïve or dogmatic science could provide a *complete* metaphysical account of its domain.

Husserl's view is made clear when he points out that science "does not investigate Evidenz, justification of perception, experience, etc., but rather the subject matter of its field. It needs those sources of justification, but it does not investigate them."[21] But science does indeed already *have* what it needs, namely perception, experience, and other "sources of justification." Phenomenology's discoveries, including its discoveries about the nature of knowledge, occur only *after* such acts have already taken place in the unreflective natural attitude. A successful phenomenology of evidence and knowledge does not first bring them into existence, but discloses what they already were. Originary intuition is evidence-providing in virtue of its nature.[22]

That the Principle of All Principles is a source rather than a ground of knowledge should not, however, obscure the very important fact the evidential quality of acts of fulfillment is a phenomenologically salient feature of them. The evidential superiority of intuitive over armchair intentionality is not something that only becomes clear through phenomenological or epistemological reflection.[23] When B expresses doubts about A's report that the hood is scratched and decides to resolve the issue, he already and without theoretical reflection experiences his mere act of thinking as not good enough. One does not have to be an epistemologist to experience this. When Husserl characterizes Evidenz or givenness as "the quite preeminent mode of consciousness," he is characterizing the phenomenal character of the experience itself.[24]

He even provides an argument to that effect. If the evidential character of these acts was not built into them, we would have to verify that *experience verifies* and *empty thinking does not* through phenomenological and epistemological reflection. "But," Husserl argues, "to know whether experience verifies, the judgment presenting the verification must still be distinguished *in itself* from any empty talk thrown in out of the blue. And, this distinguishing is again Evidenz."[25] Just as the reflective act of seeing that *experience verifies* is "in itself" different from "empty talk," so is the first-order act of seeing the hood to be scratched different in itself from emptily thinking or saying that it is (FTL §94, 233). When we do make this difference *thematic* and *conceptualized* in reflection, we are not discovering it, but rendering explicit what was there all along. So in that sense, even some *sources* of knowledge— namely some of the features of our experiences themselves—are internal. The being-in-touch character of originary intuition is a feature of our experiences, known by acquaintance in the very having of them.[26]

One further point that should be emphasized is that the evidential character of an act is not a quale or a feeling that just happens to attach itself to an intentional content. This is part of what Husserl means when he insists that Evidenz or givenness is not a *feeling*.[27] Fulfillment, for instance, is not a belief with a certain feeling attached to it. It is not, moreover, a *seeming*, if by a "seeming" one means an experience with propositional content and a distinctive kind of "felt veridicality" (Tolhurst 1998, 298), "forcefulness" (Huemer 2001, 77), "assertiveness" (Tucker 2010, 530), or "phenomenal force" (Pryor 2000, 547, n. 37). Having the forcefulness of a seeming is neither necessary nor sufficient for fulfillment. It is not sufficient, since many seemings are not even intuitive acts. It seems to me, for instance, that human life evolved from simpler organisms and that bacteria both cause diseases and are present in my environment. But neither of these propositions is fulfilled for me on the basis of intuitions, and neither is foundationally justified.

Seemings are also not *necessary* for fulfillment. Earl Conee (2013, 66–67) presents the case of "Seemless," a subject whose ordinary perceptual experiences no longer give rise to seemings thanks to his exposure to unsound but convincing skeptical arguments. Nevertheless, Seemless still undergoes experiences of cognitive fulfillment. And, as a consequence, he still has excellent evidence for the truth of the fulfilled propositions. "Seemless's perceptual evidence justifies his perceptual beliefs. Yet seeming truth does none of the justifying, since it does not occur" (Conee 2013, 67). That they do not seem true to him indicates that his seemings no longer track his evidence. But the bare fact that his seemings can fail to track his evidence shows that seemings are not identical with evidence or with the consciousness of evidence. They are, rather, fitting responses *to* the consciousness of evidence.[28]

On Husserl's view, and the view defended here, the evidential character of empty and intuitive acts is primarily grounded in their content or contents and, in many cases, the relations among those contents, and not a certain feeling of confidence or forcefulness. Once we compare, say, the mere thought that the car hood is scratched with an act in which that thought achieves fulfillment through a perceptual experience, "we see how ridiculous the view is which sees *Evidenz* as a merely appended index, a feeling attaching to otherwise identical experiences of judging" (LAW, 326). The epistemic character of these acts is ultimately grounded in their *contents* or *matters*. Conceptual acts are not empty in virtue of their quality or in virtue of the nature of their objects; they can share both with intuitive acts. They are empty in virtue of conceptual content itself. And intuitive acts are not intuitive or presentational in virtue of their quality or their objects; again, these can be shared with conceptual acts. They are intuitive, and evidential, in virtue of their content. And in the synthesis of fulfillment, it is the *matters* of the respective acts that are the "carriers of the synthesis" (LI 6 §16, 719). Indeed, Husserl *defines* matter as "the element in our acts which serves as a basis for identification" (LI 6 §25, 738).

9.4.4 The Principle of All Principles and Foundationalism

Foundationalism about knowledge is the position that all knowledge is either non-inferentially or immediately known, or is based on such knowledge. Husserl, at least at the time of *Ideas I*, is pretty clearly committed to foundationalism: "Every mediated justification leads back, as is well known, to an ... immediate justification."[29] One traditional argument for foundationalism, the regress argument, proceeds by arguing that the justification of one's belief that P either never terminates, is circular, or ends in foundational justification, and that only the latter option is compatible with our having knowledge. A much stronger case for this commitment of foundationalism, however, would be to actually identify some foundational cases of knowledge, and to explain why they are foundational. That is what Descartes attempts to do, and I believe succeeds in doing, in his *Meditations*. And it is what we are able to do by consulting the Principle of All Principles. Each time something is given originarily, and we form a belief that that is the way it is given, the resulting belief is foundational.

As one would expect, foundational justification is quite different from inferential justification. When A and B perceive the car hood to be scratched, and then believe that it is scratched, they are not inferring that it is scratched. One reason is that the experience, which is what justifies the belief, does not have propositional content. But inferential relations are relations among propositional contents or acts with such contents. A second reason is that in the case of noninferential experiential justification, the experience is of the same state of affairs that the belief is of. But this is almost never the case in inferential knowledge. Generally speaking, if we infer P from some set of propositions Q and R, Q and R do not have the same intentional object as P itself.[30] The most obvious reason, though, is that they do not need to appeal to any other beliefs. What is in their field of consciousness is the very fact that makes their belief true. The best conceivable evidence that the hood is scratched is the fact that it is scratched. Thanks to perception, that's the evidence to which they have access.

This version of foundationalism, then, has the virtue of actually specifying the foundations of knowledge rather than simply reasoning that they *must* exist. A second virtue of this version of foundationalism is that it is compatible with the ubiquity of knowledge. This is in part because the Principle of All Principles is, in a certain way, self-effacing; it doesn't need to be known, recognized, or believed in order for knowledge to occur. It is also because the acts in which we achieve foundational knowledge happen all the time. Thinking about the things one perceives, as the things one perceives, is an extremely common occurrence. The content of our foundational knowledge is not one proposition, or a handful of axiomatic propositions, nor is it a body of propositions that require philosophical meditation or reflection to unearth or produce. Rather, it includes the vast number of ordinary propositions that we believe on the basis of mundane perceptual encounters with the surrounding world.

Some of the most historically familiar versions of foundationalism do not seem to satisfactorily account for the ubiquity of knowledge. Descartes's *cogito*, for instance, is a foundation upon which virtually no one before or since has based their knowledge. Nothing could be further from our minds, when we see our car hood to be scratched, learn the lyrics of a song, discover a quicker route to the store, or find a dollar bill in our pocket, than the *cogito*. If knowledge must rest on a foundation, this had better not be the only one.

Fortunately, Descartes offers a more plausible foundation: clear and distinct perception (Descartes 1984, 24).

Sense datum theories also, it seems to me, do not adequately explain the ubiquity of knowledge. Thoughts about sense data do not normally occur, and are therefore not normally fulfilled. A few epistemologists might undergo such experiences of fulfillment. But this leaves the knowledge the rest of us have unaccounted for. I cannot get in shape just because a professional athlete goes to the gym on my behalf, and I cannot know anything about any subject matter just because a professional epistemologist can construct an edifice of knowledge on my behalf. If the actual pattern of our psychological acts does not even approximate the pattern laid down by an epistemological theory, then either that theory does not specify a necessary condition of knowing, or we do not know.

A third virtue of this account is that it is phenomenologically accurate. A foundationalist theory ought to specify foundations of knowledge that mature and reflective persons can recognize in their own experience. Since a familiar sort of experience will be directed towards a familiar kind of object—namely the kind of object that the kind of experience itself makes available to us—the objects which we encounter in foundational acts of knowing, and the acts in which we know them, ought to be ones which we are unsurprised to learn exist.

Once again, many versions of foundationalism do not seem to possess this feature. The sense datum theory and its many variants provide a convenient example. According to most versions of it, foundational knowledge is achieved in experiences in which we are acquainted with immaterial, private, and, in the case of vision, two-dimensional objects. Our experience of them is typically held to be adequate insofar as they actually possess all and only those properties that they are presented as having, and our knowledge of them is held to be infallible. This theory enjoys almost no phenomenological support. It is a piece of news, for the average intelligent person, that these sorts of things have been, all along, the objects of her perceptual experiences, and that her substantial body of knowledge of the world is grounded in an acquaintance with them. But if they really did serve as the foundation of her knowledge—and on a second-by-second basis, no less—then this should not be the least bit surprising. Philosophers give *arguments* for sense data, and should. But it is only in very peculiar circumstances that one would present an argument for, say, water or dirt. (The best "argument" for water and dirt is to refute an argument against them.) Michael Williams, while no friend of foundationalism, expresses the problem perfectly: "The view that sense-data are simply discovered by introspecting one's perceptual consciousness is highly implausible. But the alternative view—that they are postulated theoretical entities—seems to conflict with the requirement that they be given."[31]

Fourth and finally, a foundationalist theory of knowledge ought to specify foundations that are rich enough in content to make the vast body of scientific knowledge that we possess about the actual physical and cultural world intelligible. Although it is beyond the scope of this work to attempt to defend that claim in any detail, the fact that our foundational beliefs are directed upon the very same world that the natural and social sciences, along with the humanities, describe and treat theoretically is a much more promising foundation than propositions about sense data or one's own experiences.

9.4.5 The "Myth of the Given"

Still, one might worry that acts of originary cognitive fulfillment could not be foundational. One might, in particular, worry that the present account is a version of Sellars's famous "Myth of the Given" (Sellars 1997, 77). Simplifying his argument radically, Sellars presents us with the following dilemma.[32] Either states of givenness—originary intuition, in our parlance—have propositional content or they do not. If they do not, they cannot justify beliefs. And if they do, then they are not foundational.

We have already addressed the first horn of this dilemma in Chapter 8, §8.3.5 perceptual states are not able to justify beliefs because they have the same kinds of *contents* as beliefs, but because they can have the same kinds of *objects* as beliefs, namely states of affairs. We have not, however, addressed the second horn. According to the advocate of the given, as Sellars understands the position, givenness "presupposes no learning, no forming of associations, no setting up of stimulus-response connections" (Sellars 1997, 20). The given is what could be taken up by a mind devoid of concepts and knowledge, a blank slate (see Brandom 1997, 122). But according to Sellars, in order to know something as simple as that a patch is green, one must not only have a whole battery of color concepts, but one must also know various things about the conditions in which it is favorable to find out whether something is green (Sellars 1997, 43). That, in turn, requires knowledge that there are such things as lighting conditions, and that it affects how things appear. This is just the start. If seeing a green patch requires all that, consider what must be involved to see an event as a graduation ceremony or a funeral, to see a piece of paper as a five-dollar bill, or to hear a stream of noise as a linguistic utterance.

One response to this argument comes from Gail Soffer, who writes:

> For Sellars, the point is to found empirical knowledge, to identify the non-inferential bases for inferences. By contrast, for Husserl the category of the given serves to thematize the subjective elements of experience (the immanent) and to show how what is taken by us to be knowledge presupposes and emerges out of these subjective elements.
>
> (Soffer 2003, 310)

Despite her careful treatment of and powerful objections to Sellars's account of intentionality, I have misgivings about this response. The category of originary intuition is of fundamental epistemic importance for Husserl, which is why "Evidenz" is used more or less synonymously with "givenness" and "originary intuition" in so much of his work. Evidenz is "the giving of something itself" (FTL §59, 156). And what is given is not confined to what is really or intentionally immanent.

Evidenz or givenness comes, as we have seen, in two varieties. First, there is originary intuition itself. Second, there is originary cognitive fulfillment, an act which contains originary intuition as a proper part. Regarding the latter, it is clear that this *does* require possessing concepts, and possessing them authentically. You cannot know the proposition <the patch is green> without having the concepts <patch> and <green>. Furthermore, there is every reason to think that Sellars is right that concept possession itself requires knowledge, and very often quite extensive bodies of knowledge. As Willard points out, one must know a great deal even to have the ability to discover that one's broom is in the closet (2000b, 44).

Sellars is right, then, that a great deal of concept possession, and therefore propositional knowledge, "presupposes" concepts and knowledge. How, then, can it be noninferential or foundational? The answer is provided by William Alston. A piece of knowledge may depend on other knowledge in one of at least two ways. First, it may depend upon it for its *justification* or "epistemization" (Alston 1989b, 58). A piece of propositional knowledge that depends upon another piece of propositional knowledge for its epistemization cannot be foundational (ibid., 63).

There is a second way, however, in which a belief or piece of knowledge may depend on another, and that is for its *existence*. As Alston puts it,

> The question of what epistemizes a belief only arises once the belief is formed. That question presupposes the existence of the belief and hence presupposes any necessary conditions of that existence. It is then a further question whether the belief is epistemized and, if so, by what.
>
> (Alston 1989b, 63)

A piece of knowledge may existentially depend on other pieces of knowledge either contingently or essentially. In either case, that a piece of knowledge depends on other knowledge for its existence does not entail that it is *epistemically* dependent on that knowledge. As an example, Alston writes, "If one tried to teach a child that $2 + 3 = 5$ while keeping him ignorant of, for instance '$1 + 1 = 2$', he would fail miserably" (Alston 1989b, 63). But that does not mean that the appropriately primed child cannot have noninferential knowledge that $2 + 3 = 5$. Again, knowing that the hood of the car is scratched depends on a great deal of knowledge for its existence. But it need not depend on that knowledge for its justification. When one sees a scratched car hood, the vast array of knowledge presupposed by that ability—knowledge of what cars are, what a scratch is, and so on—does not operate as a set of premises from which we infer that it is scratched. It operates as an array of conditions that make noninferential knowledge possible (see Fales 1996, 123). In James Pryor's terms, the fact that knowledge is *immediate* does not entail that it is *autonomous*, that is, that it could exist without one's having other beliefs or other knowledge.[33]

Having the ability to know something, and even to perceive something, to have it directly given, is often a skill. Like other skills, is often one that requires both practice and knowledge to attain and perfect. Practice in a physical activity, such as playing a sport or musical instrument, does not make one's encounter with the implements or instruments somehow removed from them. Infants do not have optimal access to violins. Violinists do. And they have preeminent access to violins—"direct" or "immediate" or "authentic" access—not despite, but exactly because they have invested so much time handling and playing them. Their knowledge is what explains the immediacy of their access. No one would maintain that a *lack* of knowledge and practice is the best situation from which to approach violin playing.

It is just the same in the life of the mind. Ignorance is not the optimal epistemic condition in which to be in order to have the world given to one. Infants do not have the best access to or the purest and most unmediated encounter with the physical world, to say nothing of the cultural lifeworld or the world of idealities such as numbers and propositions. The people to whom those entities can be most authentically and adequately given are the ones with the most knowledge and the richest stock of authentic concepts. A radiologist, to give Susanna Siegel's example, sees more thanks to her knowledge (Siegel 2012, 201). Mathematicians can have mathematical facts given to them which the rest of us have to work out, or which we cannot know altogether. Hubert Dreyfus writes, "a chess grandmaster, when shown a position that could occur in an actual game, almost immediately experiences a compelling sense of the current issue and spontaneously makes the appropriate move" (Dreyfus 2014, 234). That is, she *sees* more than the rest of us *thanks to* her knowledge.[34]

Chess provides a good example in which someone can have noninferential knowledge that is constitutively, and not merely causally, dependent on other pieces of knowledge (Haugeland 1996). It takes knowledge to see chess pieces and chess moves. What someone totally ignorant of chess sees when looking at a chess board or watching a chess game are only the objects which materially constitute chess pieces and the motions that materially constitute chess moves.[35] Those familiar with chess see chess moves. Experts see which ones are good and which are bad. And they really do *see* them. It would be incorrect to claim that, for someone who knows chess, recognizing a chess piece or chess move is really a matter of inferring or otherwise emptily intending that it is a chess piece or move on the basis of a perception of what materially constitutes it. Rather, knowledge of chess allows the chess pieces and chess moves to show up immediately and intuitively as chess pieces and chess moves.

This becomes clear when we see how different the fulfilling sense of chess concepts are from the fulfilling senses of concepts of their material constituters. The actual physical properties of the materially constituting objects and motions can be varied rather dramatically without affecting what we *perceive* and *immediately know* of the chess pieces and chess moves. If, in the middle of a game, the players swapped out each wooden chess piece with a larger soapstone piece of the same game type, this need not interfere with the perception each player has *of the chess pieces* or *the game*. The *same* game— the same *particular* game, the very game between A and B—would continue, and would be experienced as continuing. But, as John Haugeland notes, to see the game as continuing, "a perceiver would have to 'abstract from' the gross and conspicuous differences of implementation, and attend only to the chess-relevant features of the configurations" (Haugeland 1996, 274). Moving a material constituter—a piece of wood or stone—just one square over, by contrast, would make it a very different game, no matter what it was made of. And if a player captures a piece by first removing the opponent's piece and then moving her own piece into the square, this is no different from a player first moving her piece to the square and then knocking the opponent's piece over. Again, whether a pawn is in the exact center of square d4 or up against the very edge of the square makes absolutely no difference when it comes to seeing the game. These very different materially constituting objects, events, and states of affairs are, from the point of view of seeing a chess game, equivalent.

Husserl writes, "givenness is givenness" (TS, 300). Whatever it is that enables an object to be given—biology, psychology, training, traditions, concepts, knowledge, enculturation, a good will, or whatever else—once that object is given, it really is *given*. That any of these can also function as *disabling* conditions for givenness may also be true, but is beside the point. Whatever enables you to see something really does allow you to *see* it. And once an object is given, we do not need to infer, deduce, or guess that it is as it is given. We have the thing itself. Thanks to knowledge, I can see a five-dollar bill and not just the paper that materially constitutes it, and recognize it as a five-dollar bill. But when I see a five-dollar bill, my knowledge that it is a five-dollar bill is noninferential. It is not, moreover, merely *psychologically* non-inferential; it is not just that I don't in fact perform any inferences. It is *epistemically* noninferential because, thanks to my knowledge, I have a mind capable of having such things given to me.

In anticipation of further discussions in the next chapter, it bears noting that the distinction between knowledge which depends on other knowledge for its *existence* and its *justification* is one that most phenomenologists, or at least those working within a broadly Husserlian framework, should insist upon. Phenomenological inquiry is itself supposed to enable us to achieve foundational, non-inferential, immediate knowledge of at least some essential features of consciousness. As Husserl puts it, the "phenomenological reduction" entails "the limitation to the sphere of *pure self-givenness*" (IdPh, 45). And yet it would be absurd to maintain that the phenomenological reduction and the subsequent investigations that it makes possible could be carried out by someone with no prior knowledge. Infants can't do it. You have to already have experienced the world in order to reflect on those experiences, subject them to the kind of "bracketing" that the phenomenological reduction demands, and then investigate their intrinsic and relational features. "The bracketing moment of the phenomenological reduction … presupposes the pre-phenomenological operation of the natural attitude" (Hopkins 2010, 111).

Furthermore, you must already know a great deal about the natures of various "transcendent" objects in order to know that they must be bracketed.[36] But if you have already experienced the world, then—unless an extremely radical version of skepticism is true—you will already have acquired knowledge of the world. And this is just the beginning. The kind of conceptual and linguistic knowledge required to even conceive of something like a phenomenological science and its appropriate methodology is considerable. If all of that knowledge whose *existence* were presupposed for performing the phenomenological reduction were *evidentially* presupposed—if it functioned as a body of premises from which phenomenologists drew conclusions—then the whole procedure would be incoherent on its face. After all, the main function of the reduction is to bar us from using what we may or may not know about real existence as a premise in our phenomenological inquiry.

9.5 Knowledge by Acquaintance

So far, our discussion of knowledge has been confined to objectifying acts with propositional content. On the traditional conception of knowledge as justified true belief minus luck, that's probably exactly where it should be confined. I, however, would like to follow up a remark by Jennifer Church: "If perception fails to meet the traditional requirements for knowledge then, it might be argued, so much the worse for those requirements" (Church 2013, 12). Church provides us with broader and narrower ways of understanding those requirements. I, however, wish to pursue a more direct path: veridical perception and other forms of originary intuition are cases of knowledge on *any* understanding of "justification," "belief," and "truth." If we construe them narrowly as properties that only mental states with propositional content could possess, then none of those features is necessary for knowledge.

Bertrand Russell distinguishes knowledge of things by acquaintance and knowledge of truths. The most fundamental knowledge of things, upon which all knowledge of truths depends, is knowledge by acquaintance. The perception of ordinary physical objects does not qualify as acquaintance on Russell's view, but that's largely because Russell has such unreasonably exacting standards for acquaintance and also thinks, for reasons having to do with perceptual relativity that we have already discussed (Chapter 5, §5.2.1), that we cannot have an originary intuitive consciousness of physical objects or properties. As Gareth Matthews points out, however, Russell is unclear whether knowledge by acquaintance and knowledge of truths are two *kinds* of knowledge, or two *senses* of the term "knowledge."[37] Both, as Matthews argues in this and several other cases, cannot be true. Saws and hammers are two kinds of tool, but not tools in two senses of "tool." And duck bills and dollar bills are bills in two senses of "bill," but not two kinds of bill.

Husserl also sometimes conflates senses and kinds in this context. He writes of *"Self-evidence [Evidenz] in the loose and strict sense"* (LI 6 §38, 764). Very roughly, we experience self-evidence in the "strict sense" when our intuition is adequate, and in the "loose sense" when it is not. He then writes, "To speak of *degrees and levels of self-evidence* then has a good sense" (ibid., 765). But if we can speak of degrees of self-evidence, with the highest degree being adequate fulfillment, then this highest degree is not self-evidence in some different *sense* of the term "self-evidence," but a different degree of one and the same thing, self-evidence. In fact, confusing senses and *degrees* is even worse than confusing senses and *kinds*.

Russell's view in *Problems* seems to be that they are two kinds of knowledge. But Russell never does provide any characterization of the genus to which they each belong. And just a short time later he stops calling knowledge by acquaintance "knowledge," adopting the term "acquaintance" instead (Russell 1984, 156). Richard Fumerton, a contemporary acquaintance theorist, has followed Russell on this (1995, 74).

That some propositional beliefs fall squarely within the traditional definition of knowledge while perceptual experiences does not seems like a good reason to rethink that traditional definition. There is a deep commonality between perception and other forms of acquaintance, on the one hand, and justified true beliefs, on the other. In fact, perception has *more* evidentially salient features in common with propositional acts of fulfillment than it does with *empty* and inferential acts of propositional knowledge. The traditional definition of knowledge provides no insight whatsoever into the essential commonality between acts of acquaintance or originary intuition, on the one hand, and acts of propositional knowledge on the other. Since perception arguably has none of the features specified in the definition, this suggests that we must simply be equivocating in calling them each "knowledge," or that we should cease calling acquaintance "knowledge" at all.

But that doesn't seem right. Perception places us into a conscious, intentional relation with reality. It secures that relation more effectively than any other type of act. All forms of acquaintance, in fact, put is in touch with being. So does propositional knowledge. There seems to be an important genus to which both belong. And as Colin McGinn (2008, 239) points out, we routinely call acts of acquaintance cases of knowing. Seeing a color, he writes, is a way of coming to know that color. He goes on: "To insist that such awareness is not *really* a type of knowledge would be strange indeed—what is it then, a type of ignorance? Acquaintance enriches one's cognitive repertoire—and that is what knowledge *is*. Whether it fits some arbitrarily chosen paradigm of knowledge is neither here nor there" (McGinn 2008, 239–240).

Here is an example that philosophers will appreciate. I think most of us would agree with Thomas Nagel (1974) that when you are in a conscious state, there's something that it's like to be in that state.[38] Furthermore, being in such a state is sufficient for *knowing* what it's like to be in that state. As Michael Tye puts it, "We experience phenomenal character, and thereby we know it. In so knowing it, we do not know a truth. We do not merely have abilities. We know a thing."[39] Suppose, for example, that I stub my toe and have the conscious experience that typically attends such an event. I now know what it's like to experience stubbing a toe. But I know this just in virtue of being in such a state, not in virtue of formulating propositions about it, or reflecting upon it, talking about it, or otherwise having various thoughts about it fulfilled. One does not need to enter the "space of reasons," the realm of thought and talk, in order to know what stubbing a toe is like. Being in that state is sufficient for knowing what it's like, but insufficient for propositional knowledge about it.

It seems to me perfectly apt to characterize this state as one of *knowing*. And it also seems that this state is not "knowledge" in some different *sense* of the term "knowledge" than propositional knowledge, as Wilfrid Sellars maintains (1997, §3, 15–16), but belongs to the same fundamental natural kind. If we ask for the characterization of that kind, it will not be justified true belief—the conscious state I am in when I stub my toe is not justified and is not true. But it is a matter of knowledge. As Husserl himself says elsewhere, "What is constituted perceptually in its ipseity and in its features, in its different facets, etc., comes to our originary knowledge" (PAS, 114). And Merleau-Ponty, even more straightforwardly, writes that "perception is an *originary* knowledge."[40]

The challenge for this view, one might think, is to find a characterization of knowledge broad enough to incorporate propositional knowledge and knowledge by acquaintance. Happily, Willard's characterization does just that. Knowledge is, recall, "the capacity to represent a respective subject matter as it is, on an appropriate basis of thought and/or experience" (Willard 2000b, 31). When I stub my toe or perceive a scratched car hood—even without conceptualizing them or forming beliefs about them—I am conscious of them as they are on an appropriate, and, in fact the most appropriate conceivable, basis of experience. I know.

Not only does Willard's characterization of knowledge capture what knowledge by acquaintance and knowledge of truths share in common, but we can treat justified true belief as a species of it. In the case of propositional knowledge, (a) all such representings must be *beliefs*, understood as a kind of propositional attitude, (b) they must be *true*, and (c) the "appropriate basis" in their case is that of *justification* plus whatever is required to eliminate Gettier cases. As we can see, this basically subsumes *justified true belief* as a species of knowledge distinguished from other species by tolerably clear differentiae.

Finally, and unlike Russell's account, Husserl's account of fulfillment provides an account of how knowledge by acquaintance and propositional knowledge are related. They are related in higher-order acts of cognitive fulfillment, in which the thing we are acquainted with is both given and meant, and given as meant. Intuition lays hold of the same kinds of things that can be thought of, including individuals, properties, relations, and facts or states of affairs.

If this is right, then acts of fulfillment are the most basic kind of *propositional* knowledge, but not the most basic kind of knowledge. More basic still is knowledge by acquaintance. Foundationally justified beliefs are justified in virtue of entering into a synthesis of fulfillment with acts of non-propositional knowledge, that is, originary intuition. Non-propositional knowledge by acquaintance can take the same *objects* as propositional knowledge, despite differing in *content*. In fulfillment, a fact can be both given and meant.

9.6 Conclusion

In light of the fundamental grounding role of originary intuition in intentionality discussed in Chapter 5, this account makes knowledge a condition of intentionality in general. As Husserl puts it, "a life of consciousness cannot exist without including evidence" (FTL §107d, 289)—and here Husserl no doubt means *veridical* evidence. Timothy Williamson, famous for advocating a "knowledge first" approach to epistemology, writes that "Knowing is the best kind of believing. Mere believing is a kind of botched knowing."[41] That, I believe, is exactly Husserl's view. Knowing is what believing is when belief is what it ought to be.

Knowledge is not just the *telos* of belief or that in whose terms belief ought to be defined. It's a condition for its possibility, even of the botched variety. Lillian Alweiss writes that "intentionality must be initially an existence entailing relation since we can only understand non-existence as a modality of existence" (2013, 463). That is right, but for even more basic reasons. If one genuinely and authentically believes that the hood of car is scratched, one must know what that proposition means. And knowing what it means is knowing what its fulfilling sense is. And knowing its fulfilling sense depends upon knowledge by acquaintance of various individuals and properties and, perhaps, other states of affairs. As Lynne Rudder Baker puts it, "When a child learns what 'brother' means, she learns what brothers are. We cannot distil our knowledge of language from our knowledge of the world" (Baker 2007, 13).

If this is right, Williamson's complaint that knowledge has been neglected in the philosophy of mind is a legitimate one.[42] Knowledge and evidence, far from being mere species of intentionality ranged alongside the others, are those in whose terms the others must be understood.[43] Acts of acquaintance, many of which are available to non-persons, are all, when veridical, cases of knowledge. Empty intentionality, when authentic, depends on having undergone experiences of acquaintance, and inauthentic intentionality is parasitic on authentic intentionality. Belief has pretensions to apprehend how things are, and those pretensions are most clearly met in the act of fulfillment, in which those things which are emptily meant are given. Empty intentionality, that is, is teleologically ordered to knowledge (see Bernet 2003, Dahlstrom 2001, 60ff). Knowledge is directly implicated in all objectifying acts. In his clearest specification of their nature, Husserl says that they "are in fact marked off from all others, in that the fulfillment-syntheses appropriate to their sphere have the character of *knowings*, of *identifications*" (LI 6, Introduction, 668). That is, an objectifying act is one whose successful fulfillment is a case of knowledge.

Objectifying acts are not all positing. But even in the case of non-positing objectifying acts knowledge is at work. Acts of phantasy are, as part of their own phenomenological character, modifications of their unmodified positing counterparts; they are acts in which everything, including the evidential relations among their original and originary counterparts, are modified. And acts of phantasy are themselves, in some cases at least, acts of straightforward positing knowledge of universals and the relations among them. Finally, non-objectifying acts such as desire, hope, fear, and others are founded on objectifying acts (LI 5 §41, 648). Hoping for warm weather is founded on an act which represents warm weather, and an authentic hope for warm weather can only occur if one has an authentic understanding—knowledge—of what it would amount to for there to be warm weather.

The primacy of knowledge extends, I believe, to other central concepts developed by post-Husserlian existential phenomenologists. Care, Understanding, Being-With, practical action, and the other important aspects of our being-in-the-world that Heidegger discusses in *Being and Time*, for instance, all seem to require intentional consciousness, and with it knowledge (see Ryle 1929, 25). Granted, as Ryle points out, this need not be theoretical knowledge, nor need it be the case that we must first make knowledge our end. That aiming at knowledge *as an end* is a "founded" mode of being-in-the-world is a valuable insight (see Heidegger 1962, §13). Nevertheless, I cannot care about what I am not conscious of, or about anything about which I cannot form some conception. Again, I cannot engage in means-ends planning or action if I have no knowledge of what it would be for the states of affairs I am aiming at to obtain or not. As Fodor puts it in a discussion of pragmatism,

> Acting on plans (as opposed to, say, merely behaving reflexively or just thrashing about) requires being able to think about the world. You can't think a plan of action unless you can think how the world would be if the action were to succeed.

(Fodor 2008, 13)

And you can't *authentically* think a plan of action unless you *know*, with some level of determinacy, how the world would be if successful.

Notes

1 A good example of an attempt to do just that can be found in Huemer 2001.
2 Rinofner-Kreidl 2013, 47. Also see Staiti 2015, 136.
3 See Ströker 1988, 255 and Willard 1984, 135.
4 IdPh, 18. Also see Luft 2012, 245.
5 See, for instance, LI Prol., §§44, 47.
6 Though as Plantinga (1992, 6–7) notes, this definition is almost impossible to locate in any texts prior to Gettier's devastation of it.
7 Linda Zagzebski (1994) argues that Gettier-style counterexamples can be generated against any theory of knowledge that does not include truth as a necessary condition for justification.
8 See FTL §58, Sweetman 1999, 236–237.
9 Also see Harald Wiltsche's (2015, 68) formulation: "If object P is exhibited to a subject S in intuitive givenness, then S has at least prima facie justification for believing that P exists and that P has those properties which are exhibited intuitively."
10 See Pollock 1974, 42–43. There he calls them "type I" and "type II" defeaters. Also see Huemer 2013, 747 and Soldati 2012, 30.
11 Huemer 2013, 747. Also see Soldati 2012, 30.
12 Ideas I §43, 76. For a very helpful discussion, see Jacobs 2015, esp. §4.
13 See Richard Feldman's case against "authoritarian epistemology" (2004, 124).
14 Lyons 2009, 23. He continues: "To say that S has some reason for believing p could be to say (a) that there is a cause of S's believing that p, (b) that S is justified to some degree in believing that p, or (c) there is something on which S's belief that p is based."
15 Lyons characterizes an evidential justifier as a mental state (2009, 23). On the view I endorse, evidence need not be a "state" of the agent, and what evidence supports is the *content* of a belief—that is, a proposition believed—and not the state of believing it. For a good discussion, see Pryor 2013, §6.
16 LI 6 §67, 837. Also see Willard 200b, 33: if I know that a certain book is in my briefcase, "What I know is something about that book, namely, that it is in my briefcase. And likewise, when I know that, I may not know that I have an 'appropriate basis' for representing it as I do—though I *might* know that too. It is enough that it *is* true, and that I *do* have an appropriate basis for representing it as I do."
17 See Van Cleve 1979, 69–70.
18 Conee 2004, 50. Also see Conee and Feldman 2004, 78 and Pryor 2000, 535. For a rather different but related view, see Alston 1988.
19 ILTK §27, 129. I also discuss these passages in Hopp 2019, 281–82.
20 See Hopp 2008b.
21 ILTK §25, 22; also see IdPh, 25 and CM §64, 153.
22 Soldati 2012, 39. Also see Pryor 2000, 519.

23 I am grateful to Ryan Sosna for impressing this point upon me.

24 CM §24, 57; also Lauer 1965, 60.

25 ILTK, 135–136, my emphasis.

26 See Jacobs 2016, 263 for an excellent discussion.

27 See, for instance, IdPh, 44. Also see Ideas I §§21 and 145; LI, Prol., §51; and LI 6 §39; FTL §58l and LAW, 326. For the most thorough treatment of Husserl's criticisms of the feeling theory of evidence, see Heffernan 1997. Also see Kasmier 2003, especially §2.5.1. For a recent and rich phenomenological defense, however, see Hickerson forthcoming.

28 See Audi 2013, 194 and Conee 2013, 57.

29 Ideas I §141, 280. See Erhard 2012, Wiltsche 2015, and Berghofer 2018 for defenses of Husserlian foundationalism. Also see Hopp 2012. For a very sophisticated discussion of fulfillment as a form of noninferential justification, see Piazza 2013.

30 See Hopp 2011, 212.

31 Williams 1977, 48. For a good example of the kind of view Williams has in mind, see Yolton 1953, 25.

32 See Bonjour (1978, 11) and Steup (2000, 90–91).

33 Pryor 2000, 533–534. See the entirety of §IV of that paper for a brief but illuminating discussion of the role that background beliefs might play in perceptual justification.

34 See Brogaard and Gatzia 2018, 553ff. for a rich discussion. Also see Poellner 2007, 420.

35 Haugeland 1996, 273. For a helpful discussion of material constitution, see Baker 2007, Chapter 2 and Chapter 8. I am indebted to James Kinkaid for making me increasingly aware of how much work appealing to material constitution can do for ontology and phenomenology. See his 2020.

36 See Ingarden 1976, 38, who presents this as an objection to Husserl's reductions. See Mohanty 1997, 41 for a discussion. Also see Bell 1990, 126. It would be an objection if phenomenology were supposed to provide us with the rest of our knowledge. I do not, however, think that it is.

37 See Matthews 1972, 152. "The word 'know' is here used in two different senses," Russell writes when introducing the distinction in Chapter 4 (29). But in Chapter 5 (31), he writes that "there are two sorts of knowledge: knowledge of things, and knowledge of truths."

38 McGinn discusses this example in 2008, 244ff.

39 Tye 2009, 117. Also see Strawson 2015, 219.

40 Merleau-Ponty 2012, 45. Alva Noë (2004, 117–118) maintains, correctly I believe, that sensorimotor skills involved in perception also constitute knowledge.

41 Williamson 2000, 47. For an illuminating discussion of the knowledge first approach in phenomenology, see Mulligan 2014.

42 Williamson 2000, 2. See Smithies 2019, however, for a conspicuous exception.

43 See de Warren 2009, 21–23.

Recommended Readings

Huemer, Michael. 2001. *Skepticism and the Veil of Perception*. Lanham: Rowman & Littlefield Publishers, Inc.

Husserl, Edmund. 1969. *Formal and Transcendental Logic*. Dorion Cairns, trans. The Hague: Martinus Nijhoff.

Husserl, Edmund. 1970. *Logical Investigations*. Two volumes. J.N. Findlay, trans. London: Routledge & Kegan Paul. See especially the Sixth Investigation.

Husserl, Edmund. 1999. *The Idea of Phenomenology*. Lee Hardy, trans. Boston: Kluwer Academic Publishers.

Lyons, Jack. 2009. *Perception and Basic Beliefs*. Oxford: Oxford University Press.

Pryor, James. 2000. "The Skeptic and the Dogmatist." *Noûs* 34: 517–549.

Van Cleve, James. 1979. "Foundationalism, Epistemic Principles, and the Cartesian Circle." *The Philosophical Review* 88: 55–91.

Sellars, Wilfrid. 1997. *Empiricism and the Philosophy of Mind*. Cambridge: Harvard University Press.

Siegel, Susanna. 2017. *The Rationality of Perception*. Oxford: Oxford University Press.

Smithies, Declan. 2019. *The Epistemic Role of Consciousness*. Oxford: Oxford University Press.

Willard, Dallas. 1984. *Logic and the Objectivity of Knowledge*. Athens, OH: Ohio University Press.

Williamson, Timothy. 2000. *Knowledge and Its Limits*. Oxford: Oxford University Press.

10 Phenomenology

Hopefully the work in the previous chapters has exhibited with tolerable clarity some of the central topics of phenomenological philosophy, and some of the methods by which they are to be treated. The task of this chapter is to specify more precisely the point and character of phenomenological inquiry and the phenomenological method.

10.1 The Things Themselves

In attempting to understand the nature of logic and logical consciousness, Husserl writes that

"Meanings inspired only by remote, confused, inauthentic intuitions—if by any intuitions at all—are not enough: we must go back to the 'things themselves'."[1] That requirement is not peculiar to phenomenology. Knowledge, for Husserl, in phenomenology and in general, must "leave the last word to the things themselves" (LI, Foreword II, 45). In accordance with the Principle of All Principles, the grounds of *any* science are to be established on the basis of originary intuition and originary cognitive fulfillment, on experiences in which the subject matters of those disciplines manifest themselves as what they themselves are.

> Judging rationally or scientifically about matters … means orienting oneself to the things themselves, or, more precisely, it means returning from talk and opinions to the things themselves, questioning them as they are themselves given, and setting aside all prejudices alien to them.
>
> (Ideas I §19, 34–35)

In the case of most sciences, especially the most advanced theoretical sciences, the ground of originary givenness is quickly left behind, and truths beyond what is or factually can be given are established through deductive, inductive, and abductive techniques. Phenomenology, by contrast, is a "descriptive" discipline.[2] That means, for Husserl, that it does not build deductive *theories*. As he puts it,

Phenomenology carries out its clarifications in acts of seeing, determining, and distinguishing sense. It compares, it distinguishes, it connects, it places in relation, it divides into parts, it separates off moments. But it does all this in the act of pure seeing. It does not engage in theory or mathematical construction; that is, it offers no explanations in the sense of deductive theories.

(IdPh, 43)

Elsewhere Husserl writes, "The 'theory' that it aspires to, is no more than a thinking over, a coming to an evident understanding of thinking and knowing as such, in their pure generic essence."[3] Phenomenology does not simply begin within the sphere of intuition. It in some fashion remains within those limits.

It will be noticed, however, that in the previous chapters a number of arguments were presented. And one finds a wealth of arguments in Husserl's work as well. How is that compatible with the demand that phenomenology remain a descriptive discipline? Husserl's answer is that "all non-intuitive ways of proceeding, have merely the methodological significance of leading us to the matters that a subsequently direct discernment of essence has to bring to the level of being given" (Ideas I §75, 135). That is, the function of arguments in phenomenological contexts is to lead us to *see* what we otherwise would not. There is another function for arguments as well. Phenomenology deals with contested issues. It is often not enough to simply to describe the matters with which it deals, but to show, sometimes via argument, why competing positions are false. Normally this is done by showing that various theories entail something incompatible with what we discover in phenomenological reflection. Almost every phenomenologist does this.

As noted in the Preface, the early phenomenologists did not all treat consciousness as the preeminent topic of phenomenology. For them, phenomenology is not a school united by shared doctrines or theoretical commitments. To practice phenomenology, rather, is to proceed *phenomenologically* in one's philosophical thinking, that is, to as far as possible orient oneself to phenomena as they manifest themselves in originary acts of intuition (see Seifert 1987, 10–12). It is a search for genuine understanding, an attempt to render objects, relations, and states of affairs intelligible. Reinach writes that "bare empirical fact never yields understanding" (2012b, 162). Things become intelligible when we see how and why connections hold in virtue of the natures of their relata. It is not just a brute fact that failing to honor a promise regarding a matter of importance leads to disappointment, anger, or resentment, as though it were just as readily conceivable that it could generate joy, pleasure, satisfaction, and gratitude. These aren't merely brute connections among emotion-atoms that could have been arranged in any other way whatsoever. The connections here are intelligible ones. We can conceive of someone rationally responding with gratitude to a broken promise, but only on the condition that we suppose them to have some other set of beliefs and desires that make this gratitude intelligible. Similarly, it is not just a matter of empirical fact that perceptual experiences motivate beliefs in what is intuitively presented by their means.

Phenomenological inquiry, then, is a search for intelligibility in philosophical subject matters, where intelligibility is principally a matter of having essences and essential relations given in acts of insight. So understood, phenomenological inquiry is opposed to top-down theory construction. It permits no worldviews, or overarching theories of everything, to function as first principles or unquestioned assumptions. It does not proceed by deducing consequences from verbal or empty definitions. Astounding, mystifying, debunking, and deflating are not among its primary or secondary aims.

Furthermore, phenomenological inquiry does not place prediction and control as paramount ends of theorizing activity, nor does it have a default preference for theories that are ontologically sparse. Its preference is to conform to the structure of being, however simple or complex that turns out to be. This explains, among other things, why virtually all of the diverse representatives of phenomenological philosophy are entirely unembarrassed by entities that more naturalistically and empirically minded philosophers have long viewed with suspicion. Probably no one can inquire without presuppositions, but phenomenologists seem unusually unencumbered by any felt need to make consciousness, meanings, material objects, numbers, values, essences, and so on "fit" into a preferred metaphysical framework. Although subsequent phenomenologists did not all inherit Husserl's own ontological commitments, virtually no major figure has exhibited the reductive or deflationary tendencies so common in the analytic tradition.[4] Herbert Spiegelberg goes so far as to characterize the phenomenological method as "a protest against reductionism" (Spiegelberg 1971, 656).

That phenomenology is concerned with essences and essential correlations means that it does not concern itself directly with any region of actual being. It does not posit anything as actual, whether physical or mental.

> From the beginning, as at all later stages, its scientific statements involve not the slightest reference to real existence: no metaphysical, scientific, and, above all, no psychological assertions can therefore occur among its premises.
>
> (LI, Introduction to Volume Two, §7, 265)

Phenomenology concerns real being indirectly, insofar as real entities and processes instantiate the essences described in phenomenological inquiry. In the same way, geometry concerns real being indirectly insofar as the real world contains spatially extended objects (see PP, 35). Nevertheless, the proper objects in the case of both sciences are not real particulars (Ideas I §79, 147). As Reinach puts it, "Everywhere it is essence laws that are at issue. Existence is never posited" (Reinach 2012b, 163).

10.2 Transcendental Phenomenology

Kant writes: "I entitle *transcendental* all knowledge which is occupied not so much with objects as with the mode of our knowledge of objects in so far as this mode of knowledge is to be possible *a priori*" (Kant 1965, A11–12/B25). He continues: "what here constitutes our subject-matter is not the nature of things, which is inexhaustible, but the understanding which passes judgment upon the nature of things; and this understanding, again, only in respect of its a priori knowledge" (Kant 1965, A12–13/B26). In Kant's view, then, transcendental philosophy is concerned with the nature of our a priori knowledge of things. Furthermore, transcendental philosophy is *itself* a field of a priori knowledge (Kant 1965 A14/B28).

Husserl's conception partially overlaps with Kant's.[5] First, he agrees with Kant that transcendental philosophy is a priori. Transcendental phenomenology is concerned with what Husserl, in by no means his sole unfortunate terminological choice, calls issues of "constitution," where

> constitution concerns the essential correlations between the object of knowledge and knowing, the consideration of the noetic interconnections in which are constituted ontic interconnections, even those between objects and concepts, truths, etc.
>
> (PAS, 643)

That is, transcendental philosophy takes a given type of object and examines how it is "constituted" or made present in "noetic interconnections," where what is "noetic" sits on the left-hand side of the consciousness-of relation. Because constitutive analyses concern themselves with "essential correlations," they are a priori.

Husserl's conception diverges from Kant's in several important respects, however. In the first place, transcendental inquiry is not just concerned with what we can know a priori of objects. There are empirical conditions for both empirical and for a priori knowledge, neither of which is of concern for transcendental philosophy. For example, the evolution of life in the universe is an empirical condition for living beings such as ourselves having any knowledge whatsoever. And there are, on Husserl's view, also a priori or essential conditions for the possibility of both a priori and empirical knowledge. It is not, for instance, a mere factual necessity that spatially extended objects can only be given inadequately, or that temporally extended objects can only be given in suitable acts of time-consciousness. Nor is it an accident that essences—the proper objects of a priori knowledge—can be given originarily in acts of phantasy. What transcendental philosophy investigates are the essential (or a priori) connections among acts, contents, and objects of *all* types (see PAS, 57).

A second, more important, difference between Husserl's position and Kant's is the former's insistence that transcendental questions be addressed *phenomenologically*. And that means that transcendental philosophy must proceed by bringing the various interconnections under discussion themselves to givenness. So, to give an example from the last chapter, a phenomenological defense of foundationalism should proceed not by arguing that knowledge *must* rest on some foundation or other, but by specifying the structure and content of possible foundational acts and well-founded noetic structures. We are not forbidden to look at our own actual cases to inform our discussion, provided each "actuality is treated as a possibility among other possibilities" (PP §9a, 55).

Transcendental phenomenology, then, is *the application of phenomenological methods to transcendental questions*. The subject matter of the field is, at the very least and as its non-negotiable core, the nature of and the essential correlations among conscious experiences, their contents, and their objects. As the previous chapters hopefully show, it is especially concerned with experiences in which objects are evidently given, and the various ways in which other types of mental acts are dependent upon them. Husserl describes how, even before his explicit development of phenomenology as transcendental philosophy, the fundamental task was:

> to go back radically and consistently from the respective categories of objectivities and ask about the modes of consciousness determinately belonging to them, about the subject acts, act-structures, foundations of lived experiences, in which objectivities of such a character become objects of consciousness, and above all become evidently self-given.
>
> (PP, 20)

Its method is to describe them in a systematic manner based on acts of seeing or originary intuition. All of the other procedures that Husserl discusses often—possibly too often—such as the epoché and the various phenomenological reductions, are most profitably understood as ways of making the relevant essences available to us for description.

10.3 The Transcendental Insight

Husserl eventually came to regard transcendental phenomenology as harboring a commitment to *"transcendental idealism"* (CM §41, 86). Whatever else Husserl's brand of transcendental idealism amounts to, sitting at its heart is what A.D. Smith calls his "transcendental insight" (2003, 28). Here are a few of Husserl's many formulations of it:

> The Objective world, the world that exists for me, that always has and always will exist for me, the only world that ever can exist for me — this world, with

all its Objects, I said, derives its whole sense and its existential status, which it has for me, from me myself, *from me as the transcendental Ego*, the Ego who comes to the fore only with transcendental-phenomenological epoché.

(CM §11, 26)

...nothing exists for me otherwise than by virtue of the actual and potential performance of my own consciousness.

(FTL §94, 234)

All objects and relations among objects only are what they are for us, through acts of thought essentially different from them, in which they become present to us, in which they stand before us as unitary items that we mean.

(LI 1 §10, 283)

Whatever I encounter as an existing object is something that... has received its whole being-sense for me from my effective intentionality.

(Ideas I §47, 85)

According to Smith, the transcendental insight permits of a "strong" and a "weak" reading. On the strong reading, "everything other than consciousness itself is but a construction thrown up by consciousness, and its existence is dependent upon consciousness" (A.D. Smith 2003, 30). The weak reading, by contrast, merely states that "something can exist 'for me' ... only if I am around" (ibid., 32). But this, Smith claims, "appear[s] to be the merest platitude, and not the world-historical revelation that Husserl clearly takes it to be" (ibid.).

These two readings are not exhaustive, and Smith himself opts for a third, but idealist, interpretation. There are, in any case, several reasons to reject the strong reading. Consider, for instance, the last formulation of the transcendental insight above. If that's an expression of *metaphysical* idealism, then Husserl must mean that the world I encounter is "but a construction thrown up," not just by consciousness, but by *my* consciousness—or perhaps by *Husserl's* consciousness. But that's a massively implausible reading, and almost every other formulation would demand that reading if the strong reading were right.

Second, the transcendental insight apparently holds for all objects of all types: all objects are what they are *for me* in virtue of my intentional acts. If this were tantamount to saying that those objects are created by or ontologically dependent on my consciousness of them, then Husserl would be saying that not only physical things, but also other people are so dependent. But surely that's an absurd result. No one depends for their being on *my* consciousness of them. Even I don't. I do not exist because I am conscious of myself; I am conscious of myself because I exist.

Third, there are passages that indicate that the idealistic interpretation could not be what Husserl has in mind. Consider this well-known passage: "Even God is for me what he is, in consequence of my own accomplishment of consciousness [*Bewusstseinsleistung*]."[6] This is plainly just a special application of the transcendental insight. But Husserl immediately goes on to reject any metaphysically idealistic conclusion: "Here too, as in the case of the other ego, [an] accomplishment of consciousness [*Bewusstseinsleistung*] will hardly signify that I invent or make this highest transcendency" (ibid., translation modified). So, both God and the class of other people fall outside this idealistic web. Husserl then adds: "The like is true of the world and all worldly causation" (ibid.). He continues: "the world with all its realities" is "constituted in mental processes and abilities of *my* ego" (ibid., my emphasis).

According to Husserl, then, God, others, and nature are not "invented" or "made" by my (or Husserl's) activities of consciousness. They are, however, "constituted" by me, in which case "constituting" an entity does not mean making or inventing it. As many other commentators have noted, "constituting" an object simply means carrying out the mental acts in which it is intended.[7] I can "constitute" an earthquake by being unfortunate to be stuck in one and conscious of being so, but I cannot make the earth or make it quake. I can't even contribute to its quaking. I can of course try to "impose" my concept of an earthquake on anything at all.[8] But in order to have that mental act add up to an earthquake, the extra ingredient can be nothing short of an earthquake. The "given" won't do, unless the given = an earthquake.

On the idealistic reading of the transcendental insight, "Physical things ... exist only insofar as perceptions of physical things occur and hang together in certain harmonious ways" (Yoshimi 2015, 3). This theory has the drawback of contradicting most of our core beliefs about the nature of and existence conditions of physical things, beliefs formed by the very consciousnesses that phenomenology wants to make sense of. On the platitudinous reading—which by Husserl's lights appears to be the correct one with respect to God, other egos, and "the world with all its realities" (FTL §99, 251)—*my consciousness of* physical things exists only insofar as my perceptions occur and are harmonious.

If the transcendental insight isn't momentous, then is it trivial, a platitude? Not exactly. It is, however, something that is rather evident on reflection (see A.D. Smith 2003, 32). The transcendental insight is just this: if an object is one of which I am conscious, that is because I am undergoing or carrying out the kind of experience or act in which that object is meant or given. Nothing whatsoever can be an object of my consciousness unless I carry out the acts required to have precisely it as an intentional object, and my being in a conscious state with a certain configuration is also a sufficient condition for my being conscious of that act's object (see A.D. Smith 2003, 41).

That claim is compatible with realism about the objects of experience. It is also compatible with the claim that the existence of an act's object might, in many cases, be a necessary condition for the existence of the act—obviously if the existence of an object is necessary for my consciousness of it, my consciousness of it is sufficient for the existence of that object, which is not at all to say that my consciousness "makes" it. Consciousness, as we have seen, is not an empty or featureless container or a pure intentional ray. Rather, it enters into relations in virtue of its own makeup. As Husserl writes,

> Perception does not consist in staring blankly at something lodged in consciousness, inserted there by some strange wonder as if something were first there and then consciousness would somehow embrace it. Rather, for every imaginable ego-subject, every objectlike existence with a specific content of sense is an accomplishment of consciousness. It is an accomplishment that must be new for every novel object. Every basic type of object in principle requires a different intentional structure.

(PAS, 57)

This point should be familiar from Chapter 4, §4.4.2. Conscious experiences are not featureless, but instead possess their determinate intentional direction in virtue of their own parts, most notably their matter and quality. And simply installing the object "in" the stream of consciousness would, in any case, make nothing about the intentionality of the act, or our knowledge of its object, intelligible.

Husserl himself highlights what he thinks is the obviousness of the transcendental insight when he writes, "The correlation between world (the world of which we always speak) and its subjective manners of givenness never evoked philosophical wonder" prior to his own *Logical Investigations*. It was, rather, "taken for granted" (Crisis §48, 165). To be "taken for granted" here could mean that everyone explicitly knew it, but never bothered arguing for it or deducing its consequences. But it could also mean that it's the kind of thing that is presupposed in thinking in general. And it is this latter sense, I think, that Husserl means. When one represents an object, it is "taken for granted" that one is representing that object and not something else, and that *its* modes of givenness, when it is given, are modes in which *it* manifests itself, and not veils or screens standing between us and the thing itself. It is taken for granted, in our experience of a scratched car hood, that it is a car hood that manifests itself in experience, and not an image, a sense datum, or something totally and categorially different from a car hood. That is why this sort of experience's content fulfills the concept <car hood>, a concept which, in turn, refers to car hoods. It is also taken for granted that car hoods are the kinds of things that don't have just one way of manifesting themselves. I understand, implicitly, that when you and I look at the same car hood from different sides, we are seeing the same thing without having the same type of experience. In "positing" acts, such as perception and belief, one also takes it for granted that one is representing things as they are, rather than as they aren't. That isn't something one thinks about. It's simply a condition of representing at all.

One might reasonably ask why we should even make the transcendental insight explicit if it is something that we can comfortably take for granted. One reason is that despite its obviousness, it is staggering when you consider it. You are only conscious of what you are conscious of. At the same time, you really are conscious of everything you are conscious of. And that claim, mind-numbingly boring when grasped as a mere verbal formula, becomes almost unbelievable when we stop to consider what we are conscious of. We are conscious of car hoods, and not just ideas or representations of car hoods. We are conscious of causation, otherwise we could not understand any argument to the effect that we cannot discover causal relations through experience. We are conscious of universals, otherwise we could not understand arguments for and against their existence. We are conscious of God, and gods, otherwise atheism would be unintelligible. We are conscious of, well, everything that we are conscious of—the whole wide world, and even more. We know that the world is much bigger than what we know, but it is only by virtue of our consciousness, however dim and inauthentic, of that unknown world that we could even think that. On the other side of what you are and have been conscious of is not just what you do not know or have never perceived, but what you have never in any way whatsoever been conscious of. It couldn't even be a Kantian thing-in-itself, seeing as you are now conscious (though necessarily inauthentically) of a Kantian thing-in-itself.

Furthermore, every single thing that you have ever been or will ever be conscious of, from your shoes to the farthest reaches of time and space, is something that you are conscious of thanks to the powers of *your* own mind.[9] This is why almost every formulation of the transcendental insight is couched in first-personal terms. Even everything that you have learned from others— and for most of us that is the bulk of our significant knowledge—is your knowledge now thanks to *your* ability to undergo the appropriate empathic experiences in virtue of which you are aware of others, and to carry out the conceptual acts in virtue of which their expressive linguistic acts are comprehensible. The point is simply that no one can carry out your intentional acts for you; *you* are the one who is conscious of everything you are conscious of. And, to repeat, the vast majority of what you are conscious of is not "in" your mind in any real sense. Neither the Roman Empire nor a single one of its rulers, citizens, aqueducts, or roads is "in" your or my mind as a part, piece, or property.

That, at any rate, is my own attempt to understand why something that is obvious enough to be taken for granted can and should evoke philosophical wonder. It is even more remarkable when you consider that for almost every object of which you are conscious, there is more than one way of being conscious of it. This is why, according to Husserl, every object of consciousness functions in phenomenology as a "transcendental clue" pointing back to the "multiplicities" of acts in which it is intended (CM §21, 50). And, finally, as discussed in Chapter 2, §2.2.1, each objectifying consciousness of an object is accompanied by a non-objectifying consciousness of itself. Corresponding to whatever complexity we *authentically* represent in an object, there is at least that much complexity on the side of our act of being conscious of it.

One further reason to bear the transcendental insight in mind when doing phenomenology is to avoid any claim that says or entails that we cannot be conscious of a certain type of object, or that we cannot be conscious of it in the way presupposed by the theory making the claim. I suspect some theories may come quite close to incoherently denying that we can be conscious of the kinds of entities that we must be conscious of in order even to understand the theories in question. If, to take a notable example, we had no idea *whatsoever* of necessary connections or the self, no conception, however vague, of what they at least *might* be if they were real, we could not understand Hume's arguments that we have no such ideas, or why he provides just the arguments he does against just *those* ideas.

Other positions violate the transcendental insight in more subtle ways. Quine's position regarding the indeterminacy of meaning or translation and the inscrutability of reference provides a convenient example. In his fight against the "pernicious mentalism" according to which speaker meaning could be determined by anything beyond "dispositions to overt behavior" (Quine 1968, 186), Quine asks us to consider a group of speakers who say "gavagai" whenever rabbits are around. Should we translate their term as "rabbit"? There are other contenders: "undetached rabbit part" and "rabbit stage" for instance (ibid., 188). Appealing to nothing more than their "behavior"—the noises and movements they make—leaves it open just what "gavagai" means. Which translation is correct in capturing the speakers' meaning is "indeterminate." And since the proposed translations above differ not only in meaning but in reference, "Reference itself proves behaviorally inscrutable" (ibid., 191). Because we learn our home language in just the way described—by observing others' behavior—"we can reproduce the inscrutability of reference at home" (ibid., 198). Finally, Quine is clear that this is not a matter of there being some fact to which we lack access. Rather, "the inscrutability of reference is not the inscrutability of a fact; there is no fact of the matter" (ibid., 198).

Quine's position violates the transcendental insight. As Searle points out, the only reason the argument above is intelligible is that we know that "rabbit" and "undetached rabbit part" *do*, as a discoverable matter of fact, differ in both meaning and reference. But that's just what we cannot know if Quine is right. As Searle puts it,

> If the indeterminacy thesis were really true, we would not even be able to understand its formulation; for when we were told there was no "fact of the matter" about the correctness of the translation between rabbit and rabbit stage, we would not have been able to hear any (objectively real) difference between the two English expressions to start with.
>
> (Searle 1987, 131, italics omitted)

If as far as we knew "rabbit" and "undetached rabbit part" meant the same thing, then the fact that we cannot decide between them would in no way support the view that meaning is indeterminate or that reference is inscrutable, since we would not think there's any deciding to do. The reason Quine's argument violates the transcendental insight is that he has helped himself to knowledge that he and his readers possess in a self-undermining bid to convince us that we could not possibly have such knowledge.

10.4 The Phenomenological Reduction

The transcendental insight is the guiding principle of all phenomenological analyses. It should look familiar. In Chapter 4, §4.4.2, we discussed how acts are of their objects in virtue of their own makeup, and why phenomenological inquiry into intentionality is not aided in any way by simply appealing to the features of the objects of which we are conscious. Keeping the transcendental insight in mind is a way of focusing phenomenological inquiry on that intentional makeup, and what it is about that intentional makeup of the act that makes it present its object in the way that it does. This is also my understanding of the main point of Husserl's methodological techniques, the epoché and the reduction.

I should say at the outset that, like many of his students at the time of the publication of Husserl's *Ideas I* (1913), I sometimes find Husserl's reduction bewildering in its execution and dismaying in its alleged results (see Ingarden 1976, 27). Nor am I convinced that it is indispensable for phenomenological inquiry. The best method for phenomenology is any method that allows us to discover the essential features of conscious states and their relations to their contents and objects. And, as Herbert Spiegelberg (1960, 137) notes, the fact that many of Husserl's most notable phenomenological insights were attained in the *Logical Investigations* without any explicit reduction strongly indicates that it is not the sole way of attaining phenomenological discoveries.

Most basically, the epoché and the reductions consist in no longer participating in the attitude of ordinary life, of not going along with the positing of the world that characterizes the "natural attitude" (Ideas I §27, 48). According to Husserl, the reduction's main function is not negative. It is, rather, to determine what, if anything, is left over after we have executed it, and to examine it in systematic fashion (Luft 2004, 207). Husserl's answer is that it is "'pure' or 'transcendental' consciousness" (Ideas I §33, 56). This is, says Husserl, a *"new region of being,"* and, moreover, "a region of *individual* being" (Ideas I §33, 57).

10.4.1 The Hands-Off Principle

Before saying more about the reduction and its results, a general remark about phenomenological methodology is in order. Whatever method we adopt, it would fail abysmally if it should turn out that in following it, any item in the intentional triad of act, content, and object were transformed into something different. That is, we should abide by a strict Hands-Off Principle. As Søren Overgaard remarks in response to the view that the phenomenological reductions are intended to "purify" our experiences of allegedly problematic positings:

> If we experience the world as "actually existing", as no doubt we do, then to purify our experience of that existential position is precisely to modify the very thing it was our task faithfully to describe.

> (Overgaard 2015, 188)

Overgaard's argument against the "purification" view is not only heavily supported textually, but, even more importantly, is philosophically decisive: the task of phenomenology is to describe our experiences exactly as they are, without any alteration whatsoever. Perhaps a given phenomenologist finds it objectionable that in the natural attitude we take ourselves to be directly aware of physical objects, and take those objects to exist independently of our consciousness of them. It is compatible with the Hands-Off Principle to discover that we are not epistemically justified in holding those beliefs. What the phenomenologist cannot do is re-describe those experiences in such a way that they are more to their liking, to treat them as "really" of something totally different.

If, for instance, A's experience is an originary intuition of a car hood, which she takes to both have hidden parts and to exist independently of her consciousness of it, then a phenomenological description of her experience cannot substitute the car hood with something else, such as a "noema," a "seen [car hood] as such," whose "*esse* consists exclusively in its '*percipi*'" (Ideas I §98, 198). What A perceives is *not* a car-as-perceived, something whose perceivedness is an intrinsic, much less essential, property of it.

Suppose this were the appropriate way to handle the objects of consciousness in phenomenological reflection. If so, then when A *thinks about* a car in the natural attitude, she will have instead a car-as-thought-of in the phenomenological attitude. But if that's right, then A could not undergo an experience of fulfillment in which the same object that she perceives is also thought of. Fulfillment requires that the object intuited and meant be identical. But since the respective noemata—the car-as-perceived and the car-as-thought-of—are not identical, fulfillment would be impossible. Similarly, when I want a new book, what I want is not a book-as-wanted. If it were, then in receiving the book I would receive something else, a book-as-received. In that case, I will not have received what I wanted. That's not right. What I want is a book, not a book-as-wanted, and if I get the book, I will get what I wanted.

I do not intend to get embroiled in the complicated debate over Husserl's "noema." On the "West Coast" or Fregean view, it is a "sense" which is about something.[10] On the "East Coast" view it is something like the object itself as considered within the phenomenological reduction, or "the Object precisely as intended in the act" (Drummond 1990, 142). These interpretations differ on the question whether the noema is on the right-hand of left-hand side of the consciousness-of relation. Furthermore, the difference between something that essentially bears intentionality and something that does not is a difference in fundamental ontological kinds. For my part, I am inclined to agree with Dallas Willard that, first, Husserl tells us a great deal about what the noema is not but not much about what it is, and, second, that most if not all phenomenological work can be accomplished by rich descriptions of acts, their contents, and their objects without any reference to noemata at all (see Willard 1992, 47).

The one point that bears noting is that among the many things that the noema of an act is *not* is the object of that act. Apart from Husserl's assurance that a tree can burn up while a tree-noema cannot (Ideas I §89, 156), one simple argument for that is Husserl's contention that all noemata "belong to one sole supreme genus" (Ideas I §128, 254). All objects of consciousness do not (see Willard 1989, 69). Therefore, noemata should not be treated as the objects of ordinary consciousness when we reflect phenomenologically on those experiences. We have to describe realists as realists, theists as theists, nominalists as nominalists, and perceivers of car hoods as perceivers of *car hoods*. To do anything less would, in Overgaard's words, "be in tension with the very idea of phenomenology" (Overgaard 2015, 187).

Unfortunately, Husserl seems at times to violate the Hands-Off Principle. When we engage in "*transcendental-phenomenological reflection*," he writes, "an essentially changed experience takes the place of the original one; accordingly it must be said that this reflection *alters* the original experience" (CM §15, 34, translation modified). But if the original experience is changed, then how could I ever find out, through phenomenology, about that experience? Husserl attempts to minimize the problem by claiming that even ordinary reflection "alters the previously naïve experience quite essentially" (ibid., translation modified). But that just makes the problem that much worse. It looks like reflection is unable in principle to apprehend experiences without turning them into something not only different, but "essentially changed," however that is possible (do they lose or acquire an *essential* property?).

Perhaps all the Husserl of the *Cartesian Meditations* means here is that one's total experiential state changes when one engages in reflection. But if not—if the Husserl of *Cartesian Meditations* is maintaining that the reflected-upon act *itself* undergoes a radical change when reflected upon—the Husserl of *Ideas I* has a response. The only way one could know, on grounds permissible to the phenomenologist, that reflection essentially alters experience is through reflection itself. But then one must have had reflective access to the unchanged experience to see that it has changed (Ideas I §79, 149–150). Reflection does, of course, change the total conscious life of the subject; it alters, by its very existence, the "unity of experience" (LI 5 §18, 580). And that's something that we can *see* in reflection and not simply theorize about. But, as we have seen (Chapter 4, §4.3), the unity of *experience* is not the same thing as the unity of an *act*. The act of seeing the car hood becomes part of a different unified experiential whole when I reflect—or when I hear a loud noise or smell coffee for that matter—but it does not thereby lose its own unity or integrity as an act. It does not, or at least need not, lose or acquire any properties or parts when it is reflected upon.[11]

10.4.2 The Reduction and Its Results

Husserl proposes many ways of performing the phenomenological reduction.[12] The most familiar is via what Husserl calls the "epoché." The phenomenological epoché is a procedure by which we modify the "natural attitude." In the natural attitude, the world of natural objects, living organisms, cultural artifacts, and other persons are present to us in acts of perception, thought, and knowledge (Ideas I §§27–29). According to Husserl, this attitude embodies a certain "general thesis" (Ideas I §30, 52). We take the world in general to exist, and to be more or less as it presents itself to us. The general thesis is not, as Husserl stresses, "*one distinctive act*" or "one articulated judgment *about* existence," but something present "prior to thinking" (Ideas I §31, 53). The world shows up to us, we might say, in interconnected experiences with a positing character.

Husserl proposes, for phenomenological purposes, that: "*Instead of remaining in this attitude, we want to alter it radically*" (Ideas I §31, 52). To modify the natural attitude, Husserl claims that it is "*always possible*" to "*attempt to doubt everything*," no matter how certain it is (Ideas I §31, 53). This includes, most importantly, the general thesis of the natural attitude. But, rather confusingly, the epoché is not a matter of doubting or even attempting to doubt.[13] As Husserl himself notes, whether we actually doubt everything or even *attempt* to doubt everything, we will no longer retain the thesis of the natural attitude: I cannot be doubtful and certain of the same subject matter at the same time (see Ideas I §31, 53–54). And even if I could, the last thing we want to do is transform our naïve confidence in the world into doubt, on pain of violating the Hands-Off Principle (see Thomasson 2005, 124).

So how do we avoid violating the Hands-Off Principle? Husserl assures us that, somehow, the epoché simultaneously changes the natural attitude "radically" and leaves it untouched:

> We do not give up the thesis that we have posited, we alter nothing in our conviction. That conviction remains in itself as it is ... And nevertheless it

> undergoes a modification—while it continues to remain in itself what it is, *we place it as it were "out of action," we "suspend it," we "bracket it."*
>
> (Ideas I §31, 53)

After the epoché "everything remains, so to speak, as before," and the objects of our awareness have "not forfeited the slightest nuance" of their appearing features (Ideas I §88, 176). The epoché involves "*a certain withholding of judgment that is compatible with the unshaken and even unshakeable (because evident) conviction of truth*" (Ideas I §31, 54–55). I can, allegedly, perform the epoché with respect to any judgment whatsoever, no matter how evident—even <1+1=2> or <The world exists>.[14]

The epoché is, at the beginning, a "universal" bracketing. If we leave it at that, though, we won't have a field of unbracketed objects about which we can make unmodified, positing assertions (Ideas I §32, 55). That is why we need to exercise, not a universal epoché, but a "phenomenological" epoché. We need to exclude or bracket everything that does not belong within the field to be disclosed, but include everything that belongs to it. The phenomenological reductions are the systematic steps by which we do that. Husserl describes them in the Fourth Chapter of the Second Section of *Ideas I*. The most important reduction is the bracketing of nature and all natural science. In addition to that, we must bracket the "pure ego" except to the extent that it is "cogiven[] with pure consciousness" (Ideas I §31, §57, 106), God (Ideas I §31, §58), "pure logic as mathesis universalis" (Ideas I §31, §59, 107) and, most puzzlingly, "material-eidetic disciplines" (Ideas I §31, §60).[15]

Before turning to the results of the epoché and reductions, it is important to emphasize that while Husserl models the epoché, in part, on Descartes's methodological doubt, he does this for a "completely different purpose."[16] For Descartes, the task is to discover truths that are absolutely impervious to doubt to function as a foundation for the rest of our knowledge. For Husserl, it is to open up a region of being to investigation, and to understand how knowledge and intentionality are possible. As Husserl writes elsewhere,

> It is naturally a ludicrous, though unfortunately common misunderstanding, to seek to attack transcendental phenomenology as "Cartesianism," as if its *ego cogito* were a premise or set of premises from which the rest of knowledge... was to be deduced, absolutely "secured." The point is not to secure objectivity but to understand it.[17]

Elsewhere he writes, that the point of the epoché "is not a matter of the constitution of a 'theory-free,' 'metaphysics-free' science by way of tracing all justification back to immediate findings" (Ideas I §32, 56). The importance of this point cannot be overestimated. Although Husserl does believe that phenomenological claims can in principle be based on the very highest degree of evidence, that is simply because phenomenological inquiry allegedly confines itself to what is "immanent." It is not because the task of phenomenological inquiry is to discover indubitable truths from which to deduce all the rest. As Husserl puts it, in exercising the epoché with respect to the natural (and eidetic) sciences, "*I refrain from adopting a single proposition that belongs to them, even if the evidence for it is perfect*" (Ideas I §32, 56). Such "perfect" evidence is abundant outside the sphere of phenomenological research. It is perfectly evident, or about as close to it as we can come, that color is compatible with extension, that some numbers are even, and that middle C is not a wet slab avalanche. These claims are so evident that few phenomenological claims rival them, and none surpasses them. And they do not require that one know the first thing about phenomenology in order to be known.

The phenomenological epoché is not a technique for discovering, much less *establishing*, the "real" foundations of knowledge in the sphere of subjectivity so that we can claw our way back out. It is not a solution to any skeptical problem (see Zahavi 2017, 56). The genuine skeptical problem is that prima facie plausible theories of knowledge entail it, not that its truth is consistent with our evidence. We have abundant knowledge in the natural attitude, a great deal of which is, as we have seen, foundational (see Chapter 9, §9.4.4). Natural sciences, and natural experience, are perfectly acceptable ways of acquiring knowledge. In fact, they are the *only* ways of acquiring knowledge of empirical matters of fact. Phenomenology cannot verify a single empirical proposition. It won't help you find your missing wallet or discover the age of a fossil. That is why, as Overgaard puts it,

> The reduction is thus not a procedure of regressing from the ordinary world back to something more immediately given. For the immediately given is nothing but the ordinary world, and the reduction takes this world as its "guiding clue" in order to be able to say something about the structures of the transcendental subject.[18]

Zahavi does write that the aim of the reduction and epoché is "to suspend or neutralize a certain dogmatic *attitude* towards reality" (2017, 57). That is right, but it should not be thought that the dogmatic attitude of the natural attitude is unjustified or problematic. The "dogmatism" of the natural attitude and the natural sciences is perfectly all right as it is (see Chapter 9, §9.1), since it is quite simply the refusal to take skepticism seriously.

> *The correct stance in the pre-philosophical and (in a good sense) dogmatic sphere of research*—to which all experiential sciences (but not only these sciences) belong—*is this: to discard, in a fully conscious way, all skepticism* ... and to accept the kinds of objects of knowledge wherever one actually encounters them.

(Ideas I §26, 46)

As for the question when you may take the brackets off, the answer is: whenever you feel like it. You had knowledge of the world before you ever performed the reduction, and continue to have it during and after performing the reduction.

Returning, then, to the results of the reduction: on the supposition that you have carried out the epoché and the reductions properly, there should still be something unbracketed left over for you to make positing assertions about. What is it? It is Husserl's answer to this question that principally alienated the realist phenomenologists in the Munich and Göttingen circles, as well as later existentialists. As we have seen, the reduction allegedly allows us to access a region of individual being, that of transcendental consciousness. This region of being "is *essentially* independent of any worldly, natural being, and it does not need the latter for its *existence*." As for nature, it is "a correlate of consciousness; it only *is* in the sense of constituting itself in rule-governed connections of consciousness" (Ideas I §51, 93). Husserl does insist that he is not a "Berkeleyan" idealist, that

> The real actuality is not "re-interpreted" or even denied but an absurd inter-pretation of it set aside. That absurd interpretation stems from construing the world *philosophically* as absolute, something that is thoroughly alien to the natural way of regarding the world.
>
> (Ideas I §55, 103)

At the same time, somehow, Husserl acknowledges that his position directly opposes "common sense talk" (Ideas I §50, 90). The whole world of nature, that is, including physical and psychological entities and processes, is second-ary to the region allegedly revealed through the phenomenological reduction, that of transcendental consciousness. Phenomenology's subject matter is the *essence* of this realm of individual being: pure consciousness and pure experience (Ideas I §75, 134).

There are two claims here that need to be distinguished. The first is that there is a realm of individual being, transcendental consciousness, that is independent of all nature. The second is the idealistic claim that nature is dependent on transcendental consciousness. Together with some plausible premises, the second, idealistic claim entails the first, but is not entailed by it. I will say something about the second claim in the next chapter. But what reason does Husserl provide for thinking that he has discovered a non-natural region of individual being?

The chief argument is the well-known thought experiment from §49 of *Ideas I* involving the "destruction" of the world. We are conscious of the world via the orderly progression of experience. Sometimes we are misled and conflicts arise, but they are nearly always resolved in one way or another, and none of them damages our confidence in the existence of the world. But, writes Husserl, it is "conceivable" that experience could become completely disordered, "that the connectedness of experience loses the fixed, regulated order of profiles, construals, appearances—that there is no longer a world" (Ideas I §49, 88). Obviously this would involve a change in our consciousness. But it would not add up to the *destruction* of our consciousness; consciousness *"would not be affected in its own existence"* (Ideas I §49, 89). And this, for Husserl, shows that consciousness requires no real, natural beings or "things" in order to exist.

I leave the evaluation of the merits of this argument to the reader, and merely submit that, first, there is more than one conclusion to draw from the existence of radically disordered experiences besides the non-existence of the world, and, second, that it would be unwise to pin the fate of an entire discipline on this argument.[19] A rather more interesting argument is presented earlier in §46 of *Ideas I*. Every transcendent thing, including every physical object and property, is given inadequately. And because of that, it is dubitable; "every experience [Erfahrung], no matter how far-reaching, leaves open the possibility that the given *does not exist*" (Ideas I §49, 83). Consciousness itself, by contrast, is given adequately, and its existence is indubitable and "intrinsically undeniable" (Ideas I §49, 82). The world of things is *"only a presumptive actuality,"* while my experience of it is "an *absolute* actuality" (Ideas I §49, 83). Husserl summarizes this by saying, *"The 'contingent' thesis of the world thus stands over against the 'necessary' thesis of my pure ego and life as an ego*, a thesis that is utterly indubitable" (ibid.). He then states that he has thereby supplied, minus some "easily applied additions," the most important components for an argument in favor of "the intrinsic detachability of the entire natural world from the domain of consciousness, from experiences' sphere of being" (Ideas I §49, 84).

The first thing to note about this argument, and about Husserl's general presentation of these matters in this portion of the text, is an apparent identification of indubitability with necessity and dubitability with contingency—though it is noteworthy that Husserl puts the modal terms in scare quotes. This is a mistake (see A.D. Smith 2003, 31). The existence of my present experience of the lamp near me is indubitable for me, but is obviously metaphysically contingent. And many necessary truths are dubitable or not even known at all. Kripke cites the Goldbach Conjecture and Fermat's Last Theorem (1972, 36)—though the latter example is no longer suitable. I will say more about Husserl's claims about the "necessary" status of consciousness and the "relative" status of the world in the next chapter.

The second problematic feature of this argument is that there is an apparent move from the claim that consciousness and the self are absolutely given to the claim that they have "absolute being" (Ideas I §46, 84). Reasoning from an object's mode of givenness to its mode of being is not, of course, objectionable at all. Different objects have, in virtue of their natures, different ways of manifesting themselves to consciousness. We can learn a great deal about the nature of Ideal objects, for instance, by learning that they can manifest themselves originarily even in hallucination or phantasy. And we can learn that any two objects are distinct by showing that their perceptual manifolds are distinct. As Claudio Majolino puts it, "ontological regions of being can be distinguished by means of their correlative constitutive experiences" (2016, 163). What is not valid is inferring that because an object is given F-wise, its mode of being is *F*. We cannot, for instance, conclude that because an object is given incompletely, it *is* incomplete. Nor can we conclude that because an object is given perceptually, its mode of being is perceptual—a claim which does not even make clear sense. Nor, finally, does the fact that my present experience of a lamp is given absolutely entail that it has absolute being. It quite obviously doesn't, on most natural interpretations of what that means. The existence of my experience is contingent, and it depends both existentially and essentially on many other things. In fact, one thing that Husserl would insist it depends upon is *me*.

Finally, the fact that we can be certain of the existence of our experiences and uncertain of their objects does not entail that it is metaphysically possible for the experience to exist without its object. If we could *rationally* doubt the existence of an object while being absolutely certain of the existence of an experience of an object, this would count as us clearly conceiving of the latter to exist without the former—but *only* on condition that we know all of the relevant essential properties of both the act and the object. This is similar to Arnauld's famous objection to Descartes's argument that the latter can clearly and distinctly conceive of himself existing without a body. "How," asks Arnauld, "does it follow, from the fact that he is aware of nothing else belonging to his essence, that nothing else does in fact belong to it?"[20] In order to know that, says Arnauld, Descartes must rule out the possibility that his conception of himself as a thinking thing is "an inadequate one" (Descartes 1984, 141).

Similarly, in this case, Husserl must establish that our conception of our own experiences is adequate. It's doubtful, however, that it is, especially in the case of relational acts such as perception. Suppose that I have a perceptual experience of Stan. Knowing, at this point, that Dan has a twin, I am unsure whether my experience is of Dan, or of Stan. But that does not entail that it is possible that it is either of Dan or of Stan. If the experience is of Stan, then it is *necessarily* of Stan. Husserl himself says so: "The essence of experience itself entails not only that it is consciousness, but also of what it is the consciousness" (Ideas I §36, 63). Not only is this experience essentially not of Dan, but it is essentially not of anything else, including anything fictional or non-existent. Finally, the experience has its object, Stan, quite independently of what I know or believe it to be of (see Chapter 2, §2.1.4). If the experience were only of Stan on condition that I believe or know it to be of Stan, then when I discover it is of Stan after not knowing that it is, it would acquire an essential property. But it could not *acquire* an essential property, on pain of previously existing without one of its essential properties.

What this means is that, in the case of relational acts such as perception, if the existence of an experience is certain when that of its object is dubitable, this fact depends critically on *not* being certain about the full nature of the experience in question. If I am certain that an experience is a perceptual experience of Stan, and if perceptual acts are genuinely relational, then I should also be certain that Stan exists. So, if I am uncertain of Stan's existence, then that means I am uncertain of the exact nature of my experience—either I am uncertain that it is of Stan, or uncertain that perceptual acts are relational. And that seems to be the case. The intentional transcendence of the world bleeds back into the relational acts that are of it. As Schuhmann and Smith summarize a similar point made by Daubert, "consciousness in his view can never become 'pure' in Husserl's reductive sense of this term. Consciousness is always and inevitably in confrontation with things" (Schuhmann and Smith 1985, 776).

Finally, regarding the actual carrying out of the reduction, as often as I have read Husserl's description of it, it is never clear to me just what sort of mental state I am supposed to be in when I carry it out, and I never feel confident that I've carried it out properly when, on occasion, I try. The world looks exactly the same to me, and I find it psychologically impossible not to posit its existence continually. I still answer my phone because it is really ringing, and am still really annoyed at the real banging of the radiator as I teach the reduction in class. I've certainly never experienced a "*splitting of the Ego*" that rendered me both a "naively interested Ego" and a "*disinterested onlooker*" simultaneously.[21] I also employ arguments, and work within an ontological framework of individuals, properties, relations, and so on that is effectively baked into my home language, and cannot conceive of how to conduct any inquiry in any field if I could not help myself to these completely generic categories.

10.5 Two Modest Conceptions of the Reduction

I think it's fair to say, then, that Husserl's description of how to carry out the reduction is not entirely lucid, and that Husserl's attempt at updating Descartes's argument for the separability of consciousness, not only from material nature, but from all nature, is far from clinching.[22] Nevertheless, I think there are several more modest and comprehensible understandings of the epoché, the reduction, and the process of bracketing available.

10.5.1 The Quotation View

One way of making sense of the epoché, both as a methodological device and a procedure readily psychologically achievable by non-adepts, is to treat it as something similar to quotation.[23] If I quote what someone says, I turn my attention from what they are talking about to their manner of talking about it. I focus on the utterance's sense (D.W. Smith 2007, 246). In doing so I do not doubt or attempt to doubt the truth of what was said. But neither do I affirm it (Overgaard 2015, 191). Quoting allows me to apprehend the sense of an assertion, a sense which remains what it is, and can be grasped as what it is, whether or not what is uttered is true. And so it is with the epoché. I do not doubt my experiences, nor do I, in reflection, go along with them. Rather, I focus on their inner makeup—their matter, their quality, their structure, and so on.

There is much to be said in favor of this way of understanding the epoché and the reductions. Doing something like quoting in order to orient ourselves to the intentional content and structure of consciousness, and to take it on its own terms, is an essential first step in phenomenological inquiry. More specifically, it enables us to focus our attention on the specific makeup of intentional acts so that we can understand how they are, partially or fully in virtue of that specific makeup, directed upon their objects in the manner in which they are so directed. That is, it is to focus our attention on what is really (not intentionally) immanent, not (just) to the *stream* of consciousness, but to the *act* or acts in question.

We have to describe the object of an act in describing that act. But to account for the *intentionality* of the act, to provide a constitutive explanation of why a given act is directed upon its object, appealing to the object is not enough (see Chapter 4, §4.4.2). Most objects do not enter into the stream of consciousness as real parts or pieces. And even in the case of those that do, they are still not parts or pieces of the *acts* directed upon them. This is why we must bracket objects even when their existence is beyond all rational doubt. Provided the fact that two is even is really transcendent to consciousness, it goes in brackets, at least at the stage of phenomenological inquiry where we are concerned with describing the inner structure of an act.

The point of doing this, it bears noting, is not at all epistemological, but ontological. We want to focus specifically on the nature of the act and discern how it accomplishes what it does. The fact (if it is a fact) that consciousness itself is given adequately has nothing to do with this reason for performing the reduction. Even if consciousness were not *intentionally* immanent, we should still perform some sort of reduction in order to explain the intentionality of each act in terms of its *really* immanent parts and features.

As a description of the whole nature and point of the phenomenological reduction, however, the quotation view is problematic. If all we could posit is the experience and not its object, then we could never discover that an experience entails—or does not entail—the existence of its object. But that is something that transcendental phenomenology ought to be able to discover. Husserl manages to say quite a bit about this very topic. "It is," he writes, "an essential property *of the world of things* that no perception, however so perfect, affords something absolute in its domain" (Ideas I §46, 83, my emphasis). Again: "Each immanent perception guarantees necessarily *the existence* of its object" (Ideas I §46, 82, my emphasis). Whether those claims are true or false, the fact that Husserl discusses whether acts do or do not entail the existence of their objects at all does not seem compatible with the quotation view.

As we have seen, one of the most central topics of phenomenology—arguably the single most central topic—is knowledge. But knowledge is factive: if S knows that P, then P. If all we can do as phenomenologists is investigate the experience of believing that P without determining whether or not P, then we could never investigate knowledge. Similarly, perception is quite possibly a relational act. But that, too, is something that the quotation view seems unable to allow us to discover. If the quotation view were right, then phenomenologists should be confined to investigating subjective states that merely *seem* or *feel* like perception and knowledge. In order to do that, however, one must already have some grasp on what perception and knowledge really are. And in that case, phenomenology would presuppose the findings of some other discipline.

Peter Poellner, with whose anti-Cartesian interpretation of Husserl's philosophical project I have many sympathies, partially agrees with the quotation-interpretation. Phenomenologists, he makes clear, do not turn away from the world in order to investigate a realm of immanent shadows. Nevertheless, in their investigations of acts aimed at worldly objects, they do not inquire into questions of veridicality.

> It is *irrelevant* to us whether the representations we are using to elucidate, say, the essential structural components of the perception of spatial objects are veridical perceptions or whether they are hallucinations.
>
> (Poellner 2007, 448)

Poellner is right that it is irrelevant whether the *objects* we use to illustrate phenomenological distinctions and essences *actually exist*. But that does not mean or entail that it is irrelevant whether the experiences of those objects under discussion are *veridical* or not. Those are very different issues. Frodo Baggins has lots of experiences in the fiction of which he is a part. None of the objects of his experience exist. But his experiences are not nonveridical; it is the not the story of his hallucinations. Similarly, the car hood that has recurred throughout this work does not exist. But neither do the experiences of it. The irrelevance of the existence of the car hood, *and* of A's and B's experiences of it, is explained by the fact that we are concerned with essences rather than what factually exists. It is the whole intentional nexus's existence which is irrelevant for phenomenology. But it is of the utmost phenomenological importance whether the sample experiences of the car hood are veridical or not—not *actually* veridical, but arbitrary instances of veridical *types* of experience. The reason we do not posit the car hood in discussing these examples isn't because the experience of it might, as far as phenomenological inquiry is concerned, be hallucinatory or veridical. It's because phenomenology is an eidetic discipline that posits nothing individual—not objects, and not acts either. But it can and does posit essential relations between experiences and their objects. It cannot tell us whether a perceptual experience of a car hood exists. But it lies within its purview to establish that *if* a perceptual experience of a car hood exists, the car hood must exist, or that it may or may not exist, or even that it could not exist, as is arguably the case of the objects of phantasy. That is, phenomenology has something to say about the relations between acts and their objects, and whether they are or are not existence-entailing.

10.5.2 The Bracketing View

There is an even more straightforward modest conception of the reduction that places the investigation of factive states within phenomenology's ken, and also does not require one to engage in any sort of ego-splitting at all.[24] Bracketing various subject matters is something we do all the time without even thinking about it. When we pay attention to the geometrical properties of a triangle on a chalkboard, we typically disregard the fact that it is an individual this-here made of chalk. We exercise a reduction on the empirical reality and physical composition of the chalk figure; we reduce it, intentionally, to only those features that are geometrically pertinent. In doing so we do not *doubt* or even *attempt to doubt* anything. We don't even need to stop positing it; it's clear that the physical chalk figure exists, so why bother even trying to pretend that it doesn't? Nor do we need to take up a radical or special sort of attitude. We can, for better or for worse, leave our egos intact. Bracketing is just a matter of neglecting irrelevant information. Husserl didn't invent it. It comes with doing any science at all. A physicist can and should safely bracket information about a recent political revolution, and a biologist can safely bracket the latest stock market report, and both do so more or less automatically because it is obvious that those items do not belong to their fields. Husserl himself says that the only reason that the conscientiously performed "cumbersome reductions" are necessary when doing phenomenology is that the field of pure consciousness doesn't show up in the same "obvious" and delimited way that other fields of inquiry do (Ideas I §61, 111).

When we put the positing of the natural attitude out of action, we simply bar ourselves from using any of the contents of our experiences taking place in that attitude as evidence or premises in our reasoning as phenomenologists. The epoché *"utterly closes off for me every judgment about spatiotemporal existence"* (Ideas I §32, 56). The main reason for "bracketing" the existence of the natural world when doing phenomenology is not to question, overturn, or correct the natural sciences or the natural attitude, but to prevent any "intrusion of premises" from heterogeneous and irrelevant disciplines.[25]

Bracketing in this sense is something that philosophers and non-philosophers do all the time. When we say that several of a subject's beliefs are incompatible, for instance, we typically do not mean that the relevant belief-states cannot be had by the same person at the same time. They are not incompatible states of mind in the way that red and green are incompatible properties of a surface. In characterizing these beliefs as incompatible, we bracket factual questions of psychology, and pay attention to the relevant properties of those acts. The relevant properties are that those beliefs have intentional contents, propositions, and those propositions cannot all be *true*. We perform a *logical* reduction, focusing solely on the logical properties of the person's beliefs and neglecting the rest.

The phenomenological reduction is just like that, except that we pay attention to more than just the logical properties of mental states—just as we did in the previous chapters. We are permitted to do so because there are discoverable necessary relations among more than just the logical properties of our mental states. At this point, we should have enough of a sense of the subject matter of phenomenology to bracket irrelevancies without too much difficulty. What we want to discover are the natures of various types of intentional experiences, and the essential relations they bear to their contents, their objects, and to one another. Since this is an a priori investigation, it should be clear that we can bracket all empirical matters of fact, just as we do when we examine the geometrical properties of a chalk figure on a blackboard. In the example of A and B seeing a scratched car hood, for instance, it does not matter for phenomenological purposes whether I am talking about real individuals, real experiences, or a real car hood. What matters is that if any possible individuals have the sorts of experiences that A and B undergo, then they will be conscious of a scratched car hood in the various modes and varieties that we have treated in the previous chapters.

It is of the utmost importance to note that the phenomenological reduction does not commit us to ignoring the relations of existential dependence or independence among types of acts and their objects. Nor does it, by itself, commit us to the very substantive philosophical thesis that acts can exist even when their objects do not. In the first place, no mere methodological procedure could possibly establish something like that, and to presuppose something of that magnitude would straightforwardly beg the question against numerous plausible theories of intentionality.

Second, it's clear that there are some acts whose existence *does* entail that of their objects, even when those objects can be bracketed. We can and must, Husserl insists, bracket the world of mathematical and logical idealities when doing phenomenology (Ideas I §59). But those items necessarily exist. Therefore their existence is entailed by our awareness of them. That, however, does not prevent us from bracketing their existence for the purposes of phenomenological inquiry.

Third, the phenomenological method does not require us to bracket the existence of objects while also positing the existence of *acts* directed upon them. In fact it forbids our doing so. Comparing phenomenology with geometry, Husserl writes, "Geometry and phenomenology as sciences of pure essence make note of no determinations about real existence" (Ideas I §79, 147). And that means that phenomenology does not involve positing real mental happenings (see Ideas I §54, 102). So, when we "bracket" matters in phenomenology, an act upon which we are reflecting does not look like this:

Act → {Object}

Rather, the whole real intentional nexus goes into brackets, like this:

{Act → Object}

And it is fully compatible with the latter construal to say that the act is genuinely relational, that is, that *if* an act of that type exists, its object must also exist. This is why the phenomenological reduction still permits us to make claims about factive mental states such as perception, broadly conceived as originary intuition, and knowledge—factive states, moreover, directed at real things and not just irreal noemata. In fact those are the most fundamental subject matters of the field, since all intentionality is ultimately founded on them.

The first goal of the reduction, then, is the one that the quotation view best achieves—to enable us to focus on the inner character of intentional acts to discover what it is about them that makes them intentionally directed upon their objects in the way they are so directed. This does not involve positing either the object of the act or the experience itself.

The second goal of the reduction, and one which the quotation view does not readily allow us to carry out, is to turn to the *essential* relations among types of mental acts, their contents, and their objects rather than merely factual and contingent ones. The goal of the reduction, as Amie Thomasson puts it, is to discover "general *a priori* laws governing these 'essences' of experiences" (2005, 127). The Principle of All Principles is one example of such a law. The reason to do so is so that we can focus clearly on what is prescribed by an act's own sense, and not confuse the intentional relations with various other relations, such as causal relations, that acts and their objects may bear to one another.

This brings us to a third goal of the reduction—one which the quotation view also manages to achieve—which is to put ourselves in a position in which we can faithfully describe conscious acts without being prejudicially influenced, in those descriptions, by our theories of what *must* or *could not* be the case. As we saw in the discussion of the constancy hypothesis (Chapter 7, §7.6), for instance, the assumption that perceptual or sensory experiences simply *must* correspond 1:1 to physical stimuli leads to catastrophic phenomenological results.[26] Assumptions about how things could *not* be can be just as pernicious. Many philosophers, for instance, find libertarian free will, values, universals, physical objects, consciousness, and causation to be metaphysically problematic. You name it, there's probably a philosopher out there who doesn't believe in it. Phenomenological descriptions of the intentional contents and structures of cognitive, volitional, emotional, and perceptual acts should be uninfluenced by such metaphysical commitments.

Among other things, we should avoid reasoning that because a certain sort of act simply *could not* be nonveridical or irrational, and because it *would* be nonveridical or irrational if it were directed at an object O, it *must not* be aimed at O. Such reasoning very often winds up substituting the objects quite plainly intended in mental acts with something totally different—sense data (or noemata) instead of physical things, false propositions instead of non-obtaining states of affairs, "concepts" instead of non-intentional universals, qualia instead of colors, confidence instead of evidence, psychological connections instead of logical relations, mental images instead of fictional objects, our own feelings or preferences instead of objective values, constant conjunctions instead of objective causal relations, and so on. Husserl's own case against empiricism and naturalism, spelled out most memorably in the Prolegomena of the *Logical Investigations* and the Second Chapter of the First Section of *Ideas I*, is that it routinely falsifies our consciousness because of, among other things, its "animosity to ideas" or essences (Ideas I §18, 34). The reduction leaves it open for us to reject the existence of certain entities or the rationality of believing in them. But it's important, phenomenologically, not to treat a nonveridical, false or irrational mental act about one thing as a veridical or true mental act about something very different.

To sum it up, then, what comes into view in transcendental phenomenological inquiry are the essences of and essential relations among acts, their contents, and their objects, including the relations that hold *within* those categories, such as essential relations among acts and other acts, contents and other contents, and even objects and other objects. It is not necessary to regard these essences as being instantiated in non-natural particulars, such as the states of transcendental egos, any more than we have to regard geometrical properties as instantiated in non-natural particulars—though, to be clear, it could turn out that intentional properties are instantiated in something non-physical. The phenomenological reduction is just a way of making these essential features and relations stand out in relief, and to place everything irrelevant to them in brackets. There is nothing especially "radical" about the reduction. It does not require doubt or any attempt to doubt, meditation, a bifurcation of one's own self, or anything like a "religious conversion."[27] It does not require one to retreat to a quiet place, and it can be done in concert with other real people. It does not even need to involve any epoché. Provided we find a way to bracket or neglect irrelevant information, we will be on the right path.

Furthermore, it is important not to place too much emphasis upon the phenomenological reduction as the touchstone regarding what is and is not phenomenological in character. To carry the reduction out properly, to know what can be bracketed and what cannot, one must know a lot about the subject matter already. It is through phenomenological work itself that we first come to see that, for instance, many contingent psychological facts have no bearing on the logical properties of our mental states. In the same way, it is through geometrical work itself that we discover that color can be neglected and bracketed in geometry. No one who has not grasped the subject matter of transcendental phenomenology on the basis of a fairly extensive acquaintance with concrete analyses and examples would be helped at all by a description of the phenomenological method. Moreover, the possibility remains open that we should change that method as phenomenology advances. And, of course, methods are answerable to objects, not vice versa. As Josef Seifert puts it, "only by going back to the 'things' which constitute the subject-matter of our investigation can we discover methods appropriate for their exploration" (Seifert 1987, 77–78). We have to understand things before we can understand our understanding of those things, and for essential reasons: our understanding of a thing is not the intentional target of itself, and must already exist to be the target of any other act.

Finally, when it comes to what sorts of objects we can and cannot talk about and posit when we put the brackets on, the answers are straightforward. We can think and talk about any object whatsoever, without restrictions of any kind. If anyone can possibly be conscious of an object, then the consciousness of that object is something that can be discussed in phenomenological inquiry. And because one cannot describe the consciousness of something without specifying that very something, any object of which we can be conscious can be discussed in phenomenology. Nothing has to be ignored out of epistemic caution, and nothing needs to be replaced by an "immanent" phantom or a noema (though, if noemata are *also* to be found, we must also pay attention to them as well). As for which particular objects, which real individuals, states of affairs, relations, events, and so on we can *posit* in phenomenological inquiry, the answer is: none whatsoever, not even one's own conscious experiences.

10.6 Conclusion

The modest conception of the phenomenological reduction above does not constitute an interpretation of Husserl's official statements of the nature and point of the reduction. Rather, it is an attempt to spell out a conception which manages to capture much of what Husserl himself intended it to achieve, which does not depend on any highly contentious metaphysical claims such as the existence of transcendental consciousness or the truth of metaphysical idealism, and which harmonizes with both the contents and methods of the previous chapters.

Notes

1　LI, Introduction to Vol. Two, §2, 252.
2　See Ideas I §75.

3   LI, Introduction to Volume Two, §7, 263. Also see ibid., 265.
4   Regarding those tendencies, see Burge 1999 and Preston 2007, 20–22.
5   For a very clear and concise summary of Husserl's arrival at "pure phenomenology" from his initial philosophical work on arithmetical knowledge, see Hopkins 2010, Chapter 4. For a discussion of the similarities and differences among Kant's and Husserl's conception of transcendental philosophy, and in their explanations of necessities, see Jansen 2015.
6   FTL §99, 251, translation modified. The translators have "productivity of consciousness" for *Bewusstseinsleistung*.
7   See IdPh, 52, as well as Sokolowski 1964, 54, Mohanty 1989, 151–152, Willard 2006, 597–598, and Poellner 2007, 412.
8   See Lewis 1995, 240 for this way of speaking of what we do with concepts.
9   A point made very clearly by A.D. Smith 2003, 34.
10 See Føllesdal 1969 and Smith & McIntyre 1982.
11 For an alternative take on the problematic issue of reflection, I recommend Hopkins 2010, 140ff.
12 See Kern 1977 for a classic discussion. For a good sense of how complicated the nature of the reduction and the pathways to it are, see Perkins 2017.
13 For a discussion of the differences between the epoché and doubt, see Romano 2012, 436. Also see A.D. Smith 2003, 21.
14 For a very illuminating discussion, see Alweiss 2013, §1.
15 See Ingarden 1976, 35. For discussions, see Willard 1995b, §1, D.W. Smith 2004, 17, and Kinkaid 2018, 22.
16 Ideas I §31, 53. Also see Poellner 2007, 444.
17 Crisis §55, 189. For a good discussion, see Bell 1990, 125.
18 Overgaard 2008, 298. Also see Zahavi 2017, 57–58.
19 See Majolino 2016 for a unique and very interesting take on the point of Husserl's thought experiment.
20 See Descartes 1984, 140. For Descartes's own argument for dualism, see 1984, 54.
21 See CM §15, 35. For related, and significantly harsher, criticisms, see Bell 1990, 126. For an excellent and much more sympathetic discussion of Husserl's development of his distinctive account of the splitting of the ego, and his indebtedness to Moritz Geiger and others, see Averchi 2015.
22 Husserl compares his efforts with Descartes's in Ideas I,§46, 84, claiming that his argument for the "intrinsic detachability of the entire natural world from the domain of consciousness" is one in which Descartes's argument to similar effect "finally attains its legitimacy."
23 See Sokolowski 1984; D.W. Smith 2007, 244–249; Overgaard 2015, 190–192. Thanks to Søren Overgaard for alerting me to this interpretation.
24 See Willard 1991. I have also learned that Moritz Geiger endorsed a similar conception of the reduction to the one that follows. For an excellent discussion, see Averchi (forthcoming).
25 Ideas I §61, 111. Also see Sokolowski 2000, 62–63.
26 Thanks to Søren Overgaard for this example.
27 Crisis §35, 137. For a critical response with which I share some sympathies, see Bell 1990, 126.

Recommended Readings

Husserl, Edmund. 1977. *Cartesian Meditations*. Daniel O. Dahlstrom, trans. The Hague: Martinus Nijhoff.

Husserl, Edmund. 2014. *Ideas I: Ideas for a Pure Phenomenology and Phenomenological Philosophy*. Daniel O. Dahlstrom, trans. Indianapolis: Hackett.

Reinach, Adolf. 2012b. "Concerning Phenomenology." Dallas Willard, trans. In *The Apriori Foundations of the Civil Law, along with the Lecture "Concerning Phenomenology,"* 143–165. John F. Crosby, ed. Frankfurt: Ontos Verlag.

11 Phenomenology and Transcendental Idealism

In the previous chapter, we looked at the subject matter and methods of transcendental phenomenology. Now, finally, we turn to the relation between "transcendental idealism" and phenomenology. For Husserl, the connection is intimate:

> Only someone who misunderstands either the deepest sense of intentional method, or that of transcendental reduction, or perhaps both, can attempt to separate phenomenology from transcendental idealism.

(CM §41, 86)

Given the fact that many of Husserl's descriptions of his method and his characterizations of the precise content of transcendental idealism are far from lucid, one can be forgiven for thinking that perhaps the two can be separated. I will offer an interpretation, though, according to which Husserl's remark is correct. I will also argue that transcendental idealism, so construed, is perfectly compatible with metaphysical realism regarding the objects of perception and knowledge, including physical things and ideal entities such as universals. I should say at the outset that my primary concern is not to characterize what the biographical individual Edmund Husserl in fact believed, but to present a philosophical interpretation according to which the most philosophically defensible aspects of Husserl's transcendental phenomenology are compatible with, and even support, metaphysical realism.

11.1 Phenomenology and the Question of Realism

We have already touched upon the general question of metaphysical realism in Chapter 5, §5.4.1 and Chapter 10, §10.3, where it was argued that ideal verificationism and Husserl's transcendental insight, respectively, do not entail antirealism. Metaphysical realism with respect to some class of entities is the position that those entities exist, and that neither their existence nor their nature is grounded in their being the objects of experience, thought, or discourse. Epistemic realism is metaphysical realism with respect to objects that can be known.

It is worth noting that while the formulations of these positions can surely be refined, they are intelligible positions. It is often said that Husserl and other phenomenologists have somehow overcome or dissolved the question of realism. Don Ihde, for instance, writes:

> any object-in-itself and equally any subject-in-itself remains "outside" phenomenology. It is here that the Husserlian avoidance of "realism" and "idealism"—both of which are ultimately inverse sides of the same "metaphysics"—arises. "Objectivism" and "subjectivism" are both part of a "Cartesian," dualistic myth to which Husserlian phenomenology sees itself opposed as the radical alternative.
>
> (Ihde 2012, 35)

Dan Zahavi expresses a similar thought when he writes that: "the very notions of realism and idealism are so elastic as to be nearly useless. It is no coincidence that both Hans-George Gadamer and Fink have praised Husserl for overcoming the old opposition between realism and idealism, and it is certainly true that he was neither a subjective idealist nor a metaphysical realist" (Zahavi 2003a, 72). Now there is much to be said in favor of these remarks. Husserl's position constitutes a novel conception of the relation between objectivity and subjectivity that doesn't fit neatly into preexisting categories. And surely the *terms* "realism" and "idealism" are, like almost all philosophical terms, ambiguous and used in many ways. As we have already seen in the previous discussion of "Platonic realism" (Chapter 3, §3.3), what Husserl means by "real" and "realism" is not what most philosophers mean, and not what we mean here. This will prove significant in what follows.

Nevertheless, it is perfectly meaningful to ask, of a given entity or type of entity, whether it depends for its existence or nature on another entity or type of entity. It is a perfectly meaningful question to ask whether, for instance, raindrops depend on rabbits or smiles depend on faces. Provided the terms "A" and "B" pick out something at all, it is meaningful to ask whether or not the As depend for their existence or nature on Bs. Since "consciousness" does pick something out, we can sensibly ask, of anything else we can think or talk about, whether it is ontologically dependent on it.

The question of metaphysical realism makes sense. If phenomenology has nothing to say about this issue, it is not because there is no such issue. Does phenomenology address the issue? It would be astonishing if it did not. As we have seen many times, investigating the "connections between veritable being and knowing" and "the correlations between act, meaning, object" comprises "the *task of transcendental phenomenology*" (ILTK, 434). Provided phenomenology really can live up to its task, we should expect phenomenological investigations to provide answers to the questions of metaphysical and epistemic realism. Quite obviously so, for in discerning the "relations" and "connections" among the items in our intentional triad, we will thereby discover whether the items within the triad depend upon, are constructed by, or are otherwise founded on items within the others. Phenomenological inquiry into the relations between galaxies and experiences should show us, for instance, whether galaxies *are* experiences, whether they *contain* experiences as parts, whether they themselves are parts of experiences, whether they are wholly or partially *created by* experiences, whether they are *altered* by our experiences, and so on. If phenomenology is silent about that, then plainly it is not up to its appointed task.

One might think that this answer flies in the face of phenomenology's metaphysical neutrality. It does not. If, on the one hand, metaphysics tells us about the nature and structure of the actual world, then phenomenology is silent on issues of metaphysics because it does not posit the existence of anything real. That seems to be Husserl's view of metaphysics.[1] Accordingly, if the question of realism concerns the metaphysical status of existing individuals, and if, as is the case, phenomenology is concerned with essential relationships among types of entities rather than matter-of-fact relations among individuals, the question of realism cannot even be posed by the phenomenologist (see Hall 1982).

However, the question of realism is not primarily a question about the actual world. It is a question about the relation among types of things—types of mental or linguistic entities, on the one hand, and the various other kinds of things to which they refer. It is, as Berkeley points out (1975b, §3, 90), in the nature of an idea to exist in a mind. Having established that, even an empiricist won't bother collecting specimens. Typical arguments for or against realism proceed by disclosing essential or eidetic relations among *types* of mental or linguistic entities, on the one hand, and *types* of objects, on the other. Those are the kinds of question phenomenology can address. Phenomenology's silence about what *factually* exists does not entail that it must be silent on questions about essential relationships among *types* of acts, contents, and objects—all of which *exist*.. While phenomenology might not directly say that the redwood Hyperion or the planet Jupiter is metaphysically real, it is certainly capable of asking whether or not trees and planets are the *kinds* of things which are composed of, created by, or dependent on experiences of them.

If, on the other hand, we take a broader view of metaphysics whereby it encompasses formal and material ontology, disciplines which posit nothing individual or real, then phenomenology is far from metaphysically neutral. Any theory that posits types of acts of consciousness, essences, and meanings (which are just one kind of essence), as phenomenology does, is already far from neutral on questions of what exists, even if it says nothing about what *really* exists, that is, what exists in time.

Phenomenology is also committed to the possibility of objects of various types, including such things as car hoods, and is therefore committed to the existence of those respective types of objects. Otherwise, it could not address the nature of factive mental states such as perception and knowledge directed upon them. These investigations, moreover, are directly relevant to questions about what does in fact exist and its manner of existence (see Zahavi 2017, 63–64). If we want to learn whether existing planets and trees depend on consciousness, we may simply apply eidetic results to actual cases, just as we do when we apply the results of any other eidetic science. Claims about essences and properties have an immediate bearing on claims about the possible bearers of those essences and properties, and actual objects are possible objects. Phenomenology is metaphysically neutral in the same way that geometry is metaphysically neutral—it does not directly assert the existence of anything real. Together with some evident empirical propositions about what does exist, however, both disciplines have rich metaphysical consequences.

11.2 The Tension in Husserl's Thinking

We should, then, expect phenomenological considerations to go some way towards determining whether metaphysical and epistemic realism are true, and in the eyes of many of Husserl's readers, his phenomenology does in fact answer such questions. The problem is that it appears to provide inconsistent answers. The familiar story goes something as follows. In the *Logical Investigations* of 1900–01, Husserl provided a broadly realist view of, among other things, ideal entities such as numbers, logical laws, and meanings, and spatiotemporal entities such as physical objects. A few years later, he turns to transcendental phenomenology, and, with the publication of *Ideas I* in 1913, provides the first mature statement of his distinctive brand of transcendental idealism. In doing so, he alienated, and was alienated by, most of the firmly realist members of the Munich and Göttingen groups of early students and followers. He even selected Heidegger over Alexander Pfänder as his successor at Freiburg in part because of Pfänder's unwillingness to carry out his transcendental idealist program—and also, of course, because of Husserl's mistaken belief that Heidegger intended to do so.[2]

This alleged "turn" from realism to idealism on Husserl's part is comparatively superficial, however, compared with a persisting tension within his thinking *after* his alleged turn to idealism. Levinas comes close to spotting the tension when he writes,

> The Husserlian thesis of the primacy of the objectifying act ... leads to transcendental philosophy, to the affirmation (so surprising after the realist themes the idea of intentionality seemed to approach) that the object of consciousness, while distinct from consciousness, is as it were a product of consciousness, being a "meaning" endowed by consciousness, the result of *Sinngebung*.[3]

I am far from confident that Husserl ever regards the ordinary objects of consciousness as "meanings." Nevertheless, Husserl does issue a number of idealistic sounding claims about those objects. At the same time, the "realist themes" of intentionality do not go away after the transcendental turn. They persist, and they are made increasingly expansive in scope and precise in detail through investigations of the consciousness of spatiotemporal things, time, space, images, phantasy-worlds, intersubjectivity, and so on. What we seem to find in Husserl's work are increasingly detailed accounts of how consciousness manages to come into touch with entities that in no way lie within its own sphere as parts or moments, together with repeated assurances that these very entities are somehow "constituted" by consciousness itself.

To make this more precise, the alleged tension in Husserl's thinking is among the following claims:

(A)   The world presents itself to us as metaphysically real.
(B)   By the Principle of All Principles: if the world presents itself to us as metaphysically real, we are entitled to believe that it is metaphysically real.
(C)   We are not entitled to believe that the world is metaphysically real.

Since we have already discussed the Principle of All Principles in Chapter 9, §9.4, I will confine the discussion that follows to (A) and (C).

11.3 Realism in the Natural Attitude

"Everyday life," observes Steven Crowell, "is characterized by a kind of global realism, a belief in the factual existence of what I encounter."[4] Let's begin within what Husserl calls the "natural attitude," characterized by its distinctive, but fully legitimate, kind of naivety (Ideas I §26). Within that attitude, our most fundamental engagement with the world is through perceptual experience. Perceptual experience, and that alone, provides us with an "originary" experience of natural things, relations, processes, events, and states of affairs (see Ideas I §1, 9). And in the natural attitude, the objects that we take ourselves to perceive are predominantly public, objective entities, along with their relations to one another and the complexes into which they enter. We take ourselves to perceive natural objects such as trees and mountains and grass and stones, human artifacts such as buildings and cars and liquor licenses, and, of course, other animals and humans themselves. Many of these entities present themselves as owing exactly none of their properties to us or our manner of being conscious of them. The tree I see does not perceptually appear to depend upon my experience of it for its existence, nor does it seem to acquire or lose any of its features in virtue of being perceived by me. Without belaboring the point, the most natural perspective in the natural attitude is one of realism. If you are not presently a realist, I suspect that at some point you changed your mind, and that philosophical considerations, rather than the straightforward apprehension of things in the perceived world, prompted that change. Antirealists know their view to be a surprising one.

This realism carries over into the realm of what we do not presently perceive and cannot, as a matter of fact, perceive. The world that we perceive extends far beyond the portions of it that we just happen to perceive, and is grasped by us as doing so. One reason is that we continually discover this to be so—that there is more land over the next hill, more structure to the cell we see in the microscope, a "deep field" beyond the stars so far surveyed, and so on. We discover that things don't disappear when others stop observing them, and are given every conceivable indication that we are no exceptions in this respect. Despite some abiding mysteries, our empirical sciences, all of which are carried out within the natural attitude, present us with an increasingly verified, unified, and mutually cohering picture of the nature of things.

Among other notable pieces of public knowledge, this is a world whose origins predate, by many billions of years, the advent of the earliest known conscious beings. The earliest conscious beings predate, by many hundreds of millions of years, the earliest known rational beings or persons. There is no evidence whatsoever that any finite conscious beings were present at the beginning of the universe, much less that they were causally responsible for its coming to be, and even less that they were causally responsible for it through nothing more than the execution of cognitive or linguistic acts. Still less is there any evidence that any existing finite consciousnesses now are responsible for those past events. We have a decent idea of just how conscious organisms came to be, and there is overwhelming evidence that none could possibly have been present then. If all of natural reality depends on our consciousness, then our ordinary perceptual experiences are radically illusory and our best theories of the origin of the universe and the subsequent evolution and continuation of life are radically mistaken. To put it simply: if realism about the natural world is false, then we are massively and systematically deluded. It is highly unclear how that picture is supposed to be preferable to radical skepticism—a disease to which antirealism frequently proffers itself as the cure.

Well, we might say, so what if we come to realist conclusions within the natural attitude? In the first place, the natural attitude assumes realism from the outset, so any argument for it within the natural attitude is circular. Indeed, it doesn't just assume metaphysical realism, but epistemic realism: we presuppose that our acts of perceiving and thinking can lay hold of real things as they are. Second, the natural attitude is one in which the question of the ultimate relationship between act, meaning, and object cannot be raised properly. Our natural attitude is one of "infatuation" with objects at the expense of the "constituting multiplicities belonging essentially to them" on the side of consciousness (Crisis §52, 176). Only by turning our attention to the latter can we determine just what the relationship between consciousness and the world is.

In response to the first criticism, the natural attitude does not in any obvious way "assume" realism. There is another explanation of why the natural attitude is realistic, and that is that the world appears to be real. If it appeared differently—if it appeared to be a world of Humean perceptions, for instance, or if it appeared the way fictional entities appear—the natural attitude would be correspondingly different.

The second criticism, however, has more teeth. Let us assume that it is correct, that the eidetic relationships among acts, contents, and objects are ones that cannot even be properly raised within the natural attitude. Where does this leave us? Well, at least with this much: the natural attitude, and the natural sciences the take place within it, do tell us how at least part of the world is, and all of the available information is that real objects are not dependent upon *real psychological processes* carried out by any of the actual beings which fall within its purview. This of course only gives us *some* reason to reject antirealism. It is hardly conclusive, though, since there are reasons to think that natural science could not exhaustively describe reality, especially the full reality of consciousness.

11.4 Realism in the Phenomenological Attitude

What do we find, then, when we shift to the phenomenological attitude and inspect the essential relations among acts, their contents, and their objects? One tempting answer is that after performing the various phenomenological "reductions," the objects of perception and knowledge turn out to be nothing more than "noemata." The tree I see will become the "seen tree as such," whose "*esse* consists exclusively in its '*percipi*'" (Ideas I §98, 198).

Now even if that were right, that would not automatically count against the realism of the natural attitude. The phenomenological attitude according to this understanding of it appears to beg the question against realism to an even greater degree than the natural attitude allegedly does in favor of it. Of course the world will show up as nothing more than a "correlate" of subjectivity if I succeed in making every deliberate methodological effort to exclude from my consideration and knowledge every feature of it that isn't a mere correlate of subjectivity.

Apart from ruling out realism by fiat, there is a further weakness of this argument: the fact that I had to exclude or bracket anything at all argues in favor of, not against, realism. If the world were a field of noemata, if reality consisted of nothing but transcendental consciousness and its "correlates," no reductions would be called for. Instead of performing a reduction on, say, a car hood, we could simply proceed by showing that the car hood is, contrary to what almost everyone believes, dependent for its existence on our consciousness of it.

In any case, the objects of the natural attitude do not, in phenomenological reflection, show up as mere noemata. If they did, then we could not distinguish between a real tree and a tree-noema *within* the phenomenological attitude. But we can, as Husserl insists (Ideas I §89, 176–177; Crisis §70, 242). Furthermore, if all I could be aware of in phenomenological reflection were noemata, then phenomenological reflection would fail to shed light on the phenomenological character of the experiences I enjoy in the natural attitude. I can't examine the nature of being conscious of a tree if I replace the tree with a shimmering noema. Such a substitution is a clear violation of the Hands-Off Principle.

What, then, do we find when we take on the phenomenological attitude? We find that our acts of consciousness of natural objects bear a number of features that would be inexplicable if they did not aim at and sometimes hit metaphysically real objects. David Woodruff Smith (1982) describes a number of features of perceptual experience that entail that it harbors realist commitments, including the "sensuous presence" and "individuality" of the object (D.W. Smith 1982, 45), which ensure that the object is presented as something with causal properties and an independent identity. Further, related features that show up in phenomenological reflection include those that we have already discussed.

Inadequacy: the objects of perception are presented to as having more to them than what is present to us in a given experience, and more than what is meant of them in a given thought. Furthermore, our perception of them is incomplete not because the objects are presented as *being* incomplete, like an unfinished story we are composing, but because they are so much richer than what any finite number of experiences can disclose. They do not look like partial objects that we perceive and know completely, but complete objects that we perceive and know partially—not things-from-perspectives upon which we have a God's eye view, but things from very finite and human perspectives.

Intersubjectivity: physical things are presented as which could be observed in more than one way, from more than one point of view, and simultaneously by different people. The tree I see doesn't give itself as something exclusively "for me" or even "for us." It, along with each of its features, can be and often is simultaneously perceived and thought about by myself and others, and is given as something that could be perceived by still more others. It is also something about which qualified observers can come to a consensus, and the explanation of that consensus is, in part, that the object is the way they perceive and believe it to be. If there is disagreement, we take ourselves to disagree about the same thing, and know that at least one disputing party must be wrong. Finally, we often find that others continue to perceive things which we have stopped perceiving, and that we can perceive those things after they have stopped.

Fallibility: physical objects are the kinds of things that we could coherently recognize ourselves to be mistaken about. Things might look or seem otherwise than they are. It makes sense to say "It looked taller than the other tree, but in fact they're the same size." This is not, of course, an argument for skepticism—far from it. But it is an argument for epistemic caution of a certain type. And epistemic caution is called for exactly when the nature and existence of one's intentional object is not fully determined by one's experiences or thoughts of it. We don't need to exercise a similar caution about imagined objects, since whatever seems to us to be the case with them is the case. If I imagine a dragon with two wings, I don't need to worry that it really has four; if it did, it would be because I said so (see Sartre 2010, 132).

The absence of any acts of "constructing" or "shaping" most of the objects of awareness: if epistemic realism is true, the objects of knowledge neither come into existence nor acquire properties in virtue of being perceived or known. If non-eliminative antirealism is true with respect to some object, then the appropriate kind of consciousness of that object either brings it into existence, or at least bestows some set of properties on it. A number of philosophical views, more or less remotely inspired by Kant, maintain that cognizers play an indispensable role in the configuration of the world that we experience and know. Kant claims that his so-called "categories," which he treats as certain distinctive *concepts*, enable us to know something about objects a priori, but only in virtue of "prescribing laws to nature, and even of making nature possible" (Kant 1965, B 159–160). The natural objects that we perceive and know—and indeed "all objects of any experience possible to us"—"are nothing but appearances, that is, mere representations, which, in the manner in which they are represented, as extended beings, or as series of alterations, have no independent existence outside our thoughts" (Kant 1965, A 490–01/B 518–19). Kant admits that these things are "real," but adds that: "they are nothing but representations, and cannot exist outside our mind" (Kant 1965, A 492/B 520).

More than a few philosophers have followed Kant in treating concepts, conceptual schemes, and/or the languages in which they are expressed as forming some sort of barrier between minds and an independent world. Putnam, as we have seen, holds that "'Objects' do not exist independently of conceptual schemes. *We* cut up the world into objects when we introduce one or another scheme of description."[5] Donald Davidson, discussing the possibility of "a confrontation between what we believe and reality," claims that: "the idea of such a confrontation is absurd" (Davidson 2001, 137). Perhaps one reason for Davidson's astonishing statement—after all, we seem to confront *something* all the time, and most of what we confront sure *seems* real and independently so—is his view that "if the mind can grapple without distortion with the real, the mind itself must be without categories and concepts" (Davidson 1984, 185). This means that if the mind has concepts, it can only have access to something real if the latter has been "distorted" by some process of "grappling" (Willard 2002, 72).

Davidson's and Putnam's positions provide especially clear examples of the "Midas touch" theory of mind (Willard 2000b, 38). Whatever else might be said in favor of or against Midas-touch antirealism, I suspect that, first, it is an incoherent account of intentionality, and, second, that no *phenomenological* defense of such a view is possible.[6]

Beginning with the first point, no act of consciousness could *itself* be the transformation or distortion of *its* object (Willard 2000b, 38). A perceptual experience of a chair is *of* a *chair*. It is not the perception of any transformation of something else, O, into a chair. If it were, it would be a perception of *O's transformation into a chair*. We can conceive of an act whose object is *O's transformation into a chair*, or *the transformation of O into a chair by the imposition of concepts*. But then such acts would be of *those* objects *without* transformation or distortion.

If, moreover, a class of objects showed themselves to be dependent on our minds or conceptual schemes, then that's what such objects really are, in themselves. That sensations depend on the consciousness of them, for instance, is a true statement of how they *really are*. Similarly, Davidson's claim that real objects are "distorted" by "concepts" is almost impossible to read as anything less than a claim about how they *really* are. Whatever else Midas-touch views say about the impossibility of representing things as they really are, they always seem to manage to say things about the nature of consciousness, concepts, or language and its relation to reality without "distortion" as *those* matters *really* are (see Willard 2000b, 39).

Second, there could not possibly be phenomenological evidence for a *general* Midas-touch theory. Conscious transformation requires that one be conscious of what was there before and after the transformation. If we *consciously* "cut up the world into objects when we introduce one or another scheme of description" (Putnam 1981, 52), then we must be conscious of the world as it is before we have cut it up. But then we can be conscious of something—"the world," no less—*without* distortion after all. The conscious construction or distortion of a chair must presuppose some other act A in which we start with a non-chair O and, through some operation, wind up with a chair as the object of perception. But that act A would, then, either be a grasping of O as it really is or it would not. If it is, then something, namely O, can be grasped as it is without distortion. Furthermore, we are owed an explanation of why exactly O can be perceived or known without distortion while a chair cannot—bearing in mind that such non-distorting contact would be no more or less intelligible if O were a sensation, an idea, or anything "inside" or "internal to" the mind, language, or a conceptual scheme. And if O is not grasped as what it itself is, then we have to give a similar story with respect to the relation between A and O—that is, we must appeal to yet another act A*, and some object distinct from O, O*, which undergoes transformation or distortion into O. If intentionality "imparted a property to its object" (Willard 1995, 156), then the only way we could know so on phenomenological grounds is if we compared the object without that imparted property to the object with the imparted property. But if that were possible, then we could be conscious of and know the object without imparting a property to it after all.

As far as I can tell, one of the major motivations behind Midas-touch antirealism is anti-essentialism, the rejection of the view that things have mind-independent essential properties (see Wolterstorff 1987, 249). Locke claims that *"essential, and not essential, relate only to our abstract Ideas, and the names annexed to them"* (Locke 1975, 441). Kant claims that "nothing in *a priori* knowledge can be ascribed to objects save what the thinking subject derives from itself" (Kant 1965, Bxxiii). Quine writes that "Being necessarily or possibly thus and so is in general not a trait of the object concerned, but depends on the manner of referring to the object" (Quine 1961b, 148). One type of argument to support this view comes from Putnam, who writes that:

> it only makes sense to speak of an "essential property" relative to a description. Relative to the description "that statue", a certain shape is an essential property of the object; relative to the description "that piece of clay", the shape is not an essential property (but being clay is). The question "what are the essential properties of a thing in itself" is a nonsensical one.[7]

In Putnam's view, the mind, or language, appears to endow objects with essences.

The problem is that on one interpretation Putnam's view appears to be incoherent. Exactly *which thing* is it that can be *correctly* described as both essentially shaped F-wise and as *not* essentially shaped F-wise? It cannot be the statue, since it cannot be truly described as not essentially shaped F-wise; it is essentially shaped F-wise. And it cannot be the lump of clay, since it cannot be truly described as being essentially shaped F-wise. Since the statue is essentially shaped F-wise, while the clay is not, the two are distinct, in which case there is no third thing x that is identical with both. As David Wiggins puts it,

> What is this substance out there that can be conceptualized in radically different ways, which can be seized upon in thought by the anti-essentialist, but can have radically different principles of existence and persistence ascribed to it? This is surely an entity with inconsistent properties.
>
> (Wiggins 2001, 148)

The idea that we can correctly "impose" incompatible essential properties— or incompatible contingent properties, for that matter—on the same thing is incoherent. Since the statue and the lump do have different essential properties, the conclusion to draw is that they are not identical. They are, therefore, not both identical with some third neutral thing-in-itself.

There is another way of taking Putnam's point, however, which is not that we somehow endow things with their essential properties, but that things simply do not have essential properties at all. That's a problematic view as well. If every property the statue has is accidental, then it seems that we could swap them out for any properties whatsoever without destroying it. That, I take it, is the force of Wiggins's question when he asks, "Of *what* could one ever be speaking if one allowed that it might equally well have been a fire shovel or a prime number, thought it was in fact neither?" (Wiggins 2001, 147). But even if anti-essentialism were true, this would not support the Midas-touch view. If, on the one hand, we do ascribe essential properties to things, then the conclusion to draw is not that we are *right* about mind- or language-dependent objects, but that we are *wrong* about the things in the world. And if, on the other hand, we deny that objects have essential properties, then we would be getting things right about how things really are. Finally, if Putnam himself is in a position to know that things in themselves do not have essential properties, or that they only have them relative to our concepts, then he has managed to represent them as they are.

At most, then, thinking, perceiving, and knowing might essentially *involve* or *presuppose* the transforming of one thing into something else or the imparting of a property, but they cannot themselves *be* acts of transforming *their objects* into something else or imparting properties to them. Whatever Davidson's "grappling" and Putnam's "cut[ting] up" with concepts might be, they are not and could not be *intentionality*.[8] Nor can intentional acts rest on a foundation of distorting grapplings all of which are conscious. If consciousness is always of the *products* of transformative processes, then the processes producing them must ultimately be unconscious. In that case there cannot be phenomenological evidence for such processes.

That we cannot know, perceive, or authentically represent *Kantian* things-in-themselves is something that Husserl undoubtedly endorses; the unknowability of Kantian things-in-themselves is definitional. If Husserl's ideal verificationism is right, it follows that they do not and could not exist. The idea of something that exists—something that has properties and stands in actual and possible relations to other things—but is essentially incapable of being known by any mind or any type, is incoherent for Husserl (Ideas I §48). And if they did exist, we could form absolutely no positive authentic conception of one, or have any possible grounds for believing in them (ibid.; Ameriks 1977, 506).

The claim that intentionality does not reach *the things themselves*, however, is incoherent. To say that an intentional act represents a thing *itself* is just to say that it represents *its* object. As Husserl writes, "the intentional object of a presentation is the same as its actual object, and on occasion as its external object, and … it is absurd to distinguish between them" (LI 5, Appendix to §§11 and 20, 595). More generally, an act either accurately represents an object O or it does not. If it does, it represents *that* object as *it* is. If it does not, it either (a) represents that object as it is not, (b) represents some other object altogether, or (c) simply does not represent anything at all. I take this to be part of the force of Hegel's critique of Kant's theory of cognition.[9] All acts that accurately represent objects, of whatever ontological type or status, represent those things themselves (as opposed to other things) as they are (rather than as they aren't). That is why Husserl says of perception that:

> It is ... a fundamental mistake to suppose that perception ... does not get at the thing itself, or to suppose that the thing is not given to us in itself and in its being-in-itself.
>
> (Ideas I §43, 76)

Scratched car hoods, numbers, meanings, sensations, and mental acts are all "things themselves" with which we can and do come into contact. Some of them are also things *in* themselves, not in the Kantian sense, but in the plain sense that their being is not grounded in their being the objects of consciousness, thought, or discourse. If, for whatever reason, our capacity to represent things as they are strikes one as strange, we should follow Willard's advice and "weigh the 'strangeness' in the balance with the 'contribution' view of mind and language." He continues: "How thought (or language) – being what it is – could by itself do anything to the entities with which it deals – being what they are (cows, trees, numbers, symphonies) – is surely very strange and mysterious."[10]

The arguments against the Midas-touch view do not apply to all forms of idealism; idealism as such is not committed to the view that the intentional objects of perception and knowledge are modified through some transformative process, nor is it phenomenologically unverifiable in principle. Nevertheless, if idealism were true, if the being of the objects of consciousness were grounded in their being objects of consciousness, this should be something that is or can become apparent phenomenologically. But it is not at all apparent phenomenologically. Rather, as we've seen, there is every indication that the objects we perceive and know are perceived and known to be independent of the acts in which we perceive and know them.

It appears, then, that there is ample evidence for realism from both the natural attitude and the phenomenological attitude. Since many of the objects of perception and knowledge, including not only physical objects, but ideal objects, present themselves as independent of our consciousness of them, we are, by the Principle of All Principles—and by numerous other plausible epistemic principles—rationally entitled to believe that they are real. We are epistemically justified in endorsing metaphysical realism, and this justification derives from two main sources of originary experience. The first is the perceptual experience of the natural attitude. The second is the intuitive givenness of the character of mental acts and their objects in phenomenological reflection. On the terms set by phenomenological epistemology itself, realism is justified.

11.5 Husserl Against "Realism"

As we saw in the last chapter (§10.4.2), Husserl maintains that the phenomenological reduction reveals a non-natural region of individual being, that of transcendental consciousness. As for nature, it is "a correlate of consciousness; it only *is* in the sense of constituting itself in rule-governed connections of consciousness" (Ideas I §51, 93).

Such claims—and there are more than a few in sections 49–55 of *Ideas I*—will forever nourish an understanding of Husserl as a metaphysical idealist who holds that the being of everything natural is straightforwardly dependent on consciousness. The evidence that he held such a view, however, is far from clear. Karl Ameriks (1977) argues that Husserl's claims regarding the "necessary and absolute being" of transcendental consciousness and the "merely contingent and relative being" of natural objects (Ideas I §49, 90) are in fact simply about their respective modes of givenness. I believe that Ameriks is probably right. The difference between consciousness and non-conscious physical realities is that the latter are always given inadequately, as we have discussed in detail (Chapter 5, §5.2). And that is exactly what one would expect of objects that do *not* depend on consciousness for their being. Most physical objects have *actual* parts, features, and sides that will never be perceived by any creature of any type. They do not have those actual parts and features because it is in principle possible to perceive them. Rather, it is possible to perceive them because they have them.

Often times, Husserl's idealistic sounding claims prove upon closer examination to look like nothing more than trivialities or versions of the transcendental insight. He writes in the volume *Transcendental Idealism*, for instance, that

> The existence of every actual being, every single "individual" (naturally including states of affairs, relations, etc.) demands the necessary co-existence of cognizing or cognitively capable subjects.

(TI, 139–140)

How this claim, interpreted as an expression of idealism, is compatible with even the rudiments of what we know about the world and our latecomer status in it is a mystery. But statements such as this receive further clarification, and in the process Husserl's view starts to sound less like a surprising claim about what it is for objects to exist, and more like an *obvious* claim about what is involved in our rationally positing them as existing.[11] He writes, for instance, that: "It is now evident: I cannot posit the ideal landscape as actual ... without at the same time positing myself as the subject of possible experience of this landscape" (TI, 168; also see TI, 140). Like most of the formulations of the transcendental insight (see Chapter 10, §10.3), this and other claims throughout the text are couched in first-personal terms. If we interpret them as claims about what it is for an object to exist, then we would not only have to interpret the being of any actual object as dependent on consciousness, but as dependent on *my* (or *Husserl's*, or *your*) consciousness.

An alternative interpretation is that these are not claims about what it is for a thing to exist. They are claims about what is involved in our rationally positing them to exist. If one posits an object as actual, one must also co-posit an actual consciousness which is the consciousness of it, namely one's own consciousness. And if, furthermore, one rationally posits an object as actual, one must co-posit real possibilities of coming to know it, at least in some fashion (see TI, 77). Of course, one need not co-posit real possibilities of having an originary intuition of it—that is ruled out in the case of countless objects that we rationally posit, given our obvious limitations.

On this interpretation, similar to that of Karl Ameriks (1977), what Husserl means in characterizing the being of consciousness as "necessary" and that of the world as "relative" is that in *positing* the existence of any actual object, one is thereby necessarily co-positing with it the actual existence of *one's own* consciousness, along with real possibilities of bearing at least some evidential relation to it. The "relative" being of the world amounts to this: when we are conscious of it, it is given as related to our consciousness of it. These are not claims about their respective ontological statuses, but claims about how they necessarily show up in and to consciousness.

This might seem trivial; I think that's a reason to recommend it. And despite its obviousness, it does rule out the *rational* positing of Kantian things-in-themselves. This, as Karl Ameriks argues, is the point of Husserl's claim that a world beyond our own is a "logical possibility" but a "material absurdity" (Ideas I §48, 87). The idea of such a world—a world of unexperienceable and unknowable entities—"is not self-contradictory but it is 'absurd' in that it involves a positing which has no justification in experience, no ties to a system of concepts we can employ" (Ameriks 1977, 506). It is, furthermore, "absurd" in the way Moore's paradox is absurd (see Moore 1993). It is absurd, though not a contradiction, to say "I believe p, but it's not true." It's also absurd, though logically consistent, to say "A exists, but my consciousness of it does not" or "A exists, but there's no possible evidence that it does." But the latter claim is a perfectly faithful report of the content of a belief in unknowable things in themselves (see D.W. Smith 1982, 48).

I am not altogether confident that this is the proper interpretation of Husserl's remarks. But I think that it's a philosophically defensible interpretation. There are three things to recommend it. The first is that it coheres well with the interpretation offered in §10.3 of Husserl's transcendental insight. The second is that it is tolerably obvious and devoid of profundity, as fundamental phenomenological claims ought to be, but philosophically significant enough to rule out some prominent philosophical positions. The third is that it is compatible with metaphysical and epistemic realism about the objects of ordinary perception and knowledge, positions that receive ample support from the epistemic achievements in both the natural attitude and phenomenological reflection.

11.5.1 Husserl Against Naturalistic Realism

Husserl does offer another argument against what he calls "realism," however, to which we now turn. It is an enduring theme of Husserl's work that when we reflect on the mind-world relation within the natural attitude, we invariably arrive at various absurd positions such as skepticism and relativism (IdPh, 18). Husserl is, contrary to some appearances, ultimately unmoved by both skepticism and relativism. Both are absurd, he thinks, and neither is a serious threat. What interests him, instead, is that natural reflection on consciousness seems destined to arrive there—proof, in his eyes, that it is not the attitude in which these subject matters can be disclosed.

Husserl's most significant argument that we cannot make sense of knowledge and objectivity within the natural attitude is that in that attitude, all the forms of intentionality, including logical reasoning and knowledge, will be treated as nothing more than psychological phenomena (IdPh, 16), bearing only real, contingent relations to one another and to things in the world. Knowledge will show up as "just *human knowledge,* bound to the *forms of the human intellect*" (IdPh, 18). Evidence will be construed as a distinctive sort of "feeling" that inclines us toward belief.[12] Perception will be construed as our merely human response to stimuli. And because of that, argues Husserl, natural reflection will wind up treating our knowledge and perception as "incapable of making contact with the very nature of things, with the things themselves" (IdPh, 18). If logical laws, for example, express nothing more than "contingent peculiarities of the human species" (IdPh, 18), and if our perceptual experiences register nothing more than the contingent and variable ways in which things beyond experience cause inner states in us, then it would be gratuitous to regard our acts of thinking or perceiving as laying hold of the true nature of things or their objective interconnections. At best, they track our contingent psychological responses to things in the forms of feelings, impressions, drives, and motivational tendencies. All of the accomplishments of consciousness "will be interpreted merely psychologically as 'what humans do'" (Moran 2008, 413).

How Husserl thinks this sort of position plays out in the theory of logic is well known: logical laws and ideal connections among meanings are conflated with contingent laws and empirical connections among the psychological states in which they function as contents. The consequences of this sort of theory with respect to perception are equally objectionable and worth dwelling on. A good example is the standard treatment of our consciousness of secondary qualities such as color. Secondary qualities are dispositional qualities of the object: they are "in truth … nothing in the Objects themselves, but Powers to produce various Sensations in us by their primary Qualities" (Locke 1975, 135). In color experience, on this family of views, we experience sensations, or sense data, or qualia—that is, subjective responses to the secondary qualities of objects. The secondary qualities in the object simply do not show up.

We have already encountered such views in Chapter 6, §6.7. What does show up is either in the mind, in some sense, or essentially related to minds. In any case, what we intuit is not physical. What belongs to the "thing itself," in the world, is some probably quite complicated set of physical features that cause such sensations in us in certain ("normal") circumstances. We have no reason whatsoever to suppose that our sensations resemble those physical features in any way. The connection between the physical features residing in the "thing itself" and what we actually sense is at best causal and merely contingent. Philosophers may fight over just which features, the physical ones or the sensuous ones, are properly *colors*, whether the physical features are dispositional or categorical, and so on. The important point is that the sensuous properties directly manifest in our perceptual experiences are taken to be distinct from any of the real, mind-independent features of the physical thing.

One glaring shortcoming of this type of theory is that it leaves out the thing perceived in color perception: color.[13] Unlike the complicated physical properties alleged to cause color sensations in us, *colors* appear (Quilty-Dunn 2013, 305). It is in their nature to be visible. And unlike sensations or qualia, colors can only be given in perspectives or inadequately in any single experience (see Ideas I §41, 72). Sitting between the adequately given "sensations" of empiricism and the unseen physical features that allegedly cause them are *colors*.

Following Berkeley (see 1975b, §§10 and 14), Husserl argues that if this is the proper treatment of the "secondary" qualities of the thing, it is the proper treatment of *all* the appearing qualities of the thing. The result is that not only the thing's secondary qualities, but "*the entire essential content of the perceived thing*, thus the entire thing standing there in person with all its qualities and all those that could ever be perceived, is a '*mere appearance*'" (Ideas I §40, 70). The "real" world, on this view, is an unperceivable realm "indicating itself only mysteriously," that is, "a *causal* reality in relation to the elapsing instances of subjective appearances and experiences experiencing them" (Ideas I §52, 98). What is drained from reality is not just color and sound, but *the entire perceivable world*.

In light of the previous chapters on perception, it should be clear why this view is objectionable. The perceived world is not in the mind. It is not given adequately; it is not private. Unlike sensations, moreover, most perceivable objects and properties are not localizable in any part of our body. Nor, however, is the world imperceptible. That is why Husserl writes that:

...it is absurd to connect the things of the senses and physical things together through *causality*. In doing so in the usual manner of realism, one confuses the sensory appearances, i.e. the appearing objects as such (that are themselves already transcendencies), by virtue of their "mere subjectivity," with the absolute experiences of appearing that constitute them, i.e. those of the experiencing consciousness in general.

(Ideas I §52, 97)

That "appearing things"—think of the things that actually do appear, such as colors and shapes, mountains and car hoods, concerts and football games— are "already transcendendies" means that they cannot be "immanent" components of the stream of consciousness. That they *appear* means that they cannot be the alleged and necessarily hidden "physical things" standing in merely causal relations with experiences. So what *are* these "appearing things"? Husserl's answer is simple: they *are* the "physical things" which this kind of "realism" has, incoherently, placed behind a barrier of ideas, and they are *not* "merely subjective." There are no further, *imperceptible* "physical things" sitting behind them. As he writes, "in the method of physical science the *perceived thing itself*, always and in principle, *is exactly the thing that the physicist investigates and scientifically determines*" (Ideas I §52, 95). Husserl is not denying the legitimacy of "physical science" or the existence of physical things, nor is he denying that physical sciences are the way to investigate and come to know about physical things. He's denying the existence of *necessarily imperceptible* physical things standing in merely causal relations with the things we do perceive. The relation between physical things and what we perceive is not (just) causality. It is identity.

The problem with "realism," as Husserl understands it, is that it only recognizes "real" connections among real entities. It is and must be blind to the *essential* or *Ideal* relations that tie conscious acts and their objects together. This sheds additional light on the importance of "bracketing" the existence of the world. The point, as we've seen, isn't to turn away from it. The point, rather, is not to conflate the essential relation between the conscious act with its intentional essence and its object with its nature, on the one hand, with whatever contingent real relations the act bears to that object, on the other. If as a phenomenologist I posit the red "moment" that I see as actual, I could easily be inclined to treat my experience as being *of* it in virtue of (reliably) bearing real causal relations to it. I may then be oblivious to the essential tie between them— oblivious to the feature of my experience, its sense or content, that makes the experience *of red*. It may then occur to me that if I had had this type of "reddish" experience, or reliably had these types of experiences, when in causal contact with *green* objects, my "reddish" experience would then have been *of green*. And now the game is up. I will have to regard what is intuitively given to me in color perception, the "reddishness," as an indication or sign of something I do not perceive at all. And this point generalizes: I will wind up treating the objects that actually manifest themselves in experience as merely subjective signs or indications of something which could not in principle manifest itself.

Despite Husserl's earlier claim, it is not absurd to think that physical objects stand in causal relations with mental states. What is absurd is to conflate those causal relations with intentional relations. The relation between the perceptual experience and the perceived is not a causal relation—though it may depend on causal relations—but something else entirely: a relation in which the perceived becomes manifest in the perceptual experience (D.W. Smith 1982, 46).

11.6 Transcendental Idealism

It should be fairly clear that Husserl's argument against "realism" is an attack on a certain brand of naturalism.[14] Realism, as he understands it, appears to be the view that everything that exists is real, that is, something "here and now" or determined in time (LI 2 §8, 351). If that's what's meant by "realism," then the insistence that there are Ideal—not *mental*, but *essential*—laws holding among act-types and object-types could be called "idealism." And that's just what Husserl means by "idealism" when he writes:

> To talk of "idealism" is of course not to talk of a metaphysical doctrine, but of a theory of knowledge which recognizes the "ideal" as a condition for the possibility of objective knowledge in general, and does not "interpret it away" in psychologistic fashion.[15]

He says this, of course, in the introduction to an investigation dedicated to arguing for the existence of universals and other ideal objects. Husserl's argument against "realism" is hardly an attack on metaphysical realism as we have understood it. Not only does the falsity of naturalist realism not entail the falsity of metaphysical realism, the truth of naturalistic realism appears to rule out epistemic realism with respect to physical things, to say nothing of essences and essential relations.

What uncontroversially comprises the heart of Husserl's transcendental idealism is, in addition to the transcendental insight, what has been emphasized repeatedly in the preceding chapters: the relation between an act and its content is an essential one, and the relation between an act's content and its object is again an essential one. And it is because of those relationships that phenomenology is not confined to an investigation of subjectivity, but of objects as well. This is one reason Dan Zahavi is correct when he writes that:

> only a complete misunderstanding of the aim of phenomenology leads us to the mistaken but often repeated claim that Husserl's phenomenology is not interested in reality or the question of being, but only in subjective meaning-formations in intentional consciousness.

(Zahavi 2003a, 63)

That acts and their objects stand in essential relations with one another is something grounded in the natures of each. "The essence of experience itself entails not only that it is consciousness, but also of what it is the consciousness, whether it be determinate or indeterminate" (Ideas I §36, 63). Furthermore, the essence of the *object* also entails what sorts of experiences could be of it, as we have seen (Chapter 5, §5.3). That an experience of spinach lodged between one's teeth could not, in any circumstances, count as a manifestation of a soccer game is partly due to the nature of a soccer game. That numbers can be—must be—known a priori is, again, partly grounded in the nature of numbers themselves.

As we have seen in our discussion of ideal verificationism (Chapter 5, §5.4)—another core component of Husserl's transcendental idealism, albeit a much more dubious one—not only does it belong to the nature of some objects to be manifestable to consciousness, but it belongs to the essence of all possible objects to be manifestable to consciousness. Every existing object has properties; everything with properties makes true some propositions; every true proposition has a fulfilling sense; every true proposition and every fulfilling sense is composed of contents instantiable in some possible experience (TI, 142). And this claim does have deep implications regarding the nature of being and reality: each object essentially has a possible *appearance*, a manner in which "it is known or apprehended" (D.W. Smith 2004a, 17). This "appearance" is what we have already discussed under the heading of an object's *perceptual manifold* (Chapter 5, §5.3). Smith, following Robert Sokolowski (2000), calls appearances "transcendentals" in the medieval sense, since an appearance belongs to all objects across all categories. Husserl himself seems to invoke just that sense at one point:

> Phenomenology is scientific investigation, namely, the purely seeing and clarifying investigation of the a priori, of each and every a priori: both the categorial and the material a priori. Hence, the investigation of all categories—transcendental investigation!
>
> (ILTK, 236)

Consciousness, despite falling under general ontological laws, is unlike anything else, and what makes it so very unlike everything else is not primarily that it houses "qualia" or that it's the locus of an "explanatory gap" (Levine 1983), but that, as Edith Stein puts it, "it is of the nature of the spirit to be open to all existents" (Stein 2002, 298; also Willard 1984, 56).

Because an appearance or intuitive manifold belongs essentially to every object, a full account of any object—and therefore of the natural world—must include an account of the appearance of that object, its essential relatability to both originary and non-originary intentional acts trained upon it. As Stein puts it, the existent is insufficiently described if we consider it only as such or as it is in itself. It pertains to its nature to *manifest* itself, i.e., to be at least accessible to the knowing intellect.[16]

Like Aquinas (and Aristotle before him), Husserl holds that "everything, in as far as it has being, so far is it knowable" (Aquinas 2018, I, Q. 16, Art. 3, 88). This is why phenomenology is not just the study of consciousness or subjectivity. It also discloses a dimension of the nature of any conceivable object of consciousness. And it does this uniquely. The objective sciences rely upon the intelligibility of objects and would be impossible without it; there cannot be a science of what is inaccessible in principle to consciousness. But they *say* nothing about it. They produce knowledge, but do not provide an account of knowledge. Their own achievements as intentional acts are not among the items in their fields of inquiry.[17] This does not make those sciences deficient at what they are supposed to do—a one-sided orientation towards the objective features of things is exactly what is called for if we wish to know about their objective features.[18] But it does mean that the sciences, to say nothing of ordinary consciousness, are not only naïve insofar as they "do not understand their own accomplishments as those of an accomplishing intentionality" (FTL, 13, translation modified), but that they are incomplete specifications of the full nature of their objects. What they leave out, moreover, is not just one property of objects alongside all the others. Manifestability, rather, is a property of each part and property of an object—reality is manifestable in principle all the way down. This is why the sciences cannot function as a final metaphysics; they "are unable to clarify the genuine being-sense of either their provinces or the concepts that comprehend their provinces" (FTL, 13). Nowhere is this stated more clearly than when Sokolowski writes:

> [W]hen we examine things philosophically, when we examine how they appear or manifest themselves, we are also examining their being. Their appearance is not something to be distinguished from the way they exist; part of their existence is to be presentable to consciousness. In medieval terminology, truth is a transcendental, a characteristic of being as such. Presentability or knowability belongs to things insofar as they are beings, not insofar as they are spatial or colored or large or small.[19]

The natural sciences might, for instance, tell us that salt dissolves in water. They do not tell us that salt bears any relation to consciousness and knowledge. But they *show* us, through their existence and achievements, that it does.

We can, then, summarize the core commitments of transcendental idealism as follows, in approximate order of their obviousness.

- The first commitment is the transcendental insight: everything of which a subject is conscious is something she or he is conscious of in virtue of the conscious acts that she or he carries out.
- Second, the relations constitutive of intentionality are essential ones, that is, relations grounded in the natures of the entities related. Acts essentially have their contents, and their contents are essentially of their objects, and their objects are essentially the kinds of things that can be given and meant in those types of acts. It is, furthermore, an essential feature of originary acts that they provide us with evidence about the nature of their objects, and an essential feature of intrinsically empty acts that they, by themselves, do not.
- The third commitment, as we have seen in Chapter 9, is that knowledge, including both originary intuition and cognitive fulfillment, is the most fundamental form of intentionality. Every other form of intentionality either presupposes a capacity for it (authentic meaning), is teleologically oriented toward it (all empty objectifying acts), or is an intentional modification of it (phantasy, memory).
- The fourth is ideal verificationism: every possible object is a possible object of knowledge and even of originary intuition.

This position can be called "transcendental idealism" for two reasons. The first is that it answers the modern, Kantian transcendental questions regarding the possibility of objective perception, knowledge, and cognition by appealing to Ideal or essential relations rather than only "real" ones. The second is that, as Stein, Sokolowski, and D.W. Smith maintain, it also discloses and investigates a transcendental property in the medieval sense, that is, an Ideal or essential characteristic held by all objects across all categories of being: their relatability to suitable acts of consciousness and knowledge.

I think it is fairly clear that the conjunction of these claims does not entail, or even clearly motivate, *metaphysical* antirealism of any kind. That is, the apparently inconsistent triad discussed in §11.2 above is not inconsistent: *metaphysical* and *epistemic* realism appear to be true, we are entitled to believe them, *and* we are entitled to reject *naturalistic* realism. As Scheler rightly points out, the claim that "comprehensibility through an act 'belongs' by essential necessity to the essence of an object" by no means entails the Kantian thesis that the objects "must 'conform' to acts and their interconnections."[20] Consciousness does not give orders to its objects, any more than a key gives orders to a lock that it opens—though if keys could philosophize, many would undoubtedly think they did.

Contrary to the Midas-touch approach, the structure of an act is not something that consciousness somehow passes on to its object. It is, rather, what must be in place if the act is to receive, grasp, or otherwise relate to that object. A given act can only apprehend an object if that act has the right parts and properties to apprehend it. I cannot think of an apple by means of the concept <pencil>, and I cannot *perceive* an apple solely by means of the concept <apple>. Neither could anyone else. This, moreover, would be true no matter what the ontological status of apples is; whether they exist in themselves or are merely phenomenal, a mind must be configured in a certain way to apprehend them. As Willard writes,

> Since the concept is a property of the act, it does not intervene between the act and its object, and does not close the mind off from the very objects or world that it was supposed to make accessible. It does not encapsulate the mind or its contents, any more than the properties of other things or events encapsulate them.
>
> (Willard 2002, 74)

As we've seen, a mind's possession of concepts and other contents does not rule out the *immediacy* of our knowledge. In the same way, it does not rule out the *objectivity* of our knowledge. No matter whether or not earthquakes are metaphysically real, seismologists have the best access to them, and that's due to the fact that their minds can take on the right shape to apprehend them as they really are. That is why, when we want to find out how things really are, we do our best to acquire concepts and bodies of knowledge, not shed them.

The closest this version of transcendental idealism comes to metaphysical idealism is that objects and conscious experiences are essentially the kinds of things that can stand in relations to one another, and their standing in those relations is grounded in the essences of each. This does not, however, mean that objects do in fact stand in relations to consciousness, or that they depend for their existence on consciousness in any way. As Willard puts it, "The connection between the act and the object is not, in general, an existential one, but is one of essences."[21] Again, for Scheler, the "ultimate principle of phenomenology" is "that there is an interconnection between the essence of an object and the essence of intentional experiencing." (Scheler 1973a, 265). Each object is, in its essence, the kind of thing that, ideally, *could be* related to consciousness. Some of them actually are, though many—no doubt the vast majority—are not and never will be. And consciousness is the kind of thing which, in its essence, ideally could be related to any object of any type.

These essential connections are not all existence-entailing. That a tree could be an object of consciousness, and that this possibility flows from its essence, does not entail that it *is* an object of consciousness, or even that there are any consciousnesses at all. It's rather like the connection between squares and circles. Circles are the kinds of things that could have squares inscribed in them, and this relation holds in virtue of the essences of circles and squares. It doesn't follow, however, that every circle has a square inscribed in it, or even that any circle does. Similarly, that each object is perceivable or knowable doesn't entail that each is actually perceived or known, much less that each of its parts is. In fact we know that it is a priori impossible, for Husserl, for any natural object to be given adequately in any finite set of experiences. No matter how much of an object is actually perceived, there are always more unrealized but realizable perspectives to be had on it.

11.7 Conclusion

This concludes our discussion of transcendental idealism, and this introduction to phenomenology. As the reader can no doubt surmise, transcendental phenomenology is a vast field of both ongoing and future possible inquiry and discovery. There is, ideally, a transcendental phenomenological account to be given of every conceivable object of thought and knowledge; each thing is a "transcendental clue" (CM §21, 50) pointing to the normally anonymous and unthematized acts of consciousness in which it is meant, given, or, in the best of cases, both. Obviously many of those phenomenological analyses are significantly more complicated than any provided in these pages. Hopefully, though, the present introduction can provide a tolerably firm footing for further inquiry.[22]

Husserl writes in the Forward to the second edition of his Sixth Logical Investigation that "One who is not afraid, will find sufficient opportunity for improving on my positions, and, if he cares to, for censuring their imperfections" (LI, 663). The same, quite obviously, applies *a forteriori* to the present work. What makes me optimistic about phenomenology is not that it is a completed and unchangeable crystal palace of finalized theory, but that there are real opportunities for, in Russell's words again, "successive approximations to the truth" (Russell 1917, 113). The work that Husserl set out even in his *Logical Investigations* is far from complete, and there is no reason to think that we have come close to exhausting the insights that could be brought to light by sustained work even on the topics presented therein—to say nothing of the many additional topics explored by him and other phenomenologists since.

There is, furthermore, plenty of reason to think that we should continue this work, even if that involves turning back in time to examine it with fresh eyes. That others have, by their own lights, moved past it is philosophically irrelevant. There is nothing inevitable, or even discernibly rational, about the history of philosophy. The demise of the Munich and Göttingen circles of phenomenology, and later the Freiburg school, the rise of existential phenomenology and, afterwards, hermeneutics and deconstruction, the falling asunder of analytic and continental traditions—none of this was destined to be by any Zeitgeist or by the inner logic of the philosophies themselves. These things happened for all too human reasons. Daubert became a farmer. Edith Stein was a victim of sexist discrimination all too common at the time, could not find employment at a university as a consequence, and was ultimately murdered at Auschwitz. Reinach perished at the height of his prowess in the

First World War. Pfänder was denied a Chair at Freiburg that he probably deserved. Heidegger, who received that Chair instead, was a gifted lecturer who in the 1920s simultaneously won Husserl's approval while undermining his work. As Peter Simons puts it, *"Sein und Zeit* (1927), while sailing under the flag of convenience 'Phenomenology', is a fundamental repudiation of most of the central tenets of Husserl's philosophy" (Simons 2001, 302). That, at any rate, is certainly how Husserl regarded it. Meanwhile, in the Anglo-American world…well, I think the point has been made. One lesson that Simons draws from this history is "that how things actually turn out has an a priori probability of almost zero" (Simons 2001, 308). In a rational world, it wouldn't.

Philosophers have the demanding and sometimes hazardous obligation of scouring every corner of logical space. Only a small minority of those spaces are worth inhabiting. I am hopeful that at least some of those discussed here, and the many others that phenomenologists have uncovered and will continue to uncover, prove to be among them.

Notes

1 I owe this point to Kevin Mulligan, conversation. See LI, Introduction to Volume Two, §7, 265. Also see Bernet, Kern, and Marbach 1993, 10.
2 Letter to Pfänder in Heidegger 2007, 400, translated by Burt C. Hopkins; Spiegelberg 1971, 175.
3 Levinas 1969, 123; also see Gorner 1991.
4 Crowell 2013, 18. See Ideas I §27. Also see Drummond 1990, 256. See D.W. Smith 1982 for an in-depth discussion of the realism that is built into the sense of our perceptual experiences.
5 Putnam 1981, 52. For an excellent critical discussion of this and related metaphors, see Wolter-storff 1987.
6 In this connection, also see James Franklin's (2002) discussion of what, according to David Stove, counts as the "worst argument in the world." The argument states that "We can know things only • as they are related to us • under our forms of perception and understanding • insofar as they fall under our conceptual schemes, etc. So, we cannot know things as they are in themselves" (Franklin 2002, 15). Thanks to Barry Smith for the pointer.
7 Putnam 1983, 206. See Locke 1975, 440–441 for a similar argument.
8 I am indebted to Colin Cmiel for impressing this point upon me.
9 According to Hegel it is "absurd" to suppose there is "a cognition which is true but does not know its subject matter as it is in itself" (Hegel 2010, 26). That is precisely Husserl's view as well. For an excellent discussion, see Sedgwick 2012, Chapter 3. Hegel's claim, incidentally, shows that not all (or even most) versions of idealism are versions of Midas-touch antirealism.
10 Willard 2000a, §XI.
11 I am heavily indebted to both James Kinkaid and Zachary Joachim for discussing the nature of Husserl's transcendental idealism with me, and for suggesting various ways in which these and other related passages may be compatible with realism.
12 IdPh, 44. Also see Ideas I §145; LI, Prolegomena, §51; and LI 6 §39. For excellent treatments, see Heffernan 1997 and 1998.
13 See LI 2, Appendix, 421, where Husserl says of the "common materialism" according to which "tones really are air-vibrations" that "theoretical hypotheses which explain the given genetically, are substituted for the given."
14 See Moran 2008 for a discussion of Husserl's case against naturalism.
15 LI 2, Introduction, 338. Thanks to James Kinkaid for bringing this passage, and its significance, to my attention.

16 Stein 2002, 297. Also see Sokolowski 1964, 219.

17 See FTL §9. Also see Zahavi 2017, §3.2 for a helpful discussion.

18 See Ideas I §26; also see Willard 1984, 135; Bernet, Kern, and Marbach 1993, 63; Sokolowski 2000, 63; and Hardy 2013, 63.

19 Sokolowski 1977, 180. Also see Zahavi 2003a, 55: "For how things appear is an integral part of what they really are."

20 Scheler 1973a, 375–376. H.A. Prichard makes a verbally different but philosophically similar point against Kant when he writes that if we want to understand how we think or know about objects, "we are not assisted by assuming that these objects must conform to the laws of our thinking. We must presuppose this conformity if we are to think at all" (1909, 14).

21 Willard 1984, 236. Also see Rinofner-Kreidl 2012, 418.

22 For an excellent and lucid recent work that does use much of realist phenomenology as a foundation for inquiries into the nature of value and our consciousness of it, see Hammond 2019.

Recommended Readings

Drummond, John. 1990. *Husserlian Intentionality and Non-Foundational Realism: Noema and Object*. Boston: Kluwer Academic Publishers.

Husserl, Edmund. 1977. *Cartesian Meditations*. Dorion Cairns, trans. The Hague: Martinus Nijhoff.

Husserl, Edmund. 2014. *Ideas I: Ideas for a Pure Phenomenology and Phenomenological Philosophy*. Daniel O. Dahlstrom, trans. Indianapolis: Hackett.

Stein, Edith. 2002. *Finite and Eternal Being*. Kurt F. Reinhardt, trans. Washington, D.C.: ICS Publications.

Willard, Dallas. 2000. "Knowledge and Naturalism." In W. L. Craig and J. P. Moreland, eds. *Naturalism: A Critical Analysis*, 24–48. New York: Routledge.

Bibliography

Works by Husserl

BP. 2006. *The Basic Problems of Phenomenology, from the Lectures, Winter Semester, 1910–1911*. Ingo Farin and James G. Hart, trans. Dordrecht: Springer.

CM. 1977a. *Cartesian Meditations*. Dorion Cairns, trans. The Hague: Martinus Nijhoff.

Crisis. 1970b. *The Crisis of European Sciences and Transcendental Phenomenology. An Introduction to Phenomenological Philosophy*. David Carr, trans. Evanston: Northwestern University Press.

EJ. 1973. *Experience and Judgment*. Ludwig Landgrebe, ed. James S. Churchill and Karl Ameriks, trans. Evanston: Northwestern University Press.

FTL. 1969. *Formal and Transcendental Logic*. Dorion Cairns, trans. The Hague: Martinus Nijhoff.

Ideas I. 2014. *Ideas I: Ideas for a Pure Phenomenology and Phenomenological Philosophy*. Daniel O. Dahlstrom, trans. Indianapolis: Hackett.

Ideas II. 1989. *Ideas Pertaining to a Pure Phenomenology and to a Phenomenological Philosophy. Second Book. Studies in the Phenomenology of Constitution*. Richard Rojcewicz and André Schuwer, trans. Dordrecht: Kluwer Academic Publishers.

IdPh. 1999. *The Idea of Phenomenology*. Lee Hardy, trans. Boston: Kluwer Academic Publishers.

ILTK. 2008. *Introduction to Logic and Theory of Knowledge: Lectures 1906/07*. Claire Ortiz Hill, trans. Dordrecht: Springer.

LAW. 1996. *Logik und Allgemeine Wissenschaftstheorie. Vorlesungen 1917/18 mit Ergänzenden Texten aus der ersten Fassung von 1910/11*. Husserliana vol. 30. Ursula Panzer, ed. Dordrecht: Kluwer Academic Publishers.

LI. 1970a. *Logical Investigations*. Two volumes. J.N. Findlay, trans. London: Routledge & Kegan Paul.

PAS. 2001. *Analyses Concerning Passive and Active Synthesis*. Anthony J. Steinbock, trans. Boston: Kluwer Academic Publishers.

PICM. 2005. *Phantasy, Image Consciousness, and Memory*. John B. Brough, trans. Dordrecht: Springer.

PCIT. 1991. *On the Phenomenology of the Consciousness of Internal Time (1893–1917)*. John B. Brough, trans. Dordrecht: Kluwer Academic Publishers.

PP. 1977b. *Phenomenological Psychology*. John Scanlon, trans. The Hague: Martinus Nijhoff.

PRS. 1965. "Philosophy as Rigorous Science." Quentin Lauer, trans. In *Phenomenology and the Crisis of Philosophy*, 71–147. New York: Harper.

TI. 2003. *Transzendentaler Idealismus: Texte aus dem Nachlass (1908–1921)*. Husserliana vol. 36. Robin D. Rollinger and Rochus Sowa, eds. Dordrecht: Kluwer Academic Publishers.

TS. 1997. *Thing and Space*. Richard Rojcewicz, trans. Boston: Kluwer Academic Publishers.

VB. 1987. *Vorlesungen über Bedeutungslehre. Sommersemester 1908*. Husserliana vol. 26. Ursula Panzer, ed. The Hague, Netherlands: Martinus Nijhoff.

All others

Addis, Laird. 1989. *Natural Signs: A Theory of Intentionality*. Philadelphia: Temple University Press.

Aldea, Andreea Smaranda. 2013. "Husserl's Struggle with Mental Images: Imaging and Imagining Reconsidered." *Continental Philosophy Review* 46: 371–394.

Ali, Rami. 2018. "Does Hallucinating Involve Perceiving?" *Philosophical Studies* 175: 601–627.

Allen, Keith. 2016. *A Naïve Realist Theory of Colour*. Oxford: Oxford University Press.

Almäng, Jan. 2014. "Perceptual Transparency and Perceptual Constancy." *Husserl Studies* 30: 1–19.

Alston, William. 1988. "An Internalist Externalism." *Synthese* 74: 265–283.

Alston, William. 1989a. "Levels Confusions in Epistemology." In *Epistemic Justification: Essays in the Theory of Knowledge*, 153–171. Ithaca: Cornell University Press.

Alston, William. 1989b. "What's Wrong with Immediate Knowledge?" In *Epistemic Justification: Essays in the Theory of Knowledge*, 57–78. Ithaca: Cornell University Press.

Alston, William. 1996. *A Realist Conception of Truth*. Ithaca: Cornell University Press.

Alston, William. 2002. "Sellars and the 'Myth of the Given'." *Philosophy and Phenomenological Research* 65: 69–86.

Alweiss, Lilian. 2009. "Between Internalism and Externalism: Husserl's Account of Intentionality." *Inquiry* 52: 53–78.

Alweiss, Lilian. 2013. "Beyond Existence and Non-Existence." *International Journal of Philosophical Studies* 21: 448–469.

Ameriks, Karl. 1977. "Husserl's Realism." *The Philosophical Review* 86: 498–519.

Aquinas, St. Thomas. 2018. *Summa Theologica: First Part*. Fathers of the English Dominican Province, trans. Anthony Uyl, ed. Woodstock, ON: Devoted Publishing.

Aristotle. 1941. "On Interpretation." In Richard McKeon, ed. *The Basic Works of Aristotle*, 40–61. New York: Random House.

Armstrong, D. M. 2004. *Truth and Truthmakers*. Cambridge: Cambridge University Press.

Armstrong, D. M. 2018. *Universals: An Opinionated Introduction*. New York: Routledge.

Audi, Robert. 2013. "Doxastic Innocence: Phenomenal Conservatism and the Grounds of Justification." In Chris Tucker, ed. *Seemings and Justification*, 180–201. Oxford: Oxford University Press.

Austin, J. L. 1964. *Sense and Sensibilia*. Oxford: Oxford University Press.

Averchi, Michele. 2015. "The Disinterested Spectator: Geiger's and Husserl's Place in the Debate on the Splitting of the Ego." *Studia Phaenomenologica* 15: 227–246.

Averchi, Michele D. M. Forthcoming. "Evidence Based Phenomenology and Certainty Based Phenomenology. Moritz Geiger's Reaction to Idealism in Ideas I." In Rodney Parker, ed. *The Reception of Husserl's Idealism*. Dordrecht: Springer.

Ayer, A.J. 1952. *Language, Truth and Logic*. New York: Dover Publications, Inc.

Bach, Kent. 2008. "On Referring and Not Referring." In Jeanette Gundel and Nancy Hedberg, eds. *Reference: Interdisciplinary Perspectives*, 13–58. Oxford: Oxford University Press.

Baker, Lynne Rudder. 2007. *The Metaphysics of Everyday Life*. Cambridge: Cambridge University Press.

Barber, Michael. 2008. "Holism and Horizon: Husserl and McDowell on Non-conceptual Content." *Husserl Studies* 24: 79–97.

Bell, David. 1979. *Frege's Theory of Judgement*. Oxford: Oxford University Press.

Bell, David. 1990. *Husserl*. New York: Routledge.

Benoist, Jocelyn. 2003. "Husserl's Theory of Meaning in the First Logical Investigation." In Daniel O. Dahlstrom, ed. *Husserl's Logical Investigations*, 17–35. Dordrecht: Kluwer Academic Publishers.

Benoist, Jocelyn 2015. "Sense and Reference, Again." In Jeffrey Bloechl and Nicolas de Warren, eds. *Phenomenology in a New Key: Between Analysis and History*, 93–113. New York: Springer.

Berghofer, Philipp. 2018. "Why Husserl is a Moderate Foundationalist." *Husserl Studies*, 34: 1–23.

Berkeley, George. 1975a. "An Essay Towards a New Theory of Vision." In *Philosophical Works*, 1–70. London: David Campbell Publishers Ltd.

Berkeley, George. 1975b. "A Treatise Concerning the Principles of Human Knowledge." In *Philosophical Works*, 71–153. London: David Campbell Publishers Ltd.

Bernet, Rudolf. 2003. "Desiring to Know Through Intuition." *Husserl Studies* 19: 153–166.

Bernet, Rudolf, Iso Kern, and Eduard Marbach. 1993. *An Introduction to Husserlian Phenomenology*. Evanston: Northwestern University Press.

Beyer, Christian. 1997. "Hussearle's Representationalism and the 'Hypothesis of the Background'." *Synthese* 112: 323–352.

Beyer, Christian. 2001. "A Neo-Husserlian Theory of Speaker's Reference." *Erkenntnis* 54: 277–297.

Beyer, Christian. 2016. "Edmund Husserl." In Edward N. Zalta, ed. *The Stanford Encyclopedia of Philosophy* (Summer 2018 Edition). https://plato.stanford.edu/archives/sum 2018/entries/husserl.

Block, Ned. 1990. "Inverted Earth." *Philosophical Perspectives* 4: 53–79.

Block, Ned. 2013. "Wittgenstein and Qualia." In Maria Baghramian, ed. *Reading Putnam*, 275–318. New York: Routledge.

Bolzano, Bernard. 1972. *Theory of Science*. Rolf George, trans. Los Angeles: University of California Press.

Bonjour, Laurence. 1978. "Can Empirical Knowledge Have a Foundation?" *American Philosophical Quarterly* 15: 1–13.

Bonjour, Laurence. 1998. *In Defense of Pure Reason*. Cambridge: Cambridge University Press.

Bonjour, Laurence. 2010. "Recent Work on the Internalism-Externalism Controversy." In Jonathan Dancy, Ernest Sosa, and Matthias Steup, eds. *A Companion to Epistemology*, 2nd Edition, 33–43. Oxford: Blackwell.

Bower, Matthew. 2014. "Affectively-Driven Perception: Toward a Non-Representational Phenomenology." *Husserl Studies* 30: 225–245.

Bower, Matthew. 2017. "Husserl on Perception: A Nonrepresentationalism That Nearly Was." *European Journal of Philosophy* 25: 1768–1790.

Bower, Matthew. 2019. "Daubert's Naïve Realist Challenge to Husserl." *Grazer Philosophische Studien* 96: 211–243.

Brandom, Robert. 1997. "Study Guide." In Wilfrid Sellars, *Empiricism and the Philosophy of Mind*, 119–181. Cambridge: Harvard University Press.

Brandom, Robert .2001. *Articulating Reasons*. Cambridge: Harvard University Press.

Brentano, Franz. 1995. *Psychology from an Empirical Standpoint.* Antos C. Rancurello, D. B. Terrell, and Linda L. McAlister, trans. New York: Routledge.

Brewer, Bill. 1999. *Perception and Reason.* Oxford: Clarendon Press.

Brewer, Bill. 2008. "How to Account for Illusion." In Adrian Haddock and Fiona Macpherson, eds. *Disjunctivism: Perception, Action, Knowledge,* 168–180. Oxford: Oxford University Press.

Brewer, Bill. 2011. *Perception and Its Objects.* Oxford: Oxford University Press.

Briscoe, Robert Eamon. 2008. "Vision, Action, and Make-Perceive." *Mind and Language* 23: 457–497.

Broad, C.D. 2000. *Five Types of Ethical Theory.* London: Routledge.

Brogaard, Berit 'Brit' and Dimitria Electra Gatzia. 2018. "The Real Epistemic Significance of Perceptual Learning." *Inquiry* 61: 543–558.

Brough, John. 1991. "Translator's Introduction." Edmund Husserl, *On the Phenomenology of the Consciousness of Internal Time (1893–1917).* Dordrecht: Kluwer Academic Publishers.

Brough, John. 2005. "Translator's Introduction." Edmund Husserl, *Phantasy, Image Consciousness, and Memory (1898–1925).* Dordrecht: Springer.

Brough, John. 2012. "Something that is Nothing but can be Anything: The Image and Our Consciousness of It." In Dan Zahavi, ed. *The Oxford Handbook of Contemporary Phenomenology,* 545–563. Oxford: Oxford University Press.

Brown, James Robert. 1991. *The Laboratory of the Mind: Thought Experiments in the Natural Sciences.* New York: Routledge.

Brown, James Rober. 2014. "Mathematical Narratives." *European Journal of Analytic Philosophy* 10: 59–74.

Burge, Tyler. 1999. "A Century of Deflation and a Moment about Self-Knowledge." *Proceedings and Addresses of the American Philosophical Association* 73: 25–46.

Burge, Tyler. 2010. *Origins of Objectivity.* Oxford: Oxford University Press.

Burgess, John. 2008. "Being Explained Away." In *Mathematics, Models, and Modality: Selected Philosophical Essays,* 85–103. Cambridge: Cambridge University Press.

Byrne, Alex. 2001. "Intentionalism Defended." *The Philosophical Review* 110: 199–240.

Byrne, Alex and Heather Logue. 2009. "Introduction." In Alex Byrne and Heather Logue, eds. *Disjunctivism: Contemporary Readings,* vii–xxix. Cambridge: The MIT Press.

Cairns, Dorion. 2013. *The Philosophy of Edmund Husserl.* Lester Embree, ed. New York: Springer.

Camp, Elisabeth. 2009. "Putting Thoughts to Work: Concepts, Systematicity, and Stimulus Independence." *Philosophy and Phenomenological Research* 78: 275–311.

Campbell, John. 2002. *Reference and Consciousness.* Oxford: Clarendon Press.

Campbell, John. 2005. "Transparency versus Revelation in Color Perception." *Philosophical Topics* 33: 105–115.

Campbell, John 2016. "The Problem of Spatiality for a Relational View of Experience." *Philosophical Topics* 44: 105–120.

Carman, Taylor. 1999. "The Body in Husserl and Merleau-Ponty." *Philosophical Topics* 27: 205–226.

Casey, Edward. 2001. *Imagining: A Phenomenological Study.* Second Edition. Bloomington: Indiana University Press.

Chalmers, David. 1996. *The Conscious Mind.* Oxford: Oxford University Press.

Chalmers, David. 2004. "The Representational Character of Experience." In Brian Leiter, ed. *The Future for Philosophy,* 153–181. Oxford: Oxford University Press.

Chalmers, David. 2010. "Facing Up to the Problem of Consciousness." In *The Character of Consciousness,* 3–34. Oxford: Oxford University Press.

Chemero, Anthony. 2009. *Radical Embodied Cognitive Science*. Cambridge: The MIT Press.

Chisholm, Roderick M. 1967. "Brentano on Descriptive Psychology and the Intentional." In Edward N. Lee and Maurice Mandelbaum, eds. *Phenomenology and Existentialism*, 1–23. Baltimore: The Johns Hopkins Press.

Christensen, Carleton B. 1993. "Sense, Subject and Horizon." *Philosophy and Phenomenological Research* 53: 749–779.

Christensen, Carleton B. 2013. "The Horizonal Structure of Perceptual Experience." *Logical Analysis & History of Philosophy* 16: 109–141.

Church, Jennifer. 2013. *Possibilities of Perception*. Oxford: Oxford University Press.

Churchland, Paul M. 1995. *The Engine of Reason, the Seat of the Soul*. Cambridge: The MIT Press.

Cobb-Stevens, Richard. 1990. *Husserl and Analytic Philosophy*. Dordrecht: Kluwer Academic Publishers.

Cobos, Javier EnriqueCarreño. 2013. "The Many Sense of Imagination and the Manifestation of Fiction: A View from Husserl's Phenomenology of Phantasy." *Husserl Studies* 29: 143–162.

Cohen, Jonathan. 2009. *The Real and the Red: An Essay on Color Ontology*. Oxford: Oxford University Press.

Cohen, Jonathan and Aaron Meskin. 2004. "On the Epistemic Value of Photographs." *The Journal of Aesthetics and Art Criticism* 2: 197–210.

Conee, Earl. 2004. "The Basic Nature of Epistemic Justification." In Earl Conee and Richard Feldman. *Evidentialism*, 37–52. Oxford: Oxford University Press.

Conee, Earl. 2013. "Seeming Justification." In Chris Tucker, ed. *Seemings and Justification*, 52–68. Oxford: Oxford University Press.

Conee, Earl and Richard Feldman. 2004. "Internalism Defended." In Earl Conee and Richard Feldman, *Evidentialism*, 53–82. Oxford: Oxford University Press.

Crane, Tim. 2009. "Is Perception a Propositional Attitude?" *The Philosophical Quarterly* 59: 452–469.

Crane, Tim. 2013. *The Objects of Thought*. Oxford: Oxford University Press.

Crane, Tim. 2014. *Aspects of Psychologism*. Cambridge: Harvard University Press.

Crane, Tim and Craig French. 2015. "The Problem of Perception." *The Stanford Encyclopedia of Philosophy* (Spring 2017 Edition), Edward N. Zalta (ed.), http://plato.stanford.edu/archives/spr2017/entries/perception-problem/.

Crowell, Steven. 2008. "Phenomenological Immanence, Normativity, and Semantic Externalism." *Synthese* 160: 335–354.

Crowell, Steven. 2013. *Normativity and Phenomenology in Husserl and Heidegger*. Cambridge: Cambridge University Press.

Crowell, Steven. 2016. "What Is It to Think?" In Thiemo Breyer and Christopher Gutland, eds. *Phenomenology of Thinking: Philosophical Investigations Into the Character of Cognitive Experiences*, 183–206. New York: Routledge.

Currie, Gregory. 1990. *The Nature of Fiction*. Cambridge: Cambridge University Press.

Currie, Gregory. 1995. *Image and Mind: Film, Philosophy and Cognitive Science*. Cambridge: Cambridge University Press.

Cussins, Adrian. 2003. "Content, Conceptual Content, and Nonconceptual Content." In York H. Gunther, ed. *Essays on Nonconceptual Content*, 133–163. Cambridge: The MIT Press.

Dahlstrom, Daniel O. 2001. *Heidegger's Concept of Truth*. Cambridge: Cambridge University Press.

Dahlstrom, Daniel O. 2006. "Lost Horizons: An Appreciative Critique of Enactive Externalism." In Alfredo Ferrarin, ed. *Passive Synthesis and Life-World*, 211–231. Pisa: Edizioni ETS.

Dahlstrom, Daniel O. 2007. "The Intentionality of Passive Experience: Husserl and a Contemporary Debate." *The New Yearbook for Phenomenology and Phenomenological Philosophy* 7: 1–18.

Dahlstrom, Daniel O. 2016. "Interoception and Self-Awareness: An Exploration in Introspective Phenomenology." In Daniel O. Dahlstrom, Andreas Elpidorou, and Walter Hopp, eds. *Philosophy of Mind and Phenomenology*, 141–164. New York: Routledge.

Dahlstrom, Daniel O. 2017. *Identity, Authenticity, and Humility*. Milwaukee: Marquette University Press.

Dahlstrom, Daniel O. 2018. "The Early Heidegger's Phenomenology." In Dan Zahavi, ed. *The Oxford Handbook of the History of Phenomenology*, 211–228. Oxford: Oxford University Press.

Dasgupta, Shamik. 2017. "Constitutive Explanation." *Philosophical Issues* 27: 74–97.

David, Marian. 1994. *Correspondence and Disquotation*. Oxford: Oxford University Press.

Davidson, Donald. 1984. "On The Very Idea of a Conceptual Scheme." In *Inquiries Into Truth and Interpretation*, 183–198. Oxford: Clarendon Press.

Davidson, Donald. 2001. "A Coherence Theory of Truth and Knowledge." In *Subjective, Intersubjective, Objective*, 137–157. Oxford: Clarendon Press.

Davis, Wayne A. 2003. *Meaning, Expression, and Thought*. Cambridge: Cambridge University Press.

Davis, Wayne A. 2005. *Nondescriptive Meaning and Reference: An Ideational Semantics*. Oxford: Oxford University Press.

DeRose, Keith. 1995. "Solving the Skeptical Problem." *The Philosophical Review* 104: 1–52.

Descartes, René. 1984. *The Philosophical Writings of Descartes, Volume II*. John Cottingham, Robert Stoothoff, and Dugald Murdoch, trans. Cambridge: Cambridge University Press.

Devitt, Michael. 1997. *Realism and Truth*, 2nd Edition. Princeton: Princeton University Press.

de Warren, Nicolas. 2009. *Husserl and the Promise of Time*. Cambridge: Cambridge University Press.

Dicey Jennings, Carolyn. 2012. "The Subject of Attention." *Synthese* 189: 535–554.

Dicey Jennings, Carolyn. 2017. "I Attend, Therefore I Am." Aeon. https://aeon.co/essays/what-is-the-self-if-not-that-which-pays-attention.

Dilworth, John. 2005. *The Double Content of Art*. New York: Prometheus Books.

Donnellan, Keith. 1966. "Reference and Definite Descriptions." *The Philosophical Review* 75: 281–304.

Dorsch, Fabian. 2010. "Transparency and Imagining Seeing." *Philosophical Explorations* 13: 173–200.

Doyon, Maxime. 2018. "Husserl on Perceptual Optimality." *Husserl Studies* 34: 171–189.

Dretske, Fred I. 1969. *Seeing and Knowing*. Chicago: The University of Chicago Press.

Dretske, Fred I. 1995. *Naturalizing the Mind*. Cambridge: The MIT Press.

Dretske, Fred I. 2000a. "Simple Seeing." In *Perception, Knowledge, and Belief*, 97–112. Cambridge: Cambridge University Press.

Dretske, Fred I. 2000b. "If You Can't Make One, You Don't Know How It Works." In *Perception, Knowledge, and Belief*, 208–226. Cambridge: Cambridge University Press.

Dretske, Fred I. 2003. "How Do You Know You are Not a Zombie?" In Brie Gertler, ed. *Privileged Access: Philosophical Accounts of Self-Knowledge*, 1–14. New York: Routledge.

Dreyfus, Hubert L. 1982. "The Perceptual Noema." In Hubert L. Dreyfus, ed. *Husserl, Intentionality, and Cognitive Science*, 97–123. Cambridge: The MIT Press.

Dreyfus, Hubert L. 2014. "Merleau-Ponty and Recent Cognitive Science." In Hubert Dreyfus and Mark Wrathall, eds. *Skillful Coping*, 231–248. Oxford: Oxford University Press.

Drummond, John. 1979. "On Seeing a Material Thing in Space: The Role of Kinaesthesis in Visual Perception." *Philosophy and Phenomenological Research* 40: 19–32.

Drummond, John. 1990. *Husserlian Intentionality and Non-Foundational Realism: Noema and Object.* Boston: Kluwer Academic Publishers.

Drummond, John. 2006. "The Case(s) of (Self-)Awareness." In Uriah Kriegel and Kenneth Williford, eds. *Self-Representational Approaches to Consciousness*, 199–220. Cambridge: The MIT Press.

Dubois, James M. 1995. *Judgment and Sachverhalt.* Dordrecht: Kluwer Academic Publishers.

Dummett, Michael. 1994. *Origins of Analytical Philosophy.* Cambridge: Harvard University Press.

Einstein, Albert. 1961. *Relativity: The Special and the General Theory.* Robert W. Lawson, trans. New York: Crown Trade Paperbacks.

Erhard, Christopher. 2011. "Empirische Bedeutung und Twin Earth—Husserls Bedeutungstheorie modifiziert." In Verena Mayer, Christopher Erhard, and Marisa Scherini, eds. *Die Aktualität Husserls*, 192–230. Freiburg/München: Verlag Karl Alber.

Erhard, Christopher. 2012. "Husserls moderater empirischer Fundamentalismus und das Verhältnis zwischen Phaenomenologie, Ontologie und Metaphysik. Kommentar zu Christian Beyer." In J. Nida-Ruemelin and E. Oezmen, eds. *Welt der Gruende*, 48–62. Hamburg: Meiner.

Evans, Gareth. 1982. *The Varieties of Reference.* Oxford: Oxford University Press.

Fales, Evan. 1996. *A Defense of the Given.* New York: Rowman & Littlefield.

Fasching, Wolfgang. 2012. "Intentionality and Presence: On the Intrinsic Of-ness of Consciousness from a Transcendental-Phenomenological Perspective." *Husserl Studies* 28: 121–141.

Feldman, Richard. 2004. "Authoritarian Epistemology." In Earl Conee and Richard Feldman. *Evidentialism*, 111–134. Oxford: Oxford University Press.

Feldman, Richard and Earl Conee. 2004. "Evidentialism." In *Evidentialism*, 83–107. Oxford: Oxford University Press.

Fish, William. 2009. *Perception, Illusion, and Hallucination.* Oxford: Oxford University Press.

Fodor, Jerry A. 1998. *Concepts: Where Cognitive Science Went Wrong.* Oxford: Oxford University Press.

Fodor, Jerry A. 2008. *LOT 2: The Language of Thought Revisited.* Oxford: Oxford University Press.

Føllesdal, Dagfinn. 1969. "Husserl's Notion of Noema." *The Journal of Philosophy* 66: 680–687.

Frank, Manfred. 2016. "Why Should We Think that Self-Consciousness is Non-Reflective?" In Sofia Miguens, Gerhard Preyer, and Clara Bravo Morando, eds. *Pre-reflective Consciousness: Sartre and Contemporary Philosophy of Mind*, 29–48. New York: Routledge.

Franklin, James. 2002. "Stove's Discovery of the Worst Argument in the World." *Philosophy* 77: 615–624.

Frege, Gottlob. 1946. "Sense and Reference." *The Philosophical Review* 57: 209–230.

Frege, Gottlob 1956. "The Thought: A Logical Inquiry." P. T. Geach, trans. *Mind* 65: 289–311.

Fumerton, Richard. 1995. *Metaepistemology and Skepticism.* Lanham, MD: Rowman & Littlefield.

Gadamer, Hans-Georg. 1975. *Truth and Method.* Joel Weinsheimer and Donald G. Marshall, trans. London: Bloomsbury Academic.

Gallagher, Shaun. 2005. *How the Body Shapes the Mind.* Oxford: Clarendon Press.

Gallagher, Shaun and Dan Zahavi. 2012. *The Phenomenological Mind*, 2nd Edition. New York: Routledge.

Gennaro, Rocco J. 2006. "Between Pure Self-Referentialism and the Extrinsic HOT Theory of Consciousness." In Uriah Kriegel and Kenneth Williford, eds. *Self-Representational Approaches to Consciousness*, 221–248. Cambridge: The MIT Press.

Gennaro, Rocco J. 2012. *The Consciousness Paradox*. Cambridge: The MIT Press.

Georgalis, Nicholas. 2006. *The Primacy of the Subjective*. Cambridge: The MIT Press.

Gertler, Brie. 2012. "Understanding the Internalism-Externalism Debate: What is the Boundary of the Thinker?" *Philosophical Perspectives* 26: 51–75.

Gettier, Edmund L. 1963. "Is Justified True Belief Knowledge?" *Analysis* 23: 121–123.

Gibson, James J. 1986. *The Ecological Approach to Visual Perception*. Hillsdale, NJ: Lawrence Erlbaum Associates, Publishers.

Goldman, Alvin I. 1999. "Internalism Exposed." *The Journal of Philosophy* 96: 271–293.

Goldman, Alvin I. 2012. "What is Justified Belief?" In *Reliabilism and Contemporary Epistemology*, 29–49. Oxford: Oxford University Press.

Gorner, Paul. 1991. "Realism and Idealism in Husserl." *Idealistic Studies* 21: 106–113.

Graham, George, Terence Horgan, and John Tienson. 2009. "Phenomenology, Intentionality, and the Unity of Mind." In Ansgar Beckermann, Brian P. McLaughlin, and Sven Walter, eds. *The Oxford Handbook of Philosophy of Mind*, 512–537. Oxford: Oxford University Press.

Grice, H.P. 1994a. "Meaning." In Robert M. Harnish, ed. *Basic Topics in the Philosophy of Language*, 21–29. Englewood Cliffs: Prentice Hall.

Grice, H.P. 1994b. "Logic and Conversation." In Robert M. Harnish, ed. *Basic Topics in the Philosophy of Language*, 57–73. Englewood Cliffs: Prentice Hall.

Grossman, Reinhardt. 1992. *The Existence of the World: An Introduction to Ontology*. New York: Routledge.

Gurwitsch, Aron. 1964. *The Field of Consciousness*. Pittsburgh: Duquesne University Press.

Gutting, Gary. 1978. "Husserl and Scientific Realism." *Philosophy and Phenomenological Research* 39: 42–56.

Hacker, P.M.S. 1987. *Appearance and Reality*. Oxford: Basil Blackwell.

Hall, Harrison. 1982. "The Philosophical Significance of Husserl's Theory of Intentionality." *Journal of the British Society for Phenomenology* 13: 79–84.

Hammond, Tanner. 2019. *Feeling Values: A Phenomenological Case for Moral Realism*. Dissertation: Boston University.

Hanks, Peter. 2015. *Propositional Content*. Oxford: Oxford University Press.

Hardy, Lee. 2013. *Nature's Suit: Husserl's Phenomenological Philosophy of the Physical Sciences*. Athens: Ohio University Press.

Harman, Gilbert. 1990. "The Intrinsic Quality of Experience." *Philosophical Perspectives* 4: 31–52.

Hasan, Ali and Richard Fumerton. 2016. "Foundationalist Theories of Epistemic Justification." In Edward N. Zalta, ed. *The Stanford Encyclopedia of Philosophy* (Winter 2016 Edition). https://plato.stanford.edu/archives/win2016/entries/justep-foundational.

Haugeland, John. 1996. "Objective Perception." In Kathleen Akins, ed. *Perception*, 268–290. Oxford: Oxford University Press.

Heck, Richard. 2000. "Nonconceptual Content and the 'Space of Reasons'." *The Philosophical Review* 109: 483–523.

Heffernan, George. 1997. "An Essay in Epistemic Kuklophobia: Husserl's Critique of Descartes' Conception of Evidence." *Husserl Studies* 13: 89–140.

Heffernan, George. 1998. "Miscellaneous Lucubrations on Husserl's Answer to the Question 'was die Evidenz sei': A Contribution to the Phenomenology of Evidence on the Occasion of the Publication of Husserliana Volume XXX." *Husserl Studies* 15: 1–75.

Hegel, Georg WilhelmFriedrich. 2010. *The Science of Logic.* Georg di Giovanni, trans. and ed. Cambridge: Cambridge University Press.

Heidegger, Martin. 1962. *Being and Time.* John Macquarrie & Edward Robinson, trans. San Francisco: HarperSanFrancisco.

Heidegger, Martin. 1985. *History of the Concept of Time.* Theodore Kisiel, trans. Bloomington: Indiana University Press.

Heidegger, Martin. 1999. *Contributions to Philosophy (From Enowning).* Bloomington & Indianapolis: Indiana University Press.

Heidegger, Martin. 2007. *Becoming Heidegger: On the Trail of his Early Occasional Writings, 1910–1927.* Theodore Kisiel and Thomas Sheehan, eds. Evanston: Northwestern University Press.

Hickerson, Ryan. Forthcoming. *Feelings of Believing: Psychology, History, Phenomenology.* New York: Lexington Books.

Hill, Christopher. 2009. *Consciousness.* Cambridge: Cambridge University Press.

Hinton, J. M. 1967. "Experiences." *The Philosophical Quarterly* 17: 1–13.

Hinton, J. M. 1973. *Experiences: An Inquiry into Some Ambiguities.* Oxford: Clarendon Press.

Holt, Edwin, Walter T. Marvin, William Pepperrell Montague, Ralph Barton Perry, William B. Pitkin, and Edward Gleason Spaulding. 1912. "Program and Platform of Six Realists." In *The New Realism,* 471–483. New York: The MacMillan Company.

Hopkins, Burt. 2010. *The Philosophy of Husserl.* Montreal: McGill-Queen's University Press.

Hopkins, Robert. 1998. *Picture, Image, and Experience.* Cambridge: Cambridge University Press.

Hopp, Walter. 2008a. "Husserl on Sensation, Perception, and Interpretation." *Canadian Journal of Philosophy* 38: 219–246.

Hopp, Walter. 2008b. "Husserl, Phenomenology, and Foundationalism." *Inquiry* 51: 194–216.

Hopp, Walter. 2011. *Perception and Knowledge: A Phenomenological Account.* Cambridge: Cambridge University Press.

Hopp, Walter. 2012. "The (Many) Foundations of Knowledge." In Dan Zahavi, ed. *The Oxford Handbook of Contemporary Phenomenology,* 327–348. Oxford: Oxford University Press.

Hopp, Walter. 2013. "No Such Look: Problems with the Dual Content Theory." *Phenomenology and the Cognitive Sciences* 12: 813–833.

Hopp, Walter. 2014. "Experiments in Thought." *Perspectives on Science* 22: 242–263.

Hopp, Walter. 2017. "Image Consciousness and the Horizonal Structure of Perception." *Midwest Studies in Philosophy* 41: 130–153.

Hopp, Walter. 2019. "Normativity and Knowledge." In Matthew Burch, Jack Marsh, and Irene McMullin, eds. Normativity, *Meaning, and the Promise of Phenomenology,* 271–289. New York: Routledge.

Horst, Steven. 1999. "Symbols and Computation: A Critique of the Computational Theory of Mind." *Minds and Machines* 9: 347–381.

Huemer, Michael. 2001. *Skepticism and the Veil of Perception.* Lanham: Rowman & Littlefield Publishers, Inc.

Huemer, Michael 2013. "Epistemological Asymmetries between Belief and Experience." *Philosophical Studies* 162: 741–748.

Hume, David. 1993. *An Enquiry Concerning Human Understanding*. Eric Steinberg, ed. Indianapolis: Hackett Publishing Company, Inc.

Hume, David. 1978. *A Treatise of Human Nature*, Second Edition. P.H. Nidditch, ed. Oxford: Clarendon Press.

Hurley, S. L. 1998. *Consciousness in Action*. Cambridge: Harvard University Press.

Husserl, Edmund, Alexander Pfänder, Moritz Geiger, Max Ferdinand Scheler, and Adolf Reinach. 1913. "Vorwort." *Jahrbuch für Philosophie und phänomenologische Forschung* 1: V–VI. Translated by Bob Sandmeyer. http://husserlpage.com/docs/hus_jahr_forward.pdf.

Ihde, Don. 2012. *Listening and Voice: Phenomenologies of Sound*. 2nd Edition. Albany: State University of New York Press.

Ingarden, Roman. 1973. *The Literary Work of Art*. George G. Grabowicz, trans. Evanston: Northwestern University Press.

Ingarden, Roman. 1976. "Probleme der Husserlschen Reduktion." In Anna-Teresa Tymieniecka, ed. *Analecta Husserliana* IV: 1–71. Dordrecht: D. Reidel Publishing Company.

Jackson, Frank. 1977. *Perception: A Representative Theory*. Cambridge: Cambridge University Press.

Jackson, Frank. 1986. "What Mary Didn't Know." *The Journal of Philosophy* 83: 291–295.

Jacobs, Hanne. 2010. "I am Awake: Husserlian Reflections on Wakefulness and Attention." *Alter. Revue de Phénoménologie* 18:183–201.

Jacobs, Hanne. 2015. "From Psychology to Pure Phenomenology." In Andrea Stait, ed. *Commentary on Husserl's Ideas I*, 95–118. Berlin: Walter de Gruyter.

Jacobs, Hanne. 2016. "Husserl on Reason, Reflection, and Attention." *Research in Phenomenology* 46: 257–276.

Jagnow, René. 2008. "Disappearing Appearances: On the Enactive Approach to Spatial Perceptual Content." *The Southern Journal of Philosophy* 46: 45–67.

James, William. 1952. *The Principles of Psychology*. Chicago: Encyclopedia Britannica, Inc.

Jansen, Julia. 2013. "Imagination, Embodiment and Situatedness: Using Husserl to Dispel (Some) Notions of 'Off-Line Thinking'." In Rasmus Thybo Jensen and Dermot Moran, eds. *The Phenomenology of Embodied Subjectivity*, 63–79. Dordrecht: Springer.

Jansen, Julia. 2015. "Transcendental Philosophy and the Problem of Necessity in a Contingent World." *Metodo. International Studies in Phenomenology and Philosophy*, Special Issue 1: 47–80.

Jansen, Julia. 2016. "Husserl." In Amy Kind, ed. *The Routledge Handbook of Imagination*, 69–81. New York: Routledge.

Janzen, Greg. 2006. "The Representational Theory of Phenomenal Character: A Phenomenological Critique." *Phenomenology and the Cognitive Sciences* 5: 321–339.

Johnston, Mark. 2004. "The Obscure Object of Hallucination." *Philosophical Studies* 120: 113–183.

Johnston, Mark. 2006. "Better than Mere Knowledge? The Function of Sensory Awareness." In Tamar Szabo Gendler and John Hawthorne, eds. *Perceptual Experience*, 260–290. Oxford: Clarendon Press.

Kasmier, David. 2003. "Husserl's Theory of A Priori Knowledge: A Response to the Failure of Contemporary Rationalism." Dissertation, University of Southern California.

Kasmier, David. 2015. "Knowability and Willard's Reality Hook." Delivered at the Conference in Honor of Dallas Willard, Boston University. https://vimeo.com/160688570.

Kant, Immanuel. 1965. *Critique of Pure Reason*. Norman Kemp Smith, trans. New York: Macmillan & Co., Ltd.

Käufer, Stephan and Anthony Chemero. 2015. *Phenomenology: An Introduction*. Malden: Polity Press.

Kelly, Sean Dorrance. 2001. "The Non-Conceptual Content of Perceptual Experience: Situation Dependence and Fineness of Grain." *Philosophy and Phenomenological Research* 62: 601–608.

Kelly, Sean Dorrance. 2008. "Content and Constancy: Phenomenology, Psychology, and the Content of Perception." *Philosophy and Phenomenological Research* 76: 682–690.

Kelly, Sean Dorrance. 2010. "The Normative Nature of Perceptual Experience." In Bence Nanay, ed. *Perceiving the World*, 146–159. Oxford: Oxford University Press.

Kennedy, John M. 1993. *Drawing and the Blind: Pictures to Touch.* New Haven: Yale University Press.

Kennedy, Matthew. 2009. "Heirs of Nothing: The Implications of Transparency." *Philosophy and Phenomenological Research* 79: 574–604.

Kern, Iso. 1977. "The Three Ways to the Transcendental Phenomenological Reduction in the Philosophy of Edmund Husserl." In Frederick Elliston, and Peter McCormick, eds. *Husserl. Expositions and Appraisals*, 126–149. Notre Dame: University of Notre Dame Press.

Kidd, Chad. 2019. "Re-examining Husserl's Non-Conceptualism in the Logical Investigations." *Archiv für Geschichte der Philosophie* 101: 407–444.

Kim, Jaegwon. 2005. *Physicalism, or Something Near Enough.* Princeton: Princeton University Press.

Kind, Amy. 2003. "What's So Transparent About Transparency?" *Philosophical Studies* 115: 225–244.

Kinkaid, James. 2018. "Heidegger's Science of Being, 1919–1930." Dissertation, Boston University.

Kinkaid, James. 2019. "Phenomenology, Idealism, and the Legacy of Kant." *British Journal for the History of Philosophy* 27: 593–614.

Kinkaid, James. 2020. "Phenomenology and the Stratification of Reality." *European Journal of Philosophy.* https://doi-org.ezproxy.bu.edu/10.1111/ejop.12546.

Koffka, K. 1935. *Principles of Gestalt Psychology.* London: Kegan Paul, Trench, Trubner & Co.

Köhler, Wolfgang. 1947. *Gestalt Psychology.* New York: New American Library.

Kriegel, Uriah and Kenneth Williford. 2006. "Introduction." In Uriah Kriegel and Kenneth Williford, eds. *Self-Representational Approaches to Consciousness*, 1–8. Cambridge: The MIT Press.

Kriegel, Uriah. 2009a. "Self-Representationalism and Phenomenology." *Philosophical Studies* 143: 357–381.

Kriegel, Uriah. 2009b. *Subjective Consciousness: A Self-Representational Theory.* Oxford: Oxford University Press.

Kriegel, Uriah. 2013. "The Phenomenal Intentionality Research Program." In Uriah Kriegel, ed. *Phenomenal Intentionality*, 1–26. Oxford: Oxford University Press.

Kripke, Saul. 1972. *Naming and Necessity.* Princeton: Princeton University Press.

Kroon, Frederick. 2013. "Phenomenal Intentionality and the Role of Intentional Objects." In Uriah Kriegel, ed. *Phenomenal Intentionality*, 137–155. Oxford: Oxford University Press.

Kuhn, Thomas. 1970. *The Structure of Scientific Revolutions*, second edition. Chicago: University of Chicago Press.

Kulvicki, John V. 2014. *Images.* New York: Routledge.

Kurg, Regina-Nino. 2014a. "Edmund Husserl's Theory of Image Consciousness, Aesthetic Consciousness, and Art." Dissertation, University of Fribourg.

Kurg, Regina-Nino. 2014b. "Seeing-in as Threefold Experience." *Postgraduate Journal of Aesthetics* 11: 18–26.

Kjosavik, Frode. 2003. "Perceptual Intimacy and Conceptual Inadequacy: A Husserlian Critique of McDowell's Internalism." In Dan Zahavi and Hans Ruin, eds. *Metaphysics,*

Facticity, Interpretation: Phenomenology in the Nordic Countries, 49–71. Dordrecht: Kluwer Academic Publishers.

Laasik, Kristjan. 2011. "Perceptual Presence." *Phenomenology and the Cognitive Sciences* 10: 439–459.

Lauer, Quentin. 1965. "Translator's Introduction to Edmund Husserl." *Phenomenology and the Crisis of Philosophy*. New York: Harper Torchbooks.

Leibniz, G. W. 1989. "Discourse on Metaphysics." In Roger Ariew and Daniel Garber, trans. *Philosophical Essays*, 35–68. Indianapolis: Hackett Publishing Company, Inc.

Leung, Ka-Wing. 2011."Meaning and Intuitive Act in the Logical Investigations." *Husserl Studies* 27: 125–142.

Levinas, Emmanuel. 1969. *Totality and Infinity*. Alphonso Lingis, trans. Pittsburgh: Duquesne University Press.

Levinas, Emmanuel. 1995. *The Theory of Intuition in Husserl's Phenomenology*, Second Edition. Andre Orianne, trans. Evanston: Northwestern University Press.

Levine, Joseph. 1983. "Materialism and Qualia: The Explanatory Gap." *Pacific Philosophical Quarterly* 64: 354–361.

Lewis, C. I. 1929. *Mind and the World Order*. New York: Dover Publications.

Lewis, C. I. 1995. "The Pragmatic Element in Knowledge." In Paul K. Moser and Arnold Vander Nat, eds. *Human Knowledge: Classical and Contemporary Approaches*, second edition, 234–245. Oxford: Oxford University Press.

Liebesman, David. 2014. "Necessarily, Sherlock Holmes is not a Person." *Analytic Philosophy* 55: 306–318.

Locke, John. 1975. *An Essay Concerning Human Understanding*. Edited by P. H. Nidditch. Oxford: Clarendon Press.

Loux, Michael J. 2006. *Metaphysics: A Contemporary Introduction*. Third Edition. New York: Routledge.

Logue, Heather. 2014. "Experiential Content and Naïve Realism: A Reconciliation." In Berit Brogaard, ed. *Does Perception Have Content?*, 220–241. Oxford: Oxford University Press.

Logue, Heather. 2015. "Disjunctivism." In Mohan Matthen, ed. *The Oxford Handbook of Philosophy of Perception*, 198–216. Oxford: Oxford University Press.

Lohmar, Dieter. 2002. "Categorial Intuition." In Dan Zahavi and Frederik Stjernfelt, eds. *One Hundred Years of Phenomenology*, 125–146. Dordrecht: Kluwer Academic Publishers.

Lotze, Hermann. 1884. *Logic*. Bernard Bosanquet, trans. Oxford: Clarendon Press.

Luft, Sebastian. 2004. "Husserl's Theory of the Phenomenological Reduction: Between Life World and Cartesianism." *Research in Phenomenology* 34: 198–234.

Luft, Sebastian. 2012. "Husserl's Method of Reduction." In Sebastian Luft and Søren Overgaard, eds. *The Routledge Companion to Phenomenology*, 243–253. New York: Routledge.

Lycan, William. 2004. "The Superiority of HOP to HOT." In Rocco J. Gennaro, ed. *Higher-Order Theories of Consciousness*, 93–114. Amsterdam: John Benjamins Publishing Company.

Lyons, Jack. 2009. *Perception and Basic Beliefs*. Oxford: Oxford University Press.

Madary, Michael. 2010. "Husserl on Perceptual Constancy." *European Journal of Philosophy* 20: 145–165.

Madary, Michael 2017. *Visual Phenomenology*. Cambridge: The MIT Press.

Majolino, Claudio. 2016. "'Until the End of the World': Eidetic Variation and Absolute Being of Consciousness—A Reconsideration." *Research in Phenomenology* 46: 157–183.

Marbach, Eduard. 1993. *Mental Representation and Consciousness*. Dordrecht: Springer.

Marbach, Eduard. 2013. "Towards a Phenomenological Analysis of Fictional Intentionality and Reference." *International Journal of Philosophical Studies* 21: 428–447.

Marchesi, Andrea. 2015. "Is There Something Like a (Raw) Visual Sensation?" *Archivio Di Filosofia* 83: 151–160.

Martin, M.G.F. 2003. "The Transparency of Experience." *Mind & Language* 17: 376–425.

Martin, M. 2006. "On Being Alienated." In Tamar Szabo Gendler and John Hawthorne, eds. *Perceptual Experience*, 354–410. Oxford: Clarendon Press.

Martin, M. 2009. "The Limits of Self-Awareness." In Alex Byrne and Heather Logue, eds. *Disjunctivism: Contemporary Readings*, 271–317. Cambridge: The MIT Press.

Matthen, Mohan. 2005. *Seeing, Doing, and Knowing*. Oxford: Clarendon Press.

Matthews, Gareth B. 1972. "Senses and Kinds." *The Journal of Philosophy* 69: 149–157.

McDowell, John. 1994. *Mind and World*. Cambridge: Harvard University Press.

McDowell, John. 1998a. "Intentionality De Re." In *Meaning, Knowledge & Reality*, 260–274. Cambridge: Harvard University Press.

McDowell, John. 1998b. "The Logical Form of an Intuition." *The Journal of Philosophy* 95: 451–470.

McDowell, John. 1998c. "De Re Senses." In *Meaning, Knowledge & Reality*, 214–227. Cambridge: Harvard University Press.

McGinn, Colin. 1996. *The Character of Mind*, Second Edition. Oxford: Oxford University Press.

McGinn, Colin. 2008. "Consciousness as Knowingness." *The Monist* 91: 237–249.

McIntyre, Ronald. 1987. "Husserl and Frege." *The Journal of Philosophy* 84: 529–535.

McIntyre, Ronald. 1999. "Naturalizing Phenomenology? Dretske on Qualia." In Jean Petitot, Francisco J. Varela, Bernard Pachoud, and Jean-Michel Roy, eds. *Naturalizing Phenomenology*, 429–439. Stanford: Stanford University Press.

McSweeney, Michaela Markham. 2019. "Logical Realism and the Metaphysics of Logic." *Philosophy Compass 14*. https://doi.org/10.1111/phc3.12563.

Merleau-Ponty, Maurice. 1968. *The Visible and the Invisible*. Claude Lefort, ed. Alphonso Lingis, trans. Evanston: Northwestern University Press.

Merleau-Ponty, Maurice. 2012. *Phenomenology of Perception*. Donald A. Landes, trans. New York: Routledge.

Millar, Alan. 1991. *Reasons and Experience*. Oxford: Clarendon Press.

Millar, Alan. 2008. "Perceptual-Recognitional Abilities and Perceptual Knowledge." In Adrian Haddock and Fiona Macpherson, eds. *Disjunctivism: Perception, Action, Knowledge*, 330–347. Oxford: Oxford University Press.

Millar, Boyd. 2014. "The Phenomenological Problem of Perception." *Philosophy and Phenomenological Research* 88: 625–654.

Miller, Izchak. 1984. *Husserl, Perception, and Temporal Awareness*. Cambridge: The MIT Press.

Millikan, Ruth Garrett. 1990. "The Myth of the Essential Indexical." *Noûs* 24: 723–734.

Mohanty, J.N. 1974. "On Husserl's Theory of Meaning." *The Southwestern Journal of Philosophy* 5: 229–244.

Mohanty, J.N. 1989 *Transcendental Phenomenology: An Analytic Account*. Oxford: Basil Blackwell Ltd.

Mohanty, J.N. 1997. *Phenomenology: Between Essentialism and Transcendental Philosophy*. Evanston: Northwestern University Press.

Mohanty, J.N. 2008. *The Philosophy of Edmund Husserl*. New Haven: Yale University Press.

Montague, Michelle. 2016. *The Given: Experience and Its Content*. Oxford: Oxford University Press.

Moore, G.E. 1903. "The Refutation of Idealism." *Mind* 12: 433–453.

Moore, G.E. 1993. "Moore's Paradox." In Thomas Baldwin, ed. *G.E. Moore: Selected Writings*, 207–212. New York: Routledge.

Mooney, Timothy. 2010. "Understanding and Simple Seeing in Husserl." *Husserl Studies* 26: 19–48.

Moran, Dermot. 2000. *Introduction to Phenomenology.* New York: Routledge.

Moran, Dermot. 2001. "Analytic Philosophy and Phenomenology." In Steven Crowell, Lester Embree, and Samuel J. Julian, eds. *The Reach of Reflection: Issues for Phenomenology's Second Century*, 409–433. http://www.electronpress.com.

Moran, Dermot. 2005. *Edmund Husserl: Founder of Phenomenology.* Cambridge: Polity Press.

Moran, Dermot .2007. "Edmund Husserl's Methodology of Concept Clarification." In Michael Beaney, ed. *The Analytic Turn: Analysis in Early Analytic Philosophy and Phenomenology*, 235–256. New York: Routledge.

Moran, Dermot. 2008. "Husserl's Transcendental Philosophy and the Critique of Naturalism." *Continental Philosophy Review* 41: 401–425.

Moreland, J.P. 1989. "Was Husserl a Nominalist?" *Philosophy and Phenomenological Research* 49: 661–674.

Moser, Paul K. 1988. "Foundationalism, the Given, and C. I. Lewis." *History of Philosophy Quarterly* 5: 189–204.

Mulligan, Kevin. 1995. "Perception." In Barry Smith and David Woodruff Smith, eds. *The Cambridge Companion to Husserl*, 168–238. Cambridge: Cambridge University Press.

Mulligan, Kevin. 2014. "Knowledge First—A German Folly?" In Julien Dutant, Davide Fassio, and Anne Meylan, eds. *Liber Amicorum Pascal Engel*, 380–400. Geneva: University of Geneva.

Mulligan, Kevin and Barry Smith. 1986. "A Relational Theory of the Act." *Topoi* 5: 115–130.

Murdoch, Iris. 1993. *Metaphysics as a Guide to Morals.* New York: Penguin Books.

Nagel, Thomas. 1974. "What Is It Like to Be a Bat?" *The Philosophical Review* 83: 435–450.

Natsoulas, Thomas. 2013. *Consciousness and Perceptual Experience: An Ecological and Phenomenological Approach.* Cambridge: Cambridge University Press.

Noë, Alva. 2004. *Action in Perception.* Cambridge: The MIT Press.

Noë, Alva. 2004. "Real Presence." *Philosophical Topics* 33: 235–264.

Noë, Alva. 2012. *The Varieties of Presence.* Cambridge: Harvard University Press.

Overgaard, Søren. 2008. "How to Analyze Immediate Experience: Hintikka, Husserl, and the Idea of Phenomenology." *Metaphilosophy* 39: 282–304.

Overgaard, Søren. 2010. "On the Looks of Things." *Pacific Philosophical Quarterly* 91: 260–284.

Overgaard, Søren. 2013. "Motivating Disjunctivism." *Husserl Studies* 29: 51–63.

Overgaard, Søren. 2015. "How to do Things with Brackets: the Epoché Explained." *Continental Philosophy Review* 48: 179–195.

Overgaard, Søren. 2018. "Perceptual Error, Conjunctivism, and Husserl." *Husserl Studies* 34: 25–45.

O'Shaughnessy, Brian. 2000. *Consciousness and the World.* Oxford: Oxford University Press.

Palmer, Stephen E. 1999. *Vision Science: From Photons to Phenomenology.* Cambridge: The MIT Press.

Pautz, Adam. 2010. "Why Explain Visual Experiences in Terms of Content?" In Bence Nanay, ed. *Perceiving the World*, 254–309. Oxford: Oxford University Press.

Peacocke, Christopher. 1992. *A Study of Concepts.* Cambridge: The MIT Press.

Peacocke, Christopher. 2001. "Does Perception Have a Nonconceptual Content?" *The Journal of Philosophy* 98: 239–264.

Perkins, Patricio A. 2017. "A Critical Taxonomy of the Theories About the Paths into the Reduction." *Husserl Studies* 33: 127–148.

Perry, John. 1979. "The Problem of the Essential Indexical." *Noûs* 13: 13–21.

Pfänder, Alexander. 1900. *Phänomenologie des Wollens: Eine Psychologische Analyse.* Leipzig: Johann Ambrosius Barth.

Pfänder, Alexander. 1967. *Phenomenology of Willing and Motivation.* Herbert Spiegelberg, trans. Evanston: Northwestern University Press.

Philipse, Herman. 1995. "Transcendental Idealism." In Barry Smith and David Woodruff Smith, eds. *The Cambridge Companion to Husserl*, 239–322. Cambridge: Cambridge University Press.

Piazza, Tommaso. 2007. *A Priori Knowledge: Toward a Phenomenological Explanation.* Frankfurt: Ontos Verlag.

Piazza, Tommaso. 2013. "The Evidence of the Senses is no Evidence from the Senses: Husserl's Sixth Logical Investigation on the Justification of Perceptual Beliefs." *Logical Analysis and History of Philosophy* 16: 174–191.

Pietersma, Henry. 1973. "Intuition and Horizon in the Philosophy of Husserl." *Philosophy and Phenomenological Research* 34: 95–101.

Pietersma, Henry. 2000. *Phenomenological Epistemology.* Oxford: Oxford University Press.

Plantinga, Alvin. 1992. *Warrant: The Current Debate.* Oxford: Oxford University Press.

Poellner, Peter. 2007. "Consciousness in the World: Husserlian Phenomenology and Externalism." In Brian Leiter and Michael Rosen, eds. *The Oxford Handbook of Continental Philosophy*, 409–460. Oxford: Oxford University Press.

Pollock, John L. 1974. *Knowledge and Justification.* Princeton: Princeton University Press.

Pollock, John L. and Iris Oved. 2005. "Vision, Knowledge, and the Mystery Link." *Philosophical Perspectives* 19: 305-31.

Preston, Aaron. 2007. *Analytic Philosophy: The History of an Illusion.* New York: Continuum.

Price, H.H. 1950. *Perception*, 2nd Edition. London: Methuen & Co. Ltd.

Prichard, H.A. 1909. *Kant's Theory of Knowledge.* Oxford: Clarendon Press.

Prior, A.N. 1971. *Objects of Thought.* P. T. Geach and A. J. P. Kenny, eds. Oxford: Clarendon Press.

Pryor, James. 2000. "The Skeptic and the Dogmatist." *Noûs* 34: 517–549.

Pryor, James. 2013. "There is Immediate Justification." In Matthias Steup and Ernest Sosa, eds. *Contemporary Debates in Epistemology*, Second Edition, 203–222. Malden, MA: Blackwell.

Putnam, Hilary. 1975. "The Meaning of 'Meaning'." *Minnesota Studies in the Philosophy of Science* 7: 131–193.

Putnam, Hilary. 1981. *Reason, Truth, and History.* Cambridge: Cambridge University Press.

Putnam, Hilary. 1983. *Realism and Reason.* Cambridge: Cambridge University Press.

Putnam, Hilary. 1990. *Realism With a Human Face.* Cambridge: Harvard University Press.

Putnam, Hilary. 1999. *The Threefold Cord: Mind, Body, and World.* New York: Columbia University Press.

Quilty-Dunn, Jake. 2013. "Was Reid a Direct Realist?" *British Journal for the History of Philosophy* 21: 302–323.

Quilty-Dunn, Jake. 2015. "Believing in Perceiving: Known Illusions and the Classical Dual Component Theory." *Pacific Philosophical Quarterly* 96: 550–575.

Quine, Willard Van Orman. 1960. *Word and Object.* Cambridge: The MIT Press.

Quine, Willard Van Orman. 1961a. "Two Dogmas of Empiricism." In *From a Logical Point of View*, 2nd edition, 20–46. New York: Harper & Row.

Quine, Willard Van Orman. 1961b. "Reference and Modality." In *From a Logical Point of View*, second edition, 139–159. New York: Harper and Row.

Quine, Willard Van Orman. 1968. "Ontological Relativity." *The Journal of Philosophy* 65: 185–212.

Reid, Thomas. 1853. *Essays on the Intellectual Powers of Man*. Sir William Hamilton, ed. Edinburgh: Maclachlan and Stewart.

Reid, Thomas 1997. *An Inquiry into the Human Mind on the Principles of Common Sense*. D.R. Brookes, ed. Edinburgh: Edinburgh University Press.

Reinach, Adolf. 1982. "On the Theory of the Negative Judgment." Barry Smith, trans. In Barry Smith, ed. *Parts and Moments: Studies in Logic and Formal Ontology*, 315–377. Munich: Philosophia Verlag.

Reinach, Adolf. 1989. "Einleitung in die Philosophie (1913)." In Karl Schuhmann and Barry Smith, eds. *Sämtliche Werke*, 369–513. München: Philosophia Verlag.

Reinach, Adolf. 2012a. *The Apriori Foundations of the Civil Law, along with the Lecture "Concerning Phenomenology."* John F. Crosby, trans. Frankfurt: Ontos Verlag.

Reinach, Adolf. 2012b. "Concerning Phenomenology." Dallas Willard, trans. In *The Apriori Foundations of the Civil Law, along with the Lecture "Concerning Phenomenology,"* 143–165. John F. Crosby, ed. Frankfurt: Ontos Verlag.

Rinofner-Kreidl, Sonja. 2012. "Moral Philosophy." In Sebastian Luft and Søren Overgaard, eds. *The Routledge Companion to Phenomenology*, 417–428. New York: Routledge.

Rinofner-Kreidl, Sonja. 2013. "Mental Contents, Transparency, Realism: News from the Phenomenological Camp." *Husserl Studies* 29: 33–50.

Roessler, Johannes. 2009. "Perceptual Experience and Perceptual Knowledge." *Mind* 118: 1013–1041.

Romano, Claude. 2012. "Must Phenomenology Remain Cartesian?" *Continental Philosophy Review* 45: 425–445.

Romano, Claude. 2015. *At the Heart of Reason*. Michael B. Smith and Claude Romano, trans. Evanston: Northwestern University Press.

Rorty, Richard. 1979. *Philosophy and the Mirror of Nature*. Princeton: Princeton University Press.

Rosado Haddock, Guillermo E. 2000. "Remarks on Sense and Reference in Husserl and Frege." In Claire Ortiz Hill and Guillermo E. Rosado Haddock. *Husserl or Frege? Meaning, Objectivity, and Mathematics*, 23–40. Peru, Ill.: Open Court Publishing Company.

Rosenthal, David. 1986. "Two Concepts of Consciousness." *Philosophical Studies* 49: 329–359.

Russell, Bertrand. 1917. "On Scientific Method in Philosophy." In *Mysticism and Logic and Other Essays*, 97–124. London: George Allen & Unwin.

Russell, Bertrand. 1984. *Theory of Knowledge: The 1913 Manuscript*. Elizabeth Ramsden Eames in collaboration with Kenneth Blackwell, eds. London: George Allen & Unwin.

Russell, Bertrand. 1999. *The Problems of Philosophy*. Mineola, New York: Dover Publications, Inc.

Ryle, Gilbert. 1929. "Review of Sein und Zeit by Martin Heidegger." *Mind* 38: 355–370.

Sacks, Oliver. 2010. *The Mind's Eye*. New York: Alfred A. Knopf.

Salice, Alessandro. 2016a. "Love and Other Social Stances in Early Phenomenology." In Thomas Szanto and Dermot Moran, eds. *Phenomenology of Sociality*, 234–247. New York: Routledge.

Salice, Alessandro. 2016b. "The Phenomenology of the Munich and Göttingen Circles." In Edward N. Zalta, ed. *The Stanford Encyclopedia of Philosophy* (Winter 2016 Edition). https://plato.stanford.edu/archives/win2016/entries/phenomenology-mg.

Sartre, Jean-Paul. 1960. *The Transcendence of the Ego: An Existentialist Theory of Consciousness.* Forrest Williams and Robert Kirkpatrick, trans. New York: Hill and Wang.

Sartre, Jean-Paul. 1970. "Intentionality: A Fundamental Idea of Husserl's Phenomenology." Joseph P. Fell, trans. *Journal of the British Society for Phenomenology* 1: 4–5.

Sartre, Jean-Paul. 2010. *The Imaginary.* Jonathan Webber, trans. New York: Routledge.

Sartre, Jean-Paul. 2018. *Being and Nothingness.* Sarah Richmond, trans. New York: Routledge.

Scheler, Max. 1973a. *Formalism in Ethics and Non-Formal Ethics of Values.* Manfred S. Frings and Roger L. Funk, trans. Evanston: Northwestern University Press.

Scheler, Max. 1973b. "The Theory of the Three Facts." In *Selected Philosophical Essays,* 202–287. David R. Lachterman, trans. Evanston: Northwestern University Press.

Schellenberg, Susanna. 2008. "The Situation-Dependency of Perception." *The Journal of Philosophy* 105: 55–84.

Schellenberg, Susanna. 2014. "The Relational and Representational Character of Perceptual Experience." In Berit Brogaard, ed. *Does Perception Have Content?,* 199–219. Oxford: Oxford University Press.

Schneider, Susan. 2012. "Non-Reductive Physicalism Cannot Appeal to Token Identity." *Philosophy and Phenomenological Research* 85: 719–728.

Schuhmann, Karl and Barry Smith. 1985. "Against Idealism: Johannes Daubert vs. Husserl's 'Ideas I'." *The Review of Metaphysics* 38: 763–793.

Schuhmann, Karl and Barry Smith. 1987. "Questions. An Essay in Daubertian Phenomenology." *Philosophy and Phenomenological Research* 48: 353–384.

Schwitzgebel, Eric. 2006. "Do Things Look Flat?" *Philosophy and Phenomenological Research* 72: 589–599.

Searle, John R. 1983. *Intentionality.* Cambridge: Cambridge University Press.

Searle, John R. 1987. "Indeterminacy, Empiricism, and the First Person." *The Journal of Philosophy* 84: 123–146.

Searle, John R. 1991. "Consciousness, Unconsciousness and Intentionality." *Philosophical Issues* 1: 45–66.

Searle, John R. 1992. *The Rediscovery of the Mind.* Cambridge: The MIT Press.

Sedgwick, Sally. 2012. *Hegel's Critique of Kant.* Oxford: Oxford University Press.

Seifert, Josef. 1987. *Back to 'Things in Themselves': A Phenomenological Foundation for Classical Realism.* New York: Routledge & Kegan Paul.

Sellars, Wilfrid. 1978. "The Role of Imagination in Kant's Theory of Experience." http://www.ditext.com/sellars/ikte. Edited in hypertext by A. Chrucky, with permission of H. W. Johnstone, Jr. Originally published in H. W. Johnstone, Jr. (Ed.), *Categories: A Colloquium.* Pennsylvania: Pennsylvania State University.

Sellars, Wilfrid. 1997. *Empiricism and the Philosophy of Mind.* Cambridge: Harvard University Press.

Shapiro, Lawrence. 2011. *Embodied Cognition.* New York: Routledge.

Shim, Michael K. 2005. "The Duality of Non-conceptual Content in Husserl's Phenomenology of Perception." *Phenomenology and the Cognitive Sciences* 4: 209–229.

Shim, Michael K. 2011. "Representationalism and Husserlian Phenomenology." *Husserl Studies* 27: 195–215.

Shoemaker, Sydney. 1968. "Self-Reference and Self-Awareness." *The Journal of Philosophy* 65: 555–567.

Shoemaker, Sydney. 1982: "The Inverted Spectrum." *The Journal of Philosophy* 79: 357–381.

Shoemaker, Sydney. 2000. "Introspection and Phenomenal Character." *Philosophical Topics* 28: 247–273.

Siegel, Susanna. 2010. *The Contents of Visual Experience.* Oxford: Oxford University Press.

Siegel, Susanna. 2012. "Cognitive Penetrability and Perceptual Justification." *Noûs* 46: 201–222.

Siegel, Susanna. 2017. *The Rationality of Perception*. Oxford: Oxford University Press.

Siewert, Charles P. 1998. *The Significance of Consciousness*. Princeton: Princeton University Press.

Siewert, Charles P. 2004. "Is Experience Transparent?" *Philosophical Studies* 117: 15–41.

Siewert, Charles P. 2006. "Is the Appearance of Shape Protean?" *Psyche 12*.

Siewert, Charles P. 2012. "Respecting Appearances: A Phenomenological Approach to Consciousness." In Dan Zahavi, ed. *The Oxford Handbook of Contemporary Phenomenology*, 48–69. Oxford: Oxford University Press.

Simons, Peter. 1995. "Meaning and Language." In Barry Smith and David Woodruff Smith, eds. *The Cambridge Companion to Husserl*, 106–137. Cambridge: Cambridge UniversityPress.

Simons, Peter. 2001. "Whose Fault? The Origins and Evitability of the AnalyticContinental Rift." *International Journal of Philosophical Studies* 9: 295–311.

Smith, A.D. 2000. "Space and Sight." *Mind* 109: 481–518.

Smith, A.D. 2001. "Perception and Belief." *Philosophy and Phenomenological Research* 62: 283–309.

Smith, A.D. 2002. *The Problem of Perception*. Cambridge: Harvard University Press.

Smith, A.D. 2003. *Routledge Philosophy Guidebook to Husserl and the Cartesian Meditations*. New York: Routledge.

Smith, Barry. 1982. "Introduction to Adolf Reinach On the Theory of the Negative Judgment." In Barry Smith, ed. *Parts and Moments: Studies in Logic and Formal Ontology*, 289–313. Munich: Philosophia Verlag.

Smith, Barry. 1987. "The Cognition of States of Affairs." In Kevin Mulligan, ed. *Speech Act and Sachverhalt: Reinach and the Foundations of Realist Phenomenology*, 189–225. Dordrecht: Martinus Nijhoff.

Smith, Barry. 1990. "Towards a History of Speech Act Theory." In Armin Burkhardt, ed. *Speech Acts, Meanings and Intentions. Critical Approaches to the Philosophy of John R. Searle*, 29–61. Berlin: de Gruyter.

Smith, Barry. 1994. "Husserl's Theory of Meaning and Reference." In Leila Haaparanta, ed. *Mind, Meaning, and Mathematics*, 163–183. Boston: Kluwer Academic Publishers.

Smith, Barry. 2000. "Logic and Formal Ontology." *Manuscrito* 23: 275–323.

Smith, Barry. 2001a. "Fiat Objects." *Topoi* 20: 131–148.

Smith, Barry. 2001b. "Husserlian Ecology." *Human Ontology (Kyoto)* 7: 9–24.

Smith, David Woodruff. 1982a. "The Realism in Perception." *Noûs* 16: 2–55.

Smith, David Woodruff 1982b. "What's the Meaning of 'This'?" *Noûs* 16: 181–208.

Smith, David Woodruff. 1989. *The Circle of Acquaintance*. Dordrecht: Kluwer Academic Publishers.

Smith, David Woodruff. 2004a. *Mind World*. Cambridge, MA: Cambridge University Press.

Smith, David Woodruff. 2004b. "The Structure of Context and Context Awareness." In Lester Embree, ed. *Gurwitsch's Relevancy for Cognitive Science*, 169–186. Contributions to Phenomenology, vol 52. Dordrecht: Springer.

Smith, David Woodruff. 2007. *Husserl*. New York: Routledge.

Smith, David Woodruff. 2018. "Phenomenology." In Edward N. Zalta, ed. *The Stanford Encyclopedia of Philosophy*. https://plato.stanford.edu/archives/sum2018/entries/phenomenology/.

Smith, David Woodruff. 2019. "Review of Dan Zahavi's Husserl's Legacy: Phenomenology, Metaphysics, & Transcendental Philosophy." *European Journal of Philosophy* 27: 284–290.

Smith, David Woodruff and Ronald McIntyre. 1982. *Husserl and Intentionality: A Study of Mind, Meaning, and Language*. Dordrecht: D. Reidel.

Smith, Joel. 2016. *Experiencing Phenomenology*. New York: Routledge.

Soames, Scott. 1999. *Understanding Truth*. Oxford: Oxford University Press.

Soames, Scott. 2010. *What is Meaning?*Princeton: Princeton University Press.

Soffer, Gail. 2003. "Revisiting the Myth: Husserl and Sellars on the Given." *The Review of Metaphysics* 57: 301–337.

Sokolowski, Robert. 1964. *The Formation of Husserl's Concept of Constitution*. The Hague: Martinus Nijhoff.

Sokolowski, Robert. 1977. "Review of Roman Ingarden's On the Motives which Led Husserl to Transcendental Idealism." *The Journal of Philosophy* 74: 176–180.

Sokolowski, Robert. 1984. "Quotation." *Review of Metaphysics* 37: 699–723.

Sokolowski, Robert. 2000. *Introduction to Phenomenology*. Cambridge: Cambridge University Press.

Soldati, Gianfranco. 2012. "Direct Realism and Immediate Justification." *Proceedings of the Aristotelian Society* 112: 29–44.

Somerville, James. 2006. "'The Table, Which We See': An Irresolvable Ambiguity." *Philosophy* 81: 33–63.

Spiegelberg, Herbert. 1971. *The Phenomenological Movement: A Historical Introduction*, Two Volumes, Second Edition. The Hague: Martinus Nijhoff.

Speaks, Jeff. 2009. "Transparency, Intentionalism, and the Nature of Perceptual Content." *Philosophy and Phenomenological Research* 79: 539–573.

Staiti, Andrea. 2015. "On Husserl's Alleged Cartesianism and Conjunctivism: A Critical Reply to Claude Romano." *Husserl Studies* 31: 123–141.

Stein, Edith. 2000. *Philosophy of Psychology and the Humanities*. Mary Catharine Baseheart and Marianne Sawicki, trans. Marianne Sawicki, ed. Washington, D.C.: ICS Publications.

Stein, Edith. 2002. *Finite and Eternal Being*. Kurt F. Reinhardt, trans. Washington, D.C.: ICS Publications.

Steup, Matthias. 2000. "Unrestricted Foundationalism and the Sellarsian Dilemma." *Grazer Philosophische Studien* 60: 75–98.

Strawson, Galen. 2015. "Real Direct Realism." In Paul Coates and Sam Coleman, eds. *Phenomenal Qualities: Sense, Perception, and Consciousness*, 214–256. Oxford: Oxford University Press.

Strawson, Galen. "A Hundred Years of Consciousness: 'A Long Training in Absurdity'." *Estudios de Filosofia* 59: 9–43.

Strawson, P.F. 1957. "Propositions, Concepts and Logical Truths." *The Philosophical Quarterly* 7: 15–25.

Strawson, P. 1959. *Individuals*. London: Methuen & Co Ltd.

Ströker, Elizabeth. 1988. "Phenomenology as First Philosophy: Reflections on Husserl." In Robert Sokolowski, ed. *Edmund Husserl and the Phenomenological Tradition*, 249–264. Washington: The Catholic University of America Press.

Sweetman, Brendan. 1999. "The Pseudo-Problem of Skepticism." In Brendan Sweetman, ed. *The Failure of Modernism: The Cartesian Legacy and Contemporary Pluralism*, 228–241. Washington, D.C.: Catholic University of America Press.

Szanto, Thomas. 2012. *Bewusstsein, Intentionalität und mentale Repräsentation*. Berlin: Walter de Gruyter GmbH & Co. KG.

Thomasson, Amie L. 2000. "After Brentano: A One-Level Theory of Consciousness." *European Journal of Philosophy* 8: 190–209.

Thomasson, Amie L. 2005. "First-Person Knowledge in Phenomenology." In David Woodruff Smith and Amie L. Thomasson, eds. *Phenomenology and Philosophy of Mind*, 115–139. Oxford: Oxford University Press.

Thomasson, Amie L. 2006. "Self-Awareness and Self-Knowledge." *Psyche 12*. http://journalpsyche.org/files/0xaaf2.pdf.

Thompson, Evan. 2007. *Mind in Life*. Cambridge: Harvard University Press.

Tieszen, Richard. 2005. *Phenomenology, Logic, and the Philosophy of Mathematics*. Cambridge: Cambridge University Press.

Tolhurst, William. 1998. "Seemings." *American Philosophical Quarterly* 35: 293–302.

Travis, Charles. 2004. "The Silence of the Senses." *Mind* 113: 57–94.

Tucker, Chris. 2010. "Why Open-Minded People Should Endorse Dogmatism." *Philosophical Perspectives* 24: 529–545.

Tye, Michael. 2000. *Consciousness, Color, and Content*. Cambridge: The MIT Press.

Tye, Michael. 2002. "Representationalism and the Transparency of Experience." *Noûs* 36: 137–151.

Tye, Michael. 2009. *Consciousness Revisited: Materialism without Phenomenal Concepts*. Cambridge: The MIT Press.

Tye, Michael. 2018. "Qualia." *The Stanford Encyclopedia of Philosophy* (Summer 2018 Edition), Edward N. Zalta, ed. https://plato.stanford.edu/archives/sum2018/entries/qualia/.

Van Cleve, James. 1979. "Foundationalism, Epistemic Principles, and the Cartesian Circle." *The Philosophical Review* 88: 55–91.

Van Cleve, James. 1985. "Epistemic Supervenience and the Circle of Belief." *The Monist* 68: 90–104.

Van Cleve, James. 1999. *Problems from Kant*. Oxford: Oxford University Press.

Van Cleve, James. 2015. *Problems from Reid*. Oxford: Oxford University Press.

Van Gulick, Robert. 2000. "Inward and Upward: Reflection, Introspection, and Self-Awareness." *Philosophical Topics* 28: 275–305.

Van Mazijk, Corijn. 2014. "Kant, Husserl, McDowell: The Non-Conceptual in Experience." *Diametros* 41: 99–114.

Van Mazijk, Corijn. 2016. "Kant and Husserl on the Contents of Perception." *Southern Journal of Philosophy* 54: 267–287.

Van Mazijk, Corijn. 2017a. "Phenomenological Approaches to Non-Conceptual Content." *Horizon. Studies in Phenomenology* 6: 58–58.

Van Mazijk, Corijn. 2017b. "Some Reflections on Husserlian Intentionality, Internalism, and Non-propositional Contents." *Canadian Journal of Philosophy* 47: 499–517.

Vinueza, Adam. 2001. "Realism and Mind Independence." *Pacific Philosophical Quarterly* 82: 51–70.

Voltolini, Alberto. 2015a. "Why, as Responsible for Figurativity, Seeing-In Can only Be Inflected Seeing-In." *Phenomenology and the Cognitive Sciences* 14: 651–667.

Voltolini, Alberto. 2015b. *A Syncretistic Theory of Depiction*. New York: Palgrave Macmillan.

Watzl, Sebastian. 2017. *Structuring Mind: The Nature of Attention and How it Shapes Consciousness*. Oxford: Oxford University Press.

Welton, Donn. 2000. *The Other Husserl*. Bloomington: Indiana University Press.

Wiesing, Lambert. 2011. "Pause of Participation. On the Function of Artificial Presence." *Research in Phenomenology* 41: 238–252.

Wiesing, Lambert. 2014. *The Philosophy of Perception: Phenomenology and Image Theory*. N.A. Roth, trans. London: Bloomsbury.

Wiggins, David. 2001. *Sameness and Substance Renewed*. Cambridge: Cambridge University Press.

Willard, Dallas. 1967. "A Crucial Error in Epistemology." *Mind* 76: 513–523.

Willard, Dallas. 1970. "Perceptual Realism." *Southwestern Journal of Philosophy* 1: 75–84.

Willard, Dallas. 1972. "The Paradox of Logical Psychologism: Husserl's Way Out." *American Philosophical Quarterly* 9: 94–100.

Willard, Dallas. 1982. "Wholes, Parts, and the Objectivity of Knowledge." In Barry Smith, ed. *Parts and Moments: Studies in Logic and Formal Ontology*, 379–400. Munich: Philosophia Verlag.

Willard, Dallas. 1983. "Why Semantic Ascent Fails." *Metaphilosophy* 14: 276–290.

Willard, Dallas. 1984. *Logic and the Objectivity of Knowledge*. Athens, OH: Ohio University Press.

Willard, Dallas. 1988. "A Critical Study of Husserl and Intentionality." *Journal of the British Society for Phenomenology* 19: 186–198 (part 1); 311–322 (part 2).

Willard, Dallas. 1989. "Review of 'Back to Things in Themselves': A Phenomenological Foundation for Classical Realism by Josef Seifert." *Canadian Philosophical Reviews IX*: 66–69.

Willard, Dallas. 1991. "Attaining Objectivity: Phenomenological Reduction and the Private Language Argument." In Liliana Albertazzi and Roberto Poli, eds. *Topics in Philosophy and Artificial Intelligence*, 15–21. Bozen: Istituto Mitteleuropa di Cultura.

Willard, Dallas. 1992. "Finding the Noema." In John J. Drummond and Lester Embree, eds. *The Phenomenology of the Noema*, 29–48. Dordrecht: Kluwer Academic Publishers.

Willard, Dallas. 1994a. "The Integrity of the Mental Act: Husserlian Reflections on a Fregean Problem." In Leila Haaparanta, ed. *Mind, Meaning, and Mathematics*, 235–262. Boston: Kluwer Academic Publishers.

Willard, Dallas. 1994b. "On the Texture and Substance of the Human Soul." Delivered to the Biola Philosophy Group. http://dwillard.org/articles/individual/on-the-texture-and-substance-of-the-human-soul.

Willard, Dallas. 1995a. "Knowledge." In Barry Smith and David Woodruff Smith, eds. *The Cambridge Companion to Husserl*, 138–167. Cambridge: Cambridge University Press.

Willard, Dallas. 1995b. "Phenomenology and Metaphysics." APA Symposium on Husserl's Ontology, San Francisco. http://www.dwillard.org/articles/individual/phenomenology-and-metaphysics.

Willard, Dallas. 1998. "The Redemption of Reason." Address given at Biola University for a symposium on "The Christian University in the Next Millennium." http://www.dwillard.org/articles/artview.asp?artID=118.

Willard, Dallas. 1999. "How Concepts Relate the Mind to its Objects: The 'God's Eye View'Vindicated?" *Philosophia Christi* 2: 5–20.

Willard, Dallas. 2000a. "The Significance of Husserl's Logical Investigations." Read before The Society for the Study of Husserl's Philosophy at the American Philosophical Association meeting in Albuquerque, April 7, 2000. http://www.dwillard.org/articles/individual/significance-of-husserls-logical-investigations-the.

Willard, Dallas. 2000b. "Knowledge and Naturalism." In W. L. Craig and J. P. Moreland, eds. *Naturalism: A Critical Analysis*, 24–48. New York: Routledge.

Willard, Dallas. 2002. "The World Well Won: Husserl's Epistemic Realism One Hundred Years Later." In Dan Zahavi and Frederick Stjernfelt, eds. *One Hundred Years of Phenomenology*, 69–78. Boston: Kluwer Academic Publishers.

Willard, Dallas. 2003a. "The Theory of Wholes and Parts and Husserl's Explication of the Possibility of Knowledge in the Logical Investigations." In Denis Fisette, ed. *Husserl's Logical Investigations Reconsidered*, 163–182. Boston: Kluwer Academic Publishers.

Willard, Dallas. 2003b. "Translator's Introduction." Husserl's *Philosophy of Arithmetic*. Dordrecht: Springer.

Willard, Dallas. 2006. "For Lack of Intentionality." In Lester Embree and Thomas Nenon, eds. *Phenomenology 2005, Volume 5: Selected Essays from North America, Part 2*, 593–611. Bucharest: Zeta Books.

Williams, Michael. 1977. *Groundless Belief: An Essay on the Possibility of Epistemology.* New Haven: Yale University Press.

Williamson, Timothy. 2000. *Knowledge and Its Limits.* Oxford: Oxford University Press.

Williford, Kenneth. 2006. "The Self-Representational Structure of Consciousness." In Uriah Kriegel and Kenneth Williford, eds. *Self-Representational Approaches to Consciousness*, 111–142. Cambridge: The MIT Press.

Williford, Kenneth. 2013. "Husserl's Hyletic Data and Phenomenal Consciousness." *Phenomenology and the Cognitive Sciences* 12: 501–519.

Wiltsche, Harald A. 2012. "What's Wrong with Husserl's Scientific Anti-Realism?" *Inquiry* 55: 105–130.

Wiltsche, Harald A. 2015. "Intuitions, Seemings, and Phenomenology." *teorema* 34: 57–77.

Wollheim, Richard. 1980. *Art and Its Objects*, Second Edition. Cambridge: Cambridge University Press.

Wollheim, Richard 1987. *Painting as an Art.* Princeton: Princeton University Press.

Wollheim, Richard 2003. "In Defense of Seeing-In." In H. Hecht, R. Schwartz and M. Atherton, eds. *Looking into Pictures: An Interdisciplinary Approach to Pictorial Space*, 3–15. Cambridge: The MIT Press.

Wolterstorff, Nicholas. 1987. "Are Concept-Users World-Makers?" *Philosophical Perspectives* 1: 233–267.

Yolton, John. 1953. "Linguistic and Epistemological Dualism." *Mind* 62: 20–42.

Yoshimi, Jeffrey. 2009. "Husserl's Theory of Belief and the Heideggerean Critique." *Husserl Studies* 25: 121–140.

Yoshimi, Jeffrey. 2015. "The Metaphysical Neutrality of Husserlian Phenomenology." *Husserl Studies* 31: 1–15.

Yoshimi, Jeffrey. 2016. *Husserlian Phenomenology: A Unifying Interpretation.* Cham, Switzerland: Springer.

Zagzebski, Linda. 1994. "The Inescapability of Gettier Problems." *The Philosophical Quarterly* 44: 65–73.

Zahavi, Dan. 1999. *Self-Awareness and Alterity.* Evanston: Northwestern University Press.

Zahavi, Dan. 2003a. *Husserl's Phenomenology.* Stanford: Stanford University Press.

Zahavi, Dan. 2003b. "Intentionality and Phenomenality: Phenomenological Take on the Hard Problem." *Canadian Journal of Philosophy 33*, supplement 1: 63–92.

Zahavi, Dan. 2008. "Internalism, Externalism, and Transcendental Idealism." *Synthese* 160: 355–374.

Zahavi, Dan. 2017. *Husserl's Legacy: Phenomenology, Metaphysics, & Transcendental Philosophy.* Oxford: Oxford University Press.

Zahavi, Dan and Uriah Kriegel. 2016. "For-Me-Ness: What It Is and What It Is Not." In Daniel O. Dahlstrom, Andreas Elpidorou, and Walter Hopp, eds. *Philosophy of Mind and Phenomenology: Conceptual and Empirical Approaches*, 36–53. New York: Routledge.

Zheng, Pirui. 2019. "Is Husserl a Conceptualist? Re-reading Husserl's Sixth Logical Investigation." Husserl Studies: Online First. https://doi-org.ezproxy.bu.edu/10.1007/s10743-019-09247-5.

Index